Enlarging Boston's SPOTLIGHT:

A call for Courage, Integrity, and Institutional Transformation

Dee Ann Miller

Grace Notes Press

© 2017

Table of Contents

Foreward

Dee Ann Miller's newest book, *Enlarging Boston's SPOTLIGHT*, is a thorough and rich summary of her life's work as an advocate, teacher, and networker among survivors of clergy abuse, their helpers, and those who purport to help but unwittingly create more individual and systemic harm. And it goes far beyond this important area of concern, providing insights for advocates, working for progressive causes, especially in politically-challenging times.

When one reads Miller's work one is reminded of E.M. Forster's words, "Only connect the prose and the passion, and both will be exalted... Live in fragments no longer (Forster, *Howards End)*." For decades, Miller has tirelessly beckoned the church and survivors to live in fragments no longer. She assists survivors of clergy to connect with other survivors and with healing professionals and lay companions committed to creating systems that heal. She teaches about the dynamics that facilitate abuse and the protection of abusers and abusive systems, so that lay and clergy leaders may be empowered to move beyond the deep, pointed shards of misinformation. She teaches about the dynamics of DIM thinking: how denial, ignorance, and minimization participate in individuals and systems colluding with abuse and further injuring survivors. Many have been empowered by the clarity of her terms, some have vigorously resisted her efforts, and many have been transformed by her teaching.

In *Enlarging Boston's SPOTLIGHT,* Miller has given us a readable narrative that at once weaves her own storied journey into the larger cultural, ecclesiastical, and historical context of her life's work. She has done an outstanding job in ensuring that the proverbial *baton* of story and context will be smoothly passed on to the next generation of survivors, advocates, and healers. This Spotlight will empower people both inside the church and those alienated by the church to find courage, hope, and resilience needed to address both systemic and personal issues inherent in sexual abuse by religious leaders. It will provide encouragement to individuals and institutions truly working for change in resistant systems, even beyond the church.

Dee Ann Miller has always been attentive to "grace notes," the small, apparently insignificant events that eventually, with God's help, become beacons of light and sources of meaning and sustenance for the journey. This attentiveness in her prose to the hand of God at work in the course of her advocacy work with both receptive and resistant persons gives the reader access to the source of her passion for truth, justice, and healing. And through this, both her prose and her passion exalt, nourish, and inspire us to continue this work as part of God's trajectory of love and justice.

Thank you, Dee.

The Rev. Dr. Sarah M. Rieth,
Chaplain and Diplomate in the American Association of Pastoral Counselors,
Southern Pines, North Carolina

Setting the Stage

When advocating for institutional change in regard to any matter of safety or health, we usually find ourselves having to navigate through deep, murky waters and on out into a much larger, turbulent sea. From long-term care to gun control and everything in between, it's all about seeing the larger picture, understanding the resistance, and staying the course.

When our work involves the community of faith, that community can be a great asset. Or, as in the case of abusive church leaders, it may be the biggest obstacle to health, safety, and justice imaginable. Because members of churches like to think of themselves as "one big, happy family," the unresolved problems of multiple "big, happy families" inevitably come into play on the institutional level. The 2016 Academy-Award-winning movie SPOTLIGHT shows us the challenge as it played out with Roman Catholics in the city of Boston.

The movie touches on the powerful role that survivors played in the story, demonstrating how individuals who are persistently advocating for a safer, healthier world can make a huge difference. What we see in this story can be applied to any issue and any institution—not only those of the community of faith. However, because faith issues are an intrical part of the complicated dynamics of sexual violence, domestic abuse, human trafficking or any other form of oppression that impacts the health of citizens, when abuse happens in the church, the spiritual dynamics are paramount to our study.

In the next thirty-eight chapters, I'll take you first into the back story where I had a ring-side view of Boston in 1993—not only to what was going on that city but far beyond, especially with the resistance to change in the largest of Protestant denominations in the world, the Southern Baptist Convention. From there, we'll go into ecumenical movements to bring about change in attitudes and responses as they specifically relate to abuse by clerics—first in America where the movement began, then across oceans and back to Africa, where my family's very personal encounter with collusion in the faith community began more than thirty years ago.

Shifting Gears in the Bowling Alley

"Sometimes ya' just step into the right puddles." With those words, my friend Nancy might as well have handed me a cup of hot fudge frosting to top off a slice of devil's food cake. Like the other morsel she'd tossed my way thirty minutes earlier, inside the bowling alley.

Unlike serious bowlers, I care less about my score than the weekly conversations each Friday morning among friends. Usually there are several of us—that day, only two. Fine with me. Nancy and I alone can cover *plenty* of territory.

More than anyone I know, she understands my chaotic process of writing, having learned the hard way two years ago, when she gave me so much of her time that I slipped her name below mine, on the cover of my last book. It takes little stretch to see how closely that piece of 19th century historical fiction, about homeless kids traumatized from vicious power tactics, closely parallels the real Spotlight story recently depicted on the big screen. Come to think of it, even the first book's title, "Just Following Orders,"[1] fits the sort of excuses bishops sometimes latch onto while sitting in their stone-walled fortresses, trying to avoid the truth about sexually-abusive priests.

Having just finished the last chapter of this book only hours before our time at the bowling alley, the idea of puddles was exactly what I needed to start this introduction. That's backwards to most folks, I know. Not for me. Nancy could easily tell you so.

Rest assured, I always start out my writing projects certain I know where I'm going. Yet by the time I finish, thanks to all the wonderful "puddles" I step into along the way, I end up with a whole keg of dynamite, off somewhere I never planned to be. So here I am, back where I started, hoping to better introduce you to what's in store.

Usually, when it's just Nancy and me, we begin talking about our current projects—her quilt and this intro, for instance. Nearly always, somewhere in the conversation, we end up touching on issues related to kids' needs or human dynamics. Between Nancy's thirty years of school-teaching and my thirty as a nurse/writer focusing on mental health, resiliency and systemic complicity with abuse in faith systems, we make quite a team.

Soon into our families, we're always hopping from one generation to the other, circling around to hubbies and in-laws. That leads us each wondering how our children all managed to grow up to the point they have in spite of us.

That particular day, about the seventh frame of our second game, having each managed a few strikes and spares in spite of me landing twice in the gutter, Nancy picked up her own ball, turned around to face me, and accidentally dropped a valuable piece of writing material right into my lap.

"It takes me a long time to warm up to anybody," she tells me.

"Oh, yeah? That's interesting." I wrinkle my forehead, trying to recall the day we first met. "Come to think of it, you were that way with *me*. Wonder why?"

"Bet it goes back to grade school!" she exclaimed like she suddenly had an epiphany. "Our little town was *re-e-all-y* segregated."

"You mean racially?"

"No, over religion. With me on the wrong side. Most of the town's Catholic. I had to barge my way into anything I wanted to do. Never got invited."

"Ooh! Making friends was a lot of work," I noted.

Nodding, she turned around for another strike before coming back to the table. "Finally, one girl who decided to be my friend said they'd learned at church that all Protestants are demons."

"That's not far from some Baptists I've known who claim Catholics aren't even Christian." I said, getting up for the next frame. "As a kid, we only had one Catholic in our whole school, far as I know, though could be some were hiding for safe-keeping. That one girl didn't get close to anyone. No wonder if she saw her whole school, like your friend, infested with infidels!"

By contrast, most Catholic survivors I've met in the last twenty-five years no longer want to be *associated* with folks who call themselves "Christian" at all, though many of these same survivors identify closer with Jesus than when they were staunch members of the Church, same as many Baptist survivors or Methodist or anyone in between may. They especially grasp the role played by clerics paralleling Pontius Pilate, as former priest Richard Sipe [1] likes to refer to when speaking of his own betrayal and ultimate experience of being treated as an outcast by bishops. On the way home, I got to thinking how the spiritual maturity of many Catholic survivors I know could easily show up most Baptists I've met.

Pulling up to a four-way stop on the drive home from the bowling alley, my mind returned to those puddles, which might just as well represent people as ideas. I thought how some dips in asphalt contain only nice clean rain water after a big storm. Those represent a lot of people I meet in the "assembly line" of writing. Otherwise, it's a mighty lonely career. Better still are all the new folks who come my way after publication, with interesting questions and comments—more puddles, that is—often making valuable contributions to my own evolution of thought. This book is filled with stories from these readers, each shared with their permission.

Sometimes it's the rather nasty mud puddles I learn from most. Antagonists are incredibly interesting, once I recover from the obnoxious mud-slinging and start examining the valuable, rich residue they leave behind.

The Most Significant Puddle

Cutting across campus one rainy afternoon at Oklahoma Baptist University, with a big bag of groceries in one hand and an umbrella in the other, I found myself facing one of the biggest mud puddles I'd ever seen. What an obstacle! I thought, having no idea how strategically placed this puddle would turn out to be.

Before me, lay three options. I could backtrack and take the long way around. I could risk losing both my umbrella and groceries as I leaped across the muddy divide. Or I could step into the soggy grass and slime around the puddle's edges. Taking my time, I carefully studied the obstacle and prepared to jump when suddenly... it dawned on me... I was not alone. The first hint, a pair of men's oxfords on the opposite side of that puddle. Raising my head ever so slowly, I found myself staring into the face of a fellow who seemed as uneasy about getting across the puddle as I was.

Somehow, we each made it and went our separate ways for several months before a mutual friend officially introduced me to the brown-eyed chap. Ron Miller, a ministerial student, I'd soon discover, had a passion to advocate for the oppressed that few men in powerful positions seem to ever grasp. Inherently, years before being ordained, he understood that the first priority in the gospel is to empower the powerless--something he began demonstrating as pastor of a most unusual Southern Baptist congregation near New Orleans Baptist Theological Seminary in the late 1960's, where he was enrolled while also working at an Episcopal neighborhood center. Every Sunday morning he preached to the only integrated Baptist crowd in the city, just down the street from the Black Panther's headquarters. Meanwhile we struggled together against immense racial bigotry on campus and in other SBC churches in that city.

Ten years later, after wading knee-deep through two other challenging pastorates, the two of us moved our family of four to Malawi, Africa, immersing ourselves linguistically and culturally to work under the largest evangelical mission board in the world for almost a decade, while residing in a nation under the militaristic control of one of the most corrupt dictatorships of that day. In spite of that, our work was fulfilling, our lives greatly enriched, until we suddenly discovered that our agency had considerable experience with "managing" sexual predators.

Today, such organizations often refer to themselves as "intentional communities" to justify the heavy-handed, control efforts they use to silence those who discover problems some of these "intentional community" have no intention of really owning. While intentions in communities that bear such a slogan may indeed be highly ethical, the exact opposite is often the case as their easily-threatened leaders circle the wagons to hide things they do not want known. Such was the case with the largest evangelical mission board in the world—yes the one we thought we could trust with our very lives.

In the end, it cost us our careers when we refused to "follow orders" to keep quiet about what we knew. Yet we retained something far more valuable—our integrity, our voices, and a determination to make a difference on a wide ecumenical basis. Soon this led to a study of the complex dynamics that contribute to collusion, a problem considered by many survivors to be far more devastating than the initial abuse itself.

You'll find me referring to big chunks of our personal story in the book you are about to read. Yet this book, *Enlarging Boston's SPOTLIGHT*, can best be understood by those who've read its predecessor, *How Little We Knew: Collusion and Confusion with Sexual Misconduct*.[2] It was that book which had me on morning drive-time radio in 1993, as "all of Boston was reeling," according to the show's host. That's where the first chapter of this book takes you.

As the Spotlight story clearly shows, Boston soon went back to sleep for eight years after the conviction of their most infamous child predator, illustrating profoundly my prophetic words during that 1993 interview.

Why the slumber? That's the question left largely unanswered in the movie, the one I trust you may begin to answer for yourself by the end of this book. It's one I've been wrestling with for over thirty years. And I've found the answer to be far more complicated than the question.

*****

[1] *Just Following Orders: Escape from Guerrilla Warfare in 1863* is the middle school version of the same story for grades 4 and 5, with the title *Might TALL Orders*. For much more info, see http://justfollowingorders.takecourage.org/

[2] Richard Sipe, the advisor on the telephone in the Spotlight movie, is a world-renowned, former priest and foremost expert on the Roman Catholic Church's problem with sexual abuse. Much more about him is interspersed throughout this book, beginning in Chapter 3.

[3] Much more on *How Little We Knew: Collusion and Confusion with Sexual Misconduct* and other writings can be found at http://www.takecourage.org/

"If it takes a village to raise a child,
it takes a village to abuse one." [1]

Chapter 1:
Small Comfort for Boston and Beyond

"You'll be on the most popular drive-time radio program in Boston tomorrow morning," said the publicist calling in 1993 from Prescott Press in Lafayette, Louisiana, to arrange the mid-December interview. "Seems the host thinks you might offer them some sort of *comfort* since you're not Catholic," she added with a slight giggle.

Like everyone in Lafayette, Lisa knew how much the people of Boston needed comfort. Eight years earlier her city of less than 50,000 had been forced to bear the brunt of the news that went out around the world. For years, local Church officials had failed to protect the children from a sexually-predatory priest named Gilbert Gauthe'. Adding to their shame, over $100,000,000 had been taken from the coffers that local Catholics had helped accrue.

Prescott had recently published the biography of J. Minos Simon, also a local guy who was the lawyer, now world renowned, for his success after taking it all on, thereby setting a precedent for many more to come. So the publisher had been more than happy to help broaden the education of America with a story of a Protestant American missionary-predator who'd managed to remain in Africa for a quarter of a century before officials of the mission board began stumbling all over one another, trying to justify the gross mismanagement of a case that held the same dynamics now being revealed in Catholic cases popping up across the nation.

The release of *How Little We Knew: Collusion and Confusion with Sexual Misconduct,* the story of injustice served to our family after being caught in the crossfire of this case, was turning out to be perfectly timed. Not only to broaden the education of Boston, but far beyond.

For much of the last two years, I'd been watching from our Iowa parsonage as the city of Boston was painfully assaulted with shocking revelations of Catholic officials' long-term mishandling of their now most-infamous priest and child molester.

It all culminated on December 6 in the twenty-year sentence that the perpetrator, former priest James Porter, had been able to plea bargain. In a side-bar next to the big story came an additional shock. John Doherty, one of hundreds of Porter's victims, was forfeiting $5000 of escrow money being held to silence him, alongside scores of other victims who had signed an agreement the previous summer with the diocese of nearby Fall River, not to speak of this settlement for at least a year. Where would this all end?

The original hero in the Boston story was Frank Fitzpatrick. By running want ads in key cities, simply asking, "Remember Father Porter?" he'd received calls from scores of victims like his own four children, who he'd been shocked to discover were all second-generation survivors of the same guy who had assaulted him in his own youth,

Porter's sentence was nothing, Fitzpatrick and thousands of other Catholic victims were rightfully saying to themselves, as they waited with bated breath to speak their own personal truths.

Over the past six weeks, Lisa's voice had become very familiar in our household. I was averaging two radio interviews per week from stations responding to a tiny ad Prescott had placed in a publication geared to programmers. Several stations even played recordings of syndicated programs in the wee hours of the morning, I discovered from a member of our congregation, waiting to tell me one Sunday as I walked into the sanctuary of the church my husband was pastoring. Unable to sleep a few hours earlier, she'd flipped the radio on to the sound of my pre-recorded voice, providing a strong reminder of how our words may continue working in spoken or written form, even while we're resting.

Many people find it anxiety-producing, talking to an unseen audience. Even if the topic is a common one like gardening and on a local TV program the speaker sees frequently, it can be unnerving. If you're an author who's written on a very controversial topic, talking to both an invisible host and a silent, invisible audience, you have to hope not to be literally "turned off" for saying something that upsets listeners. When it comes to being critical of a "sacred cow" like institutional religion, the chances are very high.

The author, no matter how prestigious, is at the mercy of the interviewer, who may have a hidden agenda. In fact, I was concerned most about someone purposely inviting me on to attack me verbally in order to help destroy the credibility of the emerging survivor movement.

While I can be very gracious and friendly, I'm not averse to taking on opposition. During that process, I work hard not to exhibit a "poor me" attitude. In fact, I don't want anyone's sympathy. I speak as one privileged and always appreciative of the opportunity, but make it clear I'm representing those who have not survived or still may need to remain voiceless.

I actually have a bit of a Pop-eye attitude. You remember how "the sailor man" was able to confidently declare "I yam what I yam?" And how he used spinach to fortify himself when he was ready to give out? Well, I certainly know who I am and believe it's all I need to be. My "spinach" is *what* I know with confidence, my story and the stories of so many others who have served as my own educators. It's a no-nonsense approach that most intellectually well-rounded hosts respected, whether on secular or Christian programs, with a surprising number of them seeming to be more knowledgeable than the average minister.

While I always want to be more than "Ron's wife," I generally prefer blending into ordinary life. Still, I allowed Lisa the liberty of using the "wife-and-daughter-of-a-minister card" in the "suggested introduction," sent with a review copy to interviewers to use whenever there was ample lead time. This added to my credibility, especially on Christian programs, where I was seen as "still an inside believer."

Since 1988, I'd availed myself of two tracks of intense study—not only to be more effective with patients, but also to enhance my additional work in which I was commonly referred to in bylines as a "psychosocial nurse writer." I'd gone back to school to finish course work started twenty-five years earlier toward a degree in behavioral science with community mental health emphasis, and also obtained an RNC status, having obtained official certification in psychiatric nursing through the American Nurses' Association. This qualified me to provide therapeutic services beyond most of my nursing colleagues. In the process, I'd learned much from clinical social workers and other members of the inter-disciplinary teams with whom I'd worked.

All the while I'd determined the horrors our family had been forced to endure, before being left like roadkill following our forced resignations, were going to serve as an educational piece—not only for us in our on-going process of spiritual and personal evolution, but also for the world, filled with people needing to awaken to what we'd been forced to discover.

Now, my latest specialty in writing was systemic complicity, often referred to as "collusion," common with sexual abuse in both families and larger institutions. In fact, that's the primary theme in the movie SPOTLIGHT—with clergy sexual abuse being obviously secondary to anyone watching closely. This set of dynamics extends to multiple destructive forces we so often choose to ignore. Yet it was now the hot-button topic in the institutional church, from which people were running from in all directions. What a place to be!

By the time *How Little We Knew* was published, I'd created an acronym that was being praised by social workers and other psychotherapists, as well as a few clergy. While I'd initially intended it to be used only to describe collusion with sexual abuse, it also works very well in substance abuse circles.

"DIM thinking" (Denial, Ignorance, Minimization)[1] is a cognitive disorder, I declared—though not found in the diagnostic manual of mental health disorders, commonly known as DSM-III. Nor would it be added to DSM-IV when it came out a few months after the Boston interview. No surprises there. I'd made it up—which was sort of bold for a woman who wasn't even qualified to diagnose a mental disorder.

Well, that's one of the fun things about being a writer—something like DIM thinking, which not a soul I've met yet has dared question, doesn't have to have official approval if it works for me as a writer. It does work, for several reasons: It's simple enough for the least educated to understand. By stating it as a disorder, it's something one would hope readers would want to address, not a phenomenon to be accepted as "normal"—same as anemia in Africa, I'd later write, adding symptoms (or common games of collusion), contributing factors, etc.[2] This thinking disorder can be corrected with education so that all of us can learn to recognize the problem and nip it in the bud when we spot it. "Call it," in other words. Flesh it out quickly, examine it, and externalize the problem, if need be, before owning it and seeing how it easily lodges within each of us as one of our many implicit biases, such as white privilege.

Since the original Spotlight story broke in 2002, adding to the wealth of publicity on professional sexual abuse, there have been few excuses for adults of average intelligence to remain naïve. If a person comes to tell another professional she or he has been abused by another professional these days, no matter what the age of the victim and no matter what the profession—there's no excuse at all for turning a deaf ear. And it makes no difference the degree of physical evidence or violence. The professional is the one responsible anytime he or she crosses the line, no matter who is said to have "made the first move." This was being held up with increasing frequency in the courts, and the test cases brought by courageous survivors who'd managed to find the courage and resources to bring these cases forward were not going away.

Yet in 1993, there was an especially great knowledge deficit in regard to abuse of adult women seeking professional services than there is even today. So, I was trying to hit that hard, whenever opportunity arose, as I also talked about the abuse of minors and sexual harassment and assault of adult women.

Our story was highly unusual, with the ages of victims of the same perpetrator ranging from fifteen to a grandmother in her late forties. This, with the perpetrator, in all but one of the known cases, so impulsive he didn't take time for "grooming"—all together clearly demonstrating how much many church officials may be willing to ignore in order to protect the status quo of the institution, even in cases like this where there had been extensive corroboration.

The Boston host began with a typical, fast intro that I can still recall close to verbatim: "Today we have a Protestant author, Dee Ann Miller, eager to tell us about her new book, *How Little We Knew: Collusion and Confusion with Sexual Misconduct*. Good to have you, Dee, to help us make sense of what we're hearing. The people of this city were already reeling from the Porter case. Now, if we can believe what we read, there are quite a few others 'round here. Help us understand how this can be."

How glad I was that he started out that way! Not only did it bring me up to date, since I'd not seen this latest article. It did the same for quite a few listeners who might also have missed it. With genuine empathy, totally void of surprise, my response came without missing a beat.

"I understand the city is shocked and sad, yet none of this surprises me in the least. In fact, experts predict we're going to soon hear of a lot more stories like this across the country in every denomination," I began.

*****

[1] A choice quote from McCarthy and Singer's movie *Spotlight*

[2] See http://takecourage.defining.htm

Chapter 2
Decisions, Decisions, Decisions

The most stressful part of the Boston interview came when the host pressured me to name the denomination we'd worked under. I refused, explaining that if I named a specific denomination, all other Protestants would say "That's just them, not us." I'd thought long and hard about this and was standing firm.

Most hosts supported this decision. In fact, several had validated it on the air. Not this one. I understood. After all, with Catholics in the acute phase of overwhelming shame and degradation, it would certainly be helpful to have others in the gutter with them.

Fortunately for me, with his tight schedule, there wasn't much time for the host to argue. I breathed a sigh of relief as I left for my office at the nursing agency. Overall things had gone remarkably smooth.

Double-Binds in Decision Making and Other Issues

From the very instant the first inappropriate move is made by a sexual offender a victim is instantly placed in a double-bind. With silence, safety for the criminal is assured. Unlike any other crime, a survivor must struggle alone with the secret, and often does for years. Most people don't even want to think that this might happen to them. Few have any idea how many decisions must be made over the course of a lifetime, how much energy it takes to keep quiet or how dangerous it is to speak out. Most survivors do not realize how they've come to live their lives inside this "pressure cooker" until they begin contemplating how to break the codes of secrecy.

Females tend to stuff that energy, often totally internalizing their feelings and ending up in deep, chronic depression. Males are more prone to act out aggressively when their anger overwhelms them. Due to homophobia, the stigma of emasculation, and the commonly-held myth that most male victims automatically turn into perpetrators, there's an entirely different set of issues to keep men silent, as well.

If a person gets robbed in the parking lot of a shopping mall, things aren't nearly as complicated unless the robber has kidnapped the victim.

You yell for attention and usually the crime is reported as you supply police with every detail you can remember. Nobody expects secrecy—not even the criminal. Even if a victim is unfairly blamed due to carelessness, nobody declares carelessness to be immoral or a sign the victim wanted to be robbed.

Yet a person not immediately reporting sexual assault will inevitably be blamed for *not* doing so. It's considered a sign you somehow "knew you were to blame" or "obviously didn't think it was as serious as you're now making it out to be."

If you do report, awkwardness and humiliation is always there in the reporting process, even if you have the rare understanding you're totally innocent, as I did the moment I drove away from my assailant's front door. There's also a strong chance others will blame you, anyway, due to the common belief "every victim does *something* to cause this."

When going public, in addition to the reason I stated in the Boston interview for not naming the denomination, there's often the legitimate concern for other, more fragile victims in the very same case. Mostly, I was still worried, in 1993, about one of the teenage victims in our story, now a single mom with a precious little boy to raise.

In spite of the deep betrayal we'd suffered when our former colleagues failed to join us in confronting a system that had messed up so badly, I honestly had no desire to further alienate or embarrass them by naming the small country where we'd served. None of us had ever been forewarned we might encounter a perpetrator among our colleagues. While by today's standards, this sounds very naïve, such naivety was practically universal in the 1980's, only reflective of how deeply hidden these secrets were. Even the eyes of the most progressive journalists were still hard to open. It was much too risky. After all, their own livelihood, especially in large Catholic communities or small towns across America, was invariably on the line

Still, I placed sufficient hints in *How Little We Knew* to make the story quite transparent to anyone in the evangelical world. Not only were Southern Baptists widely known for their size relative to other mission boards. SBC missionaries were considered most fortunate in not having to raise personal funds. We were well supported compared to other groups and, generally, had far more autonomy to choose where we went, how we did furlough, whether our children went to boarding school or not—all of these factors I made sure to place in the first few pages so that anyone in mission circles who wanted to reach out to me would be able to do so knowingly aware of who I was. However, I also had a realistic fear of personal retaliation. Knowing the sinister tactics used toward another SBC mission family, I would put nothing past this system I'd practically worshiped for forty years.

Late in 1988, we'd talked to Diana Wade and her attorney in a conference call after reading of her family's ordeal. She and her oldest daughter had filed a multi-million-dollar law suit against the Board.

In this case, the perpetrator was the children's father, George Thomas Wade, Jr., now serving a prison sentence for unspeakable acts for which his children would suffer lifelong scars.

In fact, the Board official who was directly complicit in this case was a man Ron and I knew personally as "Bud"—officially Dr. Marion Jerome Fray, Jr. In 1982, when the Wade's oldest daughter Renee courageously turned to her housemother and later to Fray to report that her father had molested her, "Bud," as Renee would also have known him, instructed the teenager not to tell her mother of the abuse. Even more unconscionable, he agreed to allow George to continue his work while avoiding counseling even after admitting guilt. As a result, two other children went on to endure the same fate as their big sister until the truth finally began coming out and the family returned to the United States in 1984. George was convicted of child abuse and sent to serve a twelve-year prison sentence the following year.

This had all transpired already, unbeknown to us in early 1987, as Davis Saunders, the man in charge of all of SBC mission work in East Africa, sat across from us with a toothpick hanging from his mouth as he blatantly lied to us: "I'm naïve. I've never had a case like yours." No, he hadn't. He'd had one even worse in many ways, and he'd not learned a thing! Yet he was about to be replaced—or conveniently relocated himself. That's what we learned at the end of this harrowing conversation after we'd spent so much energy thinking we were talking to the very man who would be making the final decision. Instead we'd be soon starting much of the process over with another we'd never met!

I tried to keep in touch with Diana after we first spoke in the fall of 1988, but never got a reply to any of my follow-up attempts. The Virginia State Supreme Court eventually sided with the Board in 1991, a year after a lower court awarded the Wade's the $1.5 million. In so doing, they left the sorrowing family with nothing after all they'd been through!

I wish now I had possessed the courage and had felt free to say all I knew in 1993. Knowing the power of this system, however, despite the tremendous courage I did have, I remained intimidated by this powerful system. This, in spite of our attorney's assurance that I had nothing to fear in the way of a lawsuit. What did he know in comparison to the powerful guys hired by the Foreign Mission Board of the Southern Baptist Convention, I couldn't help but wonder? The double-binds were incredible, the ethical dilemmas beyond belief.

Wade's attorney had further assured us we had no legal recourse, even if we wanted to consider such, considering the complications at that time with all cases of sexual harassment of adults that involve male-to-female Americans overseas except on embassy or military property on top of proving intent with retaliation.

The Wade family's situation was different he explained. In the end, it didn't matter so far as whether I used their already-public story or not. Not being able to contact them, fearing I would only add to their pain, I elected to do no more than merely mention that there'd been another case that hadn't turned out any better than ours.

If only I'd known what was ongoing with the Wade's, I would certainly have included much more of their story in *How Little We Knew*. In fact, it would be another twelve years before I'd learn anything more of their tragedies than what I've just written. And only in the process of writing this book did I discover much, much more through Debra McKinney, an Alaskan journalist who managed to stay involved with the family much longer than I, and supplied me with news of the unintended death of one of the Wade's grandchildren months before I was on Boston radio in 1993. The tragedy was directly related to the addiction of the child's mother, the news articles clearly show,[1] providing us with a chilling illustration of how the sins of "the fathers" get visited onto future generations, causing tragedies for years to come.

Several station hosts, based on concerns having nothing to do with the Wade case, also feared liability in even interviewing me. They wanted to ascertain I wasn't going to name the perpetrator on the air or anyone who had covered up for him, since he'd not been officially convicted in a court of law.

Thus, I simply did not name names at all. Neither did I name the denomination or location—following the same course as Marie Fortune after she served as an advocate. She turned that story into a case study *Is Nothing Sacred?* [2] in 1989, in a case where she'd been called in as an advocate for a much more theologically-moderate congregation.

More Back Story

Whenever airtime was ample, I pointed out how isolation, especially from inadequate law enforcement, increases the likelihood of both abuse and collusion. This we see in rural areas, as well as mission fields.

The inter-dependency of individuals in these small communities complicates reporting immensely, which was certainly the case in my own decision-making. In 1986, as more cases came to light, my colleagues and supervisors tried to make me the scapegoat, in fact, because I'd only made a local report of my assault to one female colleague initially, though I'd done so within twenty-four hours. out of concern for others. In the uncertainty, I told her I didn't know what I wanted her to do with this report, since we did not even have written guidelines to show us what protocol should be followed in these Dark Ages. She never followed up with me. Nobody did—not even the male official who brushed it off after she turned for guidance.

It had been over two years, even after I'd spoken unknowingly to another of this offender's victims, that the next person came forward, including one of our teenage daughter's best friends. In that process, a national teenager suffered a dislocated shoulder after another assault by the same offender, too embarrassed and frightened to tell the male medical assistant in the emergency room what happened. "Fortunately!" the woman to whom I'd first reported declared, clearly more interested in the well-being of the "Mission family" than the young girl.

To my amazement, once other incidents were reported, I was still the one getting scapegoated, as the most outspoken always is. Totally irrational, those in the greatest denial were claiming if I'd just made my story more widely known, all the others would have been prevented. If so, then why, after all the reports, nobody had been in a hurry to take decisive action to even to get the assailant out of the country?

Double-Binds of Reporting

Pamela Cooper-White, addresses the double-binds of a single survivor reporting sexual harassment, suggesting that speaking to another person who is in a position to provide an extra set of ears and eyes may be the best option when fear of retaliation is an issue.[3] From reports I've since gotten from clergywomen, I know it's an option many have chosen if they dare to report at all. A hostile environment is already an issue for most in the profession, merely by gender. If not in their local church, most certainly among their male counterparts in the wider community. Or the military. Or on college campuses.

Still, plenty of nuns are victims of abusive priests. Yvonne Maes, an author and friend I first met at Linkup, has written such a story in *The Cannibal's Wife*.[4] Though I've received far more previously-untold reports of nuns abusing children physically, emotionally, or even sexually while being charged with responsibilities of educating them.

Beyond Boston

"Only hitch on this one is you'll need to get up in the middle of the night," Lisa said. "It's the most popular evening talk show in Hawaii, specifically about couple relationships, so they'll need you both."

Three days later we sat chatting away, side by side, both fully alert at my over-sized desk, armed with coffee and thick bathrobes to ward off a 2 a.m. February chill.

Thirty seconds before airtime, I reached for the receiver on the phone's first ring. After a quick greeting, the lead-in music had us wide awake with a lively rendition of "The Hallelujah Chorus"—except with a different set of lyrics, all of which I've forgotten except the lyrics for the first two measure. Instead of the familiar word "Hallelujah" with the usual strongly-accented first syllable, there were four one-syllable words sung with exactly the same pulse asking: "H-o-w's your love life? H-o-w's your love life?"

I glanced at Ron and almost busted as his eyebrows shot up into his bald head, giving him the appearance of a startled jackrabbit. "We don't have to tell the congregation about this, do we?" he whispered, as timidly as the night he'd tried to propose to me on a reel-to-reel tape recorder, sneaking the big question in so quietly between familiar songs, I didn't even know he'd asked.

"No," I mouthed back. "It'll be our little secret." And it was as far as the congregation knew. Not a soul ever found out about it, even as they helped us celebrate our silver wedding anniversary. So here we now sit in Kansas, finally with the "cat out of the bag" and our golden anniversary fast approaching in late summer of this year.

The show turned out to be one of the best experiences of our lives. The host, who had taken time to familiarize himself with our story more than most hosts, said something akin to what a family therapist had a few years earlier: "After all you've been through, I'm surprised to see you still sitting in the same room and able to smile."

We answered candidly, readily admitting we'd had plenty of conflict, common for couples going through any kind of shared sorrow, especially involving dual career loss in mid-life. What helped most was keeping communication lines open. Certain this would all eventually pass somehow, we'd affirmed one another frequently, took turns being angry, and were neither totally down at the same time—perhaps most attributable to having two distinctively different personalities, something we've learned to monopolize on.

Ron talked about how hard it had been standing up to those we cared about deeply, people we believed had the same set of values we did. Being authentic as a couple was very important to each of us, as important as trying to be the best possible parents we could in the process. That was a huge challenge, too. Fortunately, we did not have small children, unable to comprehend anything of the situation we were in. Throughout the case, we'd still been in constant double-binds in regard to our teenage children. We wanted them to understand the reasons for our decisions. Yet, how much did they need to know? We also couldn't even imagine staying in any ministry, knowing what we knew now, without continuing to stand. What would this have said to our teenagers, I asked the audience aloud, if we'd chosen to remain silent?

What a balancing act it had been! No matter what we did, they would suffer—especially our daughter, being caught in the middle due to her close relationship with her "cousin" and close friend, who would suffer lifelong consequences from what she'd been through, even if the impact was never fully acknowledged.

The greatest tensions had come with mini-decisions, things we didn't always agree upon as a couple—like when and how to go about resigning. This coincides for many couples trying to decide to bring a court case or to go public, often with the spouse of the victim wanting to hold back to protect his partner from being hurt further. Many marriages break up when the stress becomes too overwhelming or the spouse joins others in blaming the victim.

What Remained Unspoken

Our resignation, in one month, ended up coinciding with the death of Ron's father, as well as the political take-over of the Southern Baptist Convention, which was the top story in religious news for that month of June, 1988. What a month of grief! Having elected not to name the denomination, we also could not tell the part about the grief that we already knew many others, like Jimmy Carter, were also feeling. It was as if our entire faith tradition had been stolen from us as moderates and liberals in the significant minority that was willing to leave from the much larger group who elected to stay rather than rock the boat on the stormy sea of fundamentalism.

Over the next two years, our decisions involved making a denominational transfer, something we knew, as social liberals, we would have eventually faced anyway, even without the immensely personal betrayal we'd experienced. In the interim, we successfully navigated near disasters due to the economic impact—this we could and did state. Both of us went back to school to enhance our skills in counseling with all four of us struggling simultaneously, figuring out how to meet college costs.

Shared Sorrows of Whistle-Blowers

As I saw it, ours was a classic whistle-blowing story above all. Overall our "love life" had remained strong, we explained to the Hawaiian host in the wee hours of that morning. It was our loss of careers, the spiritual betrayal, and being forced out of our adopted culture that was far greater than the impact of the assault for either of us. We both still missed working together closely on a daily basis. And, oh, how we all four missed Africa!

I cautioned listeners to never assume they know anyone's story before they hear it. Couples who have been through immense trauma should be asked what they need and given a chance to tell their stories, as this program was allowing us to do. That's how we all learn from resilience as much as we learn from those who suffer long-term, I stressed. No two stories are alike, though there's a tendency for some to want them to be, for it provides a convenience for those who prefer over-simplification and are prone to the annoyance of stereo-typing.

In the end, universal truths are far more important than the facts that doubters want to try to disprove.

After forty-five minutes, lines were opened for call-ins. How good it was to hear the voices of listeners with questions and comments! As the hour came to a close, with phones still ringing, the host announced how every call was first screened. Some had been too broken up to speak on the air. They were only calling in to express appreciation. He was able to extend the program an additional fifteen minutes to accommodate more callers. It was overwhelmingly positive for the two of us. If this had been the only result of our stand, it was worth the entire cost.

Near the end, the man fielding calls slipped a note for the host to read. One caller unable to speak declared herself to be a woman of deep faith, troubled that her church had not addressed these universal issues. Now, having found out through this program, she vowed to ask questions and to insist her own denomination do everything possible to put a stop to collusion.

Ten years earlier, I would have assumed this would be the reaction of every member of the laity upon finding out such evil existed. Instead, because it wasn't, these problems still flourished. People in the pews like her must now rise up, I told the audience, and stop deferring to people in positions of power who were more interested in protecting "equity" than making adequate reparations to those harmed.

Most programs have long since faded from my memory. Naturally, the two where open hostility was shown are among the most memorable. Yet each has served as a treasure for writing and teaching.

The only one with a female host turned out to be downright funny. Out on the West Coast, in a syrupy, schoolmarm voice, I got a serious scolding from our interviewer. It felt more like a scalding.

By then, I'd already done a good deal of education, even getting in Marie Fortune's very useful explanation about the difference in secrecy and confidentiality. Confidentiality is for protecting the vulnerable. Secrets, which only serve to protect power, are what must be avoided.

Our story was only one of many that had Protestant leaders starting to recognize that Catholics didn't have a monopoly on these problems, I declared before quoting Catholic survivor Dennis Gaboury, who had once told a roomful of bishops: "We're not your enemies. We're your last best hope."

My notes on DIM thinking, which I always kept near the phone, I also reached for as I named for Susie the games of collusion: pass the buck, let's make a deal, let's pretend, speak no evil, role reversal, and out-of- sight-and- out-of- mind.

She really liked all that. Yet she clearly did not like me using "a secular word like patriarchy" as I spoke of some reasons for collusion.

"There's no place for the word 'patriarchy' in a Christian discussion!" Susie exclaimed. "Sexual abuse is just plain old sin, Dee." An awkward silence fell between us.

In addition to not having to worry if my freshly-washed hair was still soaking wet when doing radio interviews remotely, I appreciated that nobody on the other end could see my gestures or facial expressions.

I gestured to Ron. Wouldn't he like to jump in? No need for my suggestion—two seconds later Susie had the same idea.

Unfortunately, for Susie, it didn't go so well from that point on, though she deserves an A+ for Attempting.

"Ron, can you help us out here?" she asked.

"Certainly, Susie," he replied in his meekest pastoral voice. "Patriarchy is actually an Old Testament concept."

Apparently. he wasn't pastoral enough.

"Thank you, Ron and Dee," were the last words we heard before the phone went dead. We never found out what Susie did with the last thirty minutes of that program, but we enjoyed an unusually long lunch hour and a few laughs with our sandwiches.

Had we been granted a few more seconds, some west coast resident might have appreciated hearing Ron humbly tell how he still struggled with his own faith some days as much as any survivors we knew. Or how he'd contemplated whether to even return to ministry for more than two years. Probably wouldn't have been a good idea, though. Susie would probably have railed him for his even backsliding in the first place.

A FEW WEEKS EARLIER, on a broadcast in Missouri, known as "Jubilee," the host kept airways open for the full hour. After twenty minutes, I was halfway thinking of hanging up on him. However, I stood my ground and ended up being glad I did. For if there were any women listening with a history of either sexual or domestic abuse, they needed to hear me take this guy on. He clearly illustrated many games and myths of DIM thinking, challenging and discounting me at every turn, like a defense attorney asking inappropriate questions, all which I managed to deflect in my charge-nurse manner without using a single "naughty word," though I actually did use "patriarchy" without getting directly scalded!

Repeatedly, he insisted collusion was primarily a Catholic problem, "not possible with *real* Christians."

I talked to Lisa. Would it be possible for me to get a recording of this show? I'd love to listen to the complete dialogue without being in the middle of it—just to learn what I could. She came through, same as always, immediately filling my request that resulted in a cassette recording of the entire interview—and more—just days later!

As soon as the program ended, in a voice as smooth as the man who played Cardinal Law in Spotlight, the host might as well have deleted everything I'd said. "I think you'll have to use some discernment here, folks. This woman is just a little too eager to sell books. In my denomination, we have things all worked out... I don't know anyone who doesn't." A little more research told me how wrong he was. The Assembly of God, despite written policies, ignored experts' recommendations with no provision for making founded allegations public. As a result, offenders were quietly allowed to find their way to "new places of service," if not within the ranks of Assemblies, in other groups, same as with Southern Baptists.

In every situation, even the most disparaging moments like this, I've always reminded myself that someone is most certainly out there somewhere, thinking of the next step to approaching these issues within their own community. If anyone had asked me why I wrote the book, in fact, I might have simply said: "To enlarge conversations wherever doors may open."

Today, in 2017, my conversations often include parts of this story we lived, for it is testimony that I've learned can serve the larger community immensely. That story primarily serves as a launching pad now, as we've opened our ears and our hearts to much more. We've come to have more empathy overall, due to the horrific persecution we personally encountered, sharing bonds with advocates working on topics found on the front cover of this book and far more—all providing for possibilities to have discussions and a variety of opportunities for expanding conversations in groups, large and small.

So, as the interviews came to an end in late spring of 1994, the stage for future ministry on a wide ecumenical basis was beginning.

Truth was marching on.

*****

[1] "MOTHER GOING TO JAIL, SON'S DEATH GETS WOMAN 23 MONTHS" from Anchorage Daily News (AK) - Thursday, December 9, 1993, Author: LIZ RUSKIN Daily News reporter ; Staff

[2] Fortune, Marie, 1989, *Is Nothing Sacred? When Sex Invades the Pastoral Relationship*, 1st edition, Harper & Row.

[3] Cooper-White, Pamela, 2012, *The Cry of Tamar: Violence Against Women and the Church's Response*, 2nd edition, Fortress Press, p. 75: "Notice any possible witnesses who might be able to corroborate your story and discuss the situation with them..... Should a pattern of repeat offenses with multiple victims emerge, this will further corroborate each of the victims' complaints."

[4] Maes, Yvonne, 1991, *The Cannibal's Wife*, Herodius.

Chapter 3
Strategic Planning

In spite of what Gary Wills wrote in his commentary for *NY Daily* in January of 2016, SNAP (Survivors Abused as Priests) wasn't the least bit "nascent" when the Spotlight team successfully uncovered the big story about hundreds of abusive priests in Boston. Anybody even half awake in Catholic circles knew this back in 2002. David Clossey, long-time executive director of the organization, confirms: "We were *far* from nascent; but it was certainly hard to attract any kind of sustained or national media before the Globe series." He and founder Barbara Blaine "worked full tilt for the next fifteen years," as now Managing Director Barbara Dorris puts it, without a hint as to how much she herself has done to respond to the flood of reports since 2002 or the tidal wave this past year after the release of the Academy-Award-winning movie.

The Linkup, another survivor organization comprised mostly of Catholics, was also very active during the ten years preceding 2002. Both encouraged survivors like Phil Saviano, who persistently kept going back to members of the press until the Globe's Spotlight team decided to disregard what others said about him and pay attention. SNAP and Linkup, through its newsletter, served as comfort to Phil each time powerful locals discounted and ignored him.

Though separate entities with somewhat different philosophies, these organizations functioned like a pair of strong twin cities. As with most twin cities, there was a degree of healthy friction between the two. Some survivors moved freely back and forth, reaping the benefits of both. In addition to their larger annual meetings, each organization added hundreds more contacts each year to those asking for support, though unable to make the trip.

SNAP had several small cells meeting regularly, like the one in Boston, even before that city was thrown into chaos due to the collaboration of the Globe's journalists with Saviano and others like him. After 2002, many more cells sprang up. Now, thanks to the Spotlight movie, they're growing even larger, now with 25,000 strong, as leaders branch out to train more volunteers. Survivors can no longer be hidden "under a bushel." [1]

To the average viewer, SPOTLIGHT is a movie about the Catholic Church. To others, it's about the problem with religion in general. To Protestants in the know, the entire elephant of Christianity deserves to be placed in the spotlight for its historic complicity with sexual abuse, along with the Jewish and Islamic communities, and on and on. Wherever we believe sexual abuse cannot possibly exist is likely one of the best places of all for it to be lurking safely in plain sight.

Of course, this is also related to the chronic crisis of sexual violence on campuses, where institutional protection has long attempted to hide the problems, assuming what's out of sight won't be on the minds of prospective students or their parents. Yet these days, wise parents and students should be most interested in those with zero tolerance policies. There's also the public school stories galore, as people at SESAME, an organization dedicated to Stopping Educator Sexual Abuse, Misconduct and Exploitation, will be quick to tell you as they discuss the problem of "passing the trash" from one school to the other. Whether the problem is found in hospitals, day care centers, nursing homes, therapists' offices, or a large extended family, the problem of complicity invariable will exist to a degree. Yet few members of these groups who do "get it" are still surprised when they encounter it, finding themselves at odds with the very people they've long believed to be trustworthy.

Spotlight invites us to ask how an entire city can sit and sleep with organized crime going on all around in the name of God. We might also ask how entire cities filled with espoused Christians can be oblivious to other forms of human trafficking—of which clergy sexual abuse is only one major form because of the way good old boys are protected by their own buddies. We are all responsible. The Spotlight message covers the whole city, not only those of formal religious affiliation, as screen writers Tom McCarthy and Josh Singer clearly show us.

Some commentators see investigative journalism as the most important part of the movie. Indeed, that's important. Yet I see much more. There were many courageous people in this story who deserve as much credit as the journalists. What about the "minor" characters—the survivors, that is? Or the man on the telephone, my friend Richard Sipe, who dared suggest problems nobody else could imagine before 1985.

Getting in on the Ground Level

As soon as Jeanne Miller, Linkup's founder, heard about *How Little We Knew*, she sent an enthusiastic letter of gratitude along with a request for Ron and me to come to the first leadership conference for Linkup, which she was in process of scheduling. This would be a widely ecumenical, collaborative effort, she explained. She had big dreams for representatives from every faith group in America to come together in hopes of creating a spiritual movement for survivors.

Eager to get involved, we took off for Collegeville, Minnesota in early June, 1994, expecting to find many other Protestants in a crowd of perhaps 100 or more. Instead, twenty-two Catholic souls showed up along with us and two other Protestants. Ron was the only Protestant man in the group. That was it. Like long-lost relatives, who'd finally found one another after years of unexplained separation, we bonded quickly. After living under the same heavy cloud of knowledge for years, some many years, we were eager to listen and eager to share.

Nobody complained of the dismal corridor designated for us to meet. Yet I couldn't help noticing how dimly-lit it was, and totally void of color.

"One of the hardest parts of this work is knowing far more than you can say," Jeanne Miller said to me, only minutes after we met. "So many stories of people afraid to talk when somebody from the press occasionally comes around, really wanting to listen."

Among the twenty-six of us, about half were men who'd been abused, as boys, by priests. There were a couple of female Catholic survivors, as well.

Of the three female Protestants, each of us represented a distinct group, common among female survivors. One who was a victim of abuse as an adult in counseling; one, a victim of childhood incest who was abused by her own father and happened to now be a lesbian clergywoman, and myself as victim of aggressive sexual harassment by a clergy colleague, whose victims included adolescents, one a national to whom we'd been sent to serve.

In stateside churches, there is a fourth category of victims very common among females in Protestant circles—those abused as teens by youth directors or ministers of music. In these cases, especially in theologically conservative circles, the victims are often older teens, equated as adults though developmentally far from adulthood, despite how state laws may classify them. The perpetrators, since they may not be ordained, may sometimes be considered less powerful than the senior pastor of a congregation in the system, yet this is often not the case at all, in the eyes of the victim.

There were several psychotherapists in the group. Richard Sipe, [2] the oldest among them, had been treating priests with all sorts of mental health problems for nearly three decades.

Peter Isley, himself a survivor, knew how difficult it was to find any counselor able to understand the unique issues of this population. Therefore, he'd set up a small one-of-a-kind inpatient unit, specifically for that purpose, in the treatment facility where he practiced.

Walter Bera, who specialized in treating male survivors of sexual abuse in general, had good reason for the smile on his face, having played a significant role in getting James Porter convicted. In collaboration with Porter's own therapist, he passed along written accounts from some of Porter's survivors, who were more than willing to help "refresh" Porter's memory.

Bill Bates and his wife Joan were there from Toronto, the only other couple present. They'd been married thirty-three years, which is an amazing feat for a survivor of childhood sexual abuse, especially when the perpetrator is a priest. From the time they met, Joan knew her husband had also suffered as the son of an alcoholic mother. Of course, Father Weaver took advantage of this emotionally needy child, taking him places and buying him anything he wanted in order to get his own needs satisfied.

Oh, how the couple had struggled to cope with the seeds of destruction the priest had sewn in that child's psyche! "It was as though this person had the power to reach into the computer of my mind, placing a virus into my immature logic," he told several church officials with Joan by his side, three months before that June meeting.

He'd been able to take that step due to the additional support and blessing of Father Greg Battafarano, who now sat beside the Bates, ready to join hands with other advocates.

How Bill managed to cope with this "virus," staying faithful to his family and church, even working alongside Joan in a vibrant, weekend youth ministry for years while raising three children of their own, is a testimony to the deep commitment in their rare relationship. Bill now credits Joan for seeing them through, calling her "my warrior."

Soon after the small intimate meeting at St. John's, the Bates would set up a Canadian branch of Linkup. Over the next few years, they welcomed childhood survivors of abuse at Church-run Indian boarding schools, one of the major scandals among a vast array of collective, ecumenical stories yet to be exposed.

In 2014, near the end of his 400-page story, *The Cemetery of My Mind*,[3] Bill makes a strong, eloquent, theological statement: "He abused my body, but I own my soul."

Reading this brought to mind Ron's constant watchword that helped him maintain his own sanity during our struggles, which pale compared to what the Bates have been through. "No one is going to own my soul."

Coming to this conclusion, no matter how long it takes, is a sign of spiritual health and the best antidote for systemic collusion. Through the years, Ron and I have come to count as our greatest treasures friendships like with the Bates, forged whenever such dear souls have briefly entered our lives due to the deepest spiritual suffering we have ever witnessed.

Jeanne's vision for Linkup was two-fold. Foremost was spiritual healing for survivors like her son. Not anything religious, for this was about healing souls *wounded by religion.* Anyone naïve enough to believe most childhood survivors of sexual abuse by priests would ever want to go back to any church needed to spend some time studying the issues. Many survivors would drive out of the way to avoid even going by a Catholic Church. And this has not changed. This is true for many Protestant survivors, as well, no matter their age at the time of their abuse. Except quite a few, often due to transitions into more theologically progressive groups, end up going to other denominations, a transition most Catholics seem unable to forge.

Jeanne's second priority was pushing cases toward resolution-- whatever it took. Ideally, advocacy and justice would still come from inside the Church. Realistically, this seldom happened. Church officials seemed to be immune to saying: "We blew it! Now, what can we do to help?"

"I'm sorry" by itself, though seldom offered, didn't cut it for most. Two-year-old's can get by with "I'm sorry" for carelessly breaking a trinket. People who carelessly disregard human lives must do much more, and they should know this without having to be taught, for Pete's sake!

Assistance with rehabilitation and likely at least a decade's compensation for therapy cost would be minimal for starters.

Instead most survivors were getting nothing but insults and little, if any, help for therapy.

"We were *ordered* into therapy!" I told Jeanne, laughing as I spoke, though it wasn't funny at the time it happened, of course. "They had the idea they could convince us it was a sign of insanity to stand up to a corrupt system like we tried to do. It depends on how you define 'insanity.'"

What *is* funny today: hearing Ron's account of a story once too painful for him to even share with anyone—how he said to colluding family mental health consultant, occupying a strategic spot in the Board's tower of commands: "Let's go together to see this psychiatrist. I'll tell him the whole story." What he would have told, had the consultant agreed to go, were the actions the consultant had chosen to cop out on. Of course, who's to say that the hand-picked psychiatrist would have been a person of greater character than the hand-picked, unscrupulous lawyers, hired to protect the status quo.

While the growing sense of humor among members of Linkup wouldn't be coming in great doses for several more months, Jeanne did joke about how, with us sharing the same last name, we should search for some biological link. "I could sure use some new cousins," she declared.

We all had questions, acknowledging there was so much to learn from one another. We were navigating a journey for which there was no script, same as in those recent radio interviews. I don't know about anyone else, but to this day I still play the "tapes" from those conversations over and over in my mind, to remind me of why I remain available to others.

On the last day, Richard Sipe talked about celibacy as one of several factors complicating priests' lives, thereby contributing to a culture of secrecy about sexuality in general. Scarcely half of priests he'd counseled were living celibate lives in the strictest sense of the word, he declared. The celibate requirement provided a convenient justification for the evil invasions they made into the souls and bodies of young men and women. Knowing how unlikely kids would be to talk, and how Catholic theology considers it a venial sin to disobey a priest, they were easy prey. To a Catholic child, they're refusing God when they refuse to submit to the wishes of a priest.

While I knew that Richard had a valid point, well-established in his 1990 book, *A Secret World: Sexuality and the Search for Celibacy*, which I planned to grab off a shelf of The College of St. Mary's in Omaha as soon as I got back home, I may have sounded argumentative when I reminded him we shouldn't forget that Protestant offenders and their buddies didn't have the celibacy requirement. We had plenty of abuse, too—and it wasn't limited to abuse of adult women by any means, as some wanted to believe. There were most definitely many minors among the victims in more theologically conservative groups like Southern Baptists. Clear validation would come from Carolyn Heggen, though I would not discover for several years how she'd pulled together the work of several scholars to clearly state:

> *"A disturbing fact continues to surface in sex abuse research. The first best predictor of abuse is alcohol or drug addiction in the father. But the second best predictor is conservative religiosity, accompanied by parental belief in traditional male-female roles. This means that if you want to know which children are most likely to be sexually abused by their father, the second most significant clue is whether or not the parents belong to a conservative religious group with traditional role beliefs and rigid sexual attitudes.*[4]

I would soon learn, however, that the number of female victims among Catholics exceeds male, same as it does with Protestants. The female victims, abused as adults or teens, many who become the mothers of priests' children, are the most closeted and unacknowledged of all Catholic survivors.

Ratios of minors to adults are similar for Protestants. The adults simply go unacknowledged and misunderstood so much more easily to this day. People do not comprehend the power differential that is still there with adult parishioners, especially when they are emotionally needy or turn to clergy in desperate need of spiritual or emotional guidance during crisis.

Patrick Wall [5] has given multiple reasons why adult women, even if abused as adolescents, don't come forward. It's partly because they are so badgered by defense attorneys to lay out every detail of their sexual history, in order to re-enforce the common beliefs in the minds of jurors that a female was most likely the seductress. This can be very damaging to current relationships, of course, if the survivor's partner does not already know all of her history.

Another factor with Catholics was their tendency to think of the "age of consent" as much lower than even the law indicates, Wall says. This is also common in other theologically conservative groups, I pointed out, especially in the Deep South, where girls have traditionally been expected to grow up and be responsible adults around the age of puberty in many cases, whereas "boys will be boys" operates much longer—actually for life in the minds of so many. Whenever I hear "boys will be boys" in reference to professional sexual misconduct, I quickly added, "Yes, and men should be men."

Wall left the priesthood a few years after this St. John's meeting, unable to tolerate what he was discovering as he was sent to "clean up" or serve as what's commonly referred to as "an after-pastor" when an abuser is removed from a pastoral post. Wall's now an expert in canon law, working in the office of Jeff Anderson, a Minnesota attorney who also served on The Linkup Board of Directors in the early years.

I would stick to the collusion piece, attempting to enlarge conversations primarily about this fascinating topic as a vital piece of both systems prevention and the survivors' essential need to see how easily otherwise very intelligent, trustworthy individuals—any of us, in fact--can so easily be complicit if we are too close to a case to clearly see what's going on.

I've often been reminded of what Richard Sipe said just before we broke up from that powerfully inspirational weekend.

"Solving this problem is going to take us all."

What he extended was a gift to us all, reminding me of what I'd encountered in Africa as I learned to truly listen to greatest of all experts, "the least of these," the disenfranchised with no formal schooling. As an "expert," working as a nurse and directing small community development projects, I found myself continually humbled by what they could teach me about extremely complex issues. More amazing, *this was how they rightfully saw themselves.* Whenever I failed to remember this, they'd find ways to show me how I might have erred. That's true wisdom!

Likewise, giving scholars and clergy sole ownership of this gigantic collective story in the search for answers is a recipe for failure. We dare not do it. As a nurse, often occupying a middle management position, looking at the "great and mighty" while also working closely with both patients and fine staff who are considered on the totem pole of life to be "the least of these," I recognize how we are graced by the contributions of the scholarly experts; but dare not fail to honor equally the other experts, those yet to find their power. This includes survivors of childhood sexual abuse by clerics. The survivors who once were lost in confusion, but have managed to find their way back to life honor me often with their presence.

The powerful and most educated among us can't learn without listening to the powerless. That's a spiritual principle. It's also justice.

"Solving this problem *is* going to take us all."

So what is *the problem*? In less than three months, most of us would be back for the second international gathering of The Linkup right there on the same campus. And much to the surprise of many, our keynote speaker would direct us toward the root of the primary problem… which as we'd discover just may be the *real problem* few viewers of Spotlight can fully grasp.

To solve the problem of clergy sexual abuse, we have to look at a lot of problems, going far beyond anything we've yet done. In that process, we'll discover many are closely connected.

Catholics must look beyond themselves, same as Baptists. In fact, the two would do well to look at how the problems play out so similarly in these two largest denominations, considering what the two have in common—which, for most, is likely to be surprisingly far greater than what initially meets the eye, standing in sharp contrast to more liberal Protestant denominations that are much smaller in number.

As we continue to enlarge the conversations, casting a wider and wider net, we'll soon understand we are only looking at symptoms of community mental health problems, far beyond issues of faith. Only then will we understand how deeply we must each look both *within and beyond* ourselves to discover hope through processes already proving to work within the faith systems of other cultures.

*****

[1] Referring to Matthew 5:15 - Nor do men light a lamp and put it under a bushel, but on a stand, and it gives light to all in the house. (RSV)

[2] Sipe, the renowned psychotherapist mentioned earlier spent eighteen years as a Benedictine monk and Catholic priest, trained specifically to deal with mental health issues of priests. He married Marianne, a former nun, also a psychiatrist, in 1970. His greatest contribution has been in research into issues the Catholic Church's teachings on sexuality and its effect on behavior. This led to growing concerns about the issues of sexual abuse and the cover-ups. He is a prolific author, whose works include Sex, Priests, and Secret Codes (Taylor Trade, 2006), co-authored by Patrick Wall.

[3] Bates, William, 2014, The Cemetery of My Mind, Create Space.

[4] Heggen, Carolyn, 2006, Sexual Abuse in Christian Homes and Churches, Wipf & Stock Pub; Reprint edition, p. 73.

[5] Wall, like Sipe, is a former priest and Benedictine monk. Wall left the priesthood in 1998, after twelve years of service, because he became weary of being shifted from one place to another to clean up messes left by sexual predators. He began working on behalf of victims of clergy abuse in 2002, using his expertise in canon law. He got his master's degree at St. John's. (see also #2 footnote above)

"Redeem me from the oppression of men that I may obey your precepts."
Psalm 119:134

Chapter 4
Understanding Real Power

"ALL WISDOM... DOES **NOT**... RESIDE... IN RANK!" Joan Chittister took a noticeable breath between her prophetic words, as she began the keynote address for the 1994 Linkup conference in late August, after the June leadership gathering. In those well-placed spaces, you could almost hear a pin drop. As she stepped back from the podium in a gesture showing her sentence was complete, the burst of applause sent her a clear return signal. She'd hit the nail on the head.

That's what Joan does best—as a deep thinker, writer, and speaker. Though normally soft-spoken, she doesn't mind being a loud, squeaky wheel in a world where the voice of dissension has been historically squelched. She would have chuckled had anyone addressed her as Mother Superior that day, yet it would have been entirely fitting, especially since she's a leader among nuns of the Order of St. Benedict.

Her starting sentence, lodged in my memory like a gold brick. To this day, it allows me to smile inwardly whenever I come face to face with hostility. After thirty years, I recognize how intense fear lies behind such hostility, a fear of being found out, even when the fear is irrational or unwarranted.

She went right into a story of a young crew member, trying to call to his ship captain's attention the fact they were fast approaching an iceberg; but the hard-headed commander refused to trust what he had not seen with his own eyes. The drama had the crowd in stitches, for we all knew where this was going. We easily recognized the words and tone of the nun's voice. It was a story we'd each lived—only in different form.

From my vantage point, slightly higher and at the back of the auditorium of St. John's, I noticed some of the male survivors bristling as the speaker followed up with the suggestion: "The Problem is patriarchy."

Without missing a beat, she confidently set out to supply her own working definition of patriarchy. It actually had nothing to do with gender, she declared. It was simply "elitism without merit."

This elitism, so inherent in clergy members, is often unrecognized by most male clerics, so that it becomes unknowingly a weapon as sharp as a sword and quickly drawn on, as we'd all witnessed, when power perceives itself to be threatened—even when the threat is not intended. Even a friendly suggestion of the possibility of a lawsuit will likely provide a dramatic reaction followed by frantic counter-threats that can be most un-nerving to witness.

Merit, as opposed to automatic entitlement, must be earned, the nun insisted. It is not earned by academic achievement or by ordination. It's earned by a constant demonstration of authenticity so there's no need to live by fear.

"There are plenty of others worrying about life after death," Chittister said in her closing remarks. "What concerns me most is that people are able to experience life *before* death."

This world-renowned nun had come as Jesus, with life-giving words.

She might just as well have said, "I come that you might have life more abundantly," quoting John 10:10. But she didn't dare. Quoting scripture to this motley crew would have been like slinging acid or a machete in the faces of her audience.

As Spotlight clearly pointed out, many survivors of sexually abusive clergy *don't survive*. In fact, they feel wooden or dead inside. Suicides and deadly addictions permeate this population at rates higher than I've found anywhere else. While some, on their darkest days, can still see tiny rays of Light coming through the grey or pitch-black clouds that permeate any trauma experience, I believe it's next to impossible for many to see such rays when both minds and souls have been slain repeatedly by this evil.

Yet it does happen. In this story, you'll find glimpses of those rays which Serene Jones, President of Union Theological Seminary, considers moments of grace.[1]

For survivors of abuse by clergy, an old, rigid theology no longer works. Having stripped away beliefs that are no longer useful, many have actually moved to a place beyond, a place of greater spirituality very difficult to explain, yet demonstrated by those who know them best. This is a result of resolution.

Still, many stay sadly stuck, unable to find what works for them, never understanding there are new possibilities while non-survivors cannot understand why the resources ordinarily taken for granted with groups that live by blind faith do not readily work for this group. This is not from a lack of character, but from the weight of the heavy burden of alienation that comes from repeated encounters with evil, especially evil from people whose own internal processes bind them so they're unable to separate from abusive systems.

Some of us who were privileged to be present on this historic occasion would pass along the nun's message in some form for years to come. Individual survivors and advocates to their counterparts, parishioners to their priests, therapists and lawyers to their clients, journalists and writers like me to readers.

The worst part about evil is how it so easily upstages every life it touches, creating a spiraling effect that can send even those with the power to act into denial. .

I saw this over and over in Malawi, with government officials, appearing incredibly good and kind as individuals. Yet the corrupt systems they served, the power they gained from status, the comfort and economic well-being they stood to lose by joining me in acknowledging tremendous needs that education would address—all of these made them quake with fear. For joining me, would require they approach the unspeakable, the widespread illiteracy, alcoholism, and rates of maternal and infant mortality rates the government refused to acknowledge.

As a woman, being forced away from the privilege of speaking truth to power to calloused faith leaders, I have frequently experienced the same phenomenon to a far greater degree than I did in those Malawi Offices of Ministry.

"Who ARE you?" a man who had previously known me only as "Ron's wife" asks. The question unarms me—not the words, but the tone. I'm not accustomed to being questioned in a manner best suited for speaking to an intruder on a dark street in the middle of the night. It comes across clearly as fear. As if the question is really, "Who on earth do you *think* you are?"

"All wisdom does not reside in rank," I remind myself, looking the man I'd offered to consult with in the eye, unsure why he seems suddenly petrified. Maybe he doesn't know either, but his fear startles me.

"Has there been some kind of misunderstanding?" I want to ask, and maybe I should. Something he thought I said? Something he heard from somebody else? Or had he been on my website and seen the verse on the sidebar?

It's not my words, but ancient ones from sacred text that come to mind: "Lord, how long shall the wicked prosper? How long... Yet they say the Lord shall not see."[2]

Whatever had him unnerved, my answer to his question would need to be short. He'd already said he was in a big hurry and what I thought I'd share about violence against women in our community, matters I assumed he'd want to know. Obviously, I misread something. Somehow.

Even as an old woman who knows all clergymen, same as my own father and husband, are mere human beings, it can still be unsettling to encounter such posturing. I find it uncanny to stand in the presence of such immense fear, seeing the dynamics of power shift before my eyes when the truth begins to dawn, even when the dawning is quickly squelched.

In the words of Billy Joel: "We didn't start this fire." Yet we understand it from the inside out. We know it is only fueled by secrecy born of fear, which starts with perpetrators of sexual violence and spreads quickly to all they touch, paralyzing the majority in its wake.

This is a three-alarm fire. It's extinguished only by the welcome of testimony and best fought when everyone gets involved. The spell is broken when the powerless stand to speak. That's the miracle, the Lazarus story.

"The dead shall rise!" Jesus wasn't the only person to come back from the dead, according to the Bible. Lazarus, already entombed, also came forth! This is what scares *people of power* to death. The dead are not supposed to rise again and speak truth to powerful people that others hold up as God's distinguished representatives.

The resurrection of our spirits *can* take place before physical death if we dare believe. This deeply profound message, interwoven in Christianity, is the hope within us all. The transformation of the masses occurs when the powerful also shout the message, speaking first of evil, taking it on, bringing it into the light of day.

For testimony always calls us forth to a place of questioning ourselves, to adjust our belief system and to act according to the preponderance of evidence.

This is precisely the message of SNAP. It was the message of Linkup, too. It's also the message every congregation needs today, same as our entire society—if only the doors are open for voices of hope to emerge from individuals whose lives have been deeply impacted by sexual and domestic abuse, substance abuse, mental illness, war, homophobia, disability, and a myriad of topics.

So why are men in power especially afraid to take on these topics? Could it be from secrets lurking in their own past—maybe unspeakable things not of their own doing? Whatever the causes, I'm totally fascinated by the fear.

It's outside the church in day-to-day conversations, perhaps in places where women gather, that we easily find many voices unwelcome inside "sacred" walls. Their truth goes far beyond "the facts" and often includes intensely powerful spiritual journeys. When one woman begins talking, there are soon others joining in. And the voices are purifying if you dare listen closely. Men seldom get in on these conversations, because we females don't often tell these stories in their presence—for doing so in the past has seldom gotten a very good reception.

It's not just survivors of abusive clergy who choose not to hang around the church for various reasons. Neither do many of their close friends and family members, who may be treated like outcasts, too. Triggers spark painful memories. They can even create emotional outbursts with full-blown episodes of post-traumatic stress disorder.

Yet, most pastors are surprised to hear what my friend, the late Diana Garland, founder and director of the School of Social Work at Baylor for many years, discovered before her death. Her ecumenical study[3] of 2008, found thirty-two people for every 400 members in congregations of every Protestant denomination whose lives have been impacted by sexually abusive clergy. And these were only the ones who were adults at the time of the abuse, though she did not separate out those whose grooming (preparation or preliminary advances made toward the victims) began before they even turned eighteen.

We still have no similar studies to identify those who were exclusively abused as minors. The common assumption among many Protestants is that abuse of minors is primarily a Catholic phenomenon.

In May, 2014—yes, in one month alone—twenty-four Protestant ministers were arrested (and only on Catholic priest) for molesting a child in the United States![4] Sadly, unless one of them submerges in the crowd that happens to still be attending church and decides to speak out publicly, there is little chance any two of these individuals will find one another. Protestant fragmentation is perhaps the primary cause.

What in an individual's past becomes a barrier to hearing even about sexual harassment from women like Anita Hill, who courageously spoke out? Could it be a past, painful, personal event or is it a belief? Is it because we assume we already know a person's story before a narration even starts? Do we think there is nothing more to learn? Or are we afraid to admit what we *don't* know?

"I've known a lot who've been through what you have," men are especially prone to imply in some awkward attempt to show understanding.

"No, you don't," a seasoned survivor might reply. If you dare listen closely, you're likely to discover uniqueness in each story. Through the unique aspects of each narration as much as the common themes we're provided with a rich education to lead us to practical approaches to complex problems.

By valuing each of the stories you're about to read, you'll soon notice exceptional responses in both survivors and responders. Whenever you hear stories like this, always look for what was most helpful? What gave this voice the courage to step out of the darkness to speak?

Why are so few men and women willing to stand out from the majority in the professional ministry and expose evil with a prophetic voice? How can this be in a group historically viewed to be beyond reproach? How can powerful men like Cardinal Law receive honorable promotions after years of protecting evil to the detriment of the children?

It's "not nice" to ask such questions. It sounds quite arrogant to some. Openly confessing the sins of complicity is a rare occasion for "men of the cloth." Neither do we see old-fashioned church discipline these days that calls for a public apology from abusers. Instead, in an odd twist of loyalty, we see what Southern Baptist leaders referred to as "social protection" twenty years ago, same as Catholic bishops unwilling to impose full consequences for the deep betrayal of the entire community, not just a betrayal of specific survivors.

Today there are exceptional voices. One is Rev. Tom Brady of First Methodist Church here in Lawrence, Kansas, who told his congregation the

Sunday after he saw Spotlight: "We Methodists have got our own work to do. We aren't immune from these problems either." It's something Tom's known since early in his ministry, when one of his co-workers went to prison for molesting young boys.

RECOVERING from insults or unfair silencing, brought on by this "elitism without merit" is much easier for me today after thirty years' experience. I've discovered there's an advantage in praying the Serenity Prayer *backwards*. Yes, you heard me. I start *at the bottom* of the prayer. I suggest you try it, too.

I learned long ago it's better for me to explore what I think I might change first. By starting at the top, I'm far too tempted to quickly decide I can't change a thing. Starting at the top puts me into the passive mode, which ends up being totally disabling in advocacy work for I can quickly get lost in the list of things I cannot change.

Words attributed to Oscar Romero say it best: "We cannot do everything, and there is a sense of liberation in realizing that. This enables us to do something and to do it very well."[5] Taking stock frequently, I often discover something I could not possibly have tackled a year earlier I'm able to take on today—not just because I've changed, but because others have.

Not that I expect everyone to be working intensely to stand up to power abuse that's disguised as "sex." I don't. There are far too many issues in this world needing our attention. We must diversify.

Yet I do expect every person in ministry to understand that what we commonly refer to as "sexual abuse" is really power abuse in disguise. It's a subtle, cowardly form of gaining power and control over another individual who holds lesser power due to any number of factors, the most obvious being differential in physical strength.

Even if the physical aspect of the abuse occurred only once, the double-bind for the victim is the same. It becomes all the more confusing to most victims and anyone else who hears later of an incident if the victim's power differential appears to be small, as in the case of an adult co-worker who experiences physical, sexual assault—or, as in the case of an adult congregant who is psychologically dependent on a pastor by the inherent nature of a pastoral-congregant relationship.

As Elizabeth Stellas[6], a UCC clergywoman, once said: "If you enter my kitchen, and I hit you over the head with an iron skillet, is it a cooking incident or an act of violence?" As society begins to get past the taboo created by believing sexual abuse is about "sex," we will disempower the abuser. We will get over our tendency to protect "elitism without merit" and our tendency to think of sexual violence as a private matter. Disentangle the two, and we disempower the perpetrator who is counting on this confusion to keep permeating society.

Lessons from Sesame Street

So where was Spotlight's screen writer Josh Singer in 1994, I wondered? We could have used that guy. Turns out he was probably a little too young for the Linkup crowd—but at twenty-two this "kid" was already writing for Sesame Street. So we *could* have used him, had we known.

The preschool lessons from the Biscotti Kid—like the ones on listening—sure would have come in handy at St. John's. Same as one of the best sayings in the entire series: "You made the mess. You clean it up."

*****

[1] "Just as the shattering effects of trauma are painfully particular to each person who suffers them, so the healing power of grace is specific to each imagination it soothes and heals....what my own writings on trauma continue to seek is a glimpse of grace at work in the interstices of imagination." from Trauma + Grace by Serene Jones, p. 22, Westminster John Knox Press, 2009.

[2] See Psalms 94: 3-7

[3] See http://www.baylor.edu/clergysexualmisconduct/index.php?id=67406

[4] See http://awkwardmomentsbible.com/shocking-pastors-on-the-prowl/

[5] Ironically these words were attributed to Oscar Romero, but were actually never spoken by him. To read all of this inspiring prayer, go to https://educationforjustice.org/pdfs/ej/romero.pdf

[6] Stellas, a United Church of Christ advocate clergywoman who was trained and worked for several years in the mid-90's at The Center for the Prevention of Sexual and Domestic Violence, now The FaithTrust Institute. See www.faithtrustinstitute.org

Chapter 5
Managing the Serpent

Tom Economus was the captain of this mighty little ship, floating along beside a stormy sea of destruction. That was obvious to anyone in the media who cared to glance his way. And quite a few did that week; one filmmaker from the Netherlands was having a field day. Tom would laugh if he could hear me speak of him as "a captain." He seemed to see himself more like the skipper. I'll admit he even looked a lot like the humble skipper on Gilligan's Island, though he was a whole lot smarter.

All of us together were creating quite a stir, calling publicly for accountability to stop the nonsensical recycling of abusers. Yet we all looked to Tom—even those of us more than ten years his senior.

To my knowledge, Tom's leadership was never in doubt. Neither was his caring. He worked hard to treat every soul with dignity, hoping to make up some for what the Church had done. At the same time, he showed more respect to disrespectful clerics than most of us ever managed to muster.

Tom had an enormous pastoral heart. Even in big meetings, he could expertly work a crowd, stopping to connect with individuals, sensing out felt needs with a genuine, warm smile, before turning his attention seamlessly back on the larger picture. And he did it with more humility than most pastors I'd ever met from living an entire lifetime inside the clerical system.

Intelligent, creative, and as charismatic as any fiery evangelist, he had twice the energy of most guys fast approaching forty. It was hard to be despondent in his presence, hard not to feel loved and accepted. For so many, he served as the pastor they'd always needed but had never had.

Tom had been through the Catholic mill all his life—actually quite a few mills. "Ordinary" survivors weren't the only ones driven to drink in the struggle of coping with devastating hypocrisy. Priests did it, too. Tom had gotten hooked himself in trying to cope with what he'd gone through—first as a kid from a troubled home who was expected to cater to every whim of the priest who literally had custody of him until he grew up and got away; then by the priest he turned to in hopes of finding empathy, yet who violently assaulted him as soon as Tom turned his back one day; and finally in seminary where what he saw going on made him so sick he had to get out.

Like many who managed to get to the conference, he knew he was just one drink away from going back to the hell his old addiction had created for him. Tom *officially* wasn't a priest—not one ordained by Roman Catholics, that is. He had no desire to be included in those ranks.

It was another very independent-minded Canadian priest, who became like an older brother to Tom, trying to make up to this inspirational soul for what he'd lost. "Who was this guy? What was his name?" I've asked several, embarrassed to have forgotten. Not one can remember. Yet everyone, including Tom Doyle, recalls the contribution he made through this role he seemed to feel privileged and humbled to be in.

Tom could still be a "true man of God" and even be ordained, the Canadian "rebel" assured him. Who should care he'd not stuck with seminary? In this case, not doing so, running from the atmosphere that turned his stomach, was an asset. So, this humble hero helped organize an ordination ceremony, called in supportive witnesses, and did the job himself.

Tom could hardly wait to introduce to Ron and me to this soft-spoken role model, who wore a very non-traditional set of vestments with sandals, reminding me more of a 1970's "Jesus freak," except he wisely did not wear his cross. Doing so would serve as a trigger for many in this group. In fact, many of the crosses that could not be removed from the seminary buildings due to permanent attachment had been respectfully covered for the conference.

Like his mentor, Tom would never have thought of wearing a collar. In fact, he often talked about "black collar crimes" and slapped that title across a couple of pages of "The Missing Link," the organization's newsletter, which read like a scandal sheet, broadcasting the names and crimes of Catholic priests, as well as a few Baptist ministers and an occasional mainline minister sent as news articles from around the country.

Making Room for the Serpent

Stephen Rubino talked about his own denial when approached by a mother about a problem he could not imagine even existed a few years earlier. Now, using his expertise in canon law, he was negotiating with the very institution he once idolized. Yes, I do mean "idolized," not idealized, because that's what he'd been taught to do all his life by the clerics who had now "fallen from grace."

When he finally allowed himself to believe the truth, realizing this mother only represented the tip of the iceberg—that was the moment "the serpent" entered. And it wasn't about to leave. It never does, once it comes into your life. Managing it is a full-time job, night and day, he'd discovered. It wasn't something you could just kill.

That serpent enters victims' lives, he realized, from the moment of abuse. As a lawyer, he was seeing firsthand how it grows much larger when collusion is encountered. To have the masses looking the other way changes everything, destroying any remnant of hope left. It requires every person, including professionals who have heard these stories over and over, to be constantly questioning what they once knew for certain.

In conclusion, he spoke of the denominational leaders' fears. "They have a lot to be afraid of," he admitted. "They think they cannot trust us, but they really can." He paused for effect… "They can trust us to tell the secrets."

The Wonders of Re-Imagining

There were plenty of secrets needing to be told. This was confirmed to me the very week *How Little We Knew* was released, as I stood with the first copy in my hands, overwhelmed to think of where I'd come on my journey only seven years after discovering a problem I could never have imagined existing in the community of faith.

Not I or anyone else in attendance could have predicted that the event in Minneapolis, for that November weekend in 1993, would rock the foundations of mainstream denominations to the very core, so much that anyone who had encouraged the funding of this event, sponsored by the World Council of Churches, would be chastised. To the majority of Christians, this was nothing short of heresy. Yet there I stood in the midst of "the heathen," about to connect with some of the most courageous, spiritually vibrant women I'd ever met or had the privilege of meeting since. It would prove to be the boldest, most radical of all mission enterprises in my life, with the largest crowd I'd yet addressed over the course of two days, though most of my speaking was to no more than a few from that crowd at one time. And I often listened far more than I spoke to some of the most heart-wrenching stories I've yet to hear after thirty years.

"When one begins to re-imagine God, then nothing is sacred—everything is on the table for reconstruction. Truth, reality, social institutions, modes of communication all fall prey to the corrosive analysis of post-modern subjectivism." Christopher Lensch [1], an outspoken critic of the controversial conference, wrote some time later.

If Mr. Lensch had been standing invisibly next to me those three days, he might have better understood why some women at the Re-Imagining Conference needed to *do* some re-imagining. They'd had the sacred ripped from their souls and needed to open up new modes of communication. While visualizing the Deity as a goddess, or one with a feminine side, to replace the God envisioned by men of old, served that purpose, as many attendees saw things. To them, "old things were passed away" and now all things were becoming new. I could relate to that in many, many ways—for I'd learned to question everything I'd been led to adopt as absolute and had discovered questioning to be remarkably good for me and many other women I knew, thereby enhancing, rather than destroying my faith.

If I'd had time and a place to put my thoughts in print back then, I would have written: "Come on, guys. Are you 'inerrant' fellows heretical enough to claim *you* see God on a daily basis? If so, you really have a problem! Unless you plan to toss John 1:18 through *your own* stain glass window."

Yet, I didn't have time to get off on a tangent, hog-wrestling theologians with nothing more than nursing credentials. I'll stick to what I understood of holistic health, which very much included the spiritual aspects. I yam what I yam.

I very quickly learned to be careful who I told about my experience of even being present for that eye-opening conference, too. Being wise as a serpent, in this case, meant incorporating Stephen Rubino's idea of "managing the serpent," learning to withhold key pieces of information from wolves in sheep's clothing. Discerning the need not to cast precious pearls before swine (or those who had no ears to hear) fit well this style of management.

The pearls I gathered at the Re-Imagining Conference combined with the fortification through The Linkup gave me a sense of being "ordained" anew to go forth and spread life-changing truths that most people sitting in pews every Sunday morning might find impossible to comprehend. This is something one has to witness and to feel deeply in the gut—or "soul" for those who can stretch the definition of the soul that far.

In Minneapolis, I couldn't fathom how this work would ever reach to the far corners of the world through something as magnificent as the Worldwide Web. It was enough just sign books to be transferred into the hands of women I knew would take them to distant shores of at least fourteen developing countries. There, I knew much better than most authors, each of those fourteen copies would be read many times, as all books are in locations where resources are scarce.

Back home, I was soon hearing this even from American readers. Since many survivors had very limited financial resources, they were passing a single book to a dozen or more people.

Oh, the power of the printed word that can lie dormant and be picked up again, even decades later! In this, there is no comparison between writing and speaking—each serves its purposes, yet writing may live on for decades before being picked up fresh again, sometimes by an individual who once laid it aside, unable to finish it because of triggers once caused at the time of purchase. Or it may get picked up by a new reader, perhaps from a library shelf, who finds the message timeless. And this is exactly what has happened, I've been humbled to learn, with *How Little We Knew*.

For me, attending Re-Imagining, then going back to the cold, cruel "real" world was like taking a college course in the various ways and means members of the clergy could punish women for the "original sin" of being born female and another to understand that spirituality did not have to be put in tiny, constricted boxes. It was all pre-requisite training that gave me the capacity to really take in Joan Chittister's message about "elitism without merit."

As I reflect on that powerful weekend, I saw God reflected in the faces of scores of women who stood in line, waiting to speak to me. Among those pouring their souls out, was a middle-aged woman, speaking in muted tones, about how she'd recently received validation for her strong suspicions of many years, that her minister-father had murdered her mother, leaving her as a preschooler, along with several older siblings, to fend for themselves.

While they came from all over the world, mostly Americans, some were citizens from very oppressive governments. Yet the stories they shared freely were mostly about highly-educated "men of God." The damage was obvious. It was psychological and spiritual, clearly visible in their countenance as they weighed every word, seemingly scanning my own face as if they were peering into a mirror, hoping to have reflected back some sign of truth and acceptance.

Uncovering Secrets

A Catholic survivor unveiled a very big secret at the Linkup Conference, one I'd missed about the Southern Baptist abuse problem. The survey was a self-report by SBC ministers. Conducted by SBC pastoral counselor Dr. Jeff Seats and published in *The Journal of Pastoral Care* in 1993, it showed more than 14% of the 256 pastors poled had admittedly "participated in sexual activities considered inappropriate for a minister." Those figures were not shocking to me, simply validating, though I wondered if the participants might have underreported. For I'd already found an unpublished, interdenominational study done by Richard Allan Blackman through Fuller Seminary, a very conservative institution, where *How Little We Knew* was now housed in the school's library. By self-report 38.6% of surveyed ministers in 1984 admitted to having had sexual contact with a church member!

I thought of a statement made by a young United Methodist clergywoman in our annual peer-led survivor group: "Secrets make us sick." What concerned me most was what, if anything, the SBC was going to try to do with Seat's findings. Stuffing it back into Pandora's box wasn't going to work if I had anything to do with it.

Time to see if I could get some editors to agree.

Ethics, Anyone?

The ethics of secrecy, a study which volumes have been written about, was a very important topic touched on by several on the program. All of us had been shamed repeatedly for "gossiping" every time we tried to talk to anyone outside the power structure. We weren't supposed to be telling anyone about the abuser's problem or to alert anyone else about the system problems either, of course. Never mind the primary failure shared and condoned by most systems is a failure to warn.

I'd been scolded personally by a "Father Superior" I'd never even met, a Baptist, just under Dr. Keith Parks in the pyramid we were a part of. Parks was then President of the Foreign Mission Board. In all fairness, Parks was walking on a high wire himself, about to be toppled by a sinister plan under the direction of some of Ron's very own classmates from seminary days. Politics beyond Belief!

Back in 1987, I received an enormous reprimand from 10,000 miles away by telephone one evening, the only phone call I'd ever received from our stateside office in Richmond, Virginia—about anything. In fact, if we wanted to talk privately to any of the guys occupying any level of power beyond our own colleagues about the Kingsley case, we had to track the official down or travel to another country to find him. Not one official initiated such a meeting. This is precisely the treatment whistle-blowers get, no matter what status they hold in the system.

Tactics like this had worked well for centuries throughout the community of faith, but they weren't going to work from here on out—this was the message those of us in The Linkup were trying to send. In essence, we were saying: "You better count us in on this conversation."

Agencies and denominational leaders had some very serious rule breakers on their hands. The unethical silencing of survivors must end.

Yet where were the Christian ethicists on all of this? That question kept popping into my mind sitting there at the conference. I wasn't even sure who to ask. Ethics certainly hadn't been my field except what little I had gotten—actually quite a lot in my clinical training, as I look back. We clearly had sexual ethics in our policies in mental health facilities, in fact—for nurses, as well as social workers, doctors, psychologists, even our techs. Nurses and other staff were to be friendly with patients and their families, of course. Yet patients were not "friends."

In fact, this was an odd piece of my father's seminary training at Southwestern Baptist Theological Seminary in Ft. Worth back in the 1950's. Dad only went to seminary one year (Many Baptist ministers are ordained with much less.) Yet I remember so many times how he would quote a professor he dearly loved—T. B. Maston, as I recall. He always said this professor taught him the practical things. He could get the theology on his own, he declared, with a lot of study; yet the practical wasn't so easy to come by. These rather elaborate rules I understood growing up before I ever started school—rules my parents explained to congregants informally. We did not invite select congregants into our home for social events, for example. We often went to their homes, but to reciprocate, according to the professor, would be to "show favoritism" and set a dangerous precedence. So we had friends from outside the congregation. Or when we moved elsewhere, past congregants sometimes invited us to be overnight guests in their homes. At that point, we did reciprocate, and this was where our strongest, long-term relationships with other families really blossomed.

Right or wrong, ethical or not—that's how I grew up understanding ministerial boundaries with congregants, and Ron and I have lived them, also. What was taught about sexual boundaries in the 1950's, if anything, I do not know. Yet my father demonstrated his understanding clearly one summer afternoon in the mid-60's, when he came storming into the house for lunch, irate at what he'd just heard about one of his colleagues. From what he said, I knew he clearly believed his colleague had committed career suicide. There was no mention of the female being to blame in the least. Somehow, I just thought that's the way the whole profession would see things, though I'd never really thought it through for myself all those years since, until I began to understand the range of philosophies on maintaining boundaries and how applies to the complex issues of the sexual abuse of adult congregants.

So in the 1990's, I was finding out all about the lack of training in ethics in the ministerial profession, as a whole. I don't know what happened with Baptists, whether things got looser on boundaries or if my father's training was more of a fluke.

Not only was the topic of sexual boundaries virtually unaddressed in seminary—Ron recalls nothing, though he did have a course in ministerial ethics. After going through the mill with Baptist ethicists in the next few years following this 1994 conference, I would remain utterly baffled until I got around to reading what Marie Fortune had to say in Sexual Violence: The Sin Revisited, published eleven years later. ".....sexual violence as an experience and as an ethical issue was largely overlooked until women ethicists began to listen to survivors and to address the issues."[2]

A couple of survivors at the conference had even taken the risk of being sued by breaking legal secrecy agreements forbidding them to speak again of their abuse in order to get a few thousand dollars to help with therapy. In some cases in the past, the Church had agreed to pay for therapy; but the moment the victim decided to sue for devastating, irretrievable damages (like the inability to concentrate enough to go to school or hold a decent, steady job), therapy was cruelly withdrawn. So the survivor would be forced to drop the lawsuit unless a therapist was willing to let the bills ride in hopes the victim might eventually recover the needed money through the court system. Linkup was working hard to have this common tactic forbidden.

Rubino was as furious as any survivor advocate-attorney about the hush money. As a lifelong, devout Catholic, he saw it serving only as institutional "damage control." In the end, it could cause institutions more damage if enough survivors decided to risk everything by breaking their contracts, of course.

Religion is supposed to give us light. Yet institutional protection, cloaked in the idea that facing and speaking the truth was hurting God, had complicated everything immensely. None of those in charge seemed to understand the greatest of all spiritual principles, "the truth shall make you free."

Caring lawyers, as much as therapists, were being forced to do the work of the Church, listening to the pain of survivors while clueless Church officials sat back, complaining it was all costing them way too much. Survivors were like robbers, draining their coffers so much that buildings had to be sold and important programs cut, they complained, as if this was the fault of survivors. Sadly, many congregants were scapegoating just the same.

Since the Church had rejected their responsibility to listen and decided healing should come with a few weeks of therapy, they were dragging survivors through the wringer. Now, in the courtroom, things were worse for all concerned, as they were *forced to listen* as traumatized people were put on the stand to have their horrific stories pulled out, piece by piece, by lawyers on both sides. As hard as it was for survivors, many were past caring about anything except speaking the truth for the sake of justice. Sometimes they were speaking for others who had lost their right to prosecute because the statutes of limitation had expired before a survivor could make up her mind.

Lawyers were dealing with people who had received minimal treatment in most cases, and this was largely why they'd come to lawyers in the first place. The general public had no idea how extensive and how expensive the therapy for such complex cases is. Most still don't. There were layers upon layers of added wounds, after the initial abuse, to peel back before getting to the inner core of these precious souls. This was especially true for those from troubled childhoods, already traumatized before they ended up being abused worse by priests.

Digging Deeper to Find the Big Questions

"Sometimes we need to question a little more when we are part of an insider group, to listen to the outsiders." Spotlight screen writer Josh Singer says as he captures the most important lesson the movie brings us.

As we move on into this story, I invite you to explore some questions we should all be asking insiders and outsiders:

1. Why do insiders who begin questioning a powerful system suddenly get reclassified as "outsiders?"

2. Who gets to decide these classifications, the ones in power or the individuals within? If it's the people in power, who gives them this power?

3. If an insider seriously injured by the system decides to leave for self-protection, is it possible for that person to ever be welcomed back as an honored guest?

To take these questions even further, we'll do well to contrast how this all plays out in hierarchies where Catholic concerns are often centered with the small to mid-size, autonomous congregations that constitute the self-governing bodies of the local, SBC congregation like I grew up in. Many of these in rural areas are smaller than some of the attendee's extended families. It's in these family congregations, in fact, where child abuse may go unchallenged even more easily than in a hierarchical system—either with Catholics, Episcopalians, or in an enormous multi-tiered organization where we discovered immense collusion in Southern Baptist missions.

Lawyers and doctors, as well as many mainline clergy, seem not to recognize that the largest number of individual congregations in the Protestant world fall are autonomous, rather than ecclesiastical systems, where a few people on a committee at the top, hopefully with at least a basic respect now for gender equity, may have received a good degree of very well-informed training in sorting out issues of abuse.

Most autonomous congregations have neither big cathedrals nor a hierarchy. They also tend to have leaders with limited educations and very limited budgets. Pastors in smaller congregations may be bi-vocational. They stumble along, same as congregants, with a sense of helplessness and hopelessness that easily leads people to believe competence in leadership is impossible to achieve. These folks operate like a family of deeply depressed individuals. Many of them *are* depressed.

Some Sundays, when there's nobody experienced to teach the kids, people are happy to have somebody step in and do the job. Or just skip Sunday School altogether if need be. When it comes to decisions in small groups, like in families, the thinking is "we can all trust one another." This is the same fallacy promoted in incestuous families.

And how many decision-makers in these small churches come from incestuous families? For that matter, how many in hierarchies who seek training come from these families? Or how many cardinals do?

So, what does this have to do with the questions on insiders and outsiders, you ask? And does it really tie into problems of systemic complicity in the faith community or elsewhere? I dare say it does.

*****

[1] from Western Reformed Seminary Journal, February, 2003. Seminary of Bible Presbyterian Church. http://wrs.edu/Materials_for_Web_Site/Journals/10-1%20Feb-2003/Lensch%20-%20Re-imagining%20Update.pdf

[2] "The limitations of a patriarchal bias and male experience (which for most male ethicists probably did not include sexual assault) meant that sexual violence as an experience and as an ethical issue was largely overlooked until women ethicists began to listen to survivors and address the issues." Marie Fortune in *Sexual Violence: the sin revisited* (The Pilgrim Press, 2005) From these words on p. 48, she refers us in her notes to the work of Lois Livezy, Toinette Eugene, Traci West and Pamela Cooper-White.

Chapter 6
Spiritual Guidance from Humble Prophets

Richard Sipe stepped to the microphone, slowly scanned the entire crowd, and timidly began: "I've been trying to figure out for days why I'm so nervous about this moment. I've decided it's because I care so much." He cleared his throat, pointed at his audience, and spoke seven words, as affirming as Joan Chittister's.

"You are the prophets of this day."

I remember thinking: "Wow! That's quite a promotion, Sipe!"

Joan, a Benedictine nun, had put patriarchy in its place. With Richard, a former Benedictine priest, now speaking with male authority, reaching out to restore the fallen.

I couldn't help grinning.

Two years before we left Africa, everyone in our Mission had taken a test, said to be reliable in determining one's spiritual gifts. What came out on top for me was "the gift of prophecy." When the man who led our group announced the results, he said something I thought odd at the time: "That's a hard one for a woman. You really have to be careful."

Strange, I thought. I'd not heard anything like that since I was a child, on a day when I'd gotten into a vigorous debate, as I was prone to do, with my minister-father, leaving him exasperated, as he often would be by the time we concluded our dialogue. This time, Mom had to remind him he was driving as he turned around, glaring at me in the back of our station wagon. Yet I didn't miss his familiar half-grin. I knew down deep, though I got the best of him often, he had an odd appreciation for the comradery, even often egging it on, to the annoyance of my mother.

"Too bad you're a girl. Otherwise, you'd make a fine lawyer someday!" he exclaimed. In my world, back in the 50's in Ft. Worth, Texas, I didn't know enough to challenge him on that point. I'd never heard of a female lawyer or a female minister—at least in the Baptist world. Truth is if I'd been a boy, he might have expected me to be next in line to keep the family tradition. Every firstborn male had been a Baptist preacher for at least three generations before I came along—maybe more.

Since the auditorium was filled with people who'd not been to church in years, Sipe wisely went to great lengths to explain how this prophecy stuff works and what prophets could expect. As soon as he did, some of the same men who had bristled at Chittister's initial mention of patriarchy were now doubling over with laughter. "Oh, so *that's* what we've been doing!" you could almost hear them say. "Sure we recognize those consequences! *Now* we get it!!"

It was such an important work, Sipe told us. He spoke with the authority of a theologian, a sociologist, and a psychotherapist—all three, he was, talking about the spiritual principles of social change, how prophets have to learn to be patient, often waiting for generations to see the desired transitions.

This derelict, who had left the priesthood in 1970 to marry a nun and soon after was challenging the long-standing requirement of celibacy in the priesthood, now stood before us, restoring a sense of empowerment to "the little ones" with a strong dose of reality. It was closely kin to group therapy and spiritual rejuvenation rolled into one.

Both he and Tom Doyle, through personal testimonies substantiated their reasons for claiming this movement as a work of prophecy. Both had been treated like enemies, encountered repeated psychological beatings, downgraded by a system clinging to elitism without merit that Chittister spoke of earlier. Their strength was from conviction, fortified with expertise.

Prophets who have lived close to patriarchy, been inside the system as honored members, are the biggest threats of all. If their message is true, then the patriarchs are merely human beings, who must be removed from manmade pedestals just as the golden calves people made into idols as they wandered in the wilderness long ago.

I don't recall Doyle mentioning how the retaliation he sustained, following his attempts to warn every bishop in the United States of the impending crisis, had driven him to drink and landed him in a treatment center. Perhaps he did and I missed it. Or maybe he just wasn't ready to reveal this in the mid-90s. However, that fact was part of the backstory McCarthy and Singer didn't get to in their abbreviated version of the SPOTLIGHT story. This sad outcome is clearly noted by Robert Kaiser in Tom's 2015 biography, *Whistle*.[1] In the book, we read all the details of how he was fired from a prominent position at the Vatican Embassy in

Washington because of his innocent act of trying to warn of the disaster he felt would certainly come if the bishops didn't wake up.

Tom was certainly sober now as he stood before Linkup members, pouring out his *sobering story*. Without exception, heart-wrenching, severed relationships are a part of every whistle-blower's journey, and one of the most painful losses for anybody in any role working for justice within the church, whether local or with the hierarchy of an ecclesiastical system.

There was a great distinction in Tom's story from most at Linkup, one Ron and I shared. Our losses weren't from deep, unspeakable childhood wounds. Our primary concern from the beginning had been for the more vulnerable, especially the kids. Like Tom, we'd been able to find success in our respective callings to professional ministries *before* being shot down. This meant we were both shot from positions of considerable strength, wounded but still able to speak with authority, while so many in the room had suffered from arrested development, preventing them from negotiating successful careers or emotional, sexual, or spiritual connections.

For all of us at Linkup, the Biblical account of The Good Samaritan story easily paled in comparison to what we had experienced, however. The bandits who had beaten us up and left us lying beside the road were "the saints," with many of the beaten bearers of bad news being from families who had been insiders—some children of parents who had been leaders.

It was especially hard if the whistle-blower's religious doctrine incorporated the idea the priest is the actual embodiment of God, a doctrine common in Catholicism and, to some degree, in other ecclesiastical systems. Even without this added barrier, however, when the most devout members of a congregation "walk by on the other side" under the direction of someone ordained, such concerted efforts manage to silence most. Only the strongest keep speaking.

Meanwhile, the pain is excruciating for those sitting on the side, faintly crying or too wounded to even call out while watching everyone else high-tailing it down the one-way road, oblivious to their likelihood of finding others lying in ditches up ahead, if only they dare look and listen. Or more thieves, perhaps even the same one who caused the injuries they've just ignored, still roaming around looking for his next victim.

Now, as a result of these leaders walking by, having repeatedly failed to acknowledge either the loudest whistle-blower's shouting or the cries of individual victims, many with no idea there were others perhaps just down the road, the Catholic Church was refusing to consider it might be in need of a re-ordering of the faith.

Nancy Biele, a Methodist social worker, stepped to the podium about 10 o'clock Sunday morning. Did anyone besides me see the subtle humor in this? Putting a Protestant woman, not even an official preacher, before this bunch of "lost sheep" at a Catholic seminary on the Sabbath, to address issues of power and privilege, was about as unconventional as a renegade priest like Economus could get.

Immediately after our June meeting at St. John's, Ron and I had stopped by to visit Nancy at her Minneapolis home. Graciously receiving us, she offered valuable insights, especially in dealing with a potential nationwide television appearance with Maury Povich I'd been asked to consider. As it turned out, I didn't have to.

The producer had a bizarre plan he'd not yet shared with Lisa, one I could have told him was half baked. He wanted to get a perpetrator on the show who now considered himself ready to return to ministry. Then, have me on the same show to join Maury in confronting the guy. Povich was wasting his time and mine, too, I told Lisa. I wasn't out to help anyone sensationalize these problems, only to help the general public realize sexual violence in the church or anywhere else is not a private matter, but a community one. Without the possibility of the Povich show, I might never have had the opportunity for this visit, though.

While Nancy was one of a handful of psychotherapists specializing in the unique care of survivors of sexually-abusive clergy, most of her clientele had been adult women who had been violated in a counseling relationship with a minister who usually had often undertaken counseling he wasn't qualified to do in the first place. Many had been as devastated as childhood incest survivors, which many of them already were. They now experienced the added burden of being shunned and blamed by everyone who heard their stories, including some survivors of child abuse. Tom, wisely, didn't go into detail about all of this nor did he point out there were a few from this category of survivors sitting among us.

Like SNAP, the need to focus on children who had experienced an interruption in their development was understandable. Yet Nancy was ready to advocate for a growing number of women who were finding the courage to step forward despite their extreme stigmatization best described in literature by Hawthorne in *The Scarlett Letter*. So was I. For these women had a whole other layer of issues for church folks to work through besides the survivors of child abuse. It wasn't that one set of issues was worse than the other. Yet collusion remains far more widespread when it comes to this group of adult women than any other group.

I was fast learning the whole canvas of people abused by clergy was almost as fragmented as the community of faith itself. I longed to convince childhood survivors, as well as professionals, to all keep their eyes wide open, to discourage the divisions in the survivor movement itself. While I could easily see how Protestant issues might have been more complicated by placing the primary emphasis on women abused as adults, I understood the reason for this. At times, I wished there had been more attention placed on childhood survivors in Protestant circles first; however, when I dared say this, the ones advocating most for women abused in counseling relationships would be upset with me, as if I was a traitor to the cause. While my story was quite different from the others, every survivor in every group I met, when we stuck to the collusion piece, could see how all these cases were, regardless of the age of the victim at the time of the abuse and regardless of the gender, very much the same. Only the "reasons" offered for colluding changed from one type of case to the other. I wanted to scream: "Collusion is collusion is collusion, no matter what the abuse looked like in the beginning!"

If one was centering only on abuse by Protestant clergy, rather than the larger group of "ministers" ordained—like ministers of music, religious education, or youth—then there was an exceedingly high percentage of Protestant victims who were adults. However, I was looking at the additional spectrum plus missionaries, as well as pastors who abused their own children. I felt the vast number of victims in these categories, most of which did not pertain to the traditional cases in Catholicism, made the number of victims in childhood and adolescents far greater than the demographics commonly used.

In fact, there's an entire organization, MK Safety Net, one chapter in the U. S., the other in Canada, filled only with adult children of missionaries (commonly referred to as "MKs"). And the damage these kids have sustained is every bit as devastating as the Catholic men, abused as boys, who came in throngs to Linkup meetings.

Nancy's words could serve as good medicine for every denomination—survivors, advocates, and resistant clergy included. Not wasting a moment before engaging her audience, she had her first applause within seconds by welcoming the fact she'd heard nothing so far at Linkup on the topic of forgiveness.

No need to explain that comment. Every person in the group had been asked multiple times to skip right past anything related to safety and accountability, suppressing their anger above all, anger that advocates for the perpetrator consistently showed when they didn't get cooperation. They also ignored what I refer to as "the real forgiveness problem," which was the persistent refusal of the system to *forgive messengers for coming with their scary stories, insisting on ethical responses to criminal behavior.*

I made a note to add a few other related ideas to Nancy's for my upcoming column:

> *Not one person suggested we "show a little mercy" or "just be patient." We hadn't been accused of being vengeful or trying to destroy the Church either. How refreshing! Not a soul suggested anyone "go get a life." Neither had we heard that "perpetrators are the real victims."*
>
> *Finally, there'd been no lessons in the need to stop throwing stones while others were sitting around, merely stone-walling.*

As to the rest of her Sunday morning message, Nancy could have just as easily been talking to the pope. She used a metaphor that could serve for an individual's broken self at the same time it described the condition of the church. It went something like this:

"Imagine you own a very large, beautiful urn. You love this urn more than anything you've ever owned. Suddenly you come home to discover someone has come into your home and taken a big hammer, pounding your treasure into a million tiny pieces. You're devastated. It's impossible to ever get it back, and you certainly can't replace it. So what do you do?

"You first sit down and cry. It's such a loss you wonder if you can even go on. You can't bear throwing it out. So you get an idea. If you work long and hard, carefully attaching pieces together one at a time, using really good glue, it might just be possible for you to get it back together at least..... Eventually.

"So you begin and work at it every day for years. Yet all the time you're working, you know there's no way it's ever going to look like the original. One day it dawns on you, after all this work, it's going to be fine—not like the pot you once treasured, but this one will actually be stronger. All that glue to re-enforce it helps. Plus, with the new seams in the mosaic you've created, you've got a uniquely wonderful piece. Definitely an original, all because you've taken your time to think through how it should be. Matter of fact, the closer you get to completion, the prouder you are of this finished product. It's fine. It's strong, you realize, and will serve you well. Then, as you sit back and admire your handiwork, you realize that you like this new urn. The glue actually adds a touch the old urn didn't have. It's beautiful and unique, reassembled by you. That's the most important thing about it."

She'd said so much in this illustration, without actually saying it. The people with sledge hammers hadn't just "made mistakes," as ignorant bystanders had often said. What they'd done wasn't "just sin" either. This was violence. There was no other word for it. The abuse was criminal. Yet being made whole was possible if a new definition of "whole" could be found. It was possible to be healthier than ever before, yet it would take a lot of hard work—for survivors, advocates, and the Church as a whole.

Nancy would readily admit, if pressed, that many in the room were never going to find a way to look at things as she'd described. Sadly, some would say it was impossible to find all the pieces. Yet the concept was useful for everyone.

It was a good image for the institutional church, as well, having been on a self-destructive course since its origin, with matters of oppression and abuse. The counselor seemed to be suggesting the shattering of the "urn" was almost complete. In shambles, victim to its own undoing. Since people at all levels of the system had failed to act with prudence, since they paid for the poor advice from goofy lawyers, refusing to listen to wise counsel from people who cared about spirituality and integrity, there was nothing to do except pay the consequences and begin the hard work of trying to re-build something far more spiritual, something stronger that would require years of hard work and diligence, paying close attention to every detail while re-examining the faith.

Meanwhile, the National Catholic Recorder in Kansas City, while faithfully documenting the persistent stone-walling among the bishops, was frequently being accused of yellow journalism. They had lost many subscribers who couldn't imagine what they were reading could possibly be true.

It would certainly appear the Church couldn't go on without people noticing how broken "the urn" was. Yet denial runs deep when people are invested in power—both in those who hold the power and those who worship it.

Juggling

Tom Economus asked me to begin writing an editorial column for each issue of *The Missing Link*. Overjoyed at this honor, I suggested the column be named "Reconnections," since so many of us were working desperately to overcome past *dis*connections as we joined this astounding, new spiritual movement. So, as I sat on the edge of my seat, taking in every word, I was also scribbling down anything I thought might be useful for readers of that column—or anyone else I might write for in the years to come.

As we walked out of a restaurant with the Bates one evening near Collegeville, Joan took note of the beautiful spire atop a cathedral-like church nearby. "You know, Dee, we've really put a hole in their stained glass window, haven't we?" she said, almost whispering.

I contemplated using her words as an introductory statement in my first column, but decided to save it for an upcoming article for Baptists.

Another much lighter moment I chose to share from the conference:

> *"Oh, no, another lawsuit!" joked Roman*
> *Paur as I recovered my step after awkwardly*
> *stumbling over a crack in the sidewalk of St.*

John's campus. Such moments of comic relief were everywhere as survivors, their family members, advocates, therapists, attorneys, and clergy convened to try to follow the first rule of the Benedictines—"to listen."

The editor chose to lift a single sentence from that same column, framing it in bold old-world style of calligraphy: *"For the first time in the history of Christendom, the very doors which to many have long symbolized horror were swung open to extend hospitality."*

I experienced something simply divine as we all sat at a banquet on Saturday with eloquent church officials as speakers. Yet it would have been offensive to many for me to have worded my feelings that way in "Reconnections."

Toward the end of the column, I did include a spiritual message I knew everyone could appreciate, however. I hoped it would be seen by a few clerics.

Listening to Bishop Hanus' marvelous address Saturday evening, it was refreshing to hear a clergyman other than my own husband express his outrage at the way survivors have been treated. I was equally touched to see Abbot Timothy weeping with survivors. These men have started down the same path which is all too familiar to every member of the Linkup. We know it will not be easy.

As this profession gets in touch with its grief, it must begin to see itself as victimized by the total devastation perpetrators have brought to the community of faith. If they are successful in completing the grief journey, they will have to temporarily resign from the job of being shepherds or even servants. Yes, they will have to "become as little children."

Only from that humiliating position in which we survivors have found ourselves can there be any hope of healing and learning. For now, there must be a temporary role reversal. The Church's pyramidal structure will have to be turned on its head, at least long enough for survivors to teach, admonish, and listen to the confessions of one of the most powerful professions in the world. Survivors will have to be viewed, not as lost sheep who have wandered away from the fold in sin, but as lost coins, who are valued treasures so carelessly misplaced by those in charge.

If Abbott Timothy (Kelly) took time to read this, I felt sure he'd notice the subtle scolding in that sentence about the lost sheep vs. the lost coins. I didn't need a seminary degree to see the enormous theological error he made, and I wanted to run up and tell him so that evening. Of course, I wouldn't have dared. It would have ruined the aura for everyone.

Still, I left with a big pebble in my shoe, even as I scolded myself for being too critical. It was still eating on me as Ron and I walked back across the beautifully-lit campus to our room that night.

"Did you notice?" I asked. "He referred to us as lost sheep 'who have wandered off in sin and need to be redeemed!'"

"No, I didn't catch it, but I see your point," he replied. "I was too busy thinking this is all too good to be true."

I slowed down to glance at my husband questioningly. What a skeptic he'd become!

Jeanne Miller told us at the leadership conference how St. John's was determined to be the exception. They had perpetrators there on campus under tight supervision while the leaders attending explored alternatives to the traditional consequences for behaviors of long ago. Yet, except for that odd reference to the lost sheep, I sensed genuineness in everything I'd heard.

When Tom Economus called to touch base a few days later, I didn't mention what Ron had said, only how I was re-framing Kelly's reference to the lost sheep for the upcoming "Reconnections" entry.

*****

[1] In Chapter Five's first paragraph of Whistle: Fr. Tom Doyle's Steadfast Witness For Victims Of Clerical Sexual Abuse, Robert Blair Kaiser writes of how Doyle was forced to leave the Vatican Embassy, yet "didn't have to look far for another job," then went on full-tie active duty in 1990 as an Air Force chaplain. "He wasn't there for very long before he came down with his own problem, a drinking problem." After being arrested on a DUI, he was fortunate to find the help he needed with a kind, compassionate master sergeant who directed the office for substance abuse.

The guest house where he was sent had cared for more than 7600 "priests and religious." Doyle describes the time he spent there as "the best four months of my life. There I found a new kind of God...."

Chapter 7
Homework

Dr. Elizabeth Wiebe never told her students in nursing that advocacy was the most important aspect. She just showed it—by example and attitude. Perhaps I picked this up intuitively. It's something I can't quite explain, yet I know it was there and has remained as the paramount concern throughout every aspect of my career... from the large city hospital to the streets of the Irish Channel in New Orleans, to government offices of "The Ministry" in Lilongwe, Malawi, down to the small class I taught in infant nutrition to fathers in that country where infant mortality was pathetically low, and on into the homes of troubled children, who often reflected the deeply-troubled childhoods of their own parents desperately seeking ways to make lives better for their children than they had it.

Advocacy is a taxing form of care-giving that task-oriented workers (those that just "go by the book" to get things done) are prone to ignore. That's what separates para-professionals from professionals, Ms. Wiebe would explain if asked to address this word "advocacy" that I never recall her even using.

Any advocate, professional or otherwise, will do well to remember that taking care of oneself must come first. To put it another way, self-advocacy or being certain that one's own oxygen mask is on with a strong support system in place, is paramount to preventing burn-out.

These things I knew as I eagerly returned from the Linkup conference that day with the name Jeff Seats at the top of my list of people to contact. I couldn't wait to thank him for this survey and find out what he planned to do with it.

Less than a week later I had the answer—a warm, sincere reply, thanking me for dropping into his life as a breath of fresh air. Eagerly, he explained how he'd already been in person, taking other therapists with him, to speak to leaders responsible for disseminating educational materials through the Sunday School Board. Another meeting had been held with top executives in the Convention.

The consensus in both settings had been the same. These issues could not be addressed at this time due to the "emotional climate" in the Convention.

Seats also left the door open for me to continue dialogue. I replied immediately, saying that I wasn't planning to sit back and wait, no matter what the "emotional climate" might be.

What I didn't say was what I'd learned long ago, in public health nursing. When pushing paradigms, going through the "appropriate channels" seldom gets anything accomplished. There will always be immense resistance. It was time for some experimentation of my own, I decided. Time to go beyond the power mongers and circle back around somehow. What did I have to lose?

Wartime!

Walking into my home office, even a casual visitor couldn't help but notice the June, 1993, cover of Parade Magazine, with the picture of Alice Vachss, a former prosecuting attorney, carrying a strong message about collusion sexual violence. "We Need to Go to War" was her message, in bold letters, that I've now appropriated into the scrapbook, that lies near my feet as I write today.

"I think we're already there," I told Ron, as soon as I saw her words. As a couple, we were struggling to stay on the high road while walking the "straight and narrow," being true to ourselves, trying to be there for our children and mothers from afar, and to those we each served locally.

Of course, Ron's first priority had to be tending his local flock with the multiple needs that come in any congregation with a membership of four to five hundred. We were fortunate in many ways. He'd been very open in his initial interviews with the search committee, as they explored the possibilities of him coming as pastor. It was a risk doing so, but it also served as a litmus test.

Odd as it may seem to outsiders, Ron didn't even ask me about sharing our very personal story. His not asking, I considered to be a complement to our relationship, not a boundary violation at all. That was just how committed we were to one another and the new "mission" of advocacy we both embraced. I wanted him to be free to tell our story, for it was ours to tell—not just mine, as so many have wanted to see it.

Looking back, I realize him being upfront served several purposes. It explained who we were. It also served as a litmus test, saying we have nothing to hide. If you want us, this is what you are getting—we're warning you that we don't play games. Anyone who thought otherwise from that point on would be in for a big surprise. And some were.

So here we were, exactly five years after arriving, at a point when many pastors are thinking already of moving on to a new church field. Yet we were there to stay. Little did we know that this would be Ron's last full-time assignment in any field—not because of theological differences or the conflicts caused by our stand as very public figures in the controversy we'd chosen to stand on. It would be circumstances totally beyond our control or anyone else's that would be determined in only seven more years.

All we did know at that moment was that there was a mountain of work to be done in advocacy alone, one that would require more than a lifetime. One without geographical or denominational borders. Ours was a universal message. And there would be no turning back on this journey—plenty of stops in the road to rest, yes. Those we'd take; and in that process, there would be refreshment. It would come to us with the many encouraging souls we were expecting to find in anticipation, woven into the unknown mysteries to be found in the rich, often scary, uncharted territory before us.

I would draw on what we'd learned together, through both formal and informal studies, about making structural changes in resistant systems, doing so the same as Ron would draw on it in the tedious work of pastoring. He would use what he'd learned to explore undercurrents of friction, common in every congregation, because of baggage left in the personal lives of each of us, as well as the baggage these things add to congregations as leaders try to sort out ways to keep from re-enacting past problems often left by a string of dysfunctional staff members from decades' past.

So, into our brokenness we walked together very openly—in some ways, much better prepared to serve as we embraced our brokenness in order to join the other "walking wounded" in town. In that process, we were careful to guard our own front door, to kindle the fires inside, to laugh often, and to take time to wait.

The Wounds that Remained

Whenever our conversation turned to the more recent past, Ron spoke about the difficult decisions he'd wrestled with before deciding to return to the pastorate. They were complicated enough due to the emotional and spiritual beating we'd both endured with the mission board, but even more so because of the on-going, unsafe political climate of the Southern Baptist Convention that kept making national news.

He often went back to 1988, only weeks after our resignation, where he seemed to be stuck for a long time. He'd taken off with his sister and brother-in-law, also an SBC minister, to the national convention in San Antonio only days after we'd buried his father. There he sat, like the grieving "child" he was, watching people bus in little children to vote for a fundamentalist takeover of the Southern Baptist Convention, which those children could not begin to understand. For him, this was the last straw, a form of collective child abuse in addition to being totally unethical politics.

Back home, in case he had further doubts about remaining in the SBC, I let him know there was no way I was going to play an active role in any SBC church, due to the glaring issue I knew I'd face, especially when the women of every congregation would lead out in the annual campaign to raise money for special needs for missionaries—the Lottie Moon Christmas Offering. What an outcast I'd be if I spoke with the integrity I needed to: when asked to talk about foreign missions, I could not help but tell them of the hypocrisy of this agency I'd idealized and invested in all my life. How could I not say, when speaking to women who had promoted in good faith the cause of missions all their lives, that I'd come to understand that women were being manhandled by some of the most irresponsible, unchristian men I'd ever met!

Sometimes, as we went back to affirm to one another the difficult decisions we'd made, we would be grieving simultaneously. Neither of us were fully resolved, even a decade after leaving Africa, to being "home" in the United States. We weren't really home. Our hearts were still in Africa, though we were doing the work of advocacy, which Ron understood also to be the most important aspect of professional ministry. We had only changed locations of necessity.

Our children were also still grieving deeply. James' favorite song in high school had been "I Miss the Rains Down in Africa." Oh, how we all missed those refreshing rains! Always coming just at the end of the dry season, when the heat was unbearable.

Rain was what we needed in this work of advocacy, too.

Continuing Education

Ron was determined to build on what he'd learned, taking advantage of every opportunity to learn more about systems. He was especially excited when Edwin Friedman, Jewish author of *Generation to Generation*, came to the Midwest. This book, one of the must-reads in pastoral counseling, had been particularly insightful in shedding light on ways leftover personal garbage from unresolved family issues comes into congregational dynamics. Translated into what we'd witnessed, we could imagine a myriad of reasons people had not had the courage to take an ethical stand. Yet if denominational leaders anywhere were drawing solid lines between the dots of personal past and collective present, we'd not yet seen evidence.

Both of us could understand how the increasingly complicated family issues, presenting themselves so often in our society, brought challenges for any pastor, especially without this understanding. We also asked ourselves what in our own past had contributed to us having such a different response than most to sexual violence in ministry. That complicated question is one we're still unable to fully answer.

While writing *How Little We Knew*, I'd gone back to additional advantages my unique nursing program offered, through pastoral counselors, on the staff at Baptist Memorial Hospital in Oklahoma City, where we were invited to sort through family-of-origin issues to determine how these might impact our professional lives. Now, in 1995, it suddenly dawned on me—if seminaries were requiring this anywhere, I'd not heard of it. Why not? However, suggesting this only served to raise eyebrows. I still wonder if anyone, anywhere is doing anything close to this. If so, I'd love to hear about it.

Beyond the Platform

As he'd done since seminary, Ron extended himself into the community. As a volunteer chaplain at the local jail and with the police department, often riding in squad cars, getting to know officers as they patrolled, and being on call for crisis intervention. Issues he ran across, especially when it came to gender-based violence and child abuse, he began integrating into his Sunday morning messages, making it clear where he stood and where he believed Jesus stood.

One Sunday morning, talking about what it was like for him to personally witness domestic violence taking place before his eyes, he said: "Seeing blood for the first time in a case like this really made it real for me!" At that point, a grandmother in our congregation got up and tore out of the auditorium with her concerned daughter right behind her. Ron understood immediately what was going on, but had not anticipated this reaction.

Not long before he'd stepped into the pastorate there, that grandmother had witnessed her own daughter's murder by a domestic partner. Yet, in spite of the trigger his message had been, it turned out to be an intervention. The two of us quickly followed up, of course, and the lady was able to move further toward resolution as she realized what a validation his message had provided.

Meanwhile, his attempts to have conversations with colleagues about the deficit in the profession when it came to holding colleagues accountable for sexual boundary violations of any kind weren't welcomed by most, except for female colleagues. In spite of growing public awareness, most folks wanted to treat this great embarrassment like a case of measles, soon to be over, rather than a chronic, systemic, deeply psychological case of mass denial that called for group therapy on a grand scale. Of course, in order for therapy of any kind to be successful, two factors are essential: a willingness to own the problem and a readiness to act to change things. Both were totally missing, it seemed.

Eventually, listening to him, it dawned on me. The profession wasn't just afraid of the issues. Individuals were afraid of *one another*. And for good reason! While our story called for action, it also showed what happens when a person takes a stand against popular opinion in colleagues, breaking the secret unwritten codes. Male privilege was deflecting responsibility in every agency of our nation, unwilling to do the hard work of holding one another responsible. Or to put it another way, "refusing to be real men." That was the bottom line. We'd seen it from the military to the local family and even in the selection of a Supreme Court justice.

Without even saying I was associated with any particular group, I'd received very warm grateful responses from leaders, speaking with strong voices of advocacy, in the African Inland Mission, Church of God, Quakers, Mennonites, Presbyterian (PCUSA), United Church of Christ, United Methodists, and American Baptists. By sharp contrast, I was still waiting to find any agency in the Southern Baptist Convention that receptive. In fact, both the Christian Life Commission, considered to be the ethical voice of Southern Baptists, and the Sunday School Board, the agency local churches depend on most for education, gave a "normal" Catholic response, referring me to lawyers, one who had led workshops on how churches could protect themselves from lawsuits. That was it!

However, representatives of marginalized groups I hardly knew were quick to respond. Ken Sehested, editor of Baptist Peacemaker and Jack Harwell, editor of Baptists Today agreed to use the few articles I'd already sent, and Stan Hastey of The Alliance of Baptists pledged to collaborate in any way possible, even though I'd initially not identified myself, wondering if even these folks more prone to challenge the status quo might be somehow retaliatory. I should have known. These three men knew full well the brutal repercussions that come from speaking truth to power.

As a couple, we were both energized and grateful for the opportunities. Yet it was all taking up much more of our time than we realized it might back in 1989, when we first vowed to one another to do all we could to work for change to address collusion with abuse in the faith community. Back then, we'd never expected to find ready-made, enthusiastic groups organizing to share in what we assumed we'd be trying to do on our own. For not until just before How Little We Knew went to press, I learned of The Linkup and Marie Fortune's organization in Seattle[1], just in time to include them in my short resource list in the back of the book.

During the Linkup conference, I'd had a growing sense of unrest. Something had to give, I told Ron as we unpacked our suitcases. I needed to be two people—three if I was going to be of any support to him.

I'd recently cut my hours to twenty-five per week with much of the work on evenings or weekends, catching families of elementary-age children, referred to me by school psychologists. I also needed the flexibility to respond to a growing number of requests for articles from small survivor groups, as well as to answer the letters I was getting from all over the country, showing there were many souls in isolated situations—some of them in high places in denominations who wanted something done, but weren't sure where to start. In addition, I'd been co-leading a weekly support group for incest survivors with a local psychologist at her office.

My encouragement continued to come from many unexpected sources, but most of what I learned about potential open doors in the SBC could be placed in a thick file, labelled "discouraging information."

While I initially had several encouraging letters from American Baptist leaders, telling me they were eager to see me working with a lady by the name of Mary Mild, I followed up only to find she was no longer in the same position. Multiple attempts to connect with ABC leaders led to discouragement, except for informal collaboration in those early years—much was due to a lot of turnover in leadership at the national level. Also, a tremendous amount of disturbing collusion with American Baptists in the Midwest. I found this very disturbing, since we did have a structure that was supposed to be equipped to handle all sorts of problems related to incompetency or the need for added support for ministers in each area.

I soon found myself on such a committee, thanks to a pastor who was himself a survivor of childhood sexual abuse. Both male and female would give great lip service to my one-on-one conversations, yet when they went into a committee to discuss boundary issues, I would be the only one willing to speak. Which made me the odd ball again.

Different Points of View

What we saw as basic integrity that should be ordinary in the profession, many others called "unusual courage." What we saw as justice and accountability and common decency, popular thinking in the church, from laity to professional ministers, often called "cruel" or "a lack of compassion." What we saw as professional responsibility, male ministers liked to say was "just your baggage." It was a lonely position we were in. Most disconcerting, the people who offered encouragement and gratitude seemed unable to demonstrate courage in the end. Was there any hope at all? Even if there was, the climb toward change was going to be much longer than we ever dreamed.

With my closest friends and colleagues in mental health, the complications religious rhetoric created for women dealing with gender-based violence was a common theme. The church was irrelevant, so many of my patients were saying—not Jesus, but the church.

I was surprised at how many women There were just too many triggers or they found little relevant to their personal struggles when they went. It was shocking how many times women named the lack of integrity of ministers or how often they felt the shaming, judgmental attitudes from church folks had intensified their own suffering.

Yet, in the world of "faith," few were willing to own the serious integrity problems of the profession that I picked up on from people who had no idea of my connection to the church (or of my recent issues). Outside of work, if I happened to meet someone new and began fielding the common questions of who I was, where I'd been, or how I'd ended up in Iowa, inevitably we'd soon be having a conversation about an intersection that person had experienced with collusion—either in the church or in family.

Sitting at a dinner with clergy and spouses in a neighboring state, someone asked what had led us to make a denominational change. We told our story and immediately heard: "Oh, you have no idea what we've been through here!"

Actually, we *did*, and I was quite sure most everyone for miles around did. In fact, this should not be private information any more than having someone's name on a sex registry. The offender, whose case had created chaos across at least two states, was a top official in the area. The case had drug on for many months. Now that it was "finally over," it really wasn't. It was like sitting in a room with a hole in the wall and nobody talking about how it got there. By the time he'd finally been forced to resign, two men of integrity had left the ministry in disillusionment. One was working for Gallup polls. The other driving a truck and not interested in ever going back to church.

Until the late 90's, having been in contact with victims from every mainline denomination in the United States along with several in other countries, those with more formal structures weren't doing much better than Baptists. From what we heard, Methodists were pouring a lot of money into at least "managing" the problems. They were working to get together a statement for The Book of Resolutions, which would be a starting place. Yet the resolution, which would not be adopted until 1996, was being discussed a lot as survivors in the Midwest continued to get spotty justice at best.

Having the largest pockets and greatest membership of any mainline group, they naturally had a very large number of victims, and some of the stories were horrendous, including one mother and twelve-year-old daughter both being victimized by the same lay pastor in Iowa. One United Methodist official declared he and his counterparts were spending far more time dealing with the backlog of cases coming to them than any other single aspect of duties.

So I could only imagine how many Southern Baptists would have waiting in the fringes—if word got out that there was an organized national plan for receiving them, that is. Or even began publishing information to indicate churches should all have open discussions on the topic and come up with a plan worked out with an expert.

Of course, I was dreaming. Southern Baptists can work together to send missionaries to the far corners of the world better than any other denomination. Yet when it came for distributing chunks of money to help small churches who couldn't afford to help survivors of sexual abuse committed by "wolves in sheep's clothing," pretending to be innocent, that is—well, forget that idea.

Since mainline denominations have bigger pockets than those with decentralized church polity, insurance companies had begun requiring ministers' attendance at day-long seminars to learn that a "boundary" is more than surveyor's mark or a fence post—all in order for the denominations to keep their insurance. By preventing abuse, cutting down on the degree of collusion, and encouraging prompt, ethical responses, litigations would be reduced. Marie Fortune presented these seminars in Iowa, and I attended, as did Ron. All the time, I kept thinking how this wasn't reaching the massive number of autonomous congregations where there are often not even policies and procedures for handling cases.

Just before leaving for Toronto to attend the 3rd international conference on professional boundary violations, known as CHASTEN, I turned in my resignation at work, a decision I'd wrestled with long and hard in consultation with Ron. He reminded me that we'd never let finances keep us from doing what we felt right. With neither of us being big spenders by nature, we'd make it.

I wasn't burning my bridges, we both knew. I could always return to nursing. Yet, in my idealism, I desperately wanted to believe I could make a living at writing, totally ignoring the fact, few people were yet interested in reading "such ridiculous material" as I was writing in 1994.

Meanwhile Ron contemplated what he might say for an article Tom had asked him to write on spirituality for survivors. I wondered myself. Considering the alarming statements he'd made about his own faith struggles to me lately, I was wondering how long he could keep going into the pulpit every Sunday while keeping body and soul together.

*****

[1] The Center for the Prevention of Sexual and Domestic Violence shifted much of its focus to clergy sexual abuse issues after UCC's Rev. Marie Fortune, as a professional counselor, sat down to dinner one day with a group of other psychotherapists and discovered that most everyone at the table had a story to tell of a clergy perpetrator. She knew she had to do something about this problem in her own profession. Later CPSDV became known as FaithTrust Institute. See how faithtrustinstitute.org is still working with their original intent, as an interfaith organization that's committed to stopping sexual and domestic abuse worldwide in all its forms.

Chapter 8
Pushing Boundaries

While perpetrators in institutions of power often retain their power, they and their supporters lose their privilege to become persons of influential power in *healthy* minds within the system. What's scary is that so many unhealthy minds become enslaved by the imposters, often for many years. This makes it impossible for healthy minds to easily stay and function within a system that uses power in unethical ways to control those who have managed to individuate—whether inside or outside of the system. "Intentional communities" often have different intentions than advocates do—that's the essence of the primary problem faced by all advocates.

Institutions of power have an enormous need to reign in those who advocate for the needs of the most vulnerable.

Threats of ex-communication had worked to silence many Catholic survivors and their terrified parents for years, though some others had come to a place where they could scoff at such nonsense. That was the problem for the Church, which had lost its chokehold on these courageous souls.

One middle-aged man at Linkup had defiantly told his priest: "Go ahead. Excommunicate me. See if I care!"

That same man later told me: "I've never felt so spiritually free in my life!"

Protestant clerics have their own way of ex-communicating survivors. Rather than cutting a person off from the church, everything possible is done to add shame and self-doubt to survivors already beaten down—projecting the shame that should have been the institutions onto anyone electing to share "privileged" information. Nowhere is information more guarded than when abuse is involved, even long after a case is founded. This is how collusion works.

A Striking Parallel in Health Care

In the medical world, what starts out as something simple can rapidly become complicated. Simply finding a med error or warning an institution that they might have liability issues, for instance, can quickly get translated into the threat of a lawsuit, thereby branding the nurse as "the enemy."

This, in fact, happened to me in the course of writing this book—as I advocated for an important change in a procedural issue that had caused an error in judgment in my mother's own care. Problem was, my knowledge was a threat to the system. Rather than saying "Thank you," the reaction came close to being "Get lost!" Despite a lifetime of living advocacy, this left me literally trembling off and on for weeks on end, afraid to even enter my mother's care facility without an advocate by *my* side.

To "get lost" would not only have created a disaster even greater than the one that rocked my world in 1988, after being forced to resign from the largest mission board in the world. It would have created havoc for my very vulnerable mother, who would have literally been out on the streets— or in my own house, which was the last place she needed to be due to her complex needs on top of those of my husband and I, as senior citizens dealing with complex health matters ourselves. She was where she needed to be—this I knew—and the problems I had discovered could be easily fixed, provided the enormous system was willing to face the truth in order to invest a small amount of money to correct things. I and my mother were expendable—the two of us together—this became the message, same as my husband and I had been expendable in 1986. Yet, this time it was a senior citizen, not a grown man, they were threatening to throw to the four winds. Suddenly, I was forced to stand my ground, prepared to fight tooth and toenail to see that this did not happen.

Another Way of Colluding

Not all collusion is easily recognized. Sometimes it comes in more subtle ways, especially in the faith community. The few who were true advocates within faith systems responded affirmatively whenever I asked them to provide my contact information to survivors needing support.

Those who held on to the power of the privileged played both sides against the middle, only pretending to care about safety.

"Oh, we can't do that! This would be breaking confidentiality."

These guys—and it was always guys who responded this way—also didn't understand empowerment. Why should they; for in the patriarchal way of thinking, to empower another is to disempower oneself. Power sharing is beyond comprehension in patriarchy.

I'd given up on reasoning, even after offering a humble apology for my apparent failure to explain. I wasn't asking for them to give ME survivor contact info at all, only to help break the isolation for those in need of support. I soon realized there was no need for explanation. Their lawyers had them well-trained to throw around the word "confidentiality," even when it wasn't applicable.

There was only one word to support such a response—SECRECY!

What the lawyers surely knew, but didn't care to explain is the ethics of secrecy that Marie Fortune had been so careful to work into her workshops. Confidentiality being for the protection and privacy of the vulnerable. Secrecy, for the protection and service of power. That came out in casual conversation the day we arrived for the CHASTEN conference.

"Can you guys keep a secret?" Walter Bera was grinning ear to ear as he strolled up to Tom Economus and I, where we stood waiting to distribute information about The Linkup. In his hand was a stack of papers he waved back and forth as if he was a kid waving a replica of the Liberty Bell instead of a psychotherapist and researcher studying the intersection of abuse, power, ethics and politics. What he had was a new, unpublished thesis, supporting some of his long-held assumptions, gleaned from his work with male survivors.

"Now, Walter, before you go any further, I must caution you," I interrupted, looking down my nose at him and attempting to sound like an old school marm. "Nobody here can be trusted. You see, we don't believe in secrets."

Tom Economus chuckled. "Exactly, Walter. That's why we've come here, you know."

Working the Crowds

Not believing in secrets was the one thing that united most everyone at this international conference on professional sexual misconduct—abuse that is most often thought of occurring in formal counseling with the counselee as an adult. There were representatives from every profession, including clergy, who shared our passion—all interested in using their skills to combat abuse and the concerted efforts of institutions that re-injured survivors for speaking out.

As I listened intently to stories of survivors from other professions, I took note of the similarities and contrasts between those originally wounded in counseling by clerics versus other professions. The spiritual wounds caused by machetes of hate when the abuse was reported ran all the way to the bone for clergy survivors. Others talked about psychological wounds added to the wounds of abuse, yet the deepest of all were from those wielded by professionals whose only defense came as another blow.

For some of us the primary abuse had been the defense tactics used by the institution to excuse the cover-up. "It was all done in good faith." Those were the exact words that were intended to justify collusion, which Economus claimed should be classified as a "hate crime."

No crosses need be burned on front lawns anywhere, yet souls had been branded with hot irons.

Such was the case with Faulkner—that was the last name of the former military official, now in in charge of Southern Baptist mission work for all of East Africa. He'd delivered the "all in good faith" blow from 10,000 miles away, not in a letter that could have provided material witness, but over the phone as an attempt to negate the systemic complicity of two individuals in middle management. In a panic, each of them, backed into separate corners by clear evidence of their own guilt, resorted to blaming their associates for inexcusable deceit.

"Faulkner," according to the urban dictionary can be used as a noun, meaning "the ability to waste copious time through the use of trivial knowledge." Perfecto!

Systemic complicity, as Spotlight clearly shows, is not "good faith." It's not an act of faith at all, theologically, ethically, or morally. It is total incompetence propped up by lies. People who ask someone to keep a secret to protect power know full well that it's wrong to do so. So do perpetrators.

Secrets on top of secrets simply dig deeper holes. Actually two holes. One is made in the heart of each whistle-blower, the other in the reputations of institutions in the epidemic that is no longer acceptable. Pandora's box is open, at long last.

Connections Unlimited

The best gift I received in Toronto was from an attorney when I told her I had not named the mission board or anyone else in our story, partly out of fear, despite assurance from our own attorney at home that I need not be concerned of legal repercussions. I was about to take the risk, I told her, because I had not received even a validation from the SBC, despite the fact it was second in size only to the Roman Catholic Church.

"You needn't worry," she assured me. "They know better than to make any noise in this case. The last thing they want is publicity."

An Empowering Get-Away

Greg Battafarano felt the same as Ron and I about how the public exposure of the abuse scandals was going to impact the Church. "Ultimately, this will be good for us," he said to the two of us, as we visited him one afternoon at his rectory during a much-needed vacation to Niagara Falls immediately following the CHASTEN conference.

As magnificent as our time with Greg, was seeing the power of the Falls. What a contrast to the sinister power Bill Bates had encountered here as a child! Altogether—our trip to Toronto, our visit with the empathetic priest and reflections back to the Bates' testimony—provided reminders of the potential power of power itself.

Well, I was thinking, this may be good for us all someday. From where things stood in the fall of 1994, my hunch was we had a lot of mighty stormy weather ahead.

As we boarded the plane for the return trip, I was thinking about all the people we needed to touch base with. For Ron, there was his best friend Karl, who had followed Ron's example, coming into the ABC, and now pastoring less than three hours from us. Within two years of accepting his new post, Karl found himself in a courtroom, helping a middle-aged, developmentally-delayed parishioner get a restraining order against a retired minister in the church. By then, others had come forward to report the same man. He'd been harassing women and teens for years, but nobody had come forward until this lady, now in court, marched into the church office one day, minutes after being groped in the church kitchen to report what happened.

Of course, she and Karl and a few victims who stood with her were "the problem," according to the "old guards," despite the restraining order obtained almost effortlessly in the court system. Ron tried to intervene, and the two of us together met to console victims. In the end, in spite of all we could do, every victim left the church. As did Karl, getting no help whatever from denominational leaders.

Karl showed up at our front door days later, very discouraged. As a widower for many years, he desperately needed a sounding board. I later incorporated a vital part of our conversation into an article, sitting on my website still today:

It seems there are three primary questions," I said. "Where is God? Where is the community of faith? And where am I?"

"Exactly," agreed my friend, who holds a doctorate in theology. "But I have another: Are the three of us even making contact?" [1]

Listening to Learn

I've often thought back to Nancy Biele's cautionary words about going public. Consider it carefully, she advised some of us at Linkup. For once you do, it's hard to turn back. You'll likely be getting a lot of stories in return. It can be very difficult, each story having the potential for hooking unresolved feelings unexpectedly.

Fortunately, I've never regretted stepping out of the shadows. Sure, this work is draining, but not nearly so much as living and responding to the needs I found out my back door many time in Africa or on the city streets of New Orleans. Pain exists everywhere, and we need not be surprised or shocked when we find it. Learning to breathe into the pain is not easy, but it becomes a daily exercise of necessity in such circumstances. Each day of the Re-Imagining Conference I'd awakened with a sense of excitement and wonder, in the same spirit I'd often felt in Africa, eager to see what was in store, grateful for the privilege of being at the helm of an engulfing work, knowing full well that listening was often all I could do, whether dealing with malnutrition, drug addiction, or victims of trauma.

While I certainly don't *enjoy* listening to pain, I find great joy in welcoming new contacts because I see each one as a sign of hope, no matter how distressed they may be initially. It's an opportunity to validate, make referrals, and often to offer resources or new ways of looking at things. For only by connections involving *communication, not ex-communication,* opening up channels....only then do we have an opportunity to find the divine in one another.

The experience of working the hotline was different than getting letters in the mail or getting a new "intake" in my inbox, which I would begin to do in 1997. Actually hearing the voice and waiting for someone to find their words, as therapists who specialize in this work do on a daily basis, takes so much emotional energy.

I already had enough experience to know this in working with "ordinary" assignments in mental health nursing. Yet the intensity required to do the work with incest survivors, as grueling as that can be, I soon realized could easily pale to working intensely with survivors of clergy sexual abuse—even, in many cases, with women who had experienced sexual violations in the pastor's office as adults.

For this reason, I made a decision that sounds cold and cruel to some. I readily set a boundary that I only bent under rare exception. Beginning early in 1995, when one deeply distraught lady managed to track me down by phone on a night when I was having some serious health issues of my own, totally unrelated to abuse, I listened to my wise husband without even a word of protest. It was time to draw the line.

There are many ways I have poured my life into this work, which is largely without pay. Providing exhausting, time-consuming free phone therapy is not one of them. I have spent many hours with my fingers flying to provide feedback and needed resources for empowering others. This, in addition to the formal writing or speaking I've been able to do IS my ministry, one that I believe is a calling as much as going to Africa or teaching a Sunday School class or working in church music or leading a group therapy session—all which I've also done with a sense of equal calling. Yet it is this work that I've done in the shadows of the institutional church that has brought the most fulfillment of all.

It flows out of my heart easily and freely and off my fingertips with such ease, in large part because my readers have graced me with a wonderful array of heart-warming stories and stimulation that adds life to my very soul! They only think I'm not getting paid. This "pay," for me, is like owning a mint.

There is good news and bad news in each of our lives. Since we know suffering is present, our primary role in advocacy is abiding, at least for a season, yet not in the sense of being another's salvation. Instead, by touching another through our presence, we may be instruments. Or we may not.

Sometimes, in spite of all I can do, I will do harm without intending to do it. That's not intentional, but it's a fact. I need not worry constantly about that, and I don't. I'm learning as I go, but so is the most experienced therapist.

Not all of the silence of bystanders, I've discovered, comes from apathy—not by any means. I believe it's often a fear of being found out for not having all the answers or the fear of unintentionally doing the wrong thing. Survivors often do not want to accept this as fact, but it's important that I try to communicate this to them.

It's also immensely important that each learn to build resources—that's one of the primary roles, in fact, for any advocate, clergy or otherwise. Survivors need to be encouraged to crawl out of their holes and begin building a team—ideally at least 3-5 people. These days, with the Web, it's so much easier. Yet in the early 90's, survivors were very fortunate to have one or two.

There is nothing more glorious than seeing someone find his or her voice, whether a survivor, a family member or friend, or a professional reticent to speak. Yet speaking out is a choice, not an obligation. There are few absolutes for survivors and no guarantees that outcomes are going to be what people hope for. Each survivor must ultimately be the one to weigh the consequences of each decision, and nobody should feel responsible for doing more than taking care of self—this I make very clear.

My philosophy in mission work in Africa was very similar to my philosophy for this work. Sometimes listening is all one person can offer. Yet that goes a long way in human suffering. Resources can be helpful. So can referrals. First, we are called upon to really listen, and not for the purpose of having answers or fixing anything. Then, we move up that Serenity Prayer after honestly sorting out whether there is any action we need to take. In the case of a child, that's always reporting the abuse, of course.

In the case of an adult abused long ago or a vulnerable adult coming to report current abuse, what to do requires that the adult survivor takes the lead as long as she or he is mentally competent to do so. If not, adult protective services (APS) should be called. In the case of professional sexual abuse that's being reported to a professional, there are regulations and laws that vary from case to case. In thirteen states, it is currently a crime for a member of the clergy to become sexually involved in any way with a person receiving counseling. In some states, like Texas, "spiritual counseling" is included.

Lessons from a Quaker

Dale, a middle-aged Quaker chaplain showed up at our church, unannounced, after a two-hour drive one Sunday morning, only weeks after the Boston interview. He very tentatively approached me after service, as I stood next to Ron in the foyer, bidding farewell to parishioners.

Weeks before, I got a most treasured letter from him, one he wasn't sure I'd even receive. It had taken him weeks to even locate a copy of HLWK since he couldn't remember the title, only that he wondered as soon as he heard me talking if we might have even met. We had not. Yet he'd mentioned the interview to someone else, who somehow had heard my story and knew the name of the book.

To this day, Dale reminds me of how it felt when he heard my voice validating his own experience in the dark of night. His abuse had occurred as a child, far from home, in his dorm room at the largest mission boarding school in the world—Rift Valley Academy, the very school attended by our own children years later, I was horrified to learn. I even knew the places where he'd wandered, trying to cope with what was going on.

Though a grown man, his approach that day was as tentative as a timid child. "I had to check things first," he often explains. "So hesitant, I almost left to drive back home even after sitting through service without identifying myself."

"What a blessing we would have missed if you had!" I've often pointed out since to this guy who is as close as a brother to me.

Dale is a musician and song-writer, just like Bette Rod[2] —in fact, the two met once and sang together for a survivor rally. In his hands that Sunday were lyrics he'd written about Joseph and the brothers who betrayed him. That creation would be the first of many more similar gifts for decades to come.

After asking if I could make a copy of his handiwork, we went down to lunch and then the two of us sat for a couple of hours afterwards as he allowed some of his journey to unfold. As with so many survivors since, I felt I was temporarily filling the shoes of his mother. He later confirmed this.

A few years earlier, he had desperately needed his own mother to hear his story. Like so many parents, her turning away, shaken and unable to respond immediately, had made his revelations seem counter-productive to him.

When I later tried to advocate for him with a personal letter to the current headmaster who I knew personally, all I got was blatant DIM thinking. If what this survivor was telling me had actually occurred, wrote Mr. Entwistle, the school would have known. He did not answer my letter of reply.

RVA has surely updated its policies by now, thanks to the work of MK Safety Net of which Dale has become a very active member. Yet policies and procedures are only good when people have done their own serious soul-searching. The results are serious attitude adjustments, also born out of training from professional advocates, whether a case occurs on the mission field or in a non-sectarian medical practice.

Dale was on my long list of Protestants yet to be invited to the 1995 Linkup conference. Each had been "ex-communicated," though not necessarily with the same understanding most Catholics give to this term. While most Protestants tremble at the thought of eternal damnation, some of us like Dale and others espousing "the priesthood of the believers" do not believe any soul on earth has the power to eternally doom anyone. All Protestants *do* hold the belief that a "right relationship with God" is the only salvation and this includes being "in fellowship" with those of one's faith tradition, these were not ordinary circumstances any more than any civil rights issue pitting Christian against Christian.

In such extra-ordinary social issues, we had a mid-20th century chorus, entitled "I Have Decided to Follow Jesus," which had endured in popularity to the present. "Though none go with me, still I will follow" one verse declared. That's what I was clinging to as I prepared to move into the realm of writing specifically for Baptists. It was past time to find re-enforcements.

*****

[1] originally published for advocateweb.org in 1998 following the life sentence given to Richard Kos of Dallas for molesting boys at several congregations http://www.takecourage.org/AWArticles/SpiritualHealing.htm

[2] You can hear samples from Bette Rod's CD "Pieces" and find ordering info at http://www.cdbaby.com/cd/betterod To hear the entire rally song, go to http://www.takecourage.org/rallysong.htm

Chapter 9
Amazing Links, Amazing Grace

In the dead of another Kansas winter, I was blessed recently by a beautiful moment of grace. Thirty moments, actually. Maybe more. I lost count, too busy basking in conversation with Phil Saviano, catching his well-deserved thrill of a victory re-lived and now honored on the screen.

Phil's the survivor whose persistent voice of truth and advocacy shined through the fog of denial in Boston until the Spotlight team listened to his compelling evidence that Cardinal Law and all his underlings could not be trusted to do anything except keep secrets.

Though I well remember Tom Economus telling me about the growing powder keg in Boston and how it would all surely blow up someday (rather than "blow over" like the diocese must have been hoping), I wanted Phil to tell me what connections he might have had with Linkup. Had he talked to Tom personally by chance?

No. The two never met, on September 28, 1999, Phil was inspired when Tom appeared to tell his story on PBS Frontline. It reinforced things he'd seen in Linkup's newsletter. Whenever "The Missing Link" arrived, "I read every word," he told me. "I still have them all stacked in my apartment from 1993 on." He also occasionally used the newsletter to get word out to other survivors about things going on with SNAP efforts in Boston. It served like an underground connection for him, as it did for so many others.

I don't know how Phil first heard of SNAP and The Linkup. It wasn't like there was a big advertising budget back in the 90's. Sadly, many survivors never did know. The Church certainly wasn't advertising for either organization, though I was trying to as a writer, whenever I managed to get published.

In the course of writing this book, I took time to stop and reach out to a couple with a story an awful lot like the Bates'. Except they aren't Catholic—never have been, yet the survivor's story (in this case the wife's) is related to the story of the lesbian pastor who showed up at Linkup's Leadership Conference. Each was sexually abused by her own minister-father.

There was no survivor movement when the two of them met in the mid-1980's at a conservative Bible school. Even if there had been, no copies of "The Missing Link" would have been placed around in their school cafeteria any more than seminaries ten years later. You can count on that. What a scandal that would have created!

Yet they would have been most welcome had they known. Instead they suffered through the first twenty years of their marriage, not realizing there was already a lot of help available to them.

Dangerous Theology

"The sign of God's will is that you will be led where you did not plan to go."

I'd never been in a Catholic book store in my life until I walked into the one at St. John's. Within seconds, I stopped dead in my tracks. Stepping around the corner, I pulled Ron over to see the words on a small poster, ready for purchase.

"I guess that's our sign," I said. "God really does have a sense of humor after all."

We didn't buy it. Not the bumper sticker. Nor the message that could as easily be found in any Baptist Book Store as this Catholic one.

Assuming that wherever a person is led to go is automatically God's will is a recipe for disaster. In fact, this common theology is used as a set-up by many a priest abuser to lead kids down a dark corridor as easily as some dealer luring them toward a killer drug.

God gets blamed for a tremendous amount of nonsense.

It did sound nice, and we felt good about claiming it for the moment. Never had we been so far from where we once planned to be as that day. Even going to Africa was something I'd envisioned doing since childhood. Over time, it was something we both yearned to do together—a calling as we perceived it.

We had not been led to leave Africa or the leave the SBC. We had been forced to choose the greater good for us in both situations. Yet we'd never been surer than today that we were in the right place as we stood in the middle of a Catholic book store, waiting to meet many new friends.

Going back to the introduction for this book and what I wrote about puddles, this felt like "a nice puddle" to step into on this particular day.

Important Links before the World-Wide Web

Jeanne Miller was a genius, coming up with "The Missing Link" for
the name. The Church had tried to leave survivors out of the information
flow, thereby discounting their most vital link to Truths beyond mere facts.
Survivors weren't "supposed" to be connected. Neither perpetrators nor
church officials ever counted on that happening. The irony was that the
newsletter held vital   missing pieces for church officials if they ever
happened to be interested in reclaiming any semblance of integrity and
authenticity. At the same time, it served as a way of re-connecting each
survivor, otherwise "missing in action" to important, life-giving messages
that, in turn, had the potential for breaking the isolation and changing each
one, regardless of what the Church decided to do.

The dynamics were as old as the scriptures. Outcast "lepers" were
individually walking out of psychologically imposed prisons in response to
the increasing outcries of others. As their *debilitating* chains fell off, a new,
more powerful, *connecting* chain of unity was formed, link by link. There
was a sense that this movement could not be extinguished and would only
grow until the world began to pay close attention. Survivors had little more
to cling to, and nothing more to lose.

Amazing Connections

Back in 1992, a grandmother had become a vital link (or puddle) for
me herself when she showed up in the incest survivors' support group I
was co-leading. With her permission, she was added a year later as
"Charlotte" in the final pages of *How Little We Knew.*

As a childhood survivor, severely abused in multiple ways by her
Baptist minister father, as well as her mother, she'd seen neither in years
and had no intentions of ever doing so again. Charlotte was one of the most
resourceful survivors I've ever met. In spite of her invisible scars she
carried with grace, including several on her ear drums from childhood
beatings, she'd managed to have a healthy marriage with an incredibly
supportive man, managed to have a successful career in the banking
business, and raised two loving children. In spite of all this, she was still in
a world of spiritual and psychological pain.

Except for her immediate family and closest friends, few knew why she had no use for religion of any kind. Everyone in her extended family—even those who knew the truth--still condemned her for not "honoring" her parents. For the past few years, thanks to the healing support of therapists, she was feeling rightfully proud of her accomplishments.

Somehow, she'd recently learned there was going to be a survivors' retreat at a Methodist camp near Okiboji, Iowa—one of the most popular resorts in the Midwest. It wasn't supposed to be religious at all. Otherwise, she wouldn't have considered it.

This was being offered to women from all over the country who had somehow experienced sexual abuse of any kind, at any age, by clergy of any denomination. What's more, Methodists were offering it practically free. Cost was $25 for the entire weekend, including room and board. This was phenomenal, considering that United Methodists were still four years away from even passing a resolution to address sexual abuse within pastoral relationships. I could hardly believe my ears!

The psychologist for the local incest survivors' group, which happened to be meeting in her office, explained my role as co-leader when I came on board. While I was there strictly as a mental health nurse, she was especially interested in me eventually sharing my experience and expertise on the topic of collusion and how it plays out with family dynamics. So I had been doing that, off and on, for several weeks when Charlotte mentioned this retreat.

I immediately saw some wavy lines on the spectrum of ethical boundaries if I even suggested going with Charlotte to the retreat, though I certainly was intrigued. To my surprise, when I broached the issues privately with the psychologist, she had no reservations at all, especially since the local support group, a time-limited one by design, was ending soon. In fact, having worked intensely one-on-one with Charlotte, she encouraged me to approach her with the possibility of us driving up together. It proved to be an excellent decision.

Soon after arriving in Okiboji, we learned this retreat ministry, an outgrowth of Marie Fortune's array of ministries,[1] was due to the initiative of a Methodist survivor I'll call Colleen. This middle-aged mother was also an employee of United Methodists in the area. She'd successfully petitioned the denomination's regional office to finance the annual event. This was the second year, and some of the attendees were talking about coming back each year. It was the most diverse group of women of faith I'd ever been a part of—before or since. Representatives from Catholic, Unitarian, Jehovah Witness, and Jewish communities, as well as Methodists, Baptists, and an array of Protestant denominations were there for a group of only twenty-five. Yet never have I felt such unity. Collusion was the most common element, for the ages and circumstances of each abuse victim filled a far greater spectrum than any one author had ever recognized. Some were abused as children, others as teenagers, and about half as adults. There were several of us who were victims of sexual harassment by a male colleague. Reactions, endurance between initial abuse and reporting, and expectations had all varied greatly from one story to the other.

With its growing success, an annual peer-led group would be added the following year at another encampment that happened to be only an hour's drive from the parsonage. I felt so fortunate. This unique sisterhood made up of women from across the nation ceased to meet formally within a few years when we were all able to get connected on the Web. To this day, several strong relationships have endured for me from the network, the oldest member now in her mid-eighties.

Charlotte was soon "turned off" by some at the retreat who "still believed too much in Santa Claus," as she saw it. So she dropped out early on. Yet, she was an amazing link for me to plug into a serendipitous, ecumenical group that I might never have known about had it not been for a single United Methodist survivor from a denomination who was willing to provide for their own, but go far beyond "the second mile," extending a welcome to those from other faith groups.

Along with several other survivors from the Okiboji retreat, a small, local women's support group formed, which Charlotte did remain a part of much longer. Soon a survivor abused by her Methodist step-father (also a pastor) joined us. This woman had shown up with her two small children at our church after seeing an article about my ministry in the local newspaper.

Sadly, when I last saw Charlotte several years later, shortly before the couple moved out of state, a huge hole of resentment and loss remained in her heart. Through no fault of her own, she'd found little relief.

"Janine," a young Catholic survivor, who spent most days at a sheltered workshop for people with chronic mental illness, attended both the local group and national, annual event. Quite a networker, she showed up one day at the local group with her favorite teddy bear in one hand and fliers for two organizations in the other. From that day forward, she loved telling people in the nearby Omaha chapter of SNAP, of which she was also a member, about this new writer-friend who'd known nothing of either The Linkup or SNAP until she came in as the missing link.

Eventually, a couple of women from the retreat group joined Linkup with my encouragement. These were the various kinds of connections sometimes forged like an "underground work" during those years when Boston lay sleeping. Together, sometimes on a local level, at times with connections across state or international lines, sparks were created that eventually led to a fire that's now stronger than ever thanks to Boston finally waking up and being found by Tom McCarthy and Josh Singer, who became a part of the much larger movement, finally bringing the Spotlight story to Hollywood.

The fire burns now like an eternal flame, despite the fact many of the original ties have been broken by death of individuals or entire organizations.

*****

[1] Many such retreats were held across the United States in the mid-1990's and on into the early years of the 21st century until the backlog began to dwindle. As a part of a settlement, survivors were encouraged to ask that travel and retreat expenses be covered by their church or denomination. Retreat leaders were usually ordained clergywomen who were trained by The Center for the Prevention of Sexual and Domestic Violence (now FaithTrust Institute)

Chapter 10
Struggles of a Dissident Writer

**It's persistence, not perfection,
that gets the job done in advocacy.**

Few members of The Linkup knew the agonizing process I'd gone through for years in trying to land a publisher. The story itself serves as an illustration of the resistance the world has to our message even today. Yet, far more twenty-five years ago! After all, who in the early 90's dared to believe that there was a widespread tendency, seldom even acknowledged in the press, for this most revered of professions to be acting like the mafia? And why should anyone who'd not experienced such assault or abuse believe? Hadn't we all originally assumed our own story was just a fluke?

For the benefit of those who've never tried to get published, one of the primary frustrations is that writers seldom get a reason for a rejection. It may very well be the writing. Or possibly the writer hasn't looked close enough at what the publisher wants. It could also be the way the proposal is pitched or what side of the bed the person receiving it may have gotten up on that day before trashing the whole proposal within thirty seconds.

Most submissions now are electronic. And even if the publisher wants more, there's a good chance what they ask for can be submitted electronically. Of course, in the Dark Ages before the Web, all proposals went by snail mail. If you waited three months without hearing anything, it was acceptable to submit the same manuscript to someone else. Most publishers frowned on simultaneous submissions, however. They liked to have the exclusive privilege of holding your proposal or manuscript hostage for weeks or months, and weren't always clear how long they could be expected to hold it.

Over the course of two years, I had already approached nearly thirty publishers and gotten very close to a contract with two. In the end, it had been like trying to kick field goals in soccer, then having the ball repeatedly bounce off the goal post at the finish line.

Then, one day, I had a mountaintop experience—literally. It turned out to be one of those moments when Light manages to shine through tiny spaces into the dark night of the soul. That's how Serene Jones speaks of "grace" that comes into our lives after trauma in *Trauma and Grace* (Westminster/John Knox, 2009).

To me, what happened that afternoon was more like experiencing a powerful flash of lightning that serves only to illuminate everything surrounding it on an otherwise stormy night.

It happened when I rounded a bend in West Virginia one afternoon in 1991, hiking alone near the retreat center where new ABC ministers and their spouses had been invited from all over the country for an orientation weekend. Sitting quietly on a concrete bench, overlooking a valley was another newcomer, warm-hearted and welcoming, who soon invited me to share her bench. We quickly bonded over conversation, sharing our unique journeys like refugees coming into a new land at midlife.

Dr. Bert Kae-Je, besides being an ordained minister, already held diplomat status with the American Association of Pastoral Counselors, and was an experienced writer in her field. Immediately, she wanted to hear more about *How Little We Knew* and my search for a publisher. Would I be willing to send her the manuscript?

I could hardly wait. Her response time was astounding. Within days, she had it back to me with personal notes of appreciation all over the margins along with comments and excellent suggestions for improvement, recommending that I send a query with sample chapters to Haworth Press, a strong academic publisher. She'd previously written for Dr. William Clements, editor of Haworth's "Journal of Religion and Psychotherapy." "You can tell him I sent you," she added.

I did, asking if she'd write a foreward in the meantime.

The rejection that followed this time was genuinely personal and extremely encouraging. Yet, to my surprise, though I'd addressed the proposal to Clements, it had apparently gotten intercepted before reaching him and had landed on the desk of the chief editor, who wrote that he'd looked it over carefully himself before concluding this book needed a major trade publisher; for he felt certain it would have a wide audience. However, if I was unable to find someone to take it on, I shouldn't hesitate to come back.

Clements did get it six months later, after my detour into a land of "failed field goals," once again. The turn-around time was astounding this time—a call telling me of the contract I'd be receiving by express mail later that day, based on the recommendations of the editor, who advised the marketing department: "Do not underestimate the potential of this book."

The following day, I found a personal letter from Clements in our mailbox. He was making this a priority on his schedule, expecting us to move quickly toward completion. Our household was a flurry of excitement, and so was the mental health office at work.

Three days later, Ron met me at the front door at the end of my busy week.

"You better sit down," he said. And I did immediately. From the look on his face, I was certain someone in the family must have died suddenly.

In his hand, he held a follow-up letter from Haworth, which he'd eagerly opened before thinking. To his utter dismay, they were retracting the offer. There was no recourse. The form letter, obviously sent to several authors, explained that the company's marketing department realized they had made a mistake by extending more contracts than they could afford to honor.

I called in disbelief. Whoever made this decision had surely not seen Clement's cautionary words, I exclaimed. Sorry, a kind lady told me. They all had. As for my particular project, only one person was needed to convince everyone else in the marketing department to place it on their newly-created black list, based on the belief that I would most likely be hesitant to market this book due to the nature of the story. I was appalled.

How could anyone think I would invest so much of life writing something so important and not being willing to do everything possible to promote it! I have since realized that many writers do just that. And many writers, on the other end of dysfunction, have gone unpublished entirely because they refuse to publish something timely like this book was, until they have "just the right" publisher. To me, I'd found just the right one after an extensive search, only to have someone with convincing power, able to slam the door in my face, even yet!

Whatever I said or thought, it didn't matter. Decisions were final. They wished me the best in my pursuit.

I made a mad dash to our master bedroom and, for the first time in my life, beat the very pillow where I laid my head every night, as I simultaneously let out blood-curdling, hysterical screams of deepest sorrow. Never had I felt such fury—neither before nor since. Despondency followed. I spent the weekend giving up. To think anyone would believe I'd written this story merely for "my own therapy." I had dreams for this "child" of mine that now seemed to have been delivered stillborn.

Ron, who stood by helplessly, finally shrugged. "OK. Give it a rest if you wish," he said in the calmest of tones I'd ever heard him utter.

I looked at him in disbelief. How *could* I go on? No way, I told him. I dropped a letter off to Marie Fortune, never expecting an answer since I'd only spoken to her for a half minute about the manuscript while at a training conference the year before. To my surprise, she wrote with a fury in response, saying of Haworth, "It is utter foolishness that this book is not lucrative to them. I hope this is just a matter of their stupidity and not something more."

It was just the words I needed to light another fire beneath me. I still wonder what she thought might have been "something more."

I started again through fourteen more publishers, coming close to another contract before the editor I was working with left the major publishing house suddenly without explanation, I later learned, dropping the ball on her way out. The only thing that *kept* me going was the host of people out there I could visualize needing our story—not just survivors, but professionals, family members, maybe even a few clergy members.

No way was I going to self-publish a book that had already been recognized for its worth by an expert in the field, I declared.

Six months later, I got a letter from Huntington House of Lafayette, Louisiana. David at Prescott Press would be calling me. That's when they told me about having just published *Law in the Cajun Nation* by J. Minos Simon, the very attorney who'd succeeded in winning the first-ever Catholic case, the one Tom Doyle used as an example in 1985, trying to get the attention of the bishops.

The staff of three would work hard on every aspect of publishing, from editing to the cover. They also promised to work as hard as any major publisher to get the word out. They'd been thrilled with the response from the local community to Simon's book and just as thrilled to think of taking on mine. They were certain it would have a much wider audience. There was just one catch.

I'd need to do a pre-purchase to the tune of $6000 for books that I could resell for nearly twice the price. My heart sank. Considering the encouragement I had from Clements, I knew I had a solid piece. This felt close to "vanity publishing" in spite of the support staff telling me it was "just what writers with such cutting-edge topics often had to resort to. Sometimes things can be too controversial, so it may take a while for a book like this to catch hold."

I felt insulted, I told Ron. This wasn't fair after all we'd been through, financially, as well as every other way. There was no way I was willing to turn loose of that much money!

"We can do this!" Ron insisted. "We'll eventually come out ahead. Don't hesitate." Sure, it would seriously drain our savings, but within a year our son would be finished with college. The two of us certainly knew how to live on a shoestring. Money wasn't the most important thing, he insisted. There was no reason not to go ahead if they would come through all they were promising in this contract.

I was skeptical about their promises, as well. Yet what finally tipped the scales was my strong sense of intuition. The timing was right, I felt certain, though I couldn't have told you why I felt as strongly about this as I had about our family moving to Africa. So I ignored my doubts, signed the contract, and tried to do what I'd always done with any previous decision, trying not to look back.

I quit worrying a week after the book's release.

Prescott kept every promise and much more. They paid for publicity, doing a great job of efficiently coordinating each request that came in, providing good coaching and tons of encouragement.

Then, suddenly, only a week before we left for the big 1994 Linkup conference, I got a shock as great as the call to cancel the Haworth contract. Without warning, an executive at Huntington House called with one of the most heartless messages I've ever received. Prescott Press was shutting down. Huntington House was picking up the pieces. They had fulfilled all their obligations with me. I was on my own!

When I protested, the conversation turned ugly. "As a Christian, you should understand more than anyone that things like this happen," he told me, without disclosing the nature of the mysterious problems that had caused the sudden shut down. My stomach turned. He had no idea how this sounded to someone who had been through what I had.

"People at Prescott made some serious mistakes," he continued. "Perhaps one was taking on your book because it has caused them to spend more time answering phone calls and coordinating interviews than any project they've had and more than most we've had here at Huntington House." He abruptly hung up. I wanted to barf at his condescension, but I didn't. Instead I burst into tears.

As I began to recover, I found myself drawing on the intangible gifts Bert had first given me. Not only did she take time to affirm my work. She directed me to an expert in the publishing world, a male gatekeeper in the publishing system, which has historically had a strong gender bias against female authors. The validation I received as a writer from Haworth, despite the outcome, instilled confidence that I would never have had otherwise.

My passion grew from that first week at the Re-Imagining Conference and with each new validation of how the story was reaching into the hearts of survivors and professionals alike. Yet, after all of the sacrifice, even sending out brochures to numerous SBC officials, and telling this story on the radio all over the United States, to my knowledge not one Southern Baptist had contacted the publisher or given indication they were among the few hundred who had ordered books.

Therefore, on November 1, 1994—exactly one year after I'd stood at the Re-Imagining Conference with my first copy of *How Little We Knew*, I knew it was time for me to go back to let my voice be heard by people still operating in the denomination of my heritage. I'd begin initiating this effort before Thanksgiving, when I'd be celebrating my liberation from a daily nursing schedule, though fully aware I'd be going to one equally demanding with me in charge.

When it came to Baptist publications, I'd be fortunate to find any editor courageous enough to allow me to tackle the monstrous truths about complicity with a story far more up close and personal for the denomination than most survivor stories would ever be.

For what they would know, same as I did, was something few Linkup members would ever understand: before our forced resignation, we were often introduced as "our cream of the crop," same as all missionaries for the Foreign Mission Board of the Southern Baptist Convention.

Well, the cream was rising once again to the top; and I'd be very hard to ignore if I could get past the gatekeepers.

I'd already run an informal survey with all the editors of state Baptist papers. Most either ignored me, or told me they weren't even printing what was being sent to them by male Baptist journalists on the topic of clergy sexual misconduct, not even Jeff Seats survey. So scratch every one of them off the list!

I'd tested the waters with a couple of editors of small Baptist publications I'd been reading for years, too. So far, they'd passed the test by being receptive to my initial messages and had even printed what I'd sent them, though I'd not gone so far as to tell them who I *really* was.

I casually referred to these as "Baptist tabloids," not because there was anything at all inappropriate about what they printed, simply because the vast majority of Southern Baptists were likely to think so. Little did I know: there was already a book[1] out that used the term "tabloid" when describing SBC Today, the predecessor, which began only in 1983, to Baptists Today. In fact, sum total of the readership of these little renegade publications was less than 1% of all Southern Baptists. Yet anyone who was anybody was likely to be sneaking a peak to see what "the radicals" were saying. I should fit right in now.

Both were lifelines for many people in CBF (Cooperative Baptist Fellowship), the "refugee" organization people like Jimmy Carter would eventually join, thanks to the increasing conservative resurgence.

Jack Harwell, editor of Baptists Today, had given me no reason to believe he would not be supportive, though I knew little yet about his own story as a denominational outcast or if he'd feel he could afford to take on anything as unsettling as my work.

Ken Sehested, editor of Baptist Peacemaker probably knew "women's issues" better than any Baptist editor alive, being married to Nancy Sehested, a Baptist woman who was successfully pastoring a Southern Baptist church that had been kicked out of the local association. Nancy had been featured in a Bill Moyer's PBS documentary about the fundamentalist takeover. That film ran shortly before our missionary service was terminated.

While I was still recovering from the 1992 Haworth rejection, I sent an anonymous letter to Harwell, identifying myself as an advocate wishing to bring to readers' attention the problem of clergy sexual abuse. He quickly responded warmly, assuring me he'd soon find a place for my letter.

He did so in the next issue, printing it in place of his usual editorial. He also mentioned to me a series of articles he was currently running by Dr. Joe Trull, an ethics professor at New Orleans Baptist Theological

Seminary, Ron's alma mater. Trull was recommending Baptists adopt a code of ethics for all ministers—a standard this profession did not have, unlike most other professions. One issue he'd touched on in the series was the problem of clergy sexual misconduct.

After my success in getting the letter in "Baptists Today," I sent a lengthy article to Ken on my work with sexually abused children, which he also promptly printed. While it said nothing about clergy issues, my hunch was his wife knew plenty on that topic. If so, this could open other doors.

Still, I figured Harwell would run the other way when he found out more about me. After all, any mention of what we'd been through was bound to maar the image of the prestigious Foreign Mission Board, an agency that was still an icon, holding a lot of respect of moderates, as well as the most conservative in the Convention, with the urban myth long being that the SBC started "because of missions."

It was a bald-faced lie—except for those who like to stretch the truth a country mile, which people had been doing for precisely 150 years. I didn't even know this myself after working for the agency nearly a decade! Truth is the SBC, which began in 1845, sixteen years before the first shots of the Civil War, did *not* start because of missions. It began because the South wanted to appoint a slave-holder to be a missionary in Africa, and Northerners refused to go along.

The other bald-faced lie was that this "conservative resurgence," which most moderates in the Convention referred to as "the fundamentalist take-over," was because of what was commonly known as "inerrancy," the belief that we had somehow been handed a message directly from God—both originally and through all the translations that had come through Scripture. Of course, there are tons of contradictions in theology, thanks to the numerous writers of the Bible. Yet each was supposed to have heard the voice of God directly, and we were somehow supposed to understand all these contradictions as being in agreement the way modern-day "authorities" had come to understand things. Now, anyone who disagreed with the new authorities, anyone who thought in a more intellectual or scientific approach, had better find someplace else to perch.

This controversy, which had created the first-ever big split in the Convention since 1845, was frequently making national news. All of this, of course, happened simultaneously with the turmoil that had been created in our personal lives with the collusion in the "Kingsley case."

One of the reasons I waited a full year before walking straight into the denomination of my heritage to confront this latest scandalous issue I'd taken on was that I feared the strange questions I anticipated getting. The worst ones were rhetorical and hard to ignore. They'd come in a round-about way from my colleagues and high-ranking officials at the Foreign Mission Board almost a decade earlier. The most common being, "Just what is *your* problem, woman?"

Oh, they didn't say it quite like that. The wording was much more subtle, but I easily got the message.

So as I anticipated shooting off queries to editors in 1994, I braced myself for rejections. I still doubted any Baptist editor would allow me to go as far as I wanted to go, even if I ever got my foot in the door with bits of our personal story. It really would be something like a miracle.

The Star Wars comparison that Signe Nestingen, a Minnesota psychotherapist, provided us at Linkup was especially helpful. She spoke of the typical reaction most whistle-blowers get when confronting a self-serving system about any matter that's seriously threatening the system's collective peace of mind. "You are flung into outer space. Re-entry is gained only by leaving your story on the doorstep."

Well, in Baptist Sunday School, I'd sang "This Little Light of Mine" almost every Sunday as a kid. The second verse of that song, the one we kids loved most, declared: "Hide it under a bushel—NO!" Each of us covered our right, index finger with our left hand for the first five words, then, shouted "NO" as our little hands shot off the "covered bushels."

That story I'd internalized well. This story of mine was like "a bushel." It wasn't evil. It was *about* evil, same as the story the SBC had kept hidden about its own origins, and still hadn't gotten around to apologizing for.

That big truth, hidden by a "bushel" needed uncovering, and so did this truth about sexually-abusive ministers (commonly referred to as CSA in survivor circles). The latter Southern Baptists weren't close to facing—not nearly as close as United Methodists and some other mainline groups.

The problem for every denomination was that people were often getting confused on this point of what's evil—the telling or the doing of evil-doers. That's why they once burned "witches" at the stake.

The other problem is that it's mighty close to home—to some degree, a story about everyone in it.

Some days I'd take a detour into a healthy sort of exploration. How could I have grown up in this denomination of nearly sixteen million, which totally dwarfs most mainline denominations, without seeing what was hiding in plain sight? How had I been so acculturated not to see beyond the smokescreens that so skillfully had kept each of us with the "original sin" of being born female in designated places? Why hadn't the women who had mentored me and unknowingly set me up for this fall not been aware? Did they not know a thing about the evils of patriarchy themselves? Or did they know and just choose to ignore it all?

On the other hand, thanks to so many of my sisters I was meeting outside the church—women who had been raised in "outer space" and had no desire to be inside this "world of fear," as many of them saw it—I was beginning to understand the joy of having choices. Like a child, I was "mesmerized by the fire," as Bette Rod[2] so vividly describes "the demon," what Rubino describes as "the serpent."

"The demon" wasn't an obsession keeping those of us who had been burned by the fire from moving on in our lives. As I saw it, like a child being "mesmerized by the fire," we had a chance to grow and become missing links as we came to understand how the process of collusion operates to silence whistle-blowers, showing the world how a dysfunctional system and all who participate in it, either actively or passively, can play havoc with the lives of others.

No longer did I feel like a child walking back into the system, however. I was an intensely curious and well-informed woman who did not need any church system for my own validation. My greatest concern was what damage had been done to the innocent faith of children and youth, many now still struggling as adults to come to grips with it all.

What I was seeking to do wasn't going to be easy even if I got my foot in the door. I knew that full well. Yet I intended to draw on a ton of experience that would allow me to take the heat without getting burned again beyond recognition.

Frequently, I found myself humming the tune to the second line of one of the most popular hymns of the Confederacy, "Onward Christian Soldiers," though with an opposite view as the one held by those who once supported slavery.

Unlike some of my more seasoned feminist friends, I'd grown up understanding that it was a weaponless "war" we were called to wage by exercising our faith—a war with evil. That understanding now served me well.

Alice Vaschh, would definitely approve. It was *time* to go to war.

*****

[1] The Conservative Resurgence in the Southern Baptist Convention by James C. Hefley, Hannibal Books, 1991.

[2] You can hear samples from Bette Rod's CD "Pieces" and find ordering info at http://www.cdbaby.com/cd/betterod To hear the entire rally song for free, go to http://www.takecourage.org/Journey.htm and listen as you explore spiritual helps by this author, Dee Ann Miller

Chapter 11
Lessons for Living with Serpents

"It's like a pebble in a shoe," Signe Nestingen explained. "Hardly noticeable at first. In fact, abuse awareness can usually be shaken to the side of the shoe, perhaps into a crevice. Eventually, when it finally gets your attention, it becomes really bothersome. That's when you stop walking, find a place to sit down and get that shoe off so you can take care of the problem."

Now, as Christmas of 1994 approached, I intended to be a pebble in Jack Harwell's shoe. I was still waiting on an answer to my query, which he seemed to be ignoring. Even if it was a rejection, I wanted it in writing, I told him un-apologetically.

To my surprise, I *got* an apology and the most welcome letter I'd seen since unsuccessfully searching from 10,000 miles away for someone who might be willing to own the real problem and offer no excuses. The query had gotten lost on his desk. Now, he wanted to know if I'd be willing to write a series of eight articles for him on the issues of collusion with clergy sexual abuse. I was thrilled.

Yet I wasn't jumping up and down that day in the least, for I was anxiously awaiting another piece of news that had nothing to do with writing—or so I thought. I got my answer that day, and it turned out to be more devastating than I had even imagined it might be.

Another serpent had invaded my life somewhere between 1988 and the present, though it had remained hidden until a few days before we got on the plane to go to Toronto. It all had to do with the pebble-size lump, I'd been startled to discover two inches to the right of my sternum.

It wasn't like I stayed in denial those glorious days in Toronto. I simply compartmentalized the likelihood I had cancer, knowing it would be at the top of my list once I got back home. There wasn't even a need to go to the doctor before finding out, I immediately concluded. I'd go straight to radiology, get the job done, and wait.

Back then, hospitals called the doctor's office for any middle-aged woman who requested a mammogram and got an order automatically, often thru an office nurse without the doctor even being bothered. That's exactly why my own doctor, considerably younger than me, was so shocked when she got the report. "This is hard to take. You are one who does everything right with lifestyle and even keeps screenings done on your own!" she exclaimed, as if cancer didn't strike the young and healthy.

Sadly, a decade later this very doctor would be dead from pancreatic cancer, leaving two young sons behind. Cancer, same as abuse, has a way of randomly invading our lives, no matter how cautionary we may be.

I've never aspired to thrive or even join in walk-a-thons for breast cancer. It's not that I don't care, but a decision I made in the first conversation I had after getting the bad news call from my doctor. Immediately after hanging up with the doctor, I'd picked up the phone again to call my friend Jan, a writer and breast cancer survivor who had let her cancer sit much too long, as so many women do, paying later because she'd ignored it. Jan was big on activism. That's fine. We need that, I told her. Still, she didn't think it odd in the least when I said, "I'll let others do that. All I want to do is get on with my life and back to the advocacy work I'm already doing, as fast as I possibly can."

"I think that's a fine choice," Jan assured me. She knew full well what I had waiting on my writing agenda.

Some cancer survivors say that cancer was the best thing that ever happened to them. I guess those are the cancer thrivers. I don't expect to ever say that. To this day, except for learning way more about the disease than I ever needed to know, I can only say two "good things" came from my struggles.

First, whenever I get inspired to take on a big project like this one, I jump in with all fours. Maybe that's not a lot different than before. I do come from a stock that tends to operate like that, anyway. Since cancer, though, there's always a little extra driving force. I think: "What if I don't live to see this finished?"

The other was really odd. I find myself being more empathetic than ever because of the way I now understand vulnerability on a gut level. I never fully got it, except intellectually, until the very moment when my surgeon explained what was ahead of me. Suddenly, I found myself crumbling into her arms like a bag of fine feathers. I believe I would have consented to anything she recommended at that moment. For the first time in my life, I questioned nothing.

Oh, well, I told myself as I looked at Harwell's letter again a few days after its arrival, staring through tears that weren't about to stop flowing. I'd combine the good news and the bad. The first article of the series of eight, which Jack Harwell was asking me to write, was going to show how to deal with both sexual abuse and cancer—head on. It wasn't scheduled to run until a couple of weeks into January, a few days after my four-hour ordeal on the operating table.

I still intended to have it in the mail right after Christmas. I promised Harwell this when I called—just in case something else unforeseen prevented me from being around when it ran. For the last thing I wanted to do was leave this earth without exposing the problem of collusion with abusive clergy in the denomination of my heritage—even though the publication, "Baptists Today," for which Harwell was now the editor, was as much a renegade publication as "The National Catholic Recorder."

Holiday Blues

Christmas of 1994 was the most dismal holiday I'd ever known. New Years' Day held no prospects for improvement. From here on out I would have two serpents to manage.

I kept thinking back to the call I first got from my doctor about the "inconclusive" report on a sonogram of my chest—showing a 97% likelihood of breast cancer. By the time I got to the surgeon, also the day Harwell's letter arrived, the likelihood was 99%. I'm an optimist, but a reasonably realistic one. I wasn't clinging to that 1% or begging for some kind of miraculous conversion of malignant cells to benign ones. I knew in my gut this was cancer—actually was quite sure the day I discovered the lump, thanks to my nursing knowledge. This was too solid, unlike most benign lumps I'd run across.

If it hadn't been for the generosity of my son and his fiancée Colleen, I would never have gotten done with the three writing assignments I was determined to finish before going in the hospital. She called her parents to say they were needed more at our house. So on December 26, I began writing.

I was beginning to see what Bob Laubach meant at the writers' conference I'd attended years earlier. "If you have a message you want to get across, you must learn to write it 1000 different times in 1000 different ways."

Since there were easily 1000 different audiences I could approach with this message, the words and approach for each would vary, depending on the nature of the clientele.

For instance, while I wrote for each audience about the parallels of dealing with two cancers—the one in my body, the other in the community of faith, I used a totally different slant and "voice" for each one of the three I dropped into the mailbox on December 29, on the way to the hospital.

Of course, one was that first contribution to Baptists Today. Another was a 4-page, feature article for Zondervan's impressive glossy magazine, The Journal of Christian Nursing. The third was my next "Reconnections" column.

For the nursing journal, I included appropriate responses for nurses when dealing with any sexual assault. That article, the only one of the three I'd be paid to write, came with an extra perk. The editor was doing a book review and providing a 25-question post-test.

JCN needed a lot of lead time. It would end up being over a year before it came out. Yet no article was more important to me because it was a heart-to-heart to people in the profession I had just left behind, at least for now. Again, if something unforeseen happened during my four hours on the operating table, I wanted to be sure to leave this legacy.

The editor chose to lift a statement for the sidebar: "I didn't know if God was even there, but I yelled at him just in case." It was a reference to our painful losses that forced us off the mission field, not breast cancer. However, I began that article, writing about breast cancer.

"'No matter what happened yesterday, today is filled with hope and promise.' These words are at the top of stationery I frequently use to write personal notes to survivors and advocates ......

"Right now, they are words I am trying to internalize. ....Well-meaning people take care of their own feelings by saying, 'Everything will be okay.' I answer, as politely as possible, 'It is *not* okay now, and it will never be okay. Cancer never is. In time, it will become acceptable, but it is *not* okay.'....

"Others say, 'This is going to make you even stronger than you are.' That validates my present interpretation of what is going on. It fits best my current journey. *Still, a part of me thinks, I don't want to get stronger this way.* I refuse to accept, as some suggest, that this is God's perfect will for my life."

In that article, I wanted nurses to know why they are even more likely to be trusted for some of the initial conversations a survivor of sexual assault may have than pastors or psychotherapists. Besides gender issues for most nurses and the obvious contact in ER after a sexual assault, there's the knowledge and power issues. Nurses are perceived by the general public to be knowledgeable on the topic of sexual violence but hold a minimum amount of power compared to doctors or chaplains. The more power one has, the scarier a person may appear to a vulnerable individual.

For this reason, I talked about what well-meaning people say, what is helpful, what is not.

In regard to the spirituality of survivors, I shared some of my personal struggles that came because of the collusion, rather than the physical violation. "It took time to remember that God had done nothing to cause all I had endured, and it is not God's job to provide protection either. This was all the failure of mankind."

I wrote of how cherished hymns, Scripture, beliefs, a cross or other religious symbols, clerical robes that might have once been acceptable and spiritual clichés—any or all of these can become poisoned by those who have been spiritually abused for whatever reason. For some, they are triggers. To others, they appear as a mockery to the hypocrisy demonstrated by bigotry.

"It is often difficult for us, as Christians, to put our own faith in the background and listen. Perhaps this is because we feel threatened. We may feel responsible for the victim's present (perhaps lifelong) spiritual damage. Yet I must warn you that I have spent many hours trying to undo what well-meaning Christians, both clergy and laity, have done to further damage survivors. In our eagerness to see instant healing, it is often easy for our messages to produce guilt, blame and feelings of abandonment. It's important to remember that victims aren't necessarily 'sick;' yet many who try to report do become victims of the 'cancer' of collusion in the community. This is why we need nurse advocates.

I encouraged nurses to remember the most helpful words of all in the wake of immediate trauma or residual pain. "I am so sorry." It's a phrase that I'd noticed had suddenly gone missing in American culture during the years we spent abroad, and I wondered if the phrase had been put on the taboo list for American business by lawyers who didn't want anybody to admit they'd messed up about anything. I pointed out how younger people now seem to equate "I am sorry" with "I did something wrong."

Older folks held a different understanding, I explained. Previously, many of us had used the "sorry" word to convey the kind of empathy that is called for with trauma, regardless of who is to blame. So I suggested adding "That shouldn't happen to anyone."

Honesty with feelings is vital, I told them. "If you are sad, you need to feel comfortable saying that. If you are feeling some outrage about what has happened to your patient, expressing this can be very validating. It's actually a sign of health if you are angry."

If I'd known of Brene Brown's work on shame, empathy, and vulnerability (work which was yet to come), I would have inserted a quote from one of Brown's many videos on the Web: "Empathy is the skill set for keeping compassion alive. It's feeling with someone, not feeling for someone." Which is why, whenever I hear the phrase: "I feel for you," I want to say: "I know you mean well, but please understand you can *only feel with me, not for me.*"

Knowing that some in this group might be tempted to give spiritual platitudes, I offered a bit of modelling myself. "Unless I know that a survivor is eager to harness a spiritual means of healing, I will simply pray silently."

Above all, I cautioned: "Resist the temptation to defend God." Spiritual issues can be internal. *My abuse must be because of who I am or something I did.* They are often interpersonal. *If these people who are supposed to be so strong cannot stand with me, how can God?* Or with the very concept of God. *I don't see how there could be a God. If so, God wouldn't allow things like this to happen to anyone.*

People of genuine faith, those who understand that only mature faith allows itself to question and not to have all the answers .... That's who I hoped I was writing for. Yet, writing is always an act of faith. You take many shots in the dark, same as speaking on live radio, not being able to take back what you say, not being able to control the outcome, and often wondering if anyone at all is listening or what their state of mind may be in, if they are. In the end it doesn't really matter. For faith is the evidence of things not seen—it's the stepping out that's important to the soul.

Chapter 12
Enlarging Conversations

Even before we're born, gatekeepers are supposed to keep us safe. With a little luck, parents and doctors do this, using wise judgment, filtering through to us the right information at the right time for us to grow and develop.

As we get older, we learn to filter things for ourselves. Yet doing so can be a daunting task. We have to sort out what to believe in advertising, for instance. Gatekeepers may withhold information about risks. The media decides what we need to know, and so do politicians. We depend on teachers for everything from kindergarten basics to complicated stuff like trigonometry. And then, we have the preachers, talking about the really big stuff like eternal life—which can get downright confusing if you try to listen to many of them.

Editors play a big role in what we read. As do investigative journalists, like Boston's SPOTLIGHT team. Same goes for screenplay writers and directors that make movies about important topics. Not all take great pains like Tom McCarthy did to be sure we are getting the closest portrayal of events in a true story. As he and Josh Singer wrote the story, they checked every detail with the investigative journalists who had lived the drama, never dreaming what they were doing would become a movie. After the casting was done, McCarthy arranged the three acting their parts to spend days with the real-life people they were to portray, studying even the finest mannerisms of each journalist in order to play their parts authentically.

Editors often have vested interests. Naturally, in order to keep being influential, they need to keep their positions, same as anyone. Under the best of circumstances, they have a lot of freedom. Under the worst, when working for a system easily threatened by outside information, they lose big-time if they step outside the lines too many times. That's exactly what had happened to Jack Harwell.

Up Against a Tsunami

Since I'd never stepped on toes with the few articles I'd had published in Baptist circles up until 1995, only mundane things like a grammar question or word count had raised any concerns with editors I'd worked with previously. Now, with me having a message that seared the hearts of the strongest of renegades among us, threatening long-held assumptions, I'd suddenly landed in an entirely different category.

While I could not prove it, I was already quite certain that predators in the SBC were being swept under the many small "rugs" that exist in this denomination with congregational polity. Unlike in Catholic or ecclesiastical circles where there are mid-size to huge wall-to-wall carpets that lawyers can more easily set out to damage if they are so inclined, thereby getting the attention of the press.

For instance, without big pockets, lawyers aren't likely to be willing to advocate for a single teenage victim of a youth pastor, when the victim is just above a state's "age of consent." And this is one of the most common stories with abuse in SBC circles. Often, it's not the senior pastor who leads a youngster "astray," as the average Baptist might define what occurs when an adult becomes sexually involved with a teen. It's more likely to be the minister of music or the youth pastor, men (and sometimes women) in Baptist circles possibly without an official ordination. Yet these are individuals with great or equal power in the eyes of young people and even many adult church members.

Most youth aren't likely to even turn to their parents until years after incidents of pastoral abuse, when the statute of limitations may have run out and the case becomes impossible to prove. After all, they're likely to say to themselves that what happened is "all my fault." In the meantime, the lives of untold numbers of other youth are likely to be impacted over time.

Neither is Dept. Of Human Services (DHS) likely to be interested in such cases involving older teens. That's what I knew that we were up against in the mid-90s, despite having a lot of proof. And this was only with minors as victims. It's what we're still up against today, in fact, in Protestant circles all over the world before we even start to think about adult victims.

As I look back, I'm amazed that anyone with Southern Baptist roots even gave me a chance to write for an audience filled with ministers, about crimes and corruption in their own profession. If I'd known in 1995 what I would learn in only two years about the belief system of some of the more liberal in the minority group of Baptists, I would probably have run for the hills. Even with publications considered to be "tabloids" by the conservative majority, the chief editors were male; and not all of them shared my understanding of things. Fortunately however, there was one who did, same as another well-known Georgia Baptist, Jimmy Carter.

Introducing Jack Harwell

A multitude of people had been greatly hurt in what the majority of Southern Baptists referred to as "the conservative resurgence," which was what moderate Baptists referred to as the "fundamentalist takeover." To me, it didn't matter which it was called. It reminded me very much of living under a regime where freedom of the press and rote learning was required, which was Malawi to a T in the '80s. No thinking outside the box was permitted. That was dangerous.

Not long after we went to Africa, Southern Baptist editors also began walking a fine line if they disagreed with staunch, anti-intellectual traditionalists who detested any semblance of what men like Harwell understood to be "progressive revelation." The staunchest of all the fundamentalists weren't necessarily in leadership, though plenty were. They were far more likely than not to be in a backwoods, country church that welcomed men who knew how to thump their Bibles, but had never been to seminary a day in their lives.

What most had in common, regardless of education, was an insistence on supporting the status quo in terms of race and gender. The "mark of the beast" among churches were those that dared to ordain a woman. It was the fastest way for any church to get kicked out of a local association that was the closest thing to a "district" or "area" among mainline churches today. Or, by comparison with Catholics, the local "diocese" with the man in charge lacking any structural power to act on his own. Equally blasphemous, and generally more so than the ordination of women, would be the ordination of a homosexual pastor. Any of these ordinations were a sure sign one did not believe in the "inerrancy" of the Scripture.

So in 1987, only months before our forced resignation, Harwell "chose" to take a very early retirement over being fired from the oldest Southern Baptist state paper in existence, with a readership of 100,000. He'd been threatened many times when he chose to expose the lust for power, deception and secrecy of the right-wing resurgent group pent on squelching any voice of freedom.

Despite this shackling in Georgia, he still found himself with a place of honor in a small crowd of renegades, when he agreed to become the second editor of a four-year-old "tabloid" of 4500. While most remaining leaders of the SBC considered it a scandal sheet, you can be certain plenty were finding ways to read the news of what they might easily have referred to as the "immoral minority." And that's how I found my own place back into a much smaller fold, to find a place at the table of the already-marginalized in a denomination of nearly eighteen million.

In a recent phone call, I told Jack that I suddenly felt like a dissident writer, taking on this topic, so many years ago.

"I felt like one, too, when I was forced out," he said.

Of course, people who get blamed and shamed for the sake of progressive causes are generally far more likely to consider welcoming those representing matters of close proximity to their own. Except that's still taking a risk. Editors with publications limping on one leg already might have to be careful about taking on causes "too far out," I figured.

Jack had been through things far worse than losing his prestigious position, however. 1994 had probably been the toughest year of his life, though I had no idea when I queried him.

It's hard to say how much his heart had been softened for what I was doing through the added suffering he'd endured while wrestling with his own emerging views on a topic with which even many Baptists Today readers were still struggling in the mid-90s.

Shadowboxing

Had I been reading every issue of "Baptists Today" in 1994, I would have known much more about the editor than how he'd been hung out to dry professionally. Of course, with the added flurries *How Little We Knew* had created that year, Ron and I were doing well to keep up with the usual routines that go with managing two demanding careers.

Halfway through the 1995 series I was writing, Jack sent me a precious gift with a hand-written, personal note attached. The gift was a small book, entitled *Shadowboxing the Grim Reaper*. It was written by his son Don while he was dying of AIDS at the age of thirty-nine. What Jack assumed I knew when he sent the book was that Don had died only months before he managed to misplace the query I thought he'd ignored and then readily accepted with more enthusiasm than I ever expected.

Three months before his son's life ended, Jack took a bold step. He'd long before resolved his own feelings about his son's sexual orientation. Oh, how proud he was of Don, he told readers of "Baptists Today" in an open letter that told of his son's many accomplishments, including the manuscript he was leaving to be published about this last, great struggle of his. He told of Don's three successful careers, his faith, his sexual orientation. And, most importantly, the cause of death. For this, he fully expected to receive hate mail from his own subscribers. Instead, I learned recently, he got 200 letters of support, some with requests for reprints in other college publications.

I was so thrilled to hear this, as we reminisced. All 1000 books were sold, he told me, except for those that went out as gifts. What a gift Jack gave me, sharing his story of his son. He went on to write in great detail a chapter that served as a contribution to *When a Child Dies: Stories of Survival and Hope by Richard Hipps*, published in 2008. In that detailed story of the suffering the entire family shared, Jack also reveals that he and Don's mother divorced during that time.

What a great gift Jack also gave to the LGBT population and families who had personally struggled with the same issues as he. How much that validation gave him the courage to take on my writing, it's hard to say.

The Dynamics of Risk-Taking

Suddenly I was seeing connection between multiple serpents— chronic issues that permeated the lives of so many, though seldom discussed in a way that might show the connections. Difficult and often shame-ridden issues that offered comparisons and contrasts in these three topics alone:

1. sexual abuse, specifically when perpetrated by religious leaders
2. cancer
3. homosexuality

The degree of shame and blame we recognize with any of these issues, or a multitude of other concerns like the ones you see on the cover of this book, will determine our understanding of collusion. How we are able to deflect or resolve the discomfort while refusing to internalize the stigma by focusing on reality will impact our ability to take risks and to function in spite of the added burden that society places on the shoulders of anyone whose life has been touched by any of these issues.

This understanding will go a long way to helping us understand the why's and wherefore's of self-destructive collusion that not only re-victimize and stigmatize "the other" but make impotent the systems that promote such faulty thinking, thereby contributing to stagnation that drives advocates wild.

In the end, our ability to bounce back as we absorb the blows that come with risk-taking must be carefully weighed as we sometimes set our sails in the direction the wind is blowing, when necessary, or move out into the storms as we renew our courage to prevail.

The Dynamics of Victim-Blaming

Collusion is a self-protective phenomenon that serves always to alienate "all us normal folk" from "the other." It also can alienate "me" from "myself" if I happen to be "the other" and choose to take on the blame the "normal folk" may project onto me, as they "shoot the messenger" (me, that is) for making a report. Such marginalization only serves "the normal folk" whose lives are not directly impacted, thereby allowing them to handle personal discomforts that are an otherwise healthy step of realizing "this could have been me or my loved one."

It's easy to see how this happens with the first two serpents on the list—sexual abuse by religious leaders and cancer. Internalized homophobia can also be an issue from inception to death, one of my good friends, speaking of her work with members of the LGBT community, points out.

In Africa, where fatalism or evil spirits most often take the blame for misfortune, family members may search diligently in hopes of deciding who put a curse on a loved one. Sometimes victims do discover that an enemy has indeed gone to a witch doctor and paid for a person to be cursed. In the event, the curse works, then the cursed victim or his family member may retaliate, either resorting to violence or by putting a payback curse on the original varmint. This cycle can go on and on.

In our society, we have our own superstitions, based on half-truths at best. We believe if we just "do all the right things" OR avoid what we perceive to be the cause. For instance, cancer victims often choose to torture themselves by gambling on strict diets promoted by industries that thrive on half-baked "science" that cannot possible provide any more guarantees of success than well-researched medical treatment that makes no dishonest claims.

Discussions at some support groups are filled with individuals who fail to recognize that being born female is the greatest factor in vulnerability with breast cancer, just as it is with sexual assault.

With breast cancer, there are multiple other biological factors that have little or nothing to do with current lifestyles and are believed to be the cause of many original occurrences and the likelihood of a recurrence. Few want to believe the truth that there are few guaranteed predictors as to who will likely suffer a recurrence once the disease is contracted.

With any cancer, relatives may say to one another: "If only she had (or hadn't) ... Or, in the case of lung cancer, "she just brought it on herself." We may even assume that any lung cancer patient indeed is a smoker, which was not the case in my husband's best friend, who never smoked a day in his life and had no known risk factors. Yet he died after a long battle with the disease.

Even if we feel a person is partially responsible for a chronic disease, we still support that individual, seeing they have the best possible medical care and emotional support. By contrast, we have much further to go with both sexual and domestic abuse, especially with adult victims.

With sexual assault, public awareness has certainly increased over the past fifty years with the 2016 Academy Awards reflecting this as a major theme—and not just with SPOTLIGHT. Also at the Academy Awards, there was Lady Gaga's impressive performance of "Till It Happens to You" and other movies like "Room" and "A Girl in the River:

The Price of Forgiveness." Still, it's as if our conversation has only begun. How often it gets shut down by DIM thinking as half-informed folks in our "enlightened society" continue to be acculturated to do so. It's very easy to forget that victims are "damned-if-you-do" and "damned-if-you-don't" when it comes to decisions about reporting.

Hard to say how many generations it may take to really turn the tide or when we might begin to dramatically lower our propensity to support the secrecy at the expense of everyone except perpetrators.

When the offender is a respected member of society, especially a "man of God," there's this strong tendency to believe that anyone self-sacrificing enough to choose such a profession couldn't possibly be responsible for committing a crime (or in states where the laws still lag behind, "just" crossing professional boundaries with a congregant). We have a tremendous amount of work to do in educating a public that still blames an adolescent male in high school for choosing to have a "consensual" relationship with an adult teacher. How much harder it is to understand the power imbalance for adults in a professional-client or congregant relationship.

In all of the above, there is a shame factor seldom acknowledged. Even when victims internalize little shame in regard to an issue, shaming and silencing tactics by outsiders often contribute to even the most open among us feeling hesitant to enlarge conversations that could be very enlightening. Some of our fears or hesitancy to talk about racial issues, for instance, is our tendency for all of us to project onto others our own fears of being shamed by silence or awkward moments. Opening conversations, even in one-on-one relationships can be difficult for both parties.

In time, as we all become more experienced at knowing what to say and what to ask, as we are willing to take the risk of attempting difficult dialogues, justice and understanding will increase gradually.

What about society's attitudes toward victims of terrorism? Why do we not blame victims of such incidents, in most cases? I believe it's because we understand these incidents as random, unpredictable acts, with multiple victims and an outsider as the culprit. We identify little with the perpetrator and a great deal with victims, especially if we perceive them to be like ourselves.

While we don't admit this, the first thing that may come to mind if life fails to go perfectly is a cross-examining of ourselves as if we are a prosecuting attorney. When something happens to a child, how fast are we to blame the parents for somehow failing to keep them safe or give them "stranger danger" preparation.

Yet parents, grandparents, and educators may also unknowingly plant the seeds of such thinking in children as we attempt to warn them of dangers—an issue that's especially difficult for parents who were themselves victims of child abuse.

Giving a child the same words of warning over and over can be counter-productive. It's important we have an ongoing dialogue rather than a single conversation, thinking we're done. Perhaps with some good role play added to the conversation.

Consider how a child who has been warned to the hilt may think when something unforeseen happens. He may automatically assume it's his fault; for, in our attempts to shelter children, we may be fearful of scaring them by suggesting that sometimes awful things happen in spite of everything we do. Yet this reality needs to be a part of our dialogue, as well.

Might we consider giving them a little advocacy training along with our lessons on "stranger danger?" When it is age-appropriate—somewhere in late elementary school, if not before, why not prepare them for the likelihood of every kid being the first person a friend turns to after being bullied or as a victim of abuse? Kids need to understand how important it is for them to not only be supportive of that friend, but also to seek support for themselves from a trustworthy adult as soon as possible. This prevents that child from carrying the burden that even adults can find very heavy. It also allows them to get help for their wounded friend. Yes, advocacy training needs to start very, very early. And it includes helping kids know when to keep a secret and when not to.

Historically, we have taught our children to naively trust teachers, doctors, and clergy. And this is exactly what has set up so many, especially in Catholic and Baptist circles, where conservative theology is itself a risk factor for children's safety, as Carolyn Heggen,[1] had already pointed out. The trust has eroded, however—at least according to the latest Gallup poll, showing professional ministers to be at an all-time low in credibility.[2]

Issues of "Original Sin"

Conditions of our birth, whether gender, nationality, skin color, sexual orientation, or birth defect, are matters over which we have absolutely no choice. Only bigotry and prejudice allow us to excuse ourselves from facing our own roles in protecting abusers in groups less privileged than our own.

For instance, there are multiple reasons, both inside the African-American communities and in general society, why sexual assault is even less likely to be reported than in Caucasian communities. It is very difficult to even establish what some believe to be a much higher percentage of victims of sexual abuse by clerics in this community. It is not a topic easily broached, even in survivor circles.

The most helpful resource I've discovered on this topic was a webinar from Faith Trust Institute, Sexual Abuse in the Black Church: An Historical Perspective Toward Practical Solutions by Rev. Dr. Sharon Ellis Davis and Rev. K. Ray Hill. Davis claims that abuse in largely African-American congregations is "escalated because we are hiding it or not speaking out." Congregants historically have idealized the church and the office of the pastor because of its role in working for civil rights, fighting Jim Crow, and discrimination in the justice system, among other things.

Part of the problem, according to Hill, is the tendency for pastors to "self-abuse," by neglecting self-care. A pastor who is a good role model isn't going to be bragging about not having a day off, he says.

"Powerful people empower others," Davis reminds us. "Healing involves conversation rather than silencing."

At the close of the webinar, one woman complained that her church was refusing to deal with abuse problems in an open manner. Davis suggested that if things did not change the lady "may need to mourn the loss of that church." The criteria for those involved, and especially for the pastor who if facing allegations, needs to be "What can men do to help women know they are safe?" she said only moments earlier. Stepping down to take a brief paid leave of absence, taking a humble approach, is what's appropriate in this case.

The late Diana Garland, founder of Baylor's School of Social Work, named in her honor, released a survey in 2009, indicating among many significant findings, that clergy sexual abuse occurs at three times the rate in African-American congregations over Caucasian. This "result," however, may need to be examined more closely, since it was done among women who reveal themselves as survivors and who also still attend church at least once monthly.

Could it be that these figures simply reflect a stronger likelihood that survivors in this group feel compelled to stay in the church because of their greater need to be a part of a faith community due to outside forces? Might we do well to ask more about the strong alliances of interdependency forged in this faith community, which allow individuals to be insulated from racism and economic disparity that is so much a part of their larger, day-to-day existence?

Caucasian women, on the other hand, are more likely to find a stronger support system outside the church, without the added oppression persons of color feel in the workplace and beyond.

By limiting the scope of the survey to those who have stayed in the church, we do not know what percentage of victims left. Nor do we know what percentage were abused as minors. That percentage, any advocate can tell you, is much higher—perhaps as high as 90% of clergy abuse victims do not darken the door of a church even once every six months. (more on this in Chapter 32)

Historical Pecking Orders

It would be nice if we could just wave a magic wand and lift the shame and blame that society has put on various groups of victims or marginalized individuals instantaneously, once and for all. Of course, being human, we each go through life lifting the cover on one issue slowly, then putting it back down when our tolerance level is reached, perhaps going on to pick the cover up again later on another issue, if not the same one—or maybe not. Maybe eventually we the energy to keep lifting those covers is depleted.

We like to believe we've come a long way on civil rights. If so, why are some of us still so hesitant or uncomfortable with opening conversations across the racial divide? Are we only comfortable with what the media is telling us, yet unable to match our actions with what we believe? I know that I often am.

Finally, assuming that our comfort zones may potentially improve over time, with victim-blaming and oppression decreasing, I believe it's helpful to look at the historical unfolding of some 20th century issues. It helps put into perspective what those of us daring to break the ice with discussions about sexual abuse by professionals have been up against.

- 1950 Civil Rights
- 1960 Child neglect and physical abuse
- 1970 Homosexuality, sexual violence, child sexual abuse
- 1973 Rehabilitation Act (ADA)
- 1980 Breast cancer awareness
- 1990 Professional sexual abuse, starting with abuse of minors

*****

[1] Cited previously with specific excerpt given in Chapter 3 from Heggen's book Sexual Abuse In Christian Homes and Churches

[2] Gallup's honesty and ethics rating for clergy dropped from 67% in 1985 to 47% in 2013. Sexual abuse has been cited as a primary reason for this drop. Yet Republicans tend to trust clergy and other public officials more than Democrats overall.

See   http://www.gallup.com/poll/166487/honesty-ratings-police-clergy-differ-party.aspx

Chapter 13
Sorting Through the Rubble

For the first seven months of 1995, writing for "Baptists Today," I worked hard to connect on a deep feeling level with the readership, many who were intensely grieving after losing important positions to the fundamentalist takeover. Nothing I'd ever written, however, reached to the depths of this collective grief. Out of my brokenness, I believe I was able to connect on a deeper level still as I penned the words of that first column that came straight from my heart.

"Struggles with cancer teach disciplines of patience, hope" Harwell chose to title the article that he introduced with a paragraph as the first in a series on how sexual abuse in the church could be faced "by taking a more honest look at this national problem."

By way of my own introduction, I began by validating the grief that we shared with so many readers of this publication, from personally being among the casualties of the Convention.

"Still we have questioned if even BAPTISTS TODAY could be ready to seriously take on what Roman Catholics say has been their greatest challenge since the Reformation.

From there I gave a brief summary of what we had learned, in general, about the problems of clergy sexual abuse and how its very mention shatters "happy myths" about the profession and the community of faith. Going on, I spoke of the challenge that I felt I was up to when Jack asked me to take on this series and then plunged into another, deeply-personal issue—breast cancer—with healthy family dynamics that are needed in facing cancer, which I hoped readers would see as parallel to those needed to take on the systemic "cancer" of abuse in the church.

UNTIMELY NEWS

I will be reeling from the shock for months to come. I have breast cancer, a disease that has been around for a long time, a disease no one talked about much until recently. Everything in me wants to scream out, "No! It can't be! I don't have time for the pain!"

But I will take time. The consequences of denial are deadly! My supportive family tells me, "We'll fight this together." Of that, I have no doubt. We have grown closer than ever these past few years in our lonely struggle with evil. Our growth has come because each family member has decided that sexual violence in the profession that has been our lifeline is too big for any one person to fight alone.

As we talk about the enemy that has so cruelly invaded our lives, we call it by name. Suddenly words alien only yesterday become a part of our conversation: mastectomy, support groups, radiation, chemotherapy and prosthesis.

We share our feelings openly and without shame. The grief work is difficult. It is painful. Yet, it is essential. It is a process, not an event.

Support surrounds us. Ron pastors a church full of wonderful people, already flooding us with love and prayers. A friend from my writers' association has walked this rocky path before me. She listens tirelessly, validating my suffering, but never minimizing. She reminds me "there is no need to re-invent the wheel." Lots of help is available.

The role reversal seems strange. As a psychiatric nurse, I have talked with many others through cancer crises. This is humbling.

RESOLUTION and HOPE

Riding home from the doctor's office yesterday, I turned to the man who suffered alongside me, even enduring two years of under-employment as we fought to find our way out of the SBC wilderness.

"This is crazy timing," I sobbed, as if there is ever a good time for cancer. He understood instantly that my words had nothing to do with the fact that it was two days before Christmas.

Jack Harwell's letter was only one of an outpouring of folks saying, "Teach us!" A month ago I quit my primary job to devote at least a year for walking through doors as fast as God opens them. Now, facing months of recovery, I wondered how I could possibly undertake the tasks at hand, starting with this article.

Like the Psalmist, I have learned in recent years the value of screaming my anger at God Almighty. Yet, early this morning, I spoke with a childlike faith of acceptance I did not know I possessed. "OK, how are You and I going to work together to make good come out of this one?"

"Just give them your story," came the answer. "Those folks can get it. They'll see the parallels between the two 'cancers.'

While some Baptist publications pay writers an honorarium, Baptists Today certainly couldn't do that. I didn't expect them to. They were happy to give me a by-line, though, for what it was worth.

I was braced to receive hate mail, same as Jack Harwell had been with his open letter to his son the year before. Compared to his 200 positive responses with not one negative, one of the first I got was the most negative I've had in over twenty years. Duane was a young pastor, ranting about my "lack of tolerance." It wasn't just me, but all the "fundamentalists on the left," he said. He didn't know why he was even subscribing to Baptists Today. As for my work, it was nothing but "Baloney!"

Responses came steadily every week, though nothing close to what Harwell got from his single editorial about Don the previous year. I sold about two dozen books over the whole six-month series.

The limited response clearly reflected the resistance folks had to hearing more. A sum total of eight letters came from ordained ministers. Not surprisingly, half from females, whose ordinations would not even have been acknowledged by most Southern Baptists.

Every single letter deserved an answer, I decided—even the cancer victim's, which turned out to be the only negative response in the whole lot. It was safe to assume that most of those who took time to write needed a word of comfort themselves.

Introducing Four Little Monkeys

In my letters of return, I often wrote of there being four little monkeys with collusion, "not three: See no evil. Speak no evil. Hear no evil. *Think* no evil. All the problems of the world will be perpetuated, in fact, if we allow those four little monkeys to sit on our shoulders while we comfortable deny the truth about things that are really evil. Of course, the most dangerous of all is to not even allow us to think about a serious problem close to home. For if we refuse to think something might exist in our little system, we'll never see it or have the courage to listen or to speak about it when it's right before our eyes.

Man-made religion embraces the monkeys, yet has demonized prophetic voices through the ages.

There were striking parallels to another truth about the presence of many gay and lesbian men and women at every turn in every community, simply wishing to be acknowledged and accepted for who they were, to be integrated into the mainstream as the whole people they were. Nobody needed to do anything but love and accept these souls. No other action was needed.

The evil was in those among us who preferred saying "not in my family," as Jack Harwell admits he once did before he faced the fact that one of his twin sons was gay while the other was not.

DIM thinking—denial, ignorance, and minimization—applies to both evil and "otherness." Getting past it, facing our fears, is a long process when it comes to things like mental illness, too. Mental illness is not a good thing. It is not acceptable any more than cancer is. Yet both are treatable, and the person who has either is not the problem.

Proactivity requires that we think on things not so acceptable, things that are among us closer than we want to believe. Proactivity exposes evil close to home, is willing to re-examine issues, and to embrace as good even some things that might once have been considered evil.

Proactivity demands that we not minimize the true danger of protecting evil. It demands that bystanders act in courage to stand in solidarity against ignorance. It demands that we teach our children the truths we do not want to even think about as soon as they are able to absorb new truths.

The Process of Constant Sorting

While bystanders with the power to act are required to do so courageously, there is no set of absolutely right decisions for a survivor beyond self-care. For, as much as we want to believe others can be counted on, crime victims, in general, can't count on there being someone else to jump in to do the right thing. Running the other way is far more common, especially when it comes to sexual and domestic abuse.

There is no guaranteed guide to success either. No two cases are exactly alike. Nor do any two individuals move through the awakening process at the same pace.

Be careful about listening to people who have all the answers, I caution survivors. Especially other survivors who believe "If everyone would just do what I do...." It's far more helpful to be told, "What worked for me....." All the better if the person with the past experience understands why this may or may not work for everyone.

Once life goes seriously off the "normal" course we've consistently counted on, how unpredictable things quickly become! It's what some refer to as "the loss of innocence." When children experience intense abuse very early in life, provided they have good support systems, they *may* be able to turn their early life experience into an asset--eventually. Notice I italicized the word "may." If positive outcomes are never seen, however, it's not because the child, the parents, or anyone else necessarily failed.

I don't like the "loss of innocence" phrase. In fact, when it comes to sexual abuse, I abhor it. The kid is *still innocent*. He didn't lose his innocence. What he lost is his right to trust unequivocally the very people who should be trustworthy—that's a terrible thing for an innocent child to lose.

When it comes to advocacy work, change is a long-term, inter-generational goal. We can persistently work our tails off for decades without seeing much change. Yet that doesn't necessarily mean we must cease trying.

Because advocacy is an act of faith, seeing evidence of change isn't essential at all. If it happens—great! We learn to celebrate even small breakthroughs. Or quit and go home.

On the other hand, a repeated sense of defeat leads to burn-out—primarily due to unrealistic expectations. We can do marathons for a while, yet pacing ourselves is essential. Otherwise, life passes us by.

The first thing to go is a sense of humor. Once we lose that and the ability to notice even small victories, we lose joy quickly and become old way too soon. By taking frequent breaks, even nonsense can give us energy sufficient to become more creative and even burst into song, whistling, or laughter to re-program our own brains for a short season.

Personally, I laugh a lot at nonsense. I even laughed at the goof-balls in Spotlight. Seeing Big Cats trying to swallow "canaries" is hilarious if you've sat in my seat for long. It's astounding how often well-educated men and women so easily succumb to foot-in-mouth disease when they actually know what needs to be done, Tom Economus often said.

Recently, Ron and I thoroughly enjoyed one of the most exciting basketball games I've ever seen in my life. One thing that made this game so special is the two of us have a little ownership in the team. Because we've helped to financially support the women's KU basketball team, commonly known as the Jayhawks, we care what happens. This year, they don't have a senior on the team. Oh, how they've struggled all season, with one defeat after another! By contrast, they made one three-point shot after another throughout this recent game, while their stronger opponents played like underdogs.

In the end, the Jayhawks lost. Yet none of us went home crying. We left instead with a sense of victory. There was absolutely no reason for any of those players to hang their heads in shame. They're getting stronger every day. That's what matters.

This same attitude is much more difficult to maintain in the face of cancer, untimely deaths, floods, experiences of war, or any trauma that forces us to either stop and take stock or pretend it never happened. Of course, pretending something doesn't exist or never happened is a recipe for disaster in most cases, especially for individuals or systems that insist on not seeing the impending disaster. Since so few want to take ownership of common problems of sexual abuse when evidence is clear, there are always multiple traumas left for survivors to suffer in isolation.

Because the system under-functions, the survivor either joins the passivity or over-functions in order to get the system to wake up.

When There's Nothing More to Lose

A profound shift occurs when a survivor suddenly realizes she has nothing more to lose, nothing that others can take away anymore. The worst has already happened, and that survivor is still alive to tell about it.

This happened with Phil Saviano. Yet, Phil thought he was about to die, literally, due to AIDS, the day the archdiocese offered him a five-figure settlement to shut him up.

He walked away, realizing he didn't want to be paid for being silent the rest of his short life. They couldn't take away his voice as long as he was alive. This disempowered the Church. They had no other bait. Not long afterward, a new drug suddenly had Phil in remission, and that gave him the energy, added to the inspiration from Economus, to walk back into the Boston Globe until somebody heard him and others eventually picked up the story and put it on the screen for the whole world to see.

I cannot imagine what it must feel like for him now! After hearing his voice on the phone last week, I think we'll have to find a new word for what he's experiencing. He's not just thriving. That man is soaring. And he deserves every bit of the glory he's getting. Yet, he knows full well that many others who have worked very hard also do, including many who gave up on life years ago after being abused by a priest. Thousands are living vicariously through this hero.

An Ethical Response

I had plenty to question as I sorted through various responses from that emotionally-charged article, published as my first of eight. After what I'd been through with the Foreign Mission Board, I wasn't sure I trusted anyone ever associated with Southern Baptists. They'd all have to prove themselves, especially any supposed expert in ministerial ethics like Joe Trull.

Jack Harwell may not have known. If he did, he didn't tell me, which was a good thing. For if I'd known Joe Trull had been a former trustee of the Foreign Mission Board, I might have been hesitant to even open his letter when it arrived as one of the first responses. I need not have been concerned. No letter from an ordained Southern Baptist minister has ever been more affirming to me. His words showed extreme empathy and admiration. Besides that, he was publicizing the book, had ordered a copy for the seminary library, and wanted permission to share my story in his classes. That courtesy wasn't necessary, of course, but I assured him it would be fine.

Audra Trull, the professor's wife, had run into a survivor at a retreat she'd recently led, who began telling *her* about How Little We Knew. So Audra included this in the book review she wrote for the seminary's next newsletter.

One couple couldn't make up for the many fierce attacks we'd sustained, coupled with the passivity of so many colleagues. Yet it was a great comfort to hear the words: "I grieve for you."

I waited for some time before telling Dr. Trull that another kind of grief was called for. The profession needed to grieve for itself—because of its failure to own the very problem it feared to address publicly, which had been cause for such self-destruction on top of harm to others. This meant that each cleric must go through a parallel process all survivors and true advocates have been forced to embark upon, first grieving for what is no more, the naivety of the past that has long refused to acknowledge what can no longer be ignored about the state of things. For members of the clergy and every member of the congregation, it involved self-examination, taking responsibility, and confessing complicity, wherever this was due.

Enter Serpent No. 3

Within a month, I was back to writing again, never imagining how quickly life would introduce another serpent. In the process, I'd have more writing material than I knew what to do with for months to come.

The third serpent came in a sixty-second phone call on April 19, 1995. It came as an interruption to what had started out for me as a very productive morning of writing. It would be three days before I could even think of writing again.

When I did, I began with that personal phone call. Oh, how I saw and felt the parallels and contrasts of this disaster that had also rocked the hearts of the world, with the other two which few could imagine!

The earth-shattering tragedy that first came to me through that personal phone call was one every reader of "The Missing Link" would have seen replayed time and again before they received my next column.

More deeply than the average American, they would have had their hearts rocked by the little children covered in blood, their anger soaring at the senselessness of it all. I knew the hearts of my readers enough to know how many of them would have connected the very visible suffering shared so publicly with the very personal suffering most bystanders did not even want to see—the suffering caused by ignorant, arrogant people claiming to be God's representatives:

I first learned the shattering news when my daughter, who lives in Oklahoma City, called. "Mom, I just want to let you know we're okay," she started. (I groped for understanding. My daughter Renita never calls at 10 a.m. on a weekday!)

"There's been a huge explosion near my office, but I'm okay." Her voice sounded frantic. "Go turn on the TV. I've got to go," she instructed.

The greatest shock came later. After weeping over the devastation in our home town, I learned my own daughter had narrowly escaped being in the Federal Building herself at the time of the bombing. Illness had kept her home, away from a 9 a.m. appointment in the Social Security Office, where so many deaths had occurred.

In the newsletter, as well as other articles I wrote to incorporate this disaster for a much wider audience than Linkup members, I explained how our personal shocks kept coming as we learned more. My husband and I now identified with the families of survivors in a very personal way.

Equally chilling, had this horrific crime been committed six years earlier, Ron and I could easily have been among the fatalities. For a few years earlier we had been in the Social Security office in that building ourselves in 1989, together with Ron's mother, as we went to help her sort out a benefit question.

We grieved more deeply when we learned an old classmate of Ron's had lost two grandchildren in the day care center. Such senselessness! How I appreciated the willingness of our President to call this "evil."

A cousin of mine in the military was one of the rescuers walking around with a mask and Vicks Vapor Rub under his nose by the third day, just to cope with the odor of decaying flesh embedded in the rubble. This is what healthy communities do in the aftermath of huge disasters where there are many victims.

I watched for three solid days, listening, reading, because I could not turn away. Then, when I returned to finish my "Reconnections" column, I added:

My life is filled with questions, not just about this tragedy, but about the contrast in responses we are seeing in Oklahoma with the turning away so many of us have experienced as we have attempted to cry out from beneath tons of rubble to both leadership and laity we once trusted. What factors, I wonder, help explain the stark contrast?

The comparisons come into sharper focus when I hear that the prime suspect is not a foreigner, but a fellow Oklahoman. My outrage is intensified.....I say to myself: "Sick and evil sometimes go together."

When survivors are asked what would make them feel better, they say: "find the perpetrators and stop them so they never have a chance to hurt anyone like this again!"

And nobody scolds them for saying that.

Suppose the citizens of Oklahoma had discovered the perpetrator to be their own governor? How much more intense would be the pain? Would the state be divided? Would anyone be able to believe the facts? Would the facts be treated as secrets?

Rather than a plea for justice, would the "good old boys" be crying for mercy, insisting that "people who do things like this cannot possibly be in their right mind?" Would the digging for survivors cease? Would those voices heard from under the rubble be silenced because they might remind us that even people in power are capable of horrendous acts? Would anyone suggest we focus on all the good the governor did for the state, send him for intensive counseling before returning him to his place of honor? I don't think so.

Some behaviors permanently disqualify people from holding places of power and honor.

Chapter 14
Let the Conversations Roll

Male-dominated systems have a lengthy set of important, unwritten and unspoken set of rules, usually quickly denied if an outsider suggests they might be operating. It would sound very worldly, for instance, that money could ever be the driving force behind the resistance to ethical, institutional change to promote gender equity in the faith community.

Truth is, male-dominated systems are needy organisms that only appear to "have it all together." No stronger example exists than the Roman Catholic Church. What keeps the system going is projecting onto underlings a convoluted message that seeks to both preserve and change the status quo as necessary as long as it's made the service of power. For the greedy system must be generously fed.

The thirst for power grows as the system does. The sense that there is not enough power to go around breeds unhealthy fear and competition. This sense was precisely what was growing astronomically in the Southern Baptist Convention, as well, during the mid 70's as we prepared to leave for Africa, while living and working on Montana, where few of our neighbors had any idea what "SBC" even stood for. Having at least a small presence in every county was vital to the vast organism.

In a male-dominated system, even when women are given a segment of the system to manage, there's lots of fear-talk for individuals—fear of being left out or ostracized, somehow becoming a victim of the system. Hang around "the water fountain" with a group of ministers or doctors for long and you can't miss it—there's a need for male peers to stick together, especially for protection against all the conniving women who are "out to get 'ya."

This paranoia and self-protection from "the other" feeds the strong tendency to immediately jump to the defense of a colleague rather than considering the likelihood that he might actually be "the real problem." After all, who's to say what poor, unsuspecting fellow will be the next to be falsely accused? These questions seldom spoken above a whisper become intensely embedded in the collective psyche of the group.

What is operating is unrealistic FEAR. Or False Evidence of Things not Real, according to the definition of Alcoholics Anonymous.

Collective power is fed first by individual men, yet also by women who blindly support such systems. Nobody is going to get far by bucking a system for the good of women and children unless it can be done with the approval of powerful men in good standing. Staying "reasonable," and in good standing, is essential for every minister in the Southern Baptist Convention or any other denomination—even the small percentage of females, for that matter.

However, the SBC takes the blue ribbon among major Protestant denominations for misogyny. Simply using the term "misogyny" will likely put a person's name on the black list.

So, the two largest Christian denominations in the world, though historically seen as diabolically opposed, have become very close cousins in how underlings are treated. And this all gets propped up by conservative theology that serves to "keep women in their place."

It's a strange set of dynamics that's always operated in the SBC, the same that supported slavery. Not that other conservative groups or independent churches don't have the same set of unwritten rules by which underlings must play to avoid serious punishment. They all do. Yet the same reasoning used by supporters of Donald Trump for President has long operated in the SBC: how can you question an individual or a system that has been enormously successful? What's amazing to me now, and sometimes a source of shame, is that it took over four decades of being immersed in that culture for me to see this. Had it not been for such a vicious awakening, I might still be sleeping.

Yet, liberal groups certainly aren't exempt either, despite giving lip service to their claim of gender equity. This claim can serve as a useful smokescreen to better hide deeper-seated misogyny, racism, homophobia, or any number of implicit biases in the system. Recently an Episcopalian, still a strong advocate who asks to remain anonymous, spoke poignantly to the denomination's recent history of collusion with sexual violations to the present day:

"Back in the mid-1990's the Diocese of Western New York developed tracts that were to be put in tract racks in each Episcopal church. The tracts informed people of the diocesan policy: what is sexual abuse, what is sexual exploitation, what is sexual harassment, and what to do if you have questions or want to make an accusation. Most churches didn't put the tracts in the racks, anyway; but some did, and I did get some calls, not from accusers but people concerned about someone they knew either there or in another diocese. So it was worthwhile, but resistance to giving people the information (and breaking the secrecy, etc.) was high.

"I am afraid that people are tired of this issue and feel they know about it and don't want to hear it or learn more," she adds. "In the end strong policies and procedures are only as good as people charged to implement them are willing to follow."

Commissions and Omissions

Below my fourth article in the "Baptist Today" series was a surprising announcement from the Baptist Sunday School Board. To a novice, they would seem to have ducks in order as they marched through the door I had just opened for them. Was this announcement a knee-jerk reaction or was its timing coincidental? I'll let you be the judge.

Almost comical, however, was that anyone with an ounce of informed training on professional sexual misconduct couldn't help noticing egg on the face of the very institution that was now stepping forward to speak.

This was the exact, same agency with whom Jeff Seats had spoken within the last year on "numerous occasions" and "been told that our denominational climate is not conductive to addressing this type of sensitive issue at the present time," seemed to have suddenly changed its tune. When I'd contacted them earlier that same year, I'd only been referred to an attorney who'd led a workshop for denominational officials on "important legal issues." Now that I was putting my announcement out about the need to get something done, the BSSB had suddenly established a National Advisory Committee on Sexual Misconduct—miracle of miracles!

Some of their plans looked great on paper—providing certified training to help churches recover, developing guidelines for personnel and pastor search committees, designing suggested policies for churches to adopt, including procedures for reporting, processing allegations, and follow-up. All of these I was certain were in the service of power. Red flags abounded without a single safety measure for survivors—nothing leading me to believe that reporting would be helpful in the least. How could I possibly recommend that a survivor report to anyone on this committee? I couldn't as long as the language was framed to suggest that issues of vulnerability were all about individual ministers and the churches they might serve. It was as if everything I'd written in the previous article had been ignored.

Seems I was definitely helping to enlarge a conversation, anyway. Though brief and disjointed, an odd sort of open dialogue was going on between me and Sunday School Board—except they never even acknowledged I existed in this earth-shattering announcement. Since I'd already turned in the next of my series, my response would have to wait until article #6, which turned out to be perfect timing.

The longest, most far-reaching response to this series, up until then, showed up right under the fifth article. It was a letter Jack printed in full, longer than anything I'd yet turned in myself. Seeing it, I laughed out loud for sheer joy.

Cynthia Huddlestun of Mobile, Alabama, wanted her name released alongside her eloquently mapped out journey as an incest survivor, telling how each step she'd taken toward recovery had been harder than the first in spite of much support from people in her church. Yet going home to the community where her abuser still lived was the hardest part of all.

"Going home should be joyful. Going home to church should be joyful, too. It shouldn't hurt," she wrote. And for her, it had been joyous to go home to church. Her church was a spiritual sanctuary as it should have been.

"Unlike my co-survivors who were abused by clergy," she continued, "I could find only comfort and solace in God's house."

Cynthia went on to address the BSSB's announcement:

> I read that article (about the new National Advisory Committee) several times, put it down, came back to it. As I typed this letter, I reread it, thinking surely I must have missed something....
>
> There is no mention of counseling and recovery help for victims. Where there is abuse .... there is a victim.

Treatment programs for sexual abusers have questionable rates of true and lasting recovery. For abused, there is much better success, especially when initiated early on.

Sexual misconduct is not limited to being tempted to have an affair with a pretty parishioner. It goes beyond denying "the teachings of Christ concerning purity."

It can be about having your first sexual experience at the malevolent hands of someone who tells you "God is love" in children's church next Sunday. It can be about going to church for help and counseling and finding systematic sexual abuse at the hands of a "person of the lie" masquerading as a man of God.

If you find this hard to read, imagine living it! It can make it almost impossible to trust again, difficult to love again. It can push away from God the very people who might need God the most....

In the same issue, Jack printed a shorter letter, written by five women in ministry, at least two were psychotherapists, who'd soon follow up with me in person. Their letter was as refreshing as the feeling of relief of those first rains we felt in Africa after the long, hot, dry, miserable season of living in a sun-parched world without air conditioning. The solidarity they offered me served as powerful punch at the male posturing so obvious in the BSSB's announcement.

Alongside the announcement, Jack printed a second by the founder of a "treatment center"[1] where Ron and I had already been told the SBC and the mission board routinely sent perpetrators for the most intense treatment course they could find—a round of "stress management." These dear ladies took on that piece, as well, saving me the precious space allotted for all I wanted to say in the next few articles.

Harwell chose "A curious omission" as the title for the epistle:

Regarding the Baptist Press News release about the Baptist Sunday School Board's national advisory committee on sexual misconduct, there is a curious omission. That is, the women and children who are victims of clergy sexual misconduct are simply never referred to—as if they do not exist or as if their experience is of no concern to Southern Baptists.

An accompanying article quoted the founder of Marble Retreat Center, Lewis McBurney—who along with his wife (the only woman named) serves on the advisory committee. The quote referring to "partners" of guilty clergy was a classic case of blaming the victim, since the emotional, spiritual and vocational power balance between a pastor and parishioner does not begin to approach equality.

As women who were simply willing to listen during one year, we became acquainted with 13 women victims of clergy sexual misconduct. The emotional pain, spiritual desolation and desecration of their faith as a result is almost impossible to put into words.

It is little wonder these women are lost to congregations. It is little wonder their friends and families cease active involvement in local churches, when they see how women who speak the truth about a minister's behavior are commonly treated.

Clergy sexual misconduct is THE primary issue of the contemporary church's credibility crisis with unchurched women. Few are willing to consider investing time, money and energy in "Christian" churches which continue to protect the guilty and throw stones at women named as "partners."

We strongly urge the BSSB advisory committee to immediately revise plans for their work in order to respond to children and women who are invisible in their initial plan. When committee members are able to be equally concerned with the pain of and restitution for victims as they are counseling for the ministers, they will have begun to move toward "the least of these."

Leslie Kendrick, Ginger Miller, Janet Tharpe, Bobbie Thomason and Mary Zimmer of Louisville, KY

Of course, it would have offered even more of a punch had there been a male writer to join these ladies. For now, my husband's words, which Jack chose to print, right after the ladies', would have to suffice.

Ron's brief remarks echoed some of Huddleston's and the other female writers. After identifying himself as a secondary victim, he asked: *"What does the committee plan to do to help restore the lives and especially the spirituality of victims and secondary victims?"*

The most promising response to my six months of work came from Dick Maples, coordinator for minister-church relations for the Baptist General Convention of Texas, which had pulled away from Southern Baptists.

Soon Joe Trull would become a part of the designated team to address issues of sexual abuse by clergy. If all went well, it might even be a place where I could refer victims in Texas. Nowhere else could I see even a flicker of hope. Still, if Texas Baptists operated anything like Catholics, they'd have some heavy-handed lawyers on board to be sure the system was "protecting itself" from vocal victims.

No matter what favors life might bring in this work—the women showing solidarity, the fundamentalist take-over that had created this welcoming publication Baptists Today, or the recent changes on Texas statutes—I'd be grateful for whatever I could get. Such is the nature of advocacy—we are treated like beggars at the gate, being thrown crumbs from the rich man's table. When coming from individuals who are working for change, those "crumbs" are most appreciated. When coming from systems pretending to be authorities, rather than humbly asking for help from true change agents, there's nothing at all to appreciate except the education that comes from such nonsense.

Until I had reason to believe otherwise, I'd pretend in my writing to assume that nobody at the Baptist General Convention of Texas was insincere, same as I had done with every visit I'd made to any African official working for the illustrious "benevolent dictator" to whom we were all forced to pay respect. In both scenarios, I'd remain realistically hopeful while in wait for something better to happen.

*****

[1] The Marble Retreat Center, located in the mountains of Colorado, still operates today and offers very short-term therapy, primarily group therapy for couples when an offending pastor, believed "only" to have abused an adult woman, comes their way. Eight days of an "intense program," declared the current director who revealed this in a 2015 email. After this intervention, recommendations are made, but a decision about putting an offender back in the pulpit is left to the denomination. This keeps the whole operation from having to assume liability, letting them off the hook, as they see it, for any future offenses.

Chapter 15
Bold Suggestions

As much as the system wanted to treat me like an outsider, I knew far too much for them to get by doing so. After all, I knew as well as most SBC ministers the intricate skeletal system of this massive denomination. This allowed me to get right down to the business in my next column, to suggest what each agency, including the two predominantly-female agencies, could choose to do if they were willing.

Before I got specific, I set out to dispel some common myths about survivors:

> *The memories for most were not repressed, but have haunted them for decades. Few have reported their abuse. But those who have were met with typical status-quo cover-ups and collusion. Most, contrary to popular belief, choose not to bring lawsuits.....*
>
> *WHAT IF the SBC were to follow the suggestion of Joe Trull, New Orleans seminary professor of Christian ethics, that a code of ethics for ministers be adopted?*
>
> *WHAT IF all seminaries required every student to attend a week-long training on professional sexual misconduct?*
>
> *WHAT IF prayer groups were organized throughout the denomination to uphold individuals and churches who have been victimized by clergy malpractice, as well as for the offenders themselves?*
>
> *WHAT IF all pastors were able to welcome psychotherapy as a part of their preventive health care plan and were willing to seek it freely?*

WHAT IF Baptists—after studying the clumsy response of Roman Catholics and mainline denominations—decided not to first run to attorneys to "fix" things?

WHAT IF authorities such as Gary Schoener of Minneapolis, Marie Fortune of Seattle or Tom Economus of Chicago were consulted for initial guidance instead?

WHAT IF every state organized training workshops at least once per year for pastors and church leaders.

WHAT IF the events were publicized as heavily as Sunday School teacher-training workshops?

WHAT IF these workshops were led by outside consultants trained to assist everyone to deal with this threatening subject?

WHAT IF pastors could get past their fears, understand that the reputation of their own profession is much more at stake than the unlikely (but greatly over-inflated) possibility of false accusations?

WHAT IF Baptist Woman's Missionary Union, true to their history of ministering to the oppressed, took on a nationwide project to train volunteers to act as advocates for SBC survivors of clergy sexual and domestic violence?

WHAT IF Baptist Women in Ministry announced openly their intent to band together to support the multitude of victims of clergy sexual misconduct suffering silently in their own ranks?

WHAT IF THE Baptist Sunday School Board encouraged every local church and institution to formulate policies and procedures, written to lessen the destructive aftermath of a clergy perpetrator; and what if those policies were distributed widely, rather than hidden?

WHAT IF every pastor in America began speaking out frequently against sexual abuse and domestic violence from the pulpit, declaring these to be "problems which plague even Christian homes and churches, including the ministerial profession?"

WHAT IF SBC laity insisted the names of ministers with founded allegations of sexual misconduct or abuse be made public in order to protection the vulnerable?

Suddenly a voice breaks in: "Horrors, lady! We'd never be the same!" On that we can all agree!

p.s.: The recent announcement by the Baptist Sunday School Board of a National Advisory Committee on Sexual Misconduct is welcomed, but full of omissions. Only one woman on the committee? Where are the laity? Its foremost concern is "helping" perpetrators? No mention is made of helping victims (or of holding perpetrators accountable).

Last fall Neil Kneirim of BSSB told me anything done for victims would have to be on the local level. I am confused. Perpetrators can be "helped" on a national level, but not victims?

Recovery cost for victims is too great for most local churches to meet; but it is a fraction of the cost incurred in trying to "restore" a perpetrator.

A Mistake of the System

In my final article, I wrapped things up by declaring myself as "a mistake of the system." That was a phrase being used to describe survivors who had not only survived, but gone on to talk of horrors perpetrated by Germany's concentration camps. The system hadn't expected me to open this conversation with thousands of readers as witnesses I proudly pointed out.

I ended the series by modelling several simple responses, as I wove in things to avoid saying, if any reader should ever have a victim come in search of support:

Your feelings will parallel those experienced by the victim ... shock, temporary paralysis, anger, guilt and fear may come in rapid succession.

A simple "I'm sorry" is the starting point, followed closely with "Thank you for taking the risk of talking to me."

You might add: "I know this is tough, but I'll be here for you." (Don't say it unless you mean it!) Above all, assure the victim of your commitment to her/his safety.

Resist the temptation to resort to old clichés. Even "God is with you" or "I'm praying for you" are often resented by the most seriously wounded.

"I am angered to know that anyone, especially someone in this profession, would take advantage of you," would be appreciated if it's sincere.

Most of all, listen to what may be a highly complicated story. Be aware the victim is testing you with small bits of information. Be sensitive to his or her fears revealed at this time.

Ask: "What can I do to help?" If the victim wants to pursue therapy, encourage this. Look for ways the church can assist with those bills.

Let the victim know what you plan to do next. In most cases, I would advise you to immediately go outside the church system to a professional counselor well-versed in abuse issues. Assure the victim you are doing everything possible to protect her anonymity.

However, if you are dealing with a minor, be aware that you are at least under ethical obligation to see that the abuse is reported to the human services department in your area. Finally, make a commitment to get back within two or three days. Whatever you do, don't leave the victim hanging a day longer than your agreement. The burden of initiating the next conversation is on you.

This was all I could do. The next step for me was to sit back and see where things went. I had established the facts to the best of my ability, laid out a course of direction that any individual or agency could pick up on.

The seeds were planted. They could immediately begin to germinate or lay dormant until others still in places of power might come to provide water and fertilizer. I could easily be located if anyone needed to reach me.

A New Voice from Baptist Women in Ministry

One and only one person from any agency responded to all of this: Malinda Fillingim, editor of Folio, a newsletter for Baptist Women in Ministry. She liked the suggestion that BWIM band together to take on this topic in some active role. Yet the sincere, reality-based, rhetorical question was "Who would help us?" Related to this voiced query, I sensed there was at least one more. "How can an organization filled with women already quaking under such intense pressure manage to band together in the face of such opposition on this topic?"

Still, she requested an article from me for the next issue of Folio. I gladly accepted, entitling it "A Monumental Challenge." I began by confessing my own naivety of a decade earlier, when I thought I'd found the one Baptist missionary who ever managed to slip through the cracks of the system. Then, going on to compare the institutional responses of denominations to that of Tailhook, I pointed out that 48% of UCC clergywomen had reported being victimized by male clergy in the workplace. From there, I went on to talk about the devastating cost to survivors whether or not they choose to report, ending with the minimal consequences for perpetrators and the ethical responsibility institutions and denominations had to work toward transformative change. I didn't need to point out how many women, after investing years in a career, same as I had, were now trapped in the very system they'd worked to enter yet now held little respect for. Many members of this organization were among them, I was certain. In fact, I'd already heard from some—a fact I did not state in the article.

Later that year, I flew to Little Rock for the national meeting of BWIM. It was easier than ever to understand the editor's question, "Who will help us?" when I saw the "crowd," no more than twenty women and one man married to a female pastor, who wasn't able to attend. What a stark comparison between the small gathering here, in a denomination where ordination of women wasn't even acknowledged, compared to United Methodists' COSROW, a national organization boldly taking on issues of gender oppression, including clergy sexual abuse!

David and Goliath this was not. What these women had already tackled paled in comparison to David's feat. This giant was a giant monster. My own attempt to enlist their active support was closer to a gnat trying to persuade a seriously wounded elephant to move out of the path of a hurricane.

Four years earlier, Ron still recalls the moment in 1991, when Elvis Presley's voice helped him identify his feelings as he reflected on our own double-binds with the Foreign Mission Board. We couldn't "go on together" with the Board, my husband declared. We were "caught in a trap" because of loving the agency too much to easily walk out. Yet, in the end, he realized he must walk out in order to take a stand and preserve his own sense of integrity. To not do so would have him in even a bigger trap—sacrificing what he believed after having witnessed the dishonesty that so permeated the organization of which he could no longer be a part.

This group of women was also caught in a double-bind of a similar nature, though much more was at stake. They could not hope to survive as an organization if they took a strong stand collectively. In such intense patriarchy, no fledgling organization could. I returned to Iowa, facing a stark reality, much more determined to remain a single voice crying in the wilderness, despite the increased isolation this experience required me to accept as reality dawned.

There would be no Baptist "Voice of the Faithful"[1] or any group willing to call the denomination to repentance for their strong tendency to "walk by on the other side." Nothing close to this Catholic organization, organized in 1995 and dedicated to "Keep the faith, Change the Church," as it carries on to this day.

Without such a group, Southern Baptists, as a whole, would remain pent on punishing anyone who questioned the increasingly rigid stances that put females, the most likely victims in the SBC, firmly in their place, even if they'd not experienced any sexual violation.

*****

[1] See http://www.votf.org/

Now faith is the substance of things hoped for, the evidence of things not seen.
Hebrews 11:1

Chapter 16
Precious Epistles

In advocacy work, a single voice speaks for thousands hidden in the darkness. For the advocacy writer, the greatest of all joys comes in hearing echoes of others who may simply be softly saying "Amen." Otherwise, it's hard to know if anyone is truly listening.

Whether we're writing or speaking publicly, voices of appreciation empower us who work many hours in silence, often to produce a few sentences for an unknown number of invisible souls. Those of us with years of experience have learned that a piece of writing is often be picked up on a library shelf to resonate anew decades later. What a joy it is when someone takes time to let us know!

Over and over, the stories I heard validated that accountability must come first. It is collusion that must be stopped. Despite what many seem to believe, we do not have to understand why an offender crosses the line, for instance, to protect others from harm. As if the reason makes a difference in what action needs to be taken to address the offense. Or that it is somehow acceptable to excuse or overlook what we do not understand.

The more I learned, the more horrified I became. Who would believe that, in a back-room conversation, with a half dozen of his colleagues present, an American Baptist who had been in ministry as a prominent pastor for twenty-five years would dare plead to me: "We can't let these things we're doing here leak out—people wouldn't understand." Yet that's what I'd heard with my own two ears, and not one person dared to challenge this man who was appealing to me not to repeat what I'd just heard.

Advocates know better than to stay silent in the face of such evil. Yet there were not enough men like Jack Harwell's around to stick their necks out to print what the system didn't want said.

Bringing the truth into the Light of Day, simply speaking the truth in love, is a spiritual process as much as a healthy, social process. Wherever clerics led the way in suppressing the truth, survivors from the community of faith have been the exceptions, daring to speak out and set examples for the general population in matters of professional sexual abuse until the press finally began to answer.

From there, this courage spilled over to other systems with the victims in the military coming forward shortly thereafter. Victims of teachers and healthcare recipients soon followed in mass along with those abused by mental health professionals in formal counseling. Together we marched out to go to war, often one person at a time standing against powerful men bent on protecting their own at the expense of their own integrity.

The Real Pay in Advocacy Writing

On my good days, I find it merely amusing when someone implies I am doing advocacy writing for the money. Otherwise, I'm sure many wonder, why would anybody put so much effort into writing what most people aren't interested in reading? That commonly-held view parallels placing no real value on parents or caregivers who choose to work without compensation beyond the sheer joy of fulfillment that comes from intensely giving oneself away for individuals who may not even be able to show an ounce of gratitude.

Truth is the world places little value on passion. Most writers believe success is measured in dollars and cents and in selling a certain number of copies. That's why the majority sit around and write without ever getting a "proper" publisher, which isn't necessary at all if advocacy and having a timely message is the writer's goal.

Writing is hard work—not something I do for fun in hopes of someday getting my message out. To sit around, expecting to say everything perfectly in order to somehow magically find someone else to make publication happen is the equivalent of having an external locus of control. There's no need to wait on others if you have a message to write or to speak. Just do it! The hard work of publicity that's necessary to do the marketing will be yours no matter if you have a large publisher or a small these days. Who cares what size audience you have? Audiences, though there is an ebb and flow, will continue to grow in number, we tell ourselves, if we indeed have anything important to say.

Every advocate has to get a vision of something unseen happening, for that's where paradigm changes start—deep in the invisible part of each of us, where it can stay a long time before we vocalize what's happening internally. Then, you have to write into what you are seeing, also be content to see nothing ever in a lifetime.

Over the years, I've been fortunate to see the change I visualized— not nearly as much as I'd like, and certainly not enough to keep most advocates committed for the long-haul. To me, success is not even about how much change we see in our world or in a system, however. It's how much change we see in the individuals who come our way and how they change us in the process.

One welcome change is the increase in the number of re- enforcements that have come in the past twenty years to relieve some of us pioneers. Being able to nurture some of these, knowing that this work is going to go on far into the future is such a relief! That's worth more to me than a six-figure income.

The Lag in Professional Expertise

"We are holding hands in the dark," Rev. Dr. Sarah Rieth wrote me from Buffalo, New York, while the series was running. Her words captured the feelings of so many other mental health professionals and advocates in that day. We were all so very few and far between.

Until the end of the twentieth century, there were very, very few psychotherapists who had experience in working with survivors of abuse by professionals, let alone those who knew how to cope with the added layers of collusion. This dearth was especially evident in the South, where it was virtually impossible to find a suitable counselor in the southern states who could look past his or her own culture and entanglement with religion to the degree that was needed.

When it came to professional abuse, especially of adults, the ignorance was multiplied. And there was so little literature or acknowledgment of clergy sexual abuse of minors in Protestant circles that these clients seemed to be the untouchables among psychotherapists. I was sick of being stereotyped, so my story needed to fit into one of two categories—either as a Protestant woman who had turned for spiritual counsel to her minister or a minor who had turned to a Catholic priest for the same. To imagine that some clergy members could be violent or sexually aggressive, rather than subtle in their actions, was unimaginable, even to what was considered in that day to be "a seasoned therapist." Nobody considered that priests also abused females, even more often than male victims, and that there were as many adult victims of Catholic priests, including many nuns, as there were among Protestant ministers. Protestants were different, according to the urban myths that still widely exist. Unthinkable that ministers—including ministers of youth, education, or music—might also abuse minors! And it was still a deep, dark secret that missionaries would. Heaven forbid! Such blasphemy to even speak of this!

Today, though stereotyping still occurs far too often, psychotherapists tend to be far more enlightened about the wide variety of behaviors and types of perpetrators in crimes and offenses against women, even among clergy. They are much more likely to ask around and to seek out information on the Web, of course. They're also more likely to understand that each survivor, whether female or male, has unique responses within a much broader range than "the typical." Whistle-blowers and secondary victims, despite the pain and suffering inflicted by the system, may be even more in need of support and psychotherapeutic services than many direct victims.

As a whole, we aren't necessarily fragile. Nor are we dangerous or obsessed because we do this work. Neither are we unreasonable in expecting that others will stand with us to also speak in solidarity. For not to speak publicly with a passionate commitment against these problems when one has the power to do so—that is passive collusion.

Contrary to commonly-held beliefs in the psychotherapeutic world, many survivors abused as adults need only information, comfort, and empowerment, rather than "treatment." Psychotherapist, Dr. Gary Schoener, with his broad experience in the field, frequently made such a comment on a list serve on advocateweb.org, for those of us working across a variety of disciplines in this field.

Uninformed, therapists can do far more harm than good, as we'd painfully discovered, as a couple. Shortly before being put on probation in

1988, Ron came home from a therapist to whom he'd turned for months, projecting such nonsense onto me that I could hardly believe my ears!

"The counselor wants you to come in and talk to him, so he can help us figure out why all of this is happening. He thinks you must have done something or said something to cause all of this reaction we're getting." Fortunately, I had a lot more equity in built-up credibility with Ron than the therapist had managed to scrape together in a brief period of time. I shudder to think where many couples would have ended up with this, however.

"I was trying to teach that therapist what I'd come to understand, and he just wasn't getting it all," Ron tells me, looking back. His understanding came partially from a caring psychiatrist, who lived near us in Africa, was also a social acquaintance, and offered to see us both without charge as soon as she realized what we were struggling with. In short order, though baffled, she pronounced us as too healthy to tolerate what she saw as a large, incestuous family.

Still, the counselor felt he could reason with this system by writing a letter on our behalf. While Ron was still convinced he could somehow help Board officials see that this had all been "a big misunderstanding" by sitting down with them once again. Of course, it had not been a big misunderstanding at all. The Board officials understood very well how to "deal" with these problems. The problem was their "understanding" wasn't going to keep working forever, same as it wasn't in all the other gigantic incestuous systems where their "understanding" has been "working well" for many years—faith-based, educational systems, hospitals, and a lot more.

By mid-1995, I'd heard from scores of professional counselors who had become victims of their own supervisors in the course of their work. Some seemed to be as wounded and deeply depressed as victims of childhood trauma.

"I can use all the support I can get these days. This process has felt like an uphill battle so far, and it is not nearly over......So, here I am in the midst of the most difficult thing I believe I've ever done in my life," a woman in a middle-management position in chaplaincy wrote me, as she considered filing a grievance.

While she'd first been inclined to take measures in hopes of only protecting herself, she soon realized this would still leave others vulnerable, those she was supervising, as well as all the patients in the facility.

Compared to what I'd known ten years earlier, this dear soul was an expert on what she faced. She wasn't jumping in with both feet, hoping for some magical response. Yet being an expert on any "serpent" has both advantages and disadvantages. An oncologist with cancer, for instance, is not naïve. She knows a lot about the journey, the problems caused by treatment, as well as the danger of doing nothing. Yet prognoses are not absolute in their outcomes. Decisions made under the best information available can still have disastrous outcomes. In some ways, simply knowing this makes decisions much more difficult.

More Echoes

Dr. Trull had ordered several copies of HLWK for the seminary library and was passing one around to other professors, he told me in a letter to me. He affirmed my "Christian spirit and disciplined response," which he noted gave me "a great deal more credibility" as opposed to those "more vindictive." While I tried to take this as a compliment, I made a mental note of what he seemed to be implying. Choosing legal action would be "unchristian." Of course, it would have been counterproductive to tell him we ourselves had explored the legal action and quickly concluded, after consulting with a lawyer, it would have been a lost cause.

Soon afterwards Mrs. Audra Trull wrote a wonderful review for the seminary newsletter, clearly expressing her own grief in reading the story and reflecting a spirit of advocacy that I longed for people to understand.

Most surprising, Dr. James Carter, had co-authored a book with Trull, released only weeks before HLWK, entitled *Ministerial Ethics: Being a Good Minister in a Not-So-Good World*. The chapter on sexual ethics, progressive by Baptist standards, offered a good, basic start for a denomination so retro on "women's issues." Yet I had serious problems with some of the finer points that I soon asked the two consider correcting in any future writing—the primary being their use of the word "wanderer" to refer to a type of offender these authors considered to be less of a concern than a predator. It was a term Gary Schoener [1] had agreed was already causing considerable confusion, a point that would be much later noted by Pamela Cooper-White.[2]

The remainder of the initial responses were very positive. They came from pastors or psychotherapists, a couple from survivors, and two from volunteers at domestic abuse shelters (with one writing to say how shocked she'd been to find minister's wives among their clientele).

They especially liked the third article, which I closed with a series of statements that I had written and posted above my desk as a daily reminder of why I was doing the work that I was:

- I believe the community of faith should be the safest place on the face of the earth.

- I believe it can be.

- I believe the community of faith has a right to demand more than approximate justice.

- I believe obtaining more than approximate justice can be a given for the majority of victims, but it will likely come only after generations of struggle.

- I believe it is very difficult for a profession strong educated and accomplished in extending grace and mercy to feel comfortable with "tough love."

- I believe a seminary education sprinkled with generous portions of tough-love thinking can help to facilitate justice.

- I believe committees dealing with violence in a professional setting must have an equal balance between peer professionals and laity, as well as male and female.

- I believe there should be required reading and extensive training for all committee members.

- I believe a violation of professional ethics is a violation of the community, and the community of faith has a right to know when this occurs.

- I believe that in order to stay committed to justice people of the community of faith must lace everything done with believing prayer.

- I believe full justice will only be achieved when we have a grassroots movement of informed advocates ready to join courageous survivors in speaking out.

*****

[1] Gary Schoener, clinical psychologist of the Walk-In Counseling Center in Minneapolis is world-renowned for his writing and advocacy work, speaking out, organizing conferences, and collaborating freely with professionals, para-professionals, and any member of society who is interested in reducing the suffering from all issues of sexual exploitation. He has been actively doing this work since the 1970's. His 1989 book, Psychotherapists' Sexual Involvement with Clients: Intervention and Prevention, published by Walk-In, is a classic.

[2] Pamela Cooper-White is a prolific author and one of the foremost authorities on the intersection of faith with issues of violence against women. She shares her views clearly on the "wanderer" in The Cry of Tamar: Violence Against Women and the Church's Response, (Fortress Press, 2012) p. 158, "The church's culture of optimism too often leads church officials to view many offenders incorrectly as belonging to the 'wanderer' or 'neurotic' categories, where they are given inappropriate latitude for supposed rehabilitation and rapid reinstatement."

Chapter 17
Putting Hospitality in Its Place

Our life, already in overdrive for five years before *How Little We Knew* was released, had been filled with reminders that we'd still not caught up with stateside current events, new trends, or technology. When it came to "women's issues," I'd been behind my entire life, like most women who grew up in the South, immersed in a theologically-conservative culture. It was embarrassing, especially among the women I met in Minneapolis at The Re-Imagining Conference.

For instance, feminist author Audre Lorde, whose recent death was still being mourned by many progressive thinkers in 1993, I'd never heard of. That surprised one of the women who had no idea how much I had to learn.

Days after arriving home, I'd driven over to the library at The College of St. Mary in Omaha, which would soon become a great resource, where I'd spend hours devouring fine publications and progressive ideas. There I found some of Lorde's writings, which became even more applicable to my own personal evolution of thought when breast cancer came into my life, same as it had Lorde's. It was astounding to see what this woman accomplished in her fifty-eight years.

As a lesbian writer, she managed to change the conversation about racism, feminism, and homosexuality. When it came to breast cancer, she had much to say, as well. She chose to make a bold statement to bystanders about the harsh reality of the disease by refusing to wear any prosthesis. At the same time, her boldness invited other survivors to know who they could count on for compassion and helpful conversation.

"I have come to believe over and over again that what is most important to me must be spoken, made verbal and shared, even at the risk of having it bruised or misunderstood," she once said.

When I read this, another set of Bette Rod's lyrics came to mind: "You can't hurt me anymore," she sings.[1] "I am stronger than you think I am." The fear of having the messages bruised or diminished is a constant concern for every advocate.

I'd seen "The Color Purple" on television only weeks after we returned to the States for the last time, though I'd failed to register the name of the story's author until sometime after Re-Imagining.

"What you're doing makes me think of Alice Walker and her statement about those who fear the truth," another woman visiting my Re-Imagining table commented. "You know the quote I'm talking about --the one from 'The Temple of My Familiar'?" She paused as a shadow of distress passed across her eyes.

"Don't you?" she asked incredulously.

Looking back, I wonder how she kept from smiling when I finally answered: "No. Who is she?"

Going out of her way, the kind lady made a special trip back to her hotel room to bring me a copy of a page from her own notes, apparently prepared for a presentation she was making to the crowd. On the page was the quote she believed I must have for the road ahead:

"As long as the people don't fear the truth, there is hope. For once they fear it, the one who tells it doesn't stand a chance. And today truth is still beautiful....but so frightening."

Speaking purposely takes us toward the suffering. We refuse to avoid it or run from it. For only as we walk through it is there hope for our own transformation and the transformation of this world of strife into a world of peace.

Since returning from Toronto, I'd welcomed calls almost every week from Tom Economus. He'd share what was going on in Catholic advocacy with the laity up in arms while a few much-needed donations arrived to help with "The Missing Link" and other endeavors at Linkup.

Then, I'd tell him about the responses trickling into my mail box from what little publicity I'd been able to do through Baptist publications, including a most welcome twenty-five dollar donation that had come from an American Baptist survivor, wanting to help with my ministry.

Far more book orders and requests for information came to me from small ecumenical newsletters in grassroots efforts. I struggled to keep up with the requests as book reviews as far away as Ireland came to my attention or mail from articles I squeezed into my schedule for a more general audience on a variety of other topics to help pay our personal bills.

Tom and I talked about this constant awareness of the massive number of victims buried under the rubble of institutional "holiness." It was difficult for him to imagine what I was seeing with Protestants. He knew the Catholic world, which to me was somewhat like a foreign country. Yet the fragmentation of Protestants that I'd grown up understanding was like a whole other continent to him.

There was a sense of an underground operation among Protestants as my contact list grew by word of mouth into the hundreds. Yet there was no central office for Protestant survivors. Many in mainline groups knew of Marie Fortune's work and The Center for the Prevention of Sexual and Domestic Violence. That organization became the single most effective, unifying force.

Yet the greatest bulk of evangelicals and conservative Protestants didn't know of Marie Fortune at all. There was no big national gathering for Protestant survivors, and I wasn't able to interest many in becoming involved in a largely-Catholic group. It wasn't the theological differences, but the sense of being swallowed up in a system with its own lingo that didn't translate well enough into Protestant systems. Even in our ecumenical women's support groups, we spent a good deal of time trying to explain to one another the terminology for understanding the varied processes from ecclesiastical systems to autonomous congregations and every combination in between.

Most survivors, unless they were still working on a church staff somehow, weren't likely to be reading church-related publications anymore. Yet there was a good chance some might be reading "The Other Side," a very popular, ecumenical magazine dedicated to "justice rooted in discipleship." It was precursor to "Sojourner Magazine," still speaking out stronger than ever in 2017, "radical" truths in a world needing to be challenged on cutting-edge issues.

I'd never heard of either of these magazines until I got into St. Mary's library in Omaha. Amazing that I discovered all of this through Catholics!

It certainly would have come in handy to have known retired Baptist missionaries, Anne and Fred Alexanders, who had published the first issue of "The Other Side" on a second-hand press in their Ohio basement in 1965, three years before Ron and I found ourselves in the heat of the civil rights movement in New Orleans.

I knew nothing about our close connection to the Alexander's until the magazine ceased publication in 2005 and Dee Dee Risher, the co-editor, wrote about their "stalwart belief that if white Christians were told the truth about racism, they would repent and change their ways." I would have laughed out loud had I read this statement by retired missionaries in 1995, considering how resistant Southern Baptists had been to any mention of the sin of racism. Yet I probably would not have recognized how this idealism paralleled my own a few years earlier when Ron and I were still thinking that most of our former colleagues and the wider community of Baptists would be easily awakened if only we spoke what we knew about collusion with CSA.

One thing I *did* know, as soon as the May/June issue of their magazine arrived in my mailbox just as the "Baptists Today" series ended, that this was where I had to go next.

In that issue was an interview with Edwina Gateley, an English Catholic only two years older than me. Gateley had begun her professional ministry as a missionary-teacher in Uganda in 1964, fifteen years before she entered seminary. By 1991, she'd returned to stateside living and had raised enough money to open Genesis House in Chicago, a residential program for prostitutes seeking a way out of their abusive lives that were usually rooted in their sexually abusive childhoods.

I underlined many of Edwina's words that resonated with my own experience, as she spoke of her calling to her own work of advocacy:

> *God is desperate, forever scraping the bottom of the barrel, looking for idiots to change the world.*

> *If we are following our consciences, doing what is right and good, we are capable of anything.*

> *It is incredible what you can do when you know your calling—when you absolutely know this is something you have to do.*

One thing I loved about Edwina's story was how it helped refute a stereotype that I was working to overcome, one that still plagues me well into the 21st century: the idea that all missionaries are colonialists. Many were and still are, I agree. Yet a lot of us had gone primarily for humanitarian reasons, understanding this to be the way to express our faith and love, not to declare our adopted culture as something evil that needed to be conquered.

My message, I hoped, was exactly the opposite. Bigotry, so common in American missions, had helped to create the problems of abuse. This story of ours showed what power abuse looks like under a microscope, serving as a good example for anyone and validating efforts to expose the sinister power.

All of this I shared with Tom as I sent off a query for an article that would appear late in 1996, never dreaming how it would help to turn the tide in everything we were trying to do. I found it fascinating to be inspired by a Catholic woman with a passion so close to the one we shared. These connecting pieces filled my heart with gratitude and hope, where despair could have taken root.

Tom's trips from Chicago to St. Louis and out to California, sometimes left him unavailable for weeks. These trips had two purposes: to support survivors and to try reasoning with Catholic Church officials. There were media requests to work in, as well. Boston was always on his mind. He was constantly guessing which of the powder kegs around the country might make national news next. It was only a matter of time, he'd say optimistically, even as he spoke of how devastating it was to see survivors being thrown under the bus by those who refused to wake up.

Each time we talked, I'd remind him: "Make taking care of yourself your first priority." I was worried, knowing how thin he was spread. He would just laugh it off as he seemed to be running on adrenaline night and day.

How much primary abuse was currently going on compared to the backlog of victims coming forward who were still alive to talk was anyone's guess. Every time the media gave any of us coverage, we heard from people wanting to break their secret. For Tom, this meant his phone was either busy or ringing 24/7 unless he turned it off to get some rest.

It was so hard for him to even consider setting time limits on guys calling in to spill their guts to someone for the first time, after having things bottled up for decades. I could understand. Tom had been there without a listening ear for so long. He was trying to do the work of a therapist, except therapists had time structures and office staff. He had neither. In addition, the callers often had no therapists themselves, often due to lack of funding. They were broke if not homeless, their lives often in shambles due to the abuse and often at risk for suicide.

Naturally, with callers trying in vain to get through, survivors and other advocates often gave up, same as I had when an organizational need came up. Lots of folks were frustrated due to the bottleneck. One board member who lived in Chicago told me to call her if I ever needed to get a message to Tom, promising she would run over to his place, as she often did, rather than even trying to call.

One day, when things seemed to be going nowhere in Catholic advocacy except for the calls coming in, Tom told me he'd learned he might be able to divert Linkup phone calls over to others in remote locations. Problem would be finding reliable volunteers to take a weekly shift of answering. I advised him to get right on the plan, certain he would be able to find volunteers to help, and assuring him I would gladly take a turn each week. Having often taken hot line phone calls while working inpatient, I'd be willing to even train volunteers without that experience.

Almost every time Tom called from that point on, I asked if he'd made progress on the plan to spread the phone calls around. Each time he'd say he was too busy to look into it. Suggesting that he might not be around to answer that phone if he kept up this pace, didn't seem to register.

Down's and Up's

The O. J. Simpson verdict was announced in July, 1995, sending ripples of despair through the survivor movement unlike anything since Anita Hill's lynching four years earlier. That wasn't all. Something much closer to the heart of Linkup members was thrown into the mix.

Tom called, devastated, soon after. He'd received allegations of sexual abuse on Kelly himself and several others at St. John's. It was like he'd been kicked in the solar plexus. Now, there was no place associated with Catholicism that he knew where survivors would feel reasonably safe. Neither was there any place to offer free hospitality, to Linkup, with trust being compromised. Since St. John's had absorbed much of the cost of the meetings they'd hosted, this was an enormous blow.

How many survivors he was talking about that afternoon ever brought their complaints forward, it's impossible to know. There were many other things on our minds, and I never asked about the follow-up on those cases. I do know, from reports of both Richard Sipe and Patrick Wall, is that there have been many cases since at St. John's and complicity has been horrific. The Interfaith Trauma Center,[1] which I turned down the invitation to be a part of in the beginning due to time constraints, did not survive long-term for multiple reasons never publicly revealed. Those who sat on their Board, however, revealed that the demise had been facilitated by the presence of perpetrators on the Board, who were highly skilled at doing double-speak, adding yet another layer of disillusionment for those committed over the long-haul to the survivor movement.

On to the Windy City

Shaking off the discouragement from dashed hopes over the problems at St. John's, we plunged ahead to plan for another exciting conference. Compared to Tom's enormous task, mine was very small. With several asking for a seminar on advocacy writing, I agreed to lead one as Tom and other board members in Chicago scrambled to find a meeting place there.

Even the name of the hotel, "The Clarion International," was perfect for the occasion as my friend, songwriter and vocalist Bette Rod and her husband David sent their own very personal, clarion call she'd written for the occasion: "Don't Let Them Take Your Light Away."

The Light within this group could not be extinguished. It showed on each face. "Living is more than trying to survive," were words we embraced, declaring further that those who had "been silenced shall lift up your voices and sing to reclaim the power so cruelly taken......" And sing we did, each time the chorus came 'round again.

> "Don't let them take your Light away.
> Don't let them have the final say.
> You're getting stronger every day.
> Don't let them take your Light away."[2]

Tom Doyle and Tom Economus, having led the way among Catholics, soon had other clerics joining our efforts with 10% of attendees being members of the clergy in 1996. This included Patricia Liberty, an American Baptist whose message one morning was about the pool of Bethesda and how often wounded people look to others, as if healing depends on some magical, external source.

One-on-One Hospitality

Dispelling the belief that survivors had no hope without the Church or some extra-special therapist, Liberty insisted that the real source of healing was already within each person.

Nobody exemplified this more to me than Rick Springer. As a Chicago cab driver who voluntarily extended hospitality to each of us who arrived at the airport like honored refugees. Warm, caring, and attentive to detail, Rick treated everyone like a celebrity, bringing life into every conversation, conveying a sense of equally sharing and bearing burdens and sharing joys—whatever might be called for.

Over a cup of coffee, soon after meeting him, he wanted to hear about our family. His eyes lit up at the mention of our two children. Without an ounce of bitterness, he then looked directly at me and said: "Not ever getting married or having a family has been one of my biggest losses related to the abuse."

Even as I write this paragraph, uninvited tears well up in my eyes as they did that day. All I could say is: "Rick, I'm so sorry."

"Oh, I'm one of the lucky ones!" he quickly responded with a sweet smile. "Many guys like me have never even found a way to make a living. I have a job I love! The best thing is the people I meet."

The reception Rick extended to us and many other survivors in Chicago was the opposite of the reception he'd received from the Church. That's why he enjoyed doing it so much, he said.

Two decades later, those who attended him on his death bed reported that his shining example of resiliency endured as he joked about the uselessness of Google maps to a guy who had the maps all memorized. He may well have been reflecting, even then, on a Linkup speaker's adage: "Living life to the fullest is the best revenge of all." Rick certainly did.

Then, along came my friend Bill. After years of isolation, sometimes living on the street, drinking and drugs, he'd made peace with his story and peace with himself. The two of us connected immediately with our shared belief that whenever something very negative happens in our lives, the redemptive value of the story often comes with the sharing. Bill's inspiring story had put him on the front page of his hometown in Arizona, with several photos helping to tell of his journey from his victimization to finding peace through photography.

Within seconds of meeting, he stated his understanding of deity, "if it exists at all," was in the desert where he loved to take pictures. At that time, I was hoping to do a sequel to How Little We Knew, never dreaming there would soon be a way to reach many more through the Web than I could ever hope to do in a single book. So William got excited about that, and I asked if I might be able to use some of his photography, perhaps as a cover. He had a better idea—he would send me digital copies of his best work.

"Thanks for being a part of my healing journey," Bill said to me in the hotel lobby as I was leaving. "There really is a God after all!"

I wrote about William in the next Reconnections, drawing on a bit of humor I'd run across in a very serious passage of the Bible. It was the kind of thing I would have totally missed, I'm sure, if I'd not worked in mental health.

"Remember your journey from *Shit*tam to Gilgal." (italics intended) ....*Shit*tam was the last place the Israelites camped before miraculously crossing the Jordan River. This was the final stage in their long journey from slavery. Gilgal was the place of celebration. ...

William, like many survivors, has inspired me with his personal commitment to move beyond Shittam.

Linkup, for survivors and advocates, coming out of isolation to find hope through the mirroring of other survivors, had become a Gilgal. Yet few regular church-goers could imagine how both Linkup and SNAP were literally saving lives.

*****

[1] The history of this well-intended organization is well archived at
http://www.saintjohnsabbey.org/interfaith-sexual-trauma-institute/about-isti/

[2] To hear this inspiring song sung by Bette Rod herself, and for more info on
her CD "Pieces," go to http://www.takecourage.org/rallysong.htm

Chapter 18
Soul Struggles

"I HAVE LOST MY FAITH IN GOD." That's exactly how Ron's column began, capital letters included. It lay directly opposite my "Reconnections"—the one about Shittam, on the same page. Everything else he had to say was close to what Robert Blair Kaiser recorded Tom Doyle saying twenty years later in Whistle. Ron wrote:

> *"The Church I once believed in and trusted in has sinned against me and refused to hear my cries. What kind of God is deaf to the cries of abused children and assaulted men and women? The Church I once trusted and loved, even as I trusted and loved God, has refused to hear my pleas and respond with love and justice; therefore, I no longer believe in God."*

> *This statement of unbelief could be your sentiments. Many survivors have no need or use for a god that lets them suffer at the hands of evil people.*

> *I do believe in God—but not the one I described above. I do not equate God and the Church any longer! The Church is comprised of fallible people who often are self-serving. The God they portray does not respond in compassion or justice. However, the God I believe in does. I believe in the God which Jesus Christ represented to the world. Jesus was moved with compassion for the oppressed and worked to overthrow the abusive church system of His day. That's why they killed Him."*

It's possible he was inspired by Jamie Taylor, one of his seven-year-old congregants. I'd come home one spring Sunday, telling him all about first and second-grade class, leading up to Easter.

"Why did Jesus die on the cross?" I'd asked the kids.

Jamie's hand shot right up, waving all around before I could even say her name.

"Because he didn't want to follow the rules," she answered, confidently.

I certainly couldn't argue with that!

Running into her father fourteen years later, it didn't surprise me to learn that Jamie had turned into quite a radical, outspoken woman, now tackling the problem of domestic abuse as a budding social worker.

Yes, Jamie. Some rules *are meant* to be broken.

Why I Stay in the Church

Recently a clergyman asked me why on earth I stay in the church after all I've witnessed. It's a good question, one I've contemplated many times myself, so it didn't take me long to answer:

"I'm still a follower of Jesus. He never let the church go. Why should I?" Then, I told him about Jamie. "It's really kids like Jamie who keep me in the church. Without them, I'd probably run away and hide."

I want to stay in the church to hear the wisdom of children there, to do my part in seeing they are protected from nonsense. I believe in planting seeds of social justice where they might otherwise not be sown—what better place to do this than in places where there's often a drought in justice seeking. Sadly, that's often in churches, where victims get blamed for not picking themselves up by their own bootstraps.

Staying in the church does not make me superior to those who have left, though—please don't get me wrong on that. For many who have been through far more than I have, without the personal resources to even consider staying, I affirm their decisions to do whatever path their own soul-searching leads them to take. I also stay for them, since I can—to stand in the gap and speak for them whenever I'm inclined and given opportunity.

Accessing Good Tools for the Long Haul

Personally, I've never cared much for fictional mysteries. The true ones fascinate me most. Who needs fantasy, anyway? I often ask Ron, who loves mystery movies and has the patience and visual aptitude to pick up all the clues he does, while I simply get lost and end up driving him nuts with my questions. It's a characteristic I share with my mother.

Unlike my mother, I do like surprises that add spice to my life. Mom wants to be sure she's prepared for whatever comes—even if it throws her life off course in a good way. Last time I tried surprising her, it ended up backfiring, though I'd assumed she would be thrilled.

It happened late one Friday morning when I showed up on her front porch unannounced, after driving hundreds of miles, and told her she only needed to grab a suitcase and be ready to go in a half hour. She was being kidnapped. Immediately she went into shock. Why hadn't I let her know I was coming?

She was most concerned about the temporary state of her housekeeping, as usual. Never mind it was her daughter, wanting to whisk her off for a luxurious weekend at a nearby, undisclosed location.

"Trust me, Mom," I told her. "We're going to have a great time."

We did—all three of us. It worked out fine even with the unexpected challenge the two of us discovered when my little sister, who I'd asked to drive up to meet us, arrived with a broken leg. Lydia doesn't mind surprises or mysteries in the least. As a matter of fact, she enjoys creating both more than I do, often keeping us all guessing.

Naturally, I also take after Dad in some ways, just not to the same degree as Lydia. A bit impulsive, he had a way of courageously jumping into the middle of things before realizing what a complicated mess he was getting into. That can be a good quality, depending on what a person wants to accomplish, as long as one isn't afraid of taking the risk. Often the results turn out much better than anticipated. Sometimes not nearly as well.

Like when Ron and I lived in southern Louisiana, with our two-year-old daughter and three-month-old son, in cloth diapers, and a broken-down washing machine that experts had failed to fix.

Dad, seldom easily intimidated, didn't know if he could do anything more than the last guy. Yet he'd had quite a lot of experience fixing things—or trying, anyway. It was all in the details, he declared, as he set to work.

Sure enough, that old machine was soon spinning the first load of clean diapers it had turned out in days. It would turn out hundreds more, too, for a long time to come--once we got all the standing water bailed out from the bare wood floor while Dad worked to attach the dangling drainpipe he'd failed to notice in the final step of the repair job.

Likewise, after studying up close the mysterious issues of complicity with abuse for nine years, I was beginning to question what was missing in all the training being done. For even those claiming to be thoroughly trained were conveying more resentment than empathy with messengers, even if they claimed to believe what survivors were telling them—which people were beginning to do more by the end of 1995. Offenders were still getting wrists slapped, secrets kept, and not many survivors were provided help with therapy beyond a few sessions, totally underestimating the needs of people with serious wounds.

While I wasn't sure how to change any of that, I did know one thing. If we didn't keep talking, nothing was going to ever change. Talking and writing, listening and reading—these things all go together to make up the best process I've ever encountered for changing things in any system, or in my own life.

So I took what I could pull together and jumped into the conversation from my default position, which is somewhat of a combination between Mom's tendency to keep life in reasonable order and my father's penchant for daring to take on something far above his head.

Yet, on the most frustrating days, I still wanted to resort to my own unique way of coping. It's a little related to my father's approach for fixing inanimate objects, though not quite as sophisticated.

My husband and children have been known to run for cover when I grab my favorite tool in the house, though I've never figured out why.

"It's all in how you swing this thing," I tell 'em. "Besides, what of value have I ever broken?" Problem is systems don't respond like an inanimate object can to a well-placed hammer.

That's why I've managed to wipe the letters off so many computer keyboards, same as the one I'm trying to use this morning. I express myself best when my fingers are flying—either in writing or at the piano, where keys are far more forgiving and hearts are, hopefully, more ready to receive what rolls out, often unexpectedly.

Determining the Most Important
Questions

Five years after our termination from formal mission service, whistle blowers from all across the faith spectrum were quietly asking: "What's going to happen if these problems of collusion aren't fixed?"

With many survivors managing to find one another, we were asking the same question lots of power-mongers in denominational positions were asking, though for a different reason than advocates: "Where is this all going to end?"

"Every time we think we've got a handle on the size of the problem, we discover we aren't even close," Tom Economus often said with a sigh.

Protestant protectionism was even harder to quantify than Catholic, due to fragmentation. The rhetorical question I kept asking of every Protestant was "Why is there such an obsession with proving our numbers are lower than the Catholics?" Even if only 3% of Protestant clerics were guilty of pedophilia, as opposed to 6% of priests, and even though the vast majority of Protestant victims were emotionally and spiritually-dependent adults at the time of their abuse, as most were saying, wasn't this cause for an outcry from the profession? Why did they want to see all of these situations as "victimless?" Or even worse, to see the pastors as victims rather than abusers--even when their victims were minors? One of the most common sentiments: a shrug, followed by efforts to blame society's "immorality" for the problem.

Adding to the confusion, even some laity in our local church, though clearly concerned about clergy sexual abuse, wanted to put homosexuality and abuse in the same cauldron. So many, even those in more liberal circles, attributed both issues to sinful, sexual deviancy. This way of deflecting made it very difficult to stay focused long enough on power differentiation to sort out the vast differences in the dialogue needed to filter truth from fiction on these two very different topics.

I was astounded at how difficult it was for people I thought knew my own story well to even notice the fact adolescents were among the victims. While I was careful to include this every time I told the story or wrote it, even those who claimed to have read every word of *How Little We Knew* often missed this vital piece. Except for survivors of sexual abuse as minors—they got it every time!

For the first few months, I kept going back into the book, trying to figure out how I'd missed writing the story clearly enough for readers to see this. Finally, I concluded many were just in that much denial over the abuse of minors, in general. It was there with both conservative evangelicals and mainliners, including some survivors abused as adults. It almost drove me nuts.

And even more so whenever a writer or journalist asked if they could mention my book or story in something they were writing. What a strange question! Almost an insult. Did they really think, after writing a book about unethical secrecy in the church, I might still wish it to remain a well-kept secret?

"My only stipulation, besides identifying me as the author, is that you include the adolescents if you use my story," I often said. Invariably, my request would still get lost—most frustrating, by journalists in major newspapers who couldn't seem to find room for the word "adolescents." Talk about minimizing!

By 1995, I'd begun to believe the justification for such misrepresentation had to do with the felt need of many to bring attention to the large number of adult victims. It was a need I shared. Yet why couldn't we do both?

Others wanted to see our family's story as "just a mission field story," which it certainly was not. The only thing different was how it put the problems multiplied by isolation under a microscope, further showing what happens when professionals confront other professionals or how dangerous it could be if one, even with status in the larger system, stood up and nobody else chose to join that individual. These were truths that needed to be faced—perhaps too scary to consider.

As the first female voice to publicly raise her voice about sexual abuse by ministers in the SBC, I eventually came to some peace about all of this. I'd not belabor these points so early in the process. Sorting out the various nuances, especially in regard to the age of victims, would come on down the line. Collusion applied to every form of abuse, and I could easily name them all whenever the opportunity arose.

For starters, the SBC needed to establish transparency rather than secrecy as the only acceptable response toward holding any abusers accountable. They also needed to recognize the victims' need for validation and assistance, if requested. Next, expose the abusers who had disqualified themselves from ministry, stating the reasons to congregations and providing assistance to them also, with high priority given to getting the abuser's own family back on its feet, as well. Then, finally, taking on the much longer assessment process to determine what hope there was for rehabilitating the offender without putting him back into the pulpit to serve a new congregation, where the most vulnerable people in the pews knew nothing of the man's past while the least vulnerable were often fully aware? Let's get real. These were tall orders that no single denomination, even the most liberal, wanted to fully take on in the mid 90's. *Even today, these issues are often ignored.*

The most frequent question Ron and I kept asking was: "How bad does the problem have to get before the majority of non-offenders wake up, start voting with their pocketbooks if need be, and publicly renouncing the old boys' code of silence in order to save the reputation of the profession and, ultimately, the integrity of the faith?" Were we alone in asking this? I intended to find out.

Never could we have predicted the Gallup polls would get involved to make the point in less than twenty years. The 2013 results showed nurses' credibility rating (at 82%), the highest of all professions, while clergy (at 47%) would reach an all-time low and still be dropping in 2015, the time of the latest survey at this writing--much of it having to do with the "crisis" created by the exposure of collusion with sexual abuse in the profession, which, of course, is not a new problem at all, but a chronic, systemic disease that must be managed.

Chapter 19
Much to Celebrate
(1995)

Jack Harwell jumped into the advocate role as soon as I told him of our need to find a new meeting place for the next Linkup conference. He didn't even ask before contacting a good friend at Emory. The man was optimistic, expecting to have approval from the university in a few weeks.

Tom Economus almost shouted. "Great! One less thing to worry about! Just imagine not having to go through buildings removing crucifixes to keep survivors from freaking out."

Eagerly waiting, we hoped to hear something in the first few days of 1996.

A Family Rejoicing

Over the holidays, our family had a lot to celebrate on its own compared to one year earlier. Two of us at the table felt fortunate just to be alive.

Our daughter Renita Swedberg, who had narrowly escaped being under the rubble in the Oklahoma City bombing, was now carrying our first grandchild. In early July, I'd be going down for the birth, at a midwifery center where mother and baby would only be staying a few hours before going home. As a pioneer Lamaze teacher and postpartum nurse, I was overjoyed with my daughter's choices and thrilled to be on board.

My oncologist assured me a recurrence was extremely unlikely. Thanks to my swift proactivity in seeking treatment, I'd been able to avoid chemo and radiation, and was left only to manage the chronic, residual, neuropathic pain that plagues one in six breast cancer patients—another seldom-talked-about issue.

Having tied the knot six months earlier, Colleen and our son James were busy establishing their careers in Kansas City. Renita had missed the wedding, which coincided with travel plans she'd previously made to travel with her husband James back to her childhood home in Malawi.

I was teaching all I needed to, often in the middle of the day since one third of my students were adults. Right away, I'd received calls from grandparents, as well as eager parents, who regretted their parents had allowed them to drop out of piano as a kid. While most teachers in town wouldn't consider working with adults, I loved teaching all ages.

The steadily growing clientele added yet another dimension to my life. My confidence soared as I wrote what I wanted to write and lived in the present, knowing full well that so much of making social change is about waiting for moments of readiness, same as in counseling. It was about staying persistent, learning to look for silver linings in the darkest clouds.

Changing systems, like changing continents, is akin to thawing icebergs. This I knew from my experience in Africa. When advocacy work begins paying off, it's usually after years of persistent efforts. I'd seen this in an irrigation project I'd pushed through our mission board and a literacy project that could not be implemented without the required government-produced materials, promised for two years before finally being made unavailable.

Nothing I experienced in Africa, except for the institutional stone-walling with the "Kingsley sexual abuse case" surpassed the degree of stone-walling so many others were now suffering in America as the ranks of survivors grew. Nor did anything I was hearing surprise me.

Not only did the survivors suffer. Their families and friends did. Though I wouldn't know it for several years, one of my own relatives, a faithful Baptist all her life, dropped out of church for quite for a season, deeply disillusioned at how her own friend was being treated after news of the friend's abuse, as a vulnerable adult, by her pastor.

Mainline denominations, from United Methodists to Episcopalians to Universalist Unitarians—it was all the same. Even when they had policies and procedures in place, designed to bring swift justice and healing for congregations, each could be counted on in most cases to defer to the lowest common denominator with folks searching (and usually finding) some flimsy, needle-in-a-haystack excuse for why this case was the exception and somehow should not require them to act to protect the vulnerable; of course, this would ultimately "protect" both perpetrator and the congregation, but leave open the possibility for even more collusion in the denomination when another buddy was faced with allegations. This fiasco then becomes as complicated as the compound sentence I just wrote.

Meanwhile, there remains to this day no standard process even recommended for Southern Baptist congregations, where abusive pastors were usually being protected by secrecy, often in little churches where half the members might be blood relatives. And removing the credentials of the pastor required "court" be held back in whatever congregation had chosen to ordain the man. No matter that he'd been gone from a little home church of his, where he'd grown up as a kid. No matter if the church had disbanded—which made things especially convenient for a perpetrator. After all, how do you convene a group that no longer exists? Yet still that group technically remains the only one that can exercise the responsibility of withdrawing that minister's ordination. Even I didn't know this until I got into this work, having spent all my life in SBC clergy households.

If I stayed committed to going the extra mile, continuing to network, plugging in wherever I could, I still could only hope to see rays of progress sometime in my lifetime. This I knew, especially when it came to the Southern Baptist Convention. Meanwhile, I would fill in the gap left by abusive pastors, not as a rescuer, but as an empowering catalyst. Serving somewhat like a spiritual advisor and attempting to be a healthy role model whenever I managed to informally touch base with my readers, I vowed to become a reality check, a connector, and to grow in spite of all I knew. No turning back—cause going back was not a choice for me. I didn't *want* to go back where I'd been! That made me a loner in my old crowd, but not in this whole new corridor lined with a great cloud of very credible witnesses where I'd be mingling frequently.

This was my vision, already being fulfilled within months of the release of *How Little We Knew*. "This is my story, this is my song" rang from the rafters of my heart, even as I sang the old hymn "Blessed Assurance." One day it dawned on me that this story held a spiritual message that had taken root and was being used in a good way as a part of my own testimony.

"Your life's work," as Lynn, the therapist I began seeing in 1994, wrote much later in a precious note, following a feature article she saw on my work in the Omaha World Herald.

Advocacy work sometimes showed up at my front door. Or in my student clientele when I often became a sounding board and shoulder of support to Catholic parents, when news about abusive area priests became public knowledge during those turbulent days.

Adventures in Writing

Releasing any manuscript for official publication gives me a feeling akin to a little girl letting go of a hundred balloons on a bright sunny day. It's exciting to think of them flying off to unknown far-away places where I've never even dreamed of going, and to think of people I've never met picking them up to give my writing a life of its own.

Rather than fearing what others may think, I'm more eager to get echoes or even discord. I want folks to get back to me for a conversation or to give me valuable feedback and new insights. In my wild imagination, I dare to believe something I say could make a positive change in a life in the future, in ways I'll never know.

Of course, there's the possibility it can all go the other way, too. Statements get misused, same as research does when original designers of the research had totally different expectations. That's what keeps me on my toes. Knowing someone may pick up an intended message even decades after I'm dead and take it to another level in a positive way is what makes this work mind-boggling.

Each time a writer is published, there's the chance some new market will open up through the inspiration of one reader. That's what happened with an organization for survivors of sexual violence, in general. It was called "In Search of Healing."

Jiivani was the only name I ever had for the editor of Survivor Press in Albuquerque used. For all I know, it was a one-woman operation. Being Zen Buddhist didn't hinder Jiivani from asking a former Baptist missionary to write for her about spiritual issues. Neither did it hinder me from enthusiastically agreeing.

Along with a request for a fresh, four-page article, would I agree for her to reprint ten pages she'd selected from *How Little We Knew*? What she wanted was a dramatic conversation Ron and I had with our immediate supervisor, the guy nervously chewing a toothpick while walking an invisible tightrope, trying to cover his own blunders without exposing those of his superiors, who had discredited him to cover their own—which, sum total, did provide some good laughs for those in the mood to chuckle.

What about a photo of me in Africa, preferably sitting in my favorite rocker I'd written about dropping into for solace on my hardest days during my most difficult days. To my surprise, I found exactly the photo she needed—one Ron must have snapped of me one day when I'd just gotten home from an exhilarating women's meeting nearby. I'm also wearing a slight smile with a pensive look of determination such as I often felt during the difficult days, facing intense collusion.

As we worked off and on for the next few weeks, the idea of spiritual role models came out one day in a phone conversation. This ended up being the first words for "In the Spirit of Queen Esther:"

> *If I had been asked six years ago who my Biblical role model might be, I would probably have bitterly answered: "Job's wife." Like that poor lady who had lost everything she held dear, I was ready to "curse God and die."*

On the back page, Jiivani lifted an excerpt, printing it in large, bold letters to describe my spiritual struggles:

> *Today my faith is not the same, but it is there, and it is stronger. I no longer see God as a god of the patriarchal system, but as one who has been trying for years to destroy the very system which continues to victimize women and children repeatedly.*

Next to the photo, the editor copied and framed another excerpt from the book of Esther, as printed in The Jerusalem Bible:

> "Do not suppose that, because you are in the king's palace, you are going to be the one Jew to escape. No; if you persist in remaining silent at such a time, relief and deliverance will come to the Jews from another place, but both you and the House of your father will perish. Who knows? Perhaps you have come to the throne for just such a time as this." Esther 4:14

Twenty years later, as Ron and I discussed the story of Esther more closely, I began to question whether I most admired Esther or her predecessor Queen Vashti. Like many women, I vacillate between the two.

Vashti was headstrong. She was a risk-taker she who had paid a heavy price for her boldness. Without her, Esther would never have succeeded in her mission to free her own people.

Esther knew how to play the system, yet she was much more submissive than Vashti. Still, she kept her predecessor in view. It was Vashti who had scorned and disobeyed the king's expectations in order to keep her own integrity.

For compensation, Jiivani sent half a dozen copies of the large newsletter to share and a beautiful card with a book mark too important to tuck into a book. I quickly distributed the extra copies to women in my local support group and posted the bookmark. "Walk on the wild side!" it said.

How could it possibly get any wilder or more ecumenical than this? It was another one of those beautiful moments of grace that keeps me smiling to this day.

Responses from Nurses

Equally wild, the editor of *The Journal of Christian Nursing*, a magazine about as far on the right as *In Search of Healing* was on the left, placed her own book review of How Little We Knew, in early 1996, near a reprint of the feature article I'd written in the final days of 1994. In addition to her review and my past article, she'd asked (also in 1994) for a second feature article, written specifically for JCN, which I'd actually ended up writing only days after my initial breast cancer diagnosis. Yet the usual lead time required for major magazine editors had pushed the actual publication of all of this to early 1996.

In the review, she reiterated reasons I'd given that nurses might have difficulty empathizing with victims of sexual assault. Personal victimization was one.

This brought a new wave of mail, mostly from appreciative nurses who were themselves survivors. It was a good reminder of how all helping professions are permeated with wounded healers.

Over the next two years, I had an article about various mental health concerns related to nursing in almost every issue of JCN.

Patience and Perseverance

By February, 1996, we experienced a painful snag at Linkup, far more painful than anyone at Emory could imagine. The policies at the university required any outside group be sponsored by a department within the university. Jack's friend at Emory had gone on a diligent search and turned up nothing. Not one department was willing to take on this bunch of renegades, now occasionally making national news.

Was it the size of our group? Jack couldn't say. Linkup's interest would more clearly fall under the jurisdiction of another department of study, several department heads at Emory declared. Ethics didn't want to take us on any more than Religion, Social Work, or Psychology.

Couldn't they all work together to co-sponsor the event, making history in the process? I asked. What a story that would make for the media! Baptists extending wide-open arms to Catholic refugees from all over the world!

No, things were set up for one department to be responsible, Jack was told. There was absolutely no interest to be found. Nobody cared to ask that an exception be made at Emory. Too risky to make history in this situation perhaps? Hard to say, but I couldn't help wondering. Whatever the logic, this felt to those of us in leadership at Linkup as an enormous blow, another example of "pass the buck," one of the most popular games of collusion.

Few of us in the movement had lucrative careers. Among the few with upper middle incomes, most everyone was financially strapped due to enormous therapy costs, which was the major reason survivors were turning to lawyers. So even with donated space for meeting and housing, there were many more members longing to come to life-saving gatherings than could afford to get there. Having to pass along catering expenses and rental fees to participants, already trying to scrape up transportation and motel rooms, naturally cut deeply into attendance.

What amazed us, however, was how steady the numbers remained. This served as a two-fold statement about the creativity of desperate survivors to prioritize and give sacrificially, as well as the growing number of spiritual refugees seeing an oasis of help and support, yet unable to quite reach it physically, after living in isolation for so long. It was as sad as any refugee crisis I'd witnessed in Africa, where death was accepted as inevitable. In this case, individuals were asked to go on living while surrounded for the rest of their lives by callousness and massive apathy.

Yet help was coming through a different media, that few even knew about. A gift from God was about to arrive—something I knew absolutely nothing about, but would experience as revolutionary as much as anybody I knew. It would also become the worst nightmare for anyone attempting to hide "precious information" about abuse in institutions worldwide .... and not just in the religious world, but in colleges and universities, public schools, the military, throughout the corporate world and even across Washington, D. C. to the White House. Nothing would ever be the same.

This history we were already making was about to take on a new life, bringing hope to the isolated and more work than any of us, already overwhelmed in our volunteer work, could imagine! The dawning was turning to noonday bright.

Chapter 20
Outer Limits

The fear, that's the stuff that still comes back in nightmares, that's the stuff that haunts you," Andrew Collins, Australian survivor speaking to journalist Margaret Burin*

One of the worst things about managing serpents is how they pop up, demanding attention, anytime we assume we're done with them, even long after experts seem to believe we *should* be. Well, who are the real experts and what do they know?

By summer's start, with an increasing number of calls coming in for potential students, I realized one art supported the other. It was a balancing act, one that had me soaring in both endeavors.

Yet nothing could surpass the immense joy of becoming a grandmother for the first time. Everything went quite smoothly as we welcomed a bouncing, dark-headed baby boy named Micah into our family in July.

Everything also checked out fine during a routine visit to my oncologist days soon after returning to Iowa. That's what the receptionist reminded me three weeks later, hearing the tremble in my voice as I asked how soon I could get back in.

"No problem. Better to be safe than sorry," replied the kind lady who, no doubt, had soothed many a frightened soul in the past. "We'll see you in the morning."

"Those three tiny lumps don't look like any cancer I've ever seen," my oncologist assured me. "Malignancies on the surface of an incision line typically show up like a pimple." He paused, giving me his usual comforting smile. "Just for your peace of mind, we'll get you in for a biopsy. I'll see you when that's done."

By this time, I'd done my homework on choice of surgeons. With the oncologist's blessing, I turned to the most skilled breast cancer surgeon in the metro. She gave me the same assessment. "But better safe than sorry," she added, with a shrug.

"I've never seen anything like this!" exclaimed the surgeon a month later, as Ron and I sat in her office, listening to her ranting, as if I was the problem instead of the freakish tissue she couldn't conquer. For four weeks, she'd been saying the same thing following each pathology report coming in from the last excision. Two of the exploratory surgeries had been under general anesthetic in the hospital's outpatient department. Still, her expertise had failed to locate "clear margins" all round the menacing tissue.

Even more disturbing, with my oncologist off on vacation, the surgeon called in half a dozen other experts. No two could agree on how to proceed or what concoction of "snake oil" was needed whenever this mysterious creature was finally extracted in its entirety. When that might be was anybody's guess.

I thought back to the first surgeon. She'd said I was the luckiest woman in the world since I was getting by without even radiation or chemo.

"No," I wanted to say. "Give me a break! The luckiest are those like you who have never had cancer."

Now, the most popular breast cancer surgeon around, was saying the opposite as the first. The tiny fingers of this mysterious monster were spreading out, making a mockery of all the best-educated guessers in the area.

"Women who have recurrences so soon after the original diagnosis don't usually have a good prognosis. We've got to hurry and get something done! There's no telling where this thing already is in your system!" she cried as I sat quietly, refusing to panic.

Trusting my gut, I'd made a call that morning to Rochester, Minnesota. They were willing to see me as a walk-in as soon as we arrived, I told her. It was time to explore other options.

Minutes after entering the consultation room at Mayo the next morning, I knew I'd made a wise decision. In their eyes, this was no mystery. Had I come to them five weeks earlier, I would have been done with one trip to the operating room, thanks to their system, with laboratories standing by for fast turnaround reports.

Three days later, we were on our way home with great news. While the original cells had mutated and become much more aggressive, the risk of doing any chemo, in the opinion of this team of experts, still outweighed any likely benefits. A full course of radiation was all they recommended.

"Just for your peace of mind," the discharging physician told me, "this type of recurrence isn't because your immune system is down. In fact, with no sign of metastasis, the opposite is true. Until we can find a way to treat cancer without ever cutting into it, we'll continue seeing this rare type of recurrence in a small percentage of patients. Go home and be well."

That message was the best "medicine" of all. For weeks, unlike with the original diagnosis, I'd beat myself up, wondering about a remark made by a casual acquaintance, suggesting the recurrence was my fault. I should have been resting more and not working so hard, in spite of the fulfillment I was finding in advocacy writing.

Not until I got to Chicago ten days later did I realize how physically and emotionally drained I was. Yet Linkup was just what I needed to renew my spirits as I prepared for three months of radiation.

This year, instead of being the cheer leader for others, I was happy to be on the receiving end. So I was sitting back, letting people come to me, when an animated woman rushed over and began conversing as if we'd already met.

Indeed we had, she told me. She'd purchased How Little We Knew a year earlier and had been searching for me ever since.

"Why aren't you on the Worldwide Web yet?" she blurted out before launching into something about another new-fangled thing called "e-mail," which sounded more like science fiction.

Yet the more she talked, the more interested I became.

Talk about "doing world missions!" I thought. If what she was describing was true, there would be no limit to the possibilities for my current mission. Of course, it would be impossible to reach rural Africa. The majority there didn't even have access to a telephone. Now, they'd be left out entirely. I didn't say any of this aloud, of course. I only listened as her sales speech seemed to be taking on ridiculous proportions.

"I hardly go to my mailbox now. Everything important comes to me as I sit in my house! Do it!" she urged. "Believe me, it will change everything!"

First I took a deep breath. Then, I thanked her. I'd look into all this when I could find the time, money, and energy to get back on the advocacy track, I said. Right now, breast cancer was draining me of all three.

Sudden Disconnections

With every issue of "The Missing Link" there were more notices about new cases than ever. Typically, we published copies of newspaper clips or some official document giving location, perpetrator's name, number who had come forward, what legal actions may have been taken, perhaps a phone number for others with information to call.

Tom joked about needing to get another dining table for the overflow—if only he had a larger dining room. With this in mind, I decided to call the editor. If he needed me to shorten the "Reconnections" column to fit the allotted space, I'd need to know right away.

As usual, he wasn't answering his phone, and I wondered, as always, if he picked up messages at all since he didn't return many. Still, I left one, explaining I was putting my latest contribution for "Reconnections" in the mail. If he needed something shorter this time, he should call and we'd talk about how to eliminate part of it.

I was both shocked and furious three weeks later when the next issue of the newsletter arrived. My column was missing! Since this one was time-sensitive, it couldn't be saved for a future issue. I'd worked extra hard on it for weeks in between my teaching and daily trips across the metro for radiation.

When Tom called later that week, telling me how little sleep he was getting, I asked if he'd made any progress at getting some shift work arranged to give him relief. I was truly worried about him.

No, he told me, same as he had several times in the past few months. He'd thought it over since we last talked and decided he wasn't comfortable doing that. Too hard to know who he could trust to do anything. Some he thought he could trust in other matters hadn't come through in the end.

"Tom, I know none of us can do the job like you. I also know if you keep this up, not taking care of yourself, you're going to get sick and there'll be nobody to pick up the slack. Please think about delegating," I urged.

For the first time since we met, he was argumentative. Still, I was persistent. This wasn't just about him. Who was taking calls when he was away?

Usually, nobody, he admitted. The answering machine picked up until it got full.

What if someone desperate needed help during those times?   I begged him to give the matter more consideration.

I also needed him to know how disappointed I was because of the article not being published. I'd tried again to call the editor and couldn't get through. Would he try and get back to me when he could find time?

To my surprise, he agreed to call immediately and was back within minutes. The editor couldn't remember receiving a thing. No matter, Tom said. With so many new cases to post, he wouldn't have had space to print it, anyway.

Momentarily, I found myself reflecting silently on Jeanne Miller's philosophy. Would she suggest, as I just had, that surely the notices could be reduced in size to allow room for at least a few words of encouragement in the midst of overwhelming evidence of evil?   With communication issues like this, what would keep this from happening again?

Inwardly irate and filled with self-pity, I struggled hard to control my temper. Trust issues were now on my front burner. Did these guys even care how much time I'd wasted on that article?   Considering I'd never missed a previous deadline, wasn't it only fair I be notified if the column hadn't arrived in a timely manner?

How I wish we could go back and start that conversation over! Or that I would have found a way to pull back from the abyss I was standing on. We were all stressed, trying to pick up the pieces from dysfunctional religion. Our reserves spent. What occurred merely reflected that, I knew, even as I hung up.

Immensely frustrated and unsure of where I fit in anymore, I pulled out of Linkup with that one phone call, thinking perhaps I'd get back as I regained my strength. Yet I never did. I should have. Standing helplessly by, Ron was as disappointed with me as I was with the situation. Today I'm quite sure I would have made a different choice.

I can hear some of my old friends saying: "Well, when God closes a door, He opens a window."

God had nothing to do with this. No more than when churches collude with the evil of sexual abuse.

Though I had good reason to be upset, closing those doors that day wasn't all my doing, but I'd done the final slamming. I didn't have half the personal baggage these guys did with all the childhood stuff they were carrying. Yet I, too, have my limits.

Actually, I'm amazed that any survivor organization endures. For those wishing to find an illustration of the grace of God, this might be a good place to start.

Devastating Outcomes

A year later, I longed to wave a magic wand filled with pixie dust over the head of this young man immensely devoted to the cause, who had done so much for me and a multitude of others.

Tom had metastatic colon cancer. I knew he would put up a fight to the end, and he did—for five long years until a few weeks after the Boston Globe story broke.

He already had that diagnosis when he went on Frontline. Phil Saviano knew this from the newsletter. Yet nobody could have guessed during that 1998 PBS appearance. That day this mighty role model was still so full of life.

Phil, now well into remission from AIDS, drew strength from Tom in that moment. He got up, got going, and kept going back into the Boston Globe, refusing to be discounted.

In stature, Tom was closer to Zaccheus than most priests. Yet he was a giant in spirit. It was a privilege just to stand in his shadow. I thought of him constantly during the movie, laughing with him at parts only insiders of the story could find amusing, even as another part of me grieved our broken relationship and all it represented.

Inspiration Born Anew

Soon after my last conversation with Tom, I got a call from a seventy-five-year-old man who had just lost his wife to breast cancer.

"Do you think there is any hope for me?" he asked. "Is it still possible I could learn to play the piano at my age?"

I assured him it was, but I'd need to call him back. I wasn't sure I could work him into my schedule, I fibbed.

Not knowing this old fellow, I was naturally inclined to check him out before giving him an answer. Years later, I would tell him as we laughed over that first encounter.

"Oh, you'll have the time of your life! Hugh is a delight!" declared one of my colleagues that Hugh told me would vouch for him. "Poor guy lost his wife from breast cancer not long ago, so I'm sure he needs something to keep him busy."

Knowing he needed time to grieve his own losses, I didn't dare tell him where I was at this fragile moment in my own recovery from the same disease. He had enough to worry about.

I soon learned he was a retired electrical engineer, who'd invented a life-saving flare used in World War II that allowed sailors lost for days to be found on the open sea. In my estimation, that was what he should be most remembered for. It didn't turn out that way.

For the next fourteen years, he made great weekly strides in piano, practicing night and day despite his struggle with Parkinson's and extensive skin cancer. Like all survivors who manage to thrive, he found little time to wallow in sorrow. After sideswiping a parked car on a busy city street, he voluntarily turned in his driver's license and made an appointment to see his doctor.

"If you'll save my spot, I'll plan to be back in six weeks," he promised at his next lesson, only days before checking into the hospital for open heart surgery. "Doc says I'm a high risk for this procedure at eighty-five, but I figure it's worth the risk. Why would I want to give up having fun and sit around the house at my age?" He hesitated. "But just in case I don't survive, I want you to know that, to me, it's worth the risk. I'm not about to give up my freedom yet. I'm having too much fun."

True to his word, he was back in six weeks, ready to pick up right where he left off, inspiring not just people of his own generation, but the youngest of my students, who couldn't wait to see what he'd do at each recital.

In the end, Hugh Marshall died of cancer himself, at 90. As an encore, he played the piano for his own funeral—via a video his daughter had recorded for other purposes.

"I'll tell you what I always tell my piano teacher," he said to his grieving audience, as he looked out over the crowd with his hands on the keyboard in front of him. "When I play, you never know what you're going to get, but here goes." After several bars of impressive jazz, he hit a sour note and abruptly turned back to face his audience without missing a beat.

"I warned you."

From that, he was off to his most favorite, Beethoven's "Moonlight Sonata," as those of us who mourned smiled through our tears.

Much to my surprise, his daughter stacked his trophies beside his casket. Almost touching his left arm, was a laminated full-page article published several years earlier in the local paper, reminding visitors how he'd re-invented himself and shared his time and music all over the city.

Hugh was a shining example of how to manage serpents. To me, he serves also as an example of how it's entirely possible for "old dogs" to learn new ways of doing things—perhaps even those at the Vatican, who've had too many tricks up their sleeves for far too long.

Memories of people like Hugh inspire me to dream on.

*****

* http://www.abc.net.au/news/2015-05-19/child-abuse-royal-commission-ballarat-victims-share-accounts/6477564

Chapter 21
Ethical and Unethical Dilemmas

Shortly before Christmas, 1996, a welcome note arrived from Dr. Foy Valentine, a well-known Baptist I'd admired since childhood and long before I even learned what an "ethicist" is expected to study. For decades, this man had been considered a forward-thinking, moral compass—not just for Baptists, but for many Christians. Everything he did as head of the SBC's Christian Life Commission, over the three decades he'd held that position, involved promoting justice or making wise personal choices for the sake of character building.

It was his popular series of booklets, each title starting with "Why I Don't," that got many teens thinking through cutting-edge issues that were starting to confront America's youth on an epidemic scale after World War II. Some challenges, like saying "no" to drugs or gambling, our sheltered parents had never faced as kids. Yet, in clear, concise statements, Valentine captured logical reasons, not platitudes, for avoiding many of the vices now commonly considered to be endangerments to health, though most Baptists simply called these "sinful" in that day.

If there were drugs in the schools of Ft. Worth, I would never have recognized them without the help of this practical tool. Now, we had *reasons* for old, unwritten taboos many parents had once been able to enforce with mere authoritarianism. For instance, "Why I Don't Smoke" was presented as a health issue, not just a "nasty habit." Valentine was quick to remind youth that the human body was a "temple of the Holy Spirit," and desecrating a temple wasn't only sinful in this case, it was self-destructive.

In that little series, everything was laid out in black and white, with each ethical dilemma placed under a separate, bright green cover, stapled around eight to ten pages of logic. That way, as long as readers paid close attention to the titles, it was easy to avoid mixing up all the rules and reasoning.

How fast things were changing from one generation to the next was obvious. Dancing and swearing still warranted considerable attention in this series; but some topics my grandparents would have included, like card playing and "women not dressing in men's apparel," (wearing trousers or jeans) didn't make the list.

Historically, Baptists have been good at pretending to "say no" to vices. Saying yes to social justice is another matter. Drumming up scriptural excuses for what is nothing but bigotry and oppression to most upstanding citizens today has often rested as acceptable "proof." These "divine orders" work to those who hold fast to "logical" and convenient old traditions that die hard. For literalists, who believe there are no errors in the Bible, even despite translations over centuries, these sprigs referring to things that applied in the context of yore stand to legitimately trump science if there appears to be a conflict on what's considered a moral issue.

In 1968, the same year Ron and I began working hard against the resistance to integrate Baptist churches in New Orleans, this ethicist, the age of my father, persuaded the Convention to adopt a very forward-thinking statement, confessing that the entire nation had allowed "cultural practices to persist," depriving American blacks and other races of many opportunities, which he spelled out, saying these practices had "damaged the personhood of blacks and whites alike."

After almost a decade in Africa and another in transition to a new denomination, I'd not kept up with Who's Who in Southern Baptist Leadership. Considering all the tumbling and turning from the political and theological squabbles, doing so would have been a full-time job for anyone. I didn't even know if Foy Valentine was still alive 'til he re-surfaced for me in 1996.

Now, he was editor of a new journal, Christian Ethics Today, according to Joe Trull, who suggested I write a query about getting published in it. When an acceptance letter came, I eagerly studied sample issues included. They were filled with long articles, many by scholars, to promote serious thought and more progressive views on cutting-edge issues. It was all in line with the person I knew this beloved editor to be.

To be asked to write a paragraph for this publication was quite an honor. Yet Foy Valentine was asking me to send him a minimum of 4000 words on the topic of my expertise, clergy sexual abuse. I was overjoyed. This would be the equivalent of a half dozen of my Baptists Today articles.

"Don't mince words," he instructed. "Do a thorough job."

Immediately I settled on a title: "Church Secrets We Dare Not Keep," as new spurts of energy emerged in between house calls to my students and my final weeks of radiation. While knitting everything together over the course of two weeks, I kept thinking, "I must be dreaming." This was a huge project that I assumed would only "pay" with the by-line promised in the acceptance letter. Not a problem for me. For Foy Valentine, I'd gladly write for free.

Feeling as confident as ever in my life, I faxed the manuscript in shortly before Christmas and returned home to wrap the first baby toys we'd had under our tree in two decades.

"What a complicated piece of work this life has turned out to be!" I sang to myself. The song right off Bette Rod's CD, "Pieces" [1], certainly fit the hour as much as the carols on the radio that year.

Hitting Bottom

A second note from the editor came in early January.

He liked the article. Nice to get something he didn't have to edit, said he. There was only *one* small problem.

I'd failed to show a "continuum of blame" for the various female victims I'd written about, all good friends of mine, who came from around the country to Iowa each year. Their nine stories covered the first 25% of the article. Their ages at the time of their abuse ranged from a preschooler to an adult congregant, whose teenage daughter was also a victim of the same perpetrator.

Though the note was disturbing, I assumed this role model of mine simply had limited understanding about the ethics of adult-pastoral relationships. Since he was past seventy, I could give him the benefit of the doubt, even admitting I'd never considered this aspect of the abuse spectrum myself until five years ago. It was something I understood now, thanks to Marie Fortune and the many women I'd met whose lives had been far more seriously impacted, in some ways, than some of my very young patients who had experienced sexual abuse in childhood, but had benefited from having fairly early interventions. This, thanks to supportive parents and good therapy.

No need to waste time, I told myself, as I picked up the phone and heard the voice, for the first time, of this man I so respected. Our conversation quickly went from cordial to awful to worse. Not only did he hold every adult woman partially responsible for her pastor crossing sexual boundaries, even the smallest child had done something to invite her abuse.

"What!" I exclaimed. "Surely you don't mean this!"

He certainly did, he assured me. "I've handled plenty of cases throughout my ministry, and every single woman *knew* she'd been partially to blame."

"Dr. Valentine," I said. "If you believe this, I assume you think even a woman who was assaulted, like I was, is to blame? Did you not read what I wrote of my story in Baptists Today?"

"Why, I certainly do think so! Don't you?" he replied, totally ignoring my second question.

I took a deep breath, grateful for a technique Ron had passed along from pastoral counseling. Pretending to be "the little professor" allowed me instantly to step back and externalize this disturbing revelation to gain perspective and a healthy, emotional distance before choosing a response.

"NO!" I literally yelled before returning to a well-modulated voice. "I certainly do not, and I cannot imagine how a man of your status and education could either. You can't possibly know my story well enough to make such a suggestion unless you've read it all. I sort of assumed you had."

Of course, I couldn't possibly make such an assumption. Since he clearly was confident he was being ethical in this, why should he care to know my story or hear what I had to say about anything else? Yet I wanted to make the point—he, of all Baptist men *should* have and *could* have.

Most horrifying of all was his claim to have "handled" many cases of clergy sexual misconduct over his lifetime. I'm sure he had—manhandled them, that is. Now, he was viewing this new set of stories through the lens of his perception. How many souls had left his counsel more troubled than they'd come?

This greatly-admired ethicist was far from finished with his condescension. "Dee, I've written several books. Have you read all of mine?" he returned sarcastically, ending the conversation for all practical purposes.

I was withdrawing the article, for he'd left me no choice, I declared seconds before beginning slowly to lower the receiver.

"Wait! Don't hang up!" he urged. "What if you send me as much as you feel you need to write to explain your reasoning? If it works for me, I'll considering printing it all."

I agreed—only to have the opportunity to speak my mind, though I had no reason to hope I'd ever change this old man's headstrong opinion.

What a waste of time! Why should I even bother, I asked myself. I'd wasted far more time with this enormous project than I had on the Linkup article that never got into print either.

Fighting the temptation to give up for good, I reached for a file containing the names and contact info for several Baptist Women in Ministry from the Little Rock conference, ran my finger down the list and soon found the woman I wanted to talk to. Herself a former missionary, the two of us had chatted all through supper one evening at the conference; and I felt totally affirmed by her for the work I was doing. Certain she'd be shocked, but supportive, I explained what had just occurred.

"Well, I totally agree with Foy," she declared with certainty.

"What! Surely you aren't saying...."

"Yes, I am," she interrupted. "Even the smallest child crawling up into a man's lap should know better! Maybe you need to talk to a relative of mine. She's a psychotherapist who often counsels Baptist missionaries herself. I'm pretty sure she would agree with me. Just tell her I recommended you talk to her."

At this point, hearing another Baptist, even a female psychotherapist, telling me why she believes a child should be blamed for her own abuse wouldn't have surprised me. I also knew it wasn't going to blow me away any further. If she counseled missionaries, this could be a very informative conversation, at least. So, I dialed in and braced myself for Round Three.

Which turned out to be a Charm! In fact, this dear woman seemed to be as thrilled to hear from me as I was to have my faith restored in humanity.

After explaining my reason for calling, we had a lovely conversation about many things I wouldn't dare write—not only about issues of sexual abuse at the mission board, but about more general, inadequately-addressed issues of missionary dysfunction, which she'd come to realize through her professional experience. The most interesting was a story she thought was common knowledge because it was in the public domain.

A missionary was strongly suspected of having murdered his wife on the exact road that I'd travelled many times, going down an escarpment toward Rift Valley Academy, the very school our own children had attended as teenagers.

Just as with Bert Kae-Je on that mountain in West Virginia five years earlier, our hearts melded together. In a hand-written follow-up letter, she told me: "I'll be retiring soon. And when I do, I may not stay a Baptist. But you can't quote me on that—not yet, anyway!"

I haven't—until now.

The most welcome news in that precious epistle was the act of advocacy the lady took on by going in to see Dr. Smith, the Board's family consultant, to talk to the man who had acted as midwife for our demise. She reported back that Smith told her there had been some major changes in how they handled cases now, all because of our persistence. And he asked she convey that to me.

I took the news with a grain of salt. A simple "I blew it. We all blew it." would have done the trick very well if only he'd had the courtesy to put it in writing or pick up the phone to say so, Ron and I agreed. The two of us have gone back repeatedly since to that important milestone on our journey, grateful to have simply had someone willing to speak on our behalf.

What I couldn't tell the psychologist, for I didn't yet know myself, was something buried so deeply inside Ron that he never told *me* until very recently. In 1988, nine years before we realized anyone cared enough to speak on our behalf, while Ron was in Richmond, the military man sent him to see Smith, who then ordered Ron to see a psychiatrist, telling him: "You're too angry to be a missionary."

Ron had been stuck in that story all these years, never showing himself as the victor. Even in 2016, when he relayed the complete story to me, he still did not see the humor I did to think of him turning to this arrogant "counselor" and saying: "OK, Truman. I'll go if you will …. Come on, let's go together, and we'll let the psychiatrist sort this whole mess out." He did so under the assumption no bonafide psychiatrist would fault him for his stand nor fail to validate his anger. Neither would many men in Ron's position have had the guts to do what he did. It was totally out of character for him, something I wish he had been able to be proud of. Instead what followed drove him further into shame that I didn't understand. Nor did he understand for twenty-eight years, until I finally saw him smile as the realization hit him like a beautiful, new skin graft for his soul after he spoke this truth that thus far had been unspeakable.

Smith had nothing more to say to Ron, of course. This ended the conversation, clarifying everything. The next communication from Richmond was the letter of probation that put the final nail in our missionary-career coffins. We simply could not be "fixed" nor could either of us be cajoled into complete silence.

Back again to 1997, as the depth of systemic collusion sank in deeper after those important phone calls, I felt like I had a four-ton elephant sitting on my lap. I kept thinking of all the families and offenders Valentine's unwise counsel had left improperly attended, going on to multiply this by the thousands of other less educated and less prestigious men who had done likewise—men who could have been taught by an expert in ethics during seminary to do the right thing, yet had obviously been led in the opposite direction. I also wondered how many deeply troubled families had gotten less than the optimal care they needed before meeting with disasters far worse than our own.

Ron seemed even more devastated than I. It was hard to imagine being in his shoes, knowing what he knew and being a part of a profession with so little integrity. This was long-standing, purposeful incompetence from the top down! We worked hard at building fun and diversion into our lives, fighting to keep a cloud of hopelessness from settling in permanently. We had to keep hope alive for ourselves and so many others who were finding their ways out of isolation and into our hearts.

While there was no solid evidence and nobody yet wanted to suggest resistance was greater in theologically conservative denominations, it was obvious to me it was. As I saw it, this was part of the issue with Catholics—the resistance to change put them in the highly-conservative theological camp, especially when it came to matters that appeared to be primarily about gender or their definition of "sexual deviancy" in others, ignoring the criminal deviancy of the sexual abuse of even minors.

Thanks to Sarah Rieth, I discovered validation from the work of James Poling[2] about this time. He's a scholar with southern roots who has long seen strong links in conservative theology, connecting misogyny to sexual violence. He humbly admits that his own acculturation is something he has been forced to face as he's laid bare his own ignorance and let

survivors teach him to see the church in a way that he was transformed—
not by the church, but by what he came to see about the church's role in
perpetuating these problems. He also speaks candidly of the way the
church has promoted a culture of sexual violence that has especially
impacted African-American due to a combination of racial and sexual
oppression stemming from white male patriarchs who refuse to change
their biases.[2]   Yet I found little interest among even moderate Southern
Baptists in a now-liberal theologian's suggestions on this topic.

Quakers and Mennonites, far ahead in acknowledging abuse of power
in their own circles, were most welcoming. Their editors were interested
more in empowering survivors and advocates with coping skills and
support, giving them freedom to make their own decisions as they worked
to integrate their personal experience into the larger story survivors of any
trauma are always "writing" as they live on. This was my approach
whenever I accepted an invitation to write for any small newsletter.

While I'd expected resistance in conservative circles like Missouri
Synod and Southern Baptists, I'd not been prepared for it in mainline
circles[3]. With the former groups, the denial that abuse even existed on a
widespread scale among them was still strongly denied. Whereas in more
moderate to liberal circles, the log in the eye of clerics was a denial about
the extent of *collusion* that still remained. United Methodists, leaders of the
Evangelical Lutheran Church of America, and even the United Church of
Christ, Marie Fortune's own denomination, quickly tired of hearing about
something they'd hardly gotten to first base in addressing.

Staying focused on reality was as hard for bystanders as it was for
most survivors who had kept secrets suppressed for decades for far more
personal reasons. Yet bystanders had difficulty seeing the parallels.
Survivors, far ahead in the process, easily saw.

Complications of Advocacy

Advocates for any worthy, but unpopular, cause must have a good
understanding of power dynamics, how they can flip back and forth at the
most unexpected times and how, with creativity, the messenger can keep
the scale balanced. "Powerful people empower others," Rev. Dr. Sharon
Ellis Davis reminds us.[4]

When a cleric abuses someone, the victim is disempowered internally. Ultimately, there's a sense of being demoted. When the disempowered regain their power, they confound the powerful, creatively re-writing the story.

Naturally, clerics do not want to go through the disempowering process. It's humiliating. They feel afflicted by prophetic, well-articulated messages. Ironically, the most effective are delivered by soft-spoken individuals, also speaking with authority and confidence that has a way of challenging privilege. Yet it's hard, even for men like David Clohessy, who has served as the leader and professional spokesperson for SNAP. Or Tom Doyle, who's been speaking to bishops, even decades after being shot down. Yet it's especially hard for a person who is also speaking with another kind of authority, telling his or her own story for the first time.

Among the first questions an aspiring advocate needs to ask: "What talents, life experiences or resources do I have that can serve as assets? How do I intend to take care of myself? What do I want my life to look like from here on out? What's realistic? How can my past, if I choose to reveal it, be used against me or the cause I represent?

There is a big dilemma for those of us who've experienced sexual harassment or other forms of abuse in any professional role, especially in the church. Going totally public can be costly, inviting stereotypes from poorly-informed individuals. On the other hand, there is a downside in acting as a professional who is also a totally closeted survivor. Opportunities may be missed for the story to be used for the good of others, either to inspire or educate.

Ron learned long ago, in the pastorate, that by revealing personal hurts and vulnerability, he was more likely to have others sharing their own. Doing so always carries risk that many members of the profession are very hesitant to take at all.

While in any professional role that allows them to speak or write with authority on issues of abuse, the vast majority of my contacts of both genders choose not to reveal such a history. Many choose instead to speak out only about consequences of marginalization they've faced from speaking merely as advocates. There are often no good choices in this work. Deciding what to say, when to say it, and how—all of these require contemplation—not only at the onset of advocacy, but at every step of the game.

Pamela Cooper-White is an ordained clergywoman, a professor of psychology and religion at Union Seminary, a scholar and outstanding writer, who admits to having experienced more than one incident of gender-based victimization. She does this in what I believe to be the best educational source on all forms of gender-based violence, The Cry of Tamar.[5]

For those who choose to keep personal histories hidden away completely, it's best to be prepared for the unexpected. What happens when someone asks: "What gives you so much passion for this cause? Were you once a victim yourself?" Inevitably, this question does come up. I've heard it posed in public to more than one advocate who ends up stammering around, having chosen "only" to be an advocate. So it's good to think ahead because inappropriate questions like this will come to anyone who is passionate. Some choose to avoid a direct answer, saying: "I know many with these issues, so it's one I care about deeply."

I do not advise either way. This was never a decision I wrestled with. What I've done, writing openly with a great deal of transparency, is a reflection of my personality. It's also how I've lived my life—not that I feel the need to put everything out in the open. Yet, one part of my Baptist upbringing that's stuck has been that we are called to "bear witness." This is an exercise, I've come to understand, means sharing both the good news and the hope that lies within us that overcoming, as a community, is possible in all things.

"This is my story. This is my song." And I was sticking to it.

The Unexpected Call

On a cold, Saturday evening in January, 1997, Ron was in his basement office of the parsonage, putting last-minute touches on his sermon, when the phone rang. Over the sound of the vacuum cleaner I was operating on the upper level, he shouted: "Dee, it's Foy Valentine!"

By the time I'd pulled the cord on the vacuum, Ron was literally on his knees, he later told me. He couldn't imagine anything good coming from that old man. Neither could I. What was he doing, interrupting our lives on a Saturday night?

Cordial from start to finish, as if we'd never had a word of disagreement, without a word of apology, he wanted to know if I'd allow him to publish not only the original, but the 500 words I'd sent after the phone call, in which I'd explained why his "partial-blame" theory wasn't going to fly. Besides that, he was printing an additional article by a psychologist, also a former missionary, to specifically explain why no adults could be blamed for abuse by a minister.

"I've wrestled with lots of issues in my lifetime, but none as much as this one. In fact, I've held up the whole issue of this journal in the process," he humbly told me. "But I've come around. I can see it all clearly now. I need to get it out Monday morning, so I need your permission, which is why I called so late on a Saturday night."

"Not so fast," I said. This ball was in my court now. If he really wanted this article, he'd play by my terms. "I want to see the full galleys, allowing me to check every word. If you FAX it to me Monday morning, I'll get back to you as soon as I can."

Not for one second did I trust what I was hearing. I had no reason to. Perhaps this was as close as he knew how to get to an apology. The important thing was to get that article out where it needed to be. It was too important to be wasted.

For the rest of the weekend, I was thinking: "This all sounds too good to be true. Something's fishy here."

It wasn't. When I called to give final approval on Monday morning, I still didn't believe him when he said, "Check's in the mail." I laughed out loud.

He wasn't kidding. What he sent didn't cover the mental anguish he'd caused. Yet, it was enough to pay for a year's supply of bread with plenty of butter to top it off.

It's difficult to not take resistance personally, especially when it's dished out so blatantly by a man of such stature. Yet I realized that winter I'd come a lot further at depersonalizing than I thought possible. Even more important, the true advocate I'd found in the process, the professional who had pledged her ongoing support .... she was priceless.

*****

[1] You can hear samples from Bette Rod's CD "Pieces" and find ordering info at http://www.cdbaby.com/cd/betterod Or listen to the entire Rally Song at http://www.takecourage.org/rallysong.htm

[2] See James Newton Poling's The Abuse of Power: A Theoloical Problem (Abingdon Press, 1991)

[3] Mainline congregations, also often referred to as mainstream churches, were historically the majority of Christians in America until the mid-twentieth century when shortly after World War II, there was a shift toward more conservative Christianity, where the sum of fundamentalist and charismatic groups began to outgrow the mainline denominations. Members of mainline churches made up the bulk of the founders of America. There is much confusion about where to draw the line today when many mainline congregations are as equally filled with moderate evangelicals as with very socially liberal Christians. While the core of mainline denominations in the United States were what is commonly called the Seven Sisters of American Protestantism. The seven commonly known are United Methodists (UMC), Evangelical Lutherans (ELCA), Presbyterian (PCUSA), Episcopalian (TEC), American Baptists (ABC), United Church of Christ (UCC) and Disciples of Christ (also commonly referred to simply as "The Christian Church," to add to the confusion that Catholics have understandably of Protestantism), there are other smaller mainline denominations of 100,000 or fewer members, such as Quakers and the fairly-new Cooperative Baptist Fellowship (CBF) mentioned frequently in this text.

As if this is not mind-boggling enough already, there are approximately 150 different Baptist denominations, with the Southern Baptist Convention (SBC) being the largest by far (approximately 15 million). Yet it is not the oldest. In fact, the SBC was the southern branch of what was often referred to as "Northern Baptists" during the Civil War era and on into the 20th century, yet historically has also been known as American Baptists. Both the ABC and CBF, which formed after the SBC "conservative resurgence" that culminated in 1988, the year of the author's forced resignation, are dwarfs in comparison to the SBC. The nearest denomination in size to the SBC is UMC, which is less than half the size of the SBC today.

[4] For more information on Davis' webinar "Sexual Abuse in the Black Church," co-presented by Rev. K. Ray Hill, see http://www.faithtrustinstitute.org/training/events/701A0000000WtHiIAK

[5] Cooper-White, Pamela, 2012, The Cry of Tamar: Violence against Women and the Church's Response, 2nd edition, Fortress Press.

Chapter 22
Wonders of the World-Wide Web

Laughter *is* a good medicine. Recently, it even helped me get through one of those obstinate recorded greetings spoken faithfully by a kind-sounding dummy who seems designed to keep consumers from finding a live person on the phone.

Desperate—this time with PayPal, due to a matter I assumed would be simple, I resorted to laughing out loud after multiple attempts to get a live person. Instantly, the dummy stopped talking and gave me what I wanted. You should try it.

Laughter was also very useful in the early days of the Web, when there was only one way for an amateur like me to set up a website. Commercial sites, offering a variety of prepared templates, weren't even available. Determined to succeed somehow, after forking out the small fortune (compared to today's prices) that was needed for any device sophisticated enough to access the Web, I certainly didn't have funds to hire help.

Running down to the book store, I hoped to find anything like "Websites for Dummies." Did I ever find a selection! Right inside the front door was a table loaded with such manuals, all with the word "simple" splashed somewhere across the cover—along with an acronym I'd never heard of: what on earth was HTML? The two together, I decided as soon as I got passed the covers, was nothing but an oxymoron, designed only to sell books. What was inside had me laughing out loud before I got to the counter. I might as well have been trying to read Greek.

After selecting a text with lots of illustrations, I rushed back home to find Ron congratulating himself. Not only had he learned to turn on our new toy, he was in process of establishing a dial-up service. From that point until the present, I was on my own when it came to anything much having to do with internet navigation; and most everything I've learned has been the hard way—trial and error, along with some wonderful mentors like our friend Karl, who had allowed me to watch over his shoulder for a few minutes a year earlier.

Anyone born in the 21st century may have difficulty imagining this, but my vague understanding of how to use a search engine was less than any intelligent five-year-old today. Imagine my ultimate delight in getting unexpected results the first time, moments after entering only two words: "clergy" and "abuse!"

Magically, what seemed to be a colorless photo of a single page appeared as the only result. That drab photo-static copy of a single page of resources was like finding a pot of gold at the end of the rainbow. Twice as long as anything I'd yet found on the topic of abusive clergy in all of my searching. Who would go to this trouble, I wondered? And how on earth did somebody ever get a photo onto a computer!

Within two minutes, I had my answers with many more to follow, thanks to the fast email reply from a Unitarian as thrilled to hear from me as I was to find her. What a resource person she turned out to be! She was an expert at HTML and a rather new-fangled piece of technology, called a scanner, that she had access to five days each week as a librarian at Vanderbilt. To top it off, she was one of the library's few experts in HTML and was totally thrilled to be able to walk me, step by step, through everything this nifty little book I'd bought would be able to help me do.

For the next few weeks, we were in daily contact—sometimes a dozen times in one hour. Thanks to her encouragement I took on things in the book she'd never tried. If I made a mess, a quick behind-the-scenes look was all she needed before coming back with a solution via email with frequent LOL's splashed across many a message.

We shared our stories, comparing how collusion had played out in her life in a very liberal setting with amazing similarities, despite the contrasts to things said in conservative circles—all in the process of seeing this new creation of mine taking form. Two months later, I had the equivalent of a small book on my website http://takecourage.org bearing the title: "Confronting Collusion with Abuse in the Faith Community."

True to the original intent of *How Little We Knew*, the focus was (and still is) on the problems and approaches for coping and reducing the community's DIM thinking[1] that protects evil, both in individuals and systems we may hesitant to take on.

Being able to spot the games of collusion is essential for any survivor, family member, psychotherapist, even those highly experienced with treating incest victims who still may not be familiar with the additional spiritual and systemic abuse that come with clergy cases. This knowledge is equally important for friends, congregants, and clergy attempting to respond appropriately.

Justice-seeking isn't only a legal process. Ideally, anyone seeking any resolution or assisting others toward achieve it, understands this from the beginning. In reality, few did twenty years ago. Many still don't today, even after years of suffering. Justice comes in many forms and isn't necessarily dependent on others' actions, either in the judicial system, in the clerical hierarchy, or even in the community. It can come from deep inside, generated by new ways of thinking that set the victim free to move on into more creative processes.

Systems can throw thousands of dollars at a survivor as a means of institutional damage control. Yet this isn't always enough to even get started. Money can go a long way, but only so far in the healing process. Holding an offender accountable, exposing his/her incompetence, and seeing that there is no chance for another offense toward anyone because of the power and privilege that is endemic in the office: these get-tough acts of justice do not take monetary investment. They take courage and integrity.

For a survivor to move on, however, extensive therapy is often needed. Imagine the layers of a large onion. That's how issues stack up, each tightly clinging to the heart and soul of a survivor like protective scar tissue on a burn victim. Before even getting to the deepest "burn" of the primary abuse, childhood survivors usually have many more layers caused by shaming others have poured onto a child's psyche since birth.

I posted many pages about DIM thinking (collusion) within days of launching the website, daring to identify this problem as a "cognitive disorder" that exhibits itself in individuals and collectively as these same individuals impact systems. Expanding concepts further than I'd taken them previously, I provided examples, the "games" played (pass the buck, let's pretend, role reversal, etc.), showed symptoms and "treatment" for the ailing system, and the close parallels of collusion or co-addictions commonly exhibited by family members of addicts. Always trying to write in a concise, non-blaming voice in the approach I'd once used in writing about alcoholism in the African village, I still put the responsibility where it was due, with people and systems blinded by their own illusions. Immediately, survivors, therapists, clergy, and family members began to recognize this as the exact set of dynamics they'd experienced or witnessed as advocates. Occasionally a graduate student or member of the press would pick parts of the DIM thinking phenomenon up and ask for further explanation. Over time the questions led to tweaking the information I had out there through the same process we were using (and still are), as advocates, constantly learn from one another.

Ending collusion wasn't going to happen through education alone, I declared. Grieving was the missing element. Every person had to grieve old ideals—professional ministers, survivors, and every other person in the community of faith—before we were going to see change. Churches had to get a new self-image, same as survivors, except in reverse.

This all offered ways to look at the problems more objectively. The nonsense that gave power to offenders must cease. Abuse cases, which the Church and its lawyers prefer to treat as brother-to-brother or peer-to-peer relationships, were being handled in the service of power. Confusion over confidentiality vs. secrecy, for instance, showed total incompetence that should be easy to correct with cognitive adjustment, provided people were willing to be educated.

Of course, what the hierarchy was most afraid of was what was most needed of all—the upending of the pyramid of power, the equivalent of overturning tables in the tabernacles, which was done by Christ himself because of financial extortion that exploited the poor. In the case of abuse, overturning the pyramid always requires that the masses, making up the largest segment at the base, adopt some revolutionary thinking—Jesus thinking, actually. This I'd also learned in Africa while using materials produced by The Hesperian Foundation, [2] a health education publishing non-profit for the most disenfranchised in the world. Their first work, for instance, was entitled "Where There Is NO Doctor." It showed that people could do many things to promote physical health without having western-trained experts always in charge. Imagine! Yet it wasn't a new idea. Many Quakers had been operating with these premises for centuries. It was subversive, of course—threatening and scary and bold, too.

That's also what the internet felt like to me in 1997. No longer did I need someone like Haworth Press or Foy Valentine to agree to put something in print. I only had to find ways to spread the word about what I knew, to promote ideas that were proven to work. What freedom!

"What will people think?" I could hear my cautious mother asking.

I really didn't care. I'd seen enough. So had a lot of others, which became evident within a few days.

One of my first visitors was Kevin Gourley of Austin, Texas. Julie McCord of the Omaha World-Herald, a journalist who had been trying hard to get her editor's permission to write an article about my work, now wrote all about it. She covered a full page and a half in the feature article of the Living section one Sunday.

If it hadn't been for "Christian Ethics Today," Kevin explained to McCord, he and his wife might still be trying to make sense of what turned their own lives upside down in early summer of 1997. A casual acquaintance, who'd also written something for the same issue in which "Church Secrets We Dare Not Keep" was published, casually handed Kevin an extra copy of the journal.

Glancing at the contents, the title of the article that almost didn't get published caught his eye, and everything began falling into place. The couple had desperately sought counsel from several professionals. Yet, very typical for the late twentieth century, not even the family therapist, who was paid well for her services, recognized what they clearly described as sexual exploitation—not the incident with the mental health worker and not the second one with the minister to whom Mrs. Gourley turned soon afterward!

It took a bachelor's level nurse to explain in an article Kevin got for free. Fireworks soon erupted from that article, fireworks that would continue lighting up in cyberspace for years to come.

Soon Kevin made plans to launch an elaborate educational website, using his skills as a software developer. A few months later, this brilliant creation known as www.advocateweb.org reached out to address sexual exploitation in *every* profession—nurses included, to my dismay.

A list-serve quickly grew from a half dozen into a multi-disciplinary team of Americans with a few Europeans and a couple from "down under" in Australia and New Zealand.

Meanwhile, a second list-serve provided survivors, often raw with emotion, a place to safely connect.

McCord captured the power of all these connections, including the Vanderbilt librarian and the catalyst the CET article turned out to be. Since we first met, she had come to understand my philosophy of advocacy. She was particularly interested in how I spoke of all acts of abuse committed by clergy—both sexual and domestic—to be violence. The general public didn't grasp this even with child sexual abuse, yet most therapists I knew certainly did. This needed to be spelled out, I'd insisted. A violation of this nature is always violence, whether physical force is used or not. Besides, when clergy are the perpetrators, wasn't this soul slaying? Not only did this advocate of advocates understand this, she made it a major focus of this feature article, which reached out across the wire.

Too bad I didn't know about the SOS acronym back then. I'm sure Julia would have spread that around, too, same as she did with DIM thinking that Sunday. SOS or "stuck on stupid," a favorite expression of some of my SNAP friends, works for me, too.

I expected some hate mail from all of this, but nothing came in except encouragement and more validation with some very sad stories. Included were messages from a couple of evangelical ministers—one male, one female. Both had been marginalized for their own stands, too. Hearing of their personal sacrifices was a healing experience for Ron and I, as well.

Where Have All the Baptists Gone?

Ironically, not one Baptist response had come from that CET article, though the target audience of this publication was theologically-moderate Baptists. Gourley's site was more than adequate pay for all the fret and worry.

I made sure to keep Joe Trull informed of anything pertaining to Baptist issues I picked up from the list-serve, hoping he'd pass it on to others. Despite his academic qualifications and the fact that he was pushing for a ministerial code of ethics to be a part of the Baptist ordination process, I remained troubled about his limitations. To Baptists, having fifteen years' experience as a pastor and another fifteen years teaching ministerial ethics in a seminary seemed like worlds of experience. Yet mental health was not a part of this mix—that's what concerned me most and also concerned people who did have this advantage. He relied on the same thinking many others in evangelical circles were—the idea that pastoral counselors with years of experience working with perpetrators automatically made them well-qualified to advise others.

In reality, the most hideous secondary abuse survivors had experienced came from men like Truman Smith or a similar counselor at the BGCT that Trull kept quoting. All were as highly "experienced," as

Foy Valentine was, and only slightly more up to date than Sigmund Freud, who considered patients with memories of incest to all be fantasizing.

If he was going to continue writing and offering training to others, I encouraged him to take advantage of workshops to provide training to trainers. "No funding" and inadequate interest in pursuing this suggestion remained persistent obstacles.

The "old-time religion" historically treasured by so many Baptists still was. "The Word of God is all anybody needs." The influence of this thinking, even by those who intellectually know better, still holds sway.

However, Baptists generally frowned on snake charmers and "faith healers" on television such as Oral Roberts. In spite of this, I found it incredibly naïve and alarming this "magical thinking" approach, under the guise of "rehabilitation," as long as a pastoral counselor was the one doing the evaluation and "treatment."

The Sad, Unexpected Outcome

In 2005, Kevin needed a break. He stepped back from his role to care for his mother, who was battling cancer. Other members of the Board of Directors managed to keep the website operating by hiring outside help until one disastrous day when it was totally wiped out due to hacking.

Stanley Spero, a Boston attorney, went on to work diligently with the help of other professionals to launch a much simpler site under the same name, www.advocateweb.org.

Advocate Web stands as a testimony to the power of connections. It still contains a few articles of mine along with many others by authors from a variety of disciplines.

Triaging

The skills of triage mental health nursing came in handy whenever I responded to a new reader, as I was soon doing often, sometimes multiple times in one day through my inbox. Each time, an informal assessment was necessary, this time without the benefit of visual or auditory cues. It all depended on what someone chose to put in writing.

I had acquired most of the triage nursing skills I possessed through a skilled colleague, working near me on an inpatient unit, who had triage as her only assignment. Triage nurses do not have to have all the answers. Nor are they likely to see the end results of their work. They never know who will walk in the door with what problem, at the oddest hours of the night. They only pick up signals, play hunches, and set priorities in hopes of getting a person going in the right direction. As a writer with a busy website, that's how I operated, strictly as a volunteer, of course. The miracle of the web was that it operated 24/7, even when I didn't. Yet I arranged my schedule to pick up emails somewhat like an "on-call" nurse.

The skills of an electrician come in handy, too—knowing how to facilitate connections, that is, to make sparks of action fly as people of like mind or similar stories show up, perhaps even in the same geographical area or denomination, who may be in need of support from a more seasoned survivor.

No longer were responses coming in at a trickle from occasional media coverage or some article someone happened to find. Nor did I need a week to get a reply out, as I had with snail mail. I made it a point to answer within twenty-four hours, if not instantly.

Since it often became difficult to recognize people I'd not met except by email, I found it helpful to assign each survivor a subject line to use with all correspondence. This way, should they return after an absence of several months, something related to their story I'd recognize before I even opened the email. For instance, I quickly designated one woman "Shouting Lady from California," much to her amusement, after she stood up and proclaimed the truth from where she sat in the congregation one morning to counteract the lies being spoken from the pulpit by a church official, who declared the pastor's leave of absence "an illness."

A great-grandmother I knew from the Iowa retreat, who graciously hosted Ron and I for a weekend in between appointments at Mayo, I named "Salty." Having nothing to do with her salt-and-pepper hair, the name was my way of showing appreciation for her ability to re-frame problems with a great deal of subversive humor, a quality hewn from her many years in Al-Anon.

It was troubling to think how many had been waiting for decades to find validation. Pent up energy, waiting to be channeled, was being unleashed in all directions, coming from every major denomination. My contacts included deeply-wounded pastors from Missouri Synod Lutheran and American Baptists who had been marginalized for standing alone to hold a colleague accountable, same as we had.

Of course, many of the cases were a part of the huge backlog. Now that journalists, lawyers, and advocates in churches were helping to get word out that help was available. Most mainstream survivors expected to be heard—this is what they were being told by denominational leaders to expect. Instead they often showed up in my inbox with wounds of collusion still raw, often suffering from PTSD whenever they even ran into someone from their former church.

While everything still seemed to be stacked against survivors in mainline circles, whether the problem was domestic abuse in the parsonage or sexual abuse in the church, there were agencies to make reports to outside of one's own community. Some, like United Methodists, even provided each survivor a person advocate, trained for the role.

Once, a lady leading a prevention workshop for clergy was asked, "Shouldn't the accused clergy member also have a trained advocate?"

"Seems there are plenty *already* well trained for that role in every case I've seen," she candidly replied. For those of us who had stopped to do the math, on an adjudicatory committee with ten members, by the simple law of averages reflected in the Fuller survey,[3] every third chair might be occupied by someone with a history of having had sexual contact with a congregant. Plus, several more who had knowingly protected a perpetrator in the past. Too bad these folks weren't screened as carefully as a jury.

For the next seven years, I saw little evidence of real change in the status-quo thinking. Even in denominations that had managed to get policies in place, entrenched misogynous attitudes and beliefs remained. While the degree of collusion was starting to ease, as evidenced by reports I got from survivors after 2004, even some advocates were being "beat up" after all the desensitization efforts on the part of so many of us. In 2007, in fact, a Presbyterian male advocate wrote: "It is hard enough to stand up to one's enemies. It is much harder to stand up to your friends and those whom you consider family."

When the system called for an initial report to be made to a designated individual, responses varied greatly. "I'll take this all 'under advisement,'" was common before months of silence. There were few swift processes and many sleepless nights for survivors.

With Baptist survivors, there was so much more naivety to deal with. Most assumed the denomination would have protocols to handle their complaint. Finding out otherwise, learning there was nobody with the power to do anything beyond people in the local congregation, was devastating to survivors hoping for empathy and an assurance the perpetrator wasn't going to be able to hurt anyone else.

Amy wasn't a direct survivor, but she was certainly traumatized. She was even facing the threat of a civil law suit when she discovered my site soon after leaders at her Chicago church (United Methodist) found out she'd reported evidence of wrongdoing she'd stumbled across on the computer in the church office, where she was volunteering. Before the pastor was found guilty and finally removed six months later, she'd been slandered. Then, a new pastor, obviously untrained to step into an "after-pastor" role,[4] joined church leaders in further ostracizing her. Understandably, she has never again returned to that church or any other after thirteen years.

Like many United Methodist survivors, however, she was given written materials and eventually experienced some sense of validation by the bishop, once he learned of her victimization.

A Sample

Since then, Amy has graced our lives over and over with her loving presence, as a guest in our home, a traveling companion, and by hosting us on several occasions in her own home. Not long after contacting me, she took off work, and spent two days on the road, staying up most of one night, to help me get a new computer system set up. I see her as a spiritual giant and one of the most mature individuals I've ever met.

A few days ago, I asked if she could help reconstruct our earliest email conversations, I was shocked when she forwarded them all back in the first message. Most striking were her well-articulated feelings expressed in two sentences:

> *"I have been deeply depressed, angry, and grieved*
> *over a situation that has stolen my faith, my peace,*
> *my joy, my support, my church and my*
> *community... I feel like I've been terrorized for a*
> *year and a half and I am finally free to speak of it."*

In return, I tried to provide answers to her questions plus comfort and hope:

> ..."*Sometimes you'll wish your eyes had never been opened, but many days you'll be so grateful they have been. In time, though-probably not soon.*
>
> ....*Your faith questions and skepticism will continue to be there, probably for the rest of your life. This is the case for Ron and me. Yet we are content and comfortable, at this point, with not having to have all the answers... Let me know where you want to go from here.*"

I've encouraged each new contact to consider reaching out to others from my growing list of individuals willing to be a part of someone else's support system. Sometimes a person from the same denomination, one with a similar story, or maybe a person living within an hour's drive of a new contact can make all the difference.

*****

[1] For a better understanding of how DIM thinking can be recognized and addressed, see http://www.takecourage.org/CollusionMain.htm

[2] Hesperian Foundation, now known as Hesperian Health Guides is a non-profit that produces amazing books, especially written for people who may not have access to highly-trained health professionals. See Hesperian.org

[3] In his 1984 doctoral dissertation, which is widely quoted, Richard Allen Blackmon, a Fuller Theological Seminary student, found that 38.6% of 300 ministers surveyed from a wide spectrum of denominations admitted to having had sexual contact with a church member. 12% of these admitted to sexual intercourse with a congregant.

[4] An after-pastor is one appointed or hired to serve either temporarily, like an interim, or to step in as the new pastor after the pulpit has been recently vacated by a sexual offender, either by the offender's choice to avoid being terminated or because of termination. In some cases, this after-pastor may not even be told the reason her or his predecessor left. In other cases, the church

may not even know why. Regardless of the circumstances, after-pastors are usually in for some very stormy weather. It's also fair to say that this may be the case for several pastors who follow because of the long-term damage done by the conflict and confusion created and often not adequately processed for many years. Pastors who find a lot of unresolved conflicts in a congregation will do well to consider the possibility they have unknowingly stepped into this role. Inquiries into this possibility with key people in the congregation can be very revealing and helpful, in the end. A professional counselor or even a team of professionals particularly trained to assist in these congregations can be key in promoting systemic healing, starting with the leadership.

Chapter 23
Triumphs and Trials
(1998-1999)

"Your spirit and attitude are exemplary," Joe Trull wrote after my first article in "Baptists Today."

I appreciated that complement almost as much as one from the psychiatrist we consulted before leaving Malawi. I don't suppose hers was intended as a complement, but as a way to help me stay grounded. If so, it's served me quite well for thirty years.

"Your expectations are reasonable. Your concerns valid," she assured me that morning as the two of us enjoyed the cool atmosphere on the side of Zomba Mountain. I could have easily sat there for days without either of us saying another word.

Now in 1998, the two complements together had me doing some *self-analysis*. Did my spirit and attitude leave me *too* reasonable with a system that seemed to be stuck on irrationality? Was reasoning ineffective with most Southern Baptists on these issues? Perhaps even useless? It would seem so, same as I gleaned from reports of Catholic advocates attempting to stop folks from casting stones at survivors.

Since this ethics professor had never met me, he had no way to know that I thrive on being called "reasonable." An exemplary spirit and attitude, which I also treasure, has always come in as second, tying with "efficient" or "ambitious" in my set of priorities. Ron knows that. Yet my mother still doesn't—something I probably should tell her next time we talk. To Mom, the greatest complement she can give me is: "You are *so* sweet." Sweet isn't high on my list of aspirations at all—totally at the opposite from reasonable, though I can also be both, provided all the stars are aligned and circumstances permit.

Seventy-five percent of women have the opposite set of preferences, according to the Myers-Briggs.[1] I'm in the minority who trust cognition and prefer it above feeling, which puts me somewhat in line with the majority of men. "Except for most members of the clergy I've met," says Ron.

Like many of his male colleagues who have done their jobs with remarkable finesse, Ron is also in the minority, by gender, in the general population. That factor among others put him in a position of needing the psychiatrist's analysis as much as I did, in 1987, while still on the mission field. He would have thrived far more on Trull's complement. Yet he has seldom gotten that or even an acknowledgement of gratitude from any male colleague to honor his own voice of advocacy. Most shy away from him even more than me, he senses, on the topic of professional abuse.

I'm not overly "nice" nor patient when I discover something I believe to be nonsense, on anything—just ask my children. "I'm not impulsive," I tell them. "I put a lot of thought into my next step, but I *do* think fast and am not inclined to mince words."

It's Ron who is really patient and kind when, in actuality, he's seething internally. He surprises himself and everyone around when he finally *loses* his patience. His strong belief that "everyone means well" leaves him frequently melancholic for extended periods of time after discovering the opposite in a person he trusts to join his efforts.

I believe this is true in 90% of female survivors. It's not a fault. Nor a flaw, as I see it; yet I do believe it complicates life as much as my own tendency to be blunt in the face of nonsense.

Doing Justice through Legislative Changes

Gary Schoener [2] was the very first advocate Kevin Gourley invited onto our list-serve and the mastermind behind international conferences like the one we attended in Toronto in 1994, addressing concerns with sexual boundary violations in *all* professions. Most everyone I know to be an expert in the field holds immense respect for this foremost pioneer who's worked as a psychotherapist since the 1970's on these issues. Peter Rutter, author of the classic, *Sex in the Forbidden Zone*, even had listed Gary separately from everyone else in his resource list.

He'd already helped lead a conference in Sydney, Australia and another in Norway. Now he was planning a return to Australia, this time to Melbourne, then to Denmark.

Schoener was an expert at "pulling down strongholds." He'd made a big impact in helping put some teeth into laws holding offenders accountable, specifically in his home state of Minnesota. Thanks to the passionate efforts of a Texas survivor, he'd also made great strides in that state, starting in 1985, making it a felony for pastors doing any kind of one-on-one counseling (including spiritual) to sexualize a relationship. Surprisingly, his efforts had been highly supported by some very conservative legislators who knew how to reach out across the aisles for this cause. Of course, getting elected officials to *prosecute* a beloved preacher is another matter. Yet the principles are on the books, ready to be used by courageous district attorneys in the Lone Star State.

These advocates went further, making sure that churches could be held liable for failing to check with past employers about a potential candidate's history, including mere allegations. And a former church, by not passing along such information, could also be held liable. By 1992, important loopholes were closed, allowing clients in counseling with a minister, whether a member of the congregation or not, to hold that man accountable.

Gary also served as an expert witness for the defense in a few Baptist court cases that were successfully prosecuted, his most well-known involving adolescent male victims in Florida.

It was hard to tell how Joe Trull felt when I shared this information with him no later than 1997, as he began thinking about writing more on this topic. He didn't say, but I assumed he'd be eager to avail himself of Gary's willingness via phone or email to respond to any questions anybody might have in the SBC.

I hate being suspicious, but I wondered if sharing my connection with Schoener and his role in all of this negated Baptist leaders from even seeking to know more of his opinion, as well as to be open to my grave concerns over their very optimistic views on the likelihood of rehabilitating offenders. Or maybe they simply didn't have use for any "secular" psychologist at all.

The BGCT certainly needed to protect itself as a newly-established entity, recently split off from the more conservative element of Baptists in the state. Yet they seemed clueless about why they needed to get out of their own closed system, relying instead on pastoral counselors and brutal attorneys, all highly experienced at "protecting" the BGCT, the churches it served, and the offenders they were bent on rehabilitating." This was evident time after time, whenever I'd attempted to have conversations with any of them, even Joe Trull, who referred to me as his "friend."

Back to Boston

Excitement grew as plans were made with lightning speed for another international conference—this one in Boston, like the one four years earlier in Toronto. What a difference the Web made in getting the word out! People were again coming from as far away as New Zealand.

I'd never been to Boston except remotely through the radio program five years earlier. So Ron and I were especially excited, and more so when asked to help with a break-out session. Of course, none of us could have imagined how strategic this city would become to enlarging conversations, first in 2002 and again thirteen years later when Hollywood would shine the spotlight on the courageous, heart-breaking struggle of Phil Saviano, which began only one year after we assembled for the big conference that fall of 1998.

Following our break-out session, Cheryl Cooney and her husband Greg stepped forward to surprise me. They'd driven from New York City to hear us share our story, though they'd already read ours and we also knew some of theirs. Totally immersed in 7th Day Adventist culture, both were even in its educational systems, elementary through college. Since Cheryl's abuse by a minister, starting in late adolescence and continuing well into her twenties, they had both come a long way toward hope and healing. Thanks to their efforts, an organization called CEASE,[3] specific for 7th-Day survivors of CSA, would soon be born.

How exciting it was to also meet Mary Ann Werner, someone I'd not yet heard from. As the mother of a survivor of educator abuse, she was there to promote an organization she'd recently started after reading *How Little We Knew*. SESAME (Stop Educator Abuse, Misconduct, and Exploitation) is still going strong, having been in national news with growing frequency since, helping turn the tide to make our schools safer from predators.

There were huge double-binds for feminists and social liberals when the antics of the President of the United States became public in 1998. Terminology chosen by the press, who framed it like as affair void of power imbalance, was especially troubling to victims of professional sexual misconduct. To this day, there has been no large-scale public discourse over labeling the scandal "the Monika Lewinsky affair" rather than "the Bill Clinton affair." Was I the only one who heard mothers talking informally among themselves of concerns this story raised about safety of young women on Capitol Hill?

Yet even experts and advocates had different ideas about how much Lewinsky should be considered a victim. I found this difficult to understand. Impeachment threats aside, most everyone I knew was greatly disturbed that this young woman was being drug through the dirt while the President, despite the scandal, was receiving a lot of support. Feminists were as divided as anyone.

Not one to skirt issues, Marie Fortune took this current event on in opening remarks of her impressive, keynote address at Boston. Many were asking her to seize the day, she explained, to correct the image the press was helping to portray of Monika. She found the situation awkward, considering that Clinton had been such an ally for women's issues, also signing into law the National Child Protection Act only days after the Porter verdict.

With utmost diplomacy, the speaker seized the moment in an unexpected way, almost bringing the house down in the process. Her usual "schoolmarm approach," as some clerics have described her mannerism of lecturing, made her remarks even funnier:

"I've decided to suffice it by saying that the President of the United States seems to have confused his rod with his staff," she declared.

Now for the Facts

Once the laughter subsided, this foremost authority in the faith community on topics of sexual and domestic abuse revealed how discouraged she was. After all her efforts to educate colleagues in ministry on boundary violations, and even where policies and procedures were in place, she'd seen very little change in attitudes or tactics used with survivors. This matched my conclusions, based on much more limited experience than hers. It was becoming increasingly evident that there was little hope for change without tighter laws, and lawyers were going to have to be the leading educators.

Out at the coffeepot in the hallway, I very briefly touched base with her, telling her of my attempts to collaborate with the Baptist General Convention of Texas and asking if any SBC agency or the BGCT had inquired about training. Not any agency so far, she told me. However an SBC pastoral counselor, Bill Sapp, had even availed himself of their training in Seattle, fully qualifying him to train others. Perhaps I should check to see if he'd gotten past the initial resistance, as he'd hoped to do, to put this training to use through national SBC agencies.

Overjoyed, I phoned him soon after returning home and suddenly felt like I'd found an old friend, though we'd never met. What a contrast to those I'd talked to at the BGCT! Yet he was no more hopeful than Jeff Seats had been five years earlier about Convention leaders being open to taking advantage of Sapp's intensive training that would lead to change. He'd be more than happy to do so, however, if I could find anyone in leadership who might be interested in even talking about our shared concerns.

It didn't take long for me to get back to Joe Trull. Sapp was a goldmine, I said. If the BGCT couldn't afford training with Marie Fortune, maybe they could make a deal with this man inside the Baptist system.

That didn't fly either. A quick phone call to Sapp a couple of years later told me so. Just like Schoener and Fortune, he'd not heard a word from anyone associated with the BGCT or any other Southern Baptist man in leadership.

Wanting to keep channels of communication open and certainly not wishing to appear pejorative, I wouldn't have dared tell any cleric, Baptist or otherwise, that the ecumenical responses so far had me sometimes reminiscent of working a unit filled with passive-aggressive adolescent males, all acting badly. I'd been a charge nurse in this situation in two different hospitals since returning to the States—one in Oklahoma, the other in Omaha, Nebraska. As long as we didn't push those kids, they merely sat around being totally irresponsible. By contrast, some exploded like a pressure cooker when expectations changed. What they needed was male leadership. That's where our well-trained psych techs, who did their best to reinforce expectations, came in handy.

Yet those kids were much easier to manage than these big men who were successfully avoiding responsibility. Invisibly spread around the country, operating without accountability or checks and balances, Southern Baptist ministers were very much like a bunch of boys left to be in charge of their out-of-control peers on a unit like I just described. Except many of the boys who had been in my charge would have probably done a better job.

The Next Phase of Education

After doing all I could, I pulled back in hopes someone else would discover a new approach to this need for education—perhaps an attorney, I was thinking.

I didn't have to wait long. *Two* Texas female attorneys waiting in the wing were ready to step forward to expose the truth in that State: one, a few years younger than me, in 1999. A second one, considerably younger, would come along five years later. Their efforts to point the way for Texas Baptists seemed to be the only hope left in this disappointing situation of totally broken trust in which we'd all found ourselves.

Personally, I knew my trust could never be totally restored, even if there was a big change of heart demonstrated in this state convention, any more than the trust of Richard Sipe's or Tom Doyle's could be with Catholic bishops and their attorneys. Yet, overall, I'm fortunate to have a healthy level of trust in people, in general.

After all I've been through, I still generally trust my assessment skills. I believe most mature people, in the general population, will choose to do the right thing 98% of the time. It's the immature we must watch out for, and there are plenty who can quickly become emotional terrorists in disorganized or convoluted religion, wherever it exists.

Calling in the Press

Deborah Dail, the first attorney, had been victimized by her pastor as an adult. She'd gone public three years after Ron and I first met her and her husband in their Texas home in 1995.

Tara Dooley of the Ft. Worth Star Telegram covered Dail's story and the stories of several others November 8, 1998. In the article, she clearly spelled out the problems of the SBC and sentiments expressed by the very conservative Richard Land, President of Southern Baptists' Ethics and Religious Liberty Commission. Land, who had been one of Ron's seminary classmates, told her that sexual misconduct went beyond immoral actions.

"'It is amplified by the fact that it is not only sexual immorality, but it is also a violation of pastoral trust, and in that sense is abuse," he said.

By the time of Dooley's article, Dail had already followed the protocol of the Texas Baptist Convention, going through the motions to make a local report of her abuse as a teenager to leaders of the First Baptist Church of Farmer's Branch, Texas. There she was met with the typical local church response, total denial.

In her article, Dooley had also covered another case where the pastor had left the congregation where a woman had been abused and gone on to pastor another, after members of his church circled the wagons in support of the pastor, same as in Dail's case. Whether those guys went through the BGCT's system and visited the pastoral counselor, Glenn Booth, I do not know.

At first glance, the Texas Christian Life Commission appeared to be ahead of everybody else in the Southern Baptist Convention. Not long before, they'd held a conference on clergy sexual abuse. Within two years, they were pledging to keep a roster of perpetrators on file, and provide assistance to victims.

In truth, I was highly suspicious, not knowing many particulars. What had them so highly motivated? I wondered. They did agree to pay reimbursement for shipping costs for a booklet I offered to prepare for the CLC, with the understanding it would be distributed at a state meeting I would love to have attended, had there been funding. I'd asked for this assistance, but been turned down.

In addition, I'd sent at least a dozen pages of information and recommendations, carefully prepared with Joe Trull's encouragement. He assured me that he would personally see copies were placed in the hands of every member of the newly formed task force for the Baptist General Convention of Texas.

While I'd never been invited to sit down with officials at the BGCT, Trull led me to believe they were finally moving in the right direction and that everything I sent was being taken into consideration. Yet I remained suspicious. Considering the cool reception Dail reported to me after she bravely spoke to the entire BGCT, it was hard to imagine anyone had even looked at my work.

I remained concerned, I told Trull, because of this group's intention to move ahead with some sort of recommendations without taking advantage of the training offered by Marie Fortune. There just wasn't enough money, he said again. Yet they had enough to pay abusive lawyers, as well as the highly-optimistic pastoral counselor, who apparently believed in "social protection" as much as the Baptist Sunday School Board. According to Dail, he'd picked up the phone and called the perpetrator in her case as soon as she left his office, after having turned to him in confidence.

Another Old Serpent Gains Strength

Since his first year in college, Ron had wrestled with serious complications from an old back injury. It was never a common, garden-variety back problem with herniated disks. He was already quite disabled, walking with a limp, even when I first met him.

It was like another serpent to manage, so much a part of our daily lives, especially in Africa, where the bumpy trails hardly able to pass for roads could leave an able-bodied person feeling beat up at the end of a day. Still, a day in the village could be so thrilling to him, well worth spending another day stretched out on the floor to recuperate when he returned.

This had also put a lot of restriction on his employment options during the challenging transition of the late 80's, adding to issues of self-esteem and financial strain. Of course, emotional stress can play havoc with back muscles, even with backs that aren't filled with scar tissue like his. All things considered, he wasn't doing well at all.

Something had to give, I told myself in 1999, as he prepared to go for his third laminectomy. Whenever I feel that way, I know it's time to sort the everyday clutter around the house. Doing this has a way of cleaning out the cobwebs in my head, too. It's an odd sort of anti-depressant, but it works and often leads to finding creative solutions for more serious matters plaguing me.

That's what I was doing—sorting clutter in a corner of the living room one day when I did something very odd for a woman who's seldom interested in outdoor recreation. I picked up one of Ron's old fishing magazines and was soon flipping through want ads, noticing cute little cottages, advertised near resorts several hours' drive from us, all for enormous prices. This brought to mind a recent conversation we'd had while driving around the bare, wintry countryside one dismal day as he showed me some of the little lakes and ponds, within an hour's drive of the parsonage, where he'd gone to unwind in years past.

Over the past two years, he'd quit going much because by the time he arrived, he'd be too exhausted and uncomfortable to enjoy the fishing. So, what if we had a get-away cottage near one of the lakes, we began thinking—maybe something in a small town we could invest in for retirement? This way, he could have a place to rest comfortably whenever he needed it and still enjoy one of his favorite pass-times.

Tearing out another advertisement in the fishing magazine, I tossed the rest of it with the pile of outgoing junk before dialing the number listed in the ad for the Iowa Dept. of Wildlife. I'd never heard of Cold Springs State Park, but it sounded lovely and a place worth exploring somewhere in our vicinity. Turns out it was a lovely secret the way the experts described it—the smallest and best-stocked fishing area for many miles around, on top of being scenic.

"Where?" our neighbors who had never lived elsewhere inquired. "In Iowa? Can't be. We never heard of it."

"All the better," I told Ron, laughing. "Aren't we looking for privacy? Better check this out."

Next day, I had real estate agents laughing. Yes, there were some sleepy, little towns nearby, but I must be dreaming if I thought I'd find any house under $30,000!

"I am dreaming," I told a lady with a scratchy voice, who was more interested in telling me about her upcoming retirement than the houses on the market. The receiver was halfway to its cradle when I stopped in midair.

"Wait! I almost forgot. I *do* have one I got only last week. It's been empty for over a year. Depends on how much elbow grease you've got."

I had a lot more elbow grease than money. "O. K. When could we have a look?" I asked.

The next afternoon found us traipsing through two feet of snow on a lovely half acre filled with magnificent overgrown trees, to peek through the first-floor windows of an ancient piece of old charm sitting within walking distance of Cold Spring's entrance.

Soon after Ron's surgery and for over a year afterwards, until he went on permanent disability retirement, "the cottage" provided what was needed—a weekly respite, allowing us to each continue in our respective ministries. The surgery, however, would end up not only unsuccessful, but the likely source of much more serious disability to come.

This cottage would serve as a spiritual "hiding place," not just for us, but for our extended family and many survivors who would soon grace our presence and refresh our souls. And in 2001, it would become our primary residence because of Ron's permanent disability.

Advocacy moved out of the parsonage, as we dropped the stresses of "church work" and picked up the freedom to carve out unique ways of doing ministry in the process. Often welcoming church refugees, showing them the wonderful, best-kept secret where we never planned to be.

"So much for making lemonade out of lemons!" exclaimed Fran Park, declaring the cottage the equivalent of turning the negatives into lemon meringue pie.

*****

[1] From Myers & Briggs Foundation's own website, http://www.myersbriggs.org/my-mbti-personality-type/mbti-basics/: "The purpose of the Myers-Briggs Type Indicator® (MBTI®) personality inventory is to make the theory of psychological types described by C. G. Jung understandable and useful in people's lives. The essence of the theory is that much seemingly random variation in the behavior is actually quite orderly and consistent ..." This instrument was first published in 1962.

[2] Gary Schoener, the foreward writer for this book, is a clinical psychologist and fore-runner since the 1970's in this work. His home base has remained The Walk-In Counseling Center of Minneapolis. This group which he led not only has networked exclusively, generously reaching out to share information with advocacy leaders and individual survivors. He had already gained world-renowned recognition and was listed in Peter Rutter's Sexual in the Forbidden Zone (Ballentine Books, 1989) as the premiere professional organization addressing sexual exploitation by professionals in positions of power. Also in 1989, Schoener and his colleagues produced "Psychotherapists Sexual Involvement with Clients," an 800-page powerhouse of information that helped shape the approach of activists, development of policies, laws, and the training of professional counselors to address these issues.

[3] See http://cease.startlogic.com/resources.htm

Chapter 24
Justice-Seeking in Mission Circles

When people in power possess elitism without merit, as described by Joan Chittister in Chapter 4, they stand on a pedestal that can easily collapse under the power of truth that's always much greater than a set of facts. Truth must come from multiple sources, however, to sweep power off its feet in patriarchal systems.

In a secure and well-educated community, hearing a concerned person say "you have liability issues here" should not be cause for alarm. It should only arouse curiosity and be perceived as a time to learn. Neither should the system feel threatened if the leaders are open to being curious, are devoted to serving the greater good, and interested in remedying a situation leaves vulnerable people in harm's way.

By contrast, an easily threatened institution or individual is often running scared for good reason. In this case, advocates are quickly seen as enemies. This can create unnecessary, unnerving distress for anyone working for progressive change.

The Downfall of Institutional Thinking--Maintaining "Stability"

The opposite of transform is "remain" or "stay," according to common definition. Not so in a system. Systems are alive—both biological ones and institutional ones. Without daily transformation, systems either die or become diseased.

The opposite of a transformed institutional system is *regressive* deformity until the system begins to destroy itself or, even worse, the people within it. Where mission organizations lay on this spectrum became obvious in the way they chose to approach their abuse problems, once the truth became clear.

Presbyterians and Methodists

I could never have imagined an outcome as spectacular and far-reaching as the one that occurred after several adult MK's (missionaries' kids), who were abused on the mission field, got in touch with me via my website.

Their story of discovery had begun more than a decade earlier. In 1987, the same year Ron discovered the Newsweek article about the growing awareness of "the Catholic problem." This was not a Southern Baptist story, though. It was Presbyterian (PCUSA), the denomination that identifies itself as "reformed and still reforming."

As Bill Pruitt got up to preach at a missionary gathering, several of his victims, by then in their 30's and 40's, made individual decisions to walk out. Their actions were not intended as a collective protest, though their individual decisions worked together to serve this purpose, once they met outside. Surprised at their common reaction, as these young ladies met in the minutes that followed, they began a conversation that would start them on the long road toward recovery, a road that would bring them back together again and again to share more and more of their collective story of betrayal while reaching out repeatedly to others.

It is unclear how much they all knew, back in 1987, about Pruitt's history. Certainly, the full story of how he had, after being confronted with allegations, been able to conveniently relocate back in the United States, was yet unknown to them. Apparently, it hadn't been discussed much among his former missionary colleagues. If so, not enough, since he was now leading the group in a worship experience!

Among the 1987 protestors was Liz Iverson, who seems to have been the most persistent of the women seeking to bring the truth to light. She was determined not to let others stay in permanent denial. Martha Faupel recently wrote: "When Liz first wrote me..... my exact quote to her was 'I am not interested because it is a scary thing to open up a can of worms. You might not be able to get all the worms out; or you may not be able to put the worms back in the can and close the lid; and then you have to learn to live with worms.' She was patient and supportive anyway!"

While waiting for more truth to be revealed, Liz and some of the others in that 1987 group of protesters were sorting out the past through formal therapy and informal talks with one another. Lots of important things were going on during those years, as there often are in cases when things seem to be at a standstill.

In fact, the problems of mission field abuse could no longer be hidden. In 1998, eleven years after the informal 1987 survivor walk-out, there was a reunion of alumnae from the boarding school where these victims of Pruitt had spent much of their childhood.

Sitting around a table, some of the Presbyterian and Methodist MK's from the Congo began casually sharing survivor stories of old times. These were more the common garden-variety stories that MK's tell. Like the time someone may have found a live critter in the half-cooked cafeteria rice or when a brave soul managed to sneak off from chapel without getting caught.

Eventually, the tone of the conversation changed when one of the women mentioned being abused by Pruitt. Soon others related their own stories. Before the reunion was over, these women resolved to tell their stories to people with power in the very system that had held them captive as children. They were tired of carrying the burden that adults of yesteryears should have carried for them!

Exceptional responses came from several PCUSA leaders, starting with Dr. Marian McClure, the director of the Worldwide Ministries Division. When she got a call from the father of one of the survivors, she didn't hesitate to respond compassionately. Immediately, she arranged for a retreat with some of the best-known leaders in retreat services for survivors of clergy sexual abuse, Rev. Pat Liberty and Mary Kuhns. The retreat was scheduled in November.

By then, Pat and I had met a couple of times at both Linkup and the Boston conference where we'd been able to share our mutual passion and frustration with our respective survivor ministries, so *How Little We Knew* was on the recommended reading list for the retreat. Pat also told them that I now had a website.

Soon Becky and other survivors were reading the book, which some said spurred them toward further resolve, realizing that their case wasn't an isolated one. Becky was the first survivor to email me from this group with everyone else soon following.

As in so many previous cases, I simply stood by, listening, validating, encouraging realistic expectations, hoping to brace my confidantes for disappointment. Even with the unusual response they'd received already, I was still skeptical, having lost count of the number of mission field cases that had come to my attention over the past five years.

In the end, I was able to help assemble an independent team of experts from a variety of denominations to form a commission for Presbyterians. In 2002, at the end of an extensive, very costly exploration, there were twenty-two founded cases with scores more of which they had knowledge too limited to include. A sense of justice was achieved for the MK's in the end, as they personally reported back to me.

As a part of this, PCUSA helped with the production of a 2006 DVD "Witnesses to Truth, Witnesses to Healing: Investigating Child Abuse in Missionary Settings," available at the Presbyterian Distribution Service 1-800-524-2612.

There was also a new set of recommendations adopted for handling all cases of sexual abuse by clerics in PCUSA.

Right in the middle of the PCUSA efforts, around 2004, other MK's were coming forward, victims of several perpetrators in various locations in Africa and Asia. This began an even more extensive set of investigations that took place over seven years, resulted in thirty more founded cases, and an additional 546-page report in 2010.

Whether MK Sean Coppedge, then 36, received any financial assistance as did the first group of PCUSA victims is unclear. What is clear, weeks after the report was issued, Coppedge sued PCUSA because some of their officials knew of another MK perpetrator at his boarding school and still allowed the abuser to return to school, where he abused Coppedge and others. In 2011, that case got thrown out in Kentucky courts. Yet it is significant on two fronts. While cases occurring on the mission field seldom had a chance of even finding legal representation in 1987, some of the loopholes involving abuse occurring overseas had been closed by 2010, allowing a good possibility of this young man winning had it not been for the archaic laws in Kentucky (and many other states) that have not removed the statute of limitations on child abuse cases.

In spite of the negative outcome in this case, to my knowledge, nothing has come close to the degree of justice extended outside the court system by the PCUSA internal process. It gives tremendous hope and flies in the face of any system, Baptist or otherwise, unwilling to act prudently, clinging to the traditions of age-old institutional protection.

Eventually Methodists followed suit, with their own study of Methodist MK's that had surfaced as a result of PCUSA's investigation.

(For a more complete story of the original cases, see
takecourage.org/pcusa.htm)

Southern Baptist Missions

There were signs of positive change at the International Mission Board of the Southern Baptist Convention, too—tangible evidence this time. It came after I was contacted by Eddie Ruble, a sibling to one of several survivors, abused as kids in Indonesia about thirty years earlier. That group had since been on a mission of their own, one I knew nothing about until shortly before they made national news when others in the group also called or emailed me as they sought to know how to proceed. I was eager to see just how much real change had taken place in attitudes, as well as approaches that I'd been told had come as a result of our persistence in the Kingsley case.

The perpetrator, William McElrath, had been terminated in 1995, with his wife being allowed to take early retirement. It happened after members of this group reported that "Mac," as William was known, had been allowed to stay on the field all those years after being reprimanded for multiple offenses in the past. Now, their concern was for the immigrant children he was being allowed to work with in a North Carolina church, where the pastor knew of his past. They wanted the board to not allow past offenders to be identified simply as "retired" or "former" missionaries, but as "terminated."

As a group, they'd managed to muster the support of a strong advocate still in a position of considerable authority with the IMB, as well as the support of journalist willing to expose the perpetrator. In the end, there were some positive signs, yet their requests, including some for personal compensation to help therapy from the disastrous life-long results of these "kids'" abuse was not realized. Most striking, the North Carolina Baptist Standard gave a full and candid report filled with unadorned truth. Things done in darkness could no longer be easily hidden! Google "McElrath missionary Baptist Standard" for much more detail.

After the consultations, I wrote the President of the IMB, Jerry Rankin, thanking him for what had been done. I noted that from the reports I received, it did appear there had been considerable changes since the Kingsley case in our Mission fifteen years earlier, and asked to see the current policies on sexual misconduct that he'd publicly said were "very strong" and allowed for "zero tolerance."

The response was cordial. Simply having written policies available was quite an improvement. Yet I had concerns about the wording of some statements and was especially concerned that there was little to no provision for what I suspected the Board would still be considering cases of "immorality" rather than the abuse of vulnerable adults or sexual harassment of colleagues. I received no satisfactory reply. I am unaware if further alterations have since been made to make a policy of "zero tolerance" an actuality in these cases.

When I recently inquired again via email, saying this was the most common type of abuse of all, I got no response. Nor can I locate anything on the site to address this problem. Apparently, they don't consider it important. Perhaps they'd say our case involving assault or molestation of several adults was only a fluke?

In 2004, as a direct result of the Indonesian MK's, the largest evangelical mission board in the world installed a hotline for reporting abuse from anywhere in the world, same as any denomination should have. The number, 1-866-292-0181, is given out to all missionaries, I'm told. With considerable searching, I did discover it also on a back page of the website. Would a national like the young girl assaulted by Kingsley be able to find it? Or an MK who might want to register concerns, now that the Board is supposedly more trauma-informed than when the Wade children were abused by their own father? Or are these possibilities still considered flukes, too?

Christian and Missionary Alliance

Rich Darr, the United Methodist pastor I met at Linkup in 1995, also an MK survivor, passed word of my work along to some of his childhood peers, including the parents of Beverly Shellrude Thompson, one of the long-time leaders of what is now MK Safety Net. This organization began in 1999, following some resolution from transactions with the Christian and Missionary Alliance, the sending agency of the Darr's, Shellrude's, and many other families whose children were required to leave home in early elementary school to attend the Mamou Boarding School.

Mamou was a place of horrors for lots of MK's. This was determined and validated after a steering committee, somewhat similar to what the Presbyterians had set up for their mission group. Though on a much smaller scale, it was made up of people both from inside and outside the system who came together to hear their cries.

These MK's also produced a film in 2008. "All God's Children," proudly introduced at the Sundance Film Festival that year, where it received a good deal of fanfare, to call attention to the plight of these abused children, left to fend for themselves far away from the watch-care of their parents "all in the name of Jesus." Then, initially cast aside by the system that is supposed to represent the ultimate in God's Love.

MK Safety Net[1] now has two branches—one stateside, one in Canada. They have supported MK's around the world from a variety of other Missions and sending agencies, reaching out in the hopes of preventing and addressing abuse, when it occurs, more efficiently and therapeutically. Their work has included retreats in recent years, during which William Paul Young, an MK survivor and author of *The Shack*,[2] was their guest speaker.

Dale Dorrell, that Quaker chaplain who showed up at our church in early 1994, has been an active part of the survivor organization, sharing selections from the large volume of songs he's written about his own spiritual journey, just as he has with Ron and I personally on so many visits to our home.

Dale, Beverly, Rich, and many others from this group, including several parents, have graced my life as we've pooled our insights and provided mutual support while searching for ways to make good come out of the evil that transpired in these mission settings.

Indian Mission Schools

Related to all of these stories, I cannot fail to mention the horrors experienced with Native Americans, going back to the nineteenth century, where suspicions abound in such schools as Shawnee Mission, a Methodist facility in Kansas, now an historic site.

Abuse in Canadian boarding schools well into the twentieth century is another huge study with ramifications very much like what MK's have experienced at boarding schools around the world. By 2003, Anglicans were bankrupt and in resignation Bishop Duncan D. Wallace had told the New York Times: "When you get down to it, all we need is a bottle of wine, a book and a table, and we are in business."[3]

Those three items may be all *they* needed to be in business. In Africa, authentic churches operated even without this much, sometimes meeting only under a shade tree. Yet authenticity requires compassion and integrity. Sadly, Canadian Anglicans weren't the only ones in Canada bankrupt in that department. Canadian Presbyterians, Roman Catholics, and the United Church were, as well.

And who among them had truly listened to the outcries of these adults, so traumatized as children? Who would even dare excuse the schemes to annihilate these children's own culture, devised in the name of Jesus, with the cooperation of the Canadian government officials? Where were the masses who should have fallen to their knees to cry alongside the sufferers who lived with the consequences of these collective sins every day of their lives?

The over-riding cry in each of the groups I've written about in this chapter needed to be: "How can we be transformed through the renewing of our minds? Lord, help us!" After years of work in hopes of change, we find sadly that precious few are there yet.

*****

[1] MKSafetynet.com

[2] William Paul Young's The Shack was once #1 on the New York Times best seller list. It has recently been made into an outstanding movie.

[3] from New York Times article, "Indian Lawsuits on School Abuse May Bankrupt Canada Churches" by James Brooke, November 2, 2000

Chapter 25
New Life in a New Century

"Abuse of power is a very simple human dynamic. It's what a kid will understand in the schoolyard: There's the kid who's stronger and bigger than everybody else, and he's abusing that power to take something from the victim, whether it's lunch money or possessions or just their dignity. You see the same dynamic in the adult world; it just manifests itself in more adult, violent ways over time and on a bigger scale," says Gary Haugen, leader of the International Justice Mission.[1]

Understanding how this applies to the faith community is daunting for all concerned. For, how can people charged with leadership responsibilities that call for a level of humility assumed to be inherent in the faith community be expected to understand how this very universal assumption also gives them power so closely aligned to that of politicians, often lauded or feared for the power they are allowed to *legitimately* claim?

Expanding Lessons in International Power Abuse

Our daughter's family of three had been living in Moscow for nearly two years. Now, in early 2000, with the birth of a second grandson fast approaching, our plans were to visit them in late spring before flying back with the family to where they would be resettling stateside. Having missed out on those precious early years in Micah's life, we were ready to jump with all fours into the joys of hands-on grand-parenting.

Yet Ron's failing health had him too exhausted to even think of making the trip. He was not recovering well from surgery, yet insisted he was well enough for me to leave him for three weeks. I did so reluctantly.

Those days of fun and frolic, taking in the wonders of Russia, were often punctuated by trips on the busy subways. I kept looking at the drawn faces. Oh, what despair they reflected! My mind often wandered to the Russian pastor who had reached out through cyberspace, concerned for the victims he'd encountered there. And sometimes to W. Africa, where I'd filled an order for *How Little We Knew* from a woman with a name I could tell was clearly African. Though I said little to my daughter about my feelings, knowing that people unable to do more than survive have little time to think of other forms of oppression in their lives, I had difficulty at times focusing on my new grandson Malachi, rather than on what I could literally do nothing about short of praying for moments of grace for those who had so deeply touched my life from afar.

Coming home, we were forced to make an unexpected stop near the east coast of Canada due to a disruptive passenger, threatening stewardesses. While this created a 24-hour delay, once we got to New York City, where we awaited new connecting flights, the alarm caused was minimal by the standards that would soon be changed due to unforeseen circumstances in the tragedy about to unfold in The Big Apple.

Providing Help in Web Time

The effects of mutual empowerment at AdvocateWeb multiplied as the group expanded. So did our ability to find local support for new contacts, coming to any one of us, often from some faraway location.

"I've got someone desperate for support near Philadelphia. She's been through several therapists already, can't find one who's ever dealt with this mess. Anyone have ideas?" Donna might ask.

For major cities in the States, suggestions ranged from an agency to an isolated survivor hoping to start a support group. Simply finding someone within a two-hour drive was the best we could hope for in most cases.

In the absence of googlemaps, geographical questions might enter into the mix. "How close is this little town to Nashville? I've got a couple of good contacts there," someone might chime in later in the day to another request.

Meanwhile, the cost of www.advocateweb.org was being driven up due to its success, creating a real strain on Kevin, who was dependent on what little (or nothing) most users were able or willing to contribute. Unlike http://takecourage.org , basically an information-only site with only email access provided for users to reach out for support, Gourley's site was running as much as $1000/month, since costs were driven up each time someone clicked onto any page, including the list-serve, where scores were chiming into the robust conversations every day. Yet most of us, already stretched with our own advocacy efforts, had little in the way of financial contributions to make. Such is the nature of most non-profits. Even Linkup was struggling, and I knew of numerous fledgling survivor groups that had folded between financial burdens and internal strife so common when wounded people with exhausted emotional resources come together for a worthy cause.

That's why I never seriously considered the advice of several of my readers, who each seemed to assume the simple act of filing for non-profit status would somehow inspire lots of contributions. In theory, it sounded like a wonderful idea. The reality is few survivors or wounded advocates have funds to do more than take care of their own needs and precious few others care to contribute to such a cause.

Financially, we were seeing light at the end of the tunnel as we slowly recuperated from publication costs, thanks to book sales. So, I certainly didn't want to get bogged down in unnecessary, bureaucratic quagmire.

By limiting my involvement and having a business that was constantly expanding sufficient to meet our needs, we were coping well in every way.

It was exciting when several doctoral students turned to me, asking for assistance in finding willing participants for research needed. Before I even inquired, I knew that many of my contacts would be thrilled to participate.

Meanwhile, at the request of some of my readers, I began thinking of another writing project. This time, a novelette.

Problems of Protestant Fragmentation

Unlike Catholics, we Protestants have not organized a national group like SNAP. Doing so could be complicated.

Protestant survivors are more likely to be split on potential approaches to healing along the same lines of their respective theological preferences. Those from very conservative groups, like Southern Baptists, who may be seeking primarily "Biblical answers" in detail, turn to persons specifically designated as "Christian counselors" or pastoral counselors.

Unfortunately, many counselors in both groups, except for some trained through the American Association of Pastoral Counselors, often dished out further doses of spiritual abuse instead of healing, having limited insight as to how patriarchy served as a contributing issue, so that many women abused as adults have already gone from childhood sexual abuse to domestic abuse with the "blessing" of their old faith group. And for them to even suggest they might be questioning their loyalty to "the faith" might be seriously frowned on by many a so-called "Christian counselor."

Survivors from moderate to liberal theological groups may be more likely to seek out a counselor who is a Christian, but without this being posted. They are likely to be offended by heavy doses of so-called "Biblical counseling," in fact. Many female pastoral counselors are in tune with the issues today much more than twenty years ago, just as many secular counselors now are aware and able to offer excellent support. Still, it's best to seek out someone with experience in this field, no matter what type of counselor is sought.

SNAP is more than happy to have Protestants join them, and quite a few have found that connection very beneficial. Not the majority of Protestants, however, since many are still turned off by the name that works well only for Episcopalians and Catholics while most Protestant survivors don't automatically understand that those abused by ministers of other faiths are also welcome despite efforts of SNAP to dispel this myth. Some who come from less ecclesiastical systems have expressed difficulty in relating to members in SNAP, since there is still an underlying current evident, at times, that prevents Catholic survivors from understanding how the wounds inflicted from the sinister tactics of Protestants can be equally as deep as those left by the "real" Church.

Yet David Clohessy, former executive director of SNAP, understands as well as anyone that conservative evangelical churches, especially mega-churches, are the new frontier in this work. Offenders in both clergy and laity easily hide among the crowd, and people seeking "only Biblical answers" are likely to find plenty of ways to multiply the use of Scriptures as weapons to support complicity if a case happens to surface.

***

"Does anyone have a contact in Omaha?" The message caught my attention the moment it flashed across my monitor.

"Omaha!" I shot back. "I'm only minutes away!"

"I thought you were in Iowa," Kevin replied.

"I am—on the border of Nebraska, though. What's up?"

"Well, this lady's coming up on the one-year anniversary of being raped and badly needs local support. Can you take it?"

Within five minutes, I had an email connection with Nobuko Oyabu. I offered to meet her anywhere she wished, immediately if need be. Not necessary. She could wait until the next evening, she assured me.

Immediately, I recognized her luxury apartment house just by name. Only fifteen minutes from my own place, I'd even gone there to visit a colleague a few years earlier.

In less than twenty-four hours, I was sitting in front of her large living room window, taking in the spectacular view of the third-largest colored fountain in the world, one of my favorite places in the Midwest, while listening to the horrific details of her account, some of which is now on her web-site, nobukoonline.com:

> *"That night, I was forced to learn how much it hurts to be violated in a very sacred place; my womb. The offender was sentenced to 20 years in prison. I am one of few lucky victims who got some sort of justice. I know the majority are not so lucky. I now cannot stop wondering how many victims are out there crying alone tonight."*

For the first time in my life, after years in mental health nursing and listening to hundreds of survivors, I heard a survivor's voice filled with far more gratitude than rage. At first, I thought she must be in a lot of denial. Yet, as I listened, I sensed she was far from it.

She could acknowledge the pain and sorrow, and knew she still had some hard work ahead. Though she appeared incredibly fragile with her petite frame, I soon recognized this beautiful woman to be as strong as nails. By nature, she's as gentle as a dove, poised as any actress, and wiser than any serpent. Yet she also had a life-long, strong faith, still intact. This, she believed, had guided her decisions from the beginning until the present.

Fearing the rapist might return as soon as she left, she'd instantaneously wrapped herself in the top bedsheet after her violent assault and dashed across the hall, where she managed to awaken a male tenant who immediately pulled her inside, locked the door, and called the police. From that moment until the day of court, when the neighbor, as her witness, was allowed to testify on her behalf without her ever going into the courtroom, Nobuko felt vindicated.

There were no long delays. The rapist was serving a twenty-year sentence. Every person along the way knew what to do and what to say, she told me. This included her co-workers, many at her church, and even people she'd never met, like those who had trained responders and laid the groundwork for justice by getting legislation passed, she explained.

None of this erased the pain she was now revisiting, telling me her sacred story. Yet it allowed her to move on without the re-injuries the majority of survivors' experience. That's why she was inspired to do something to help those less fortunate.

What she envisioned was a book, especially for people in Japan, where the subject of sexual violence was seldom discussed, even in the media. As an award-winning photojournalist, now working for the Omaha World-Herald, she'd be putting faces to sexual assault through displays and a book she hoped to publish. Her work would speak in the same way that photos of breast cancer had, saying: "This happens to real people. These aren't made-up stories".

I had a story about Japan myself. A couple of years earlier, I'd been contacted by an associate editor of a widely-read evangelical publication in Japan, asking me for an article on sexual abuse in the church. He'd need plenty of lead time to get it translated. So, I was just getting started when the man emailed again with an apology. His editor had forbidden him to go any further with such a radical project. Hearing this saddened Nobuko, but did not surprise her. The culture greatly discouraged open dialogue about sexual violence far more than in western culture, she explained.

As we visited, I enjoyed a delicious, three-course, Japanese meal that could have competed with any restaurant in town. It was Nobuko's gift to *me*, she said; yet I had come, hoping to be a blessing to *her* with a small token of my appreciation, a copy of *How Little We Knew*. Somehow, someday, I told her, it might help in her work as she encountered the

masses in the faith community unlikely to experience the justice that she
had in the courts.

Before we'd even gotten to the cream flan, I learned that Nobuko was
also a preacher's kid. Her parents had first been Baptists, but became
United Methodist when she was very young. Her father did a lot of work
with street women in Japan and often talked about this population's link to
a history of childhood sexual abuse. When she got around to telling them
of her rape, she knew they'd be supportive. Yet she'd not done so yet,
since she'd not seen them since the incident. She was now more worried
about them and how she'd cope with their pain. How hard it would be to
see them struggle with her revelation!

That night, we dreamed together, even as we shared mutual
sorrows—me old enough to be her mother with several years' experience
in advocacy, allowing her to take the lead in the conversation. When she
got into her project more, I was certain I could connect her with survivors
across the United States, Canada, and a few abroad. The problem would be
expenses for travel. She would find the way, she assured me.

Before leaving, I planted a wild idea, telling her about Lifetime TV,
the women's channel. Though she'd never heard of it and I'd never seen
anything like her project on the network, there was a remote possibility
they'd be interested.

I was one of her first photo subjects. She came to the parsonage with
all her equipment, same as she visited so many others in their own homes,
just as I'd done in hers a few months earlier. And I knew at least 20% of
her subjects by the time she finished. Several of them victims of clergy I'd
introduced her to that she'd ended up traveling, even abroad, to visit.

Later, I shared with her a set of Bette Rod's lyrics, which reminded
me so much of this courageous young woman now:

> "You can't hurt me anymore.
> I am stronger than you think I am."

By the end of 2002, three exciting things had happened in Nobuko's
life. In July, she married a supportive African-American minister named
Patrick. A short time later she fulfilled our dream when she appeared on
Lifetime TV for a documentary devoted to her award-winning

photojournalist project with the faces of several survivors from Japan to England to Manitoba and all across the United States. The project also kicked off the National Domestic Violence Awareness Month at the Russell Rotunda of the United States Senate in Washington D. C. The signs under the photos told something about each person pictured. Through all of this, she's been sure to tell people of the added layers of collusion that often come from leaders of churches, usually unprepared and too afraid to face the truth whenever they encounter an abusive member of the clergy.

In 2005, the two became the proud parents of a baby girl. Her grandparents came from Japan to visit, and the young family reciprocated with Nobuko sometimes making trips on her own before they settled down in Yokohama, Japan for both of them to get involved in various outreach projects. This amazing young woman, who still uses her camera as a tool for ministry, has also been honored with multiple advocacy awards.

In 2007, her story and photos were published in Japanese in a book entitled "Stand."[2]

In 2011, she participated in disaster relief, photographing the destruction and comforting survivors of the earthquake in Japan. And since moving back to her native land, she's been working toward establishing a support system for survivors of sexual violence and being an advocate for other disenfranchised groups locally.

Advocacy—it's a gift that just keeps giving as we give ourselves away to others.

*****

[1] Direct quote from The Rotarian, February, 2017, p. 42

[2]   https://leoadambiga.com/2012/04/16/photojournalist-nobuko-oyabus-own-journey-of-recovery-sheds-light-on-survivors-of-rape-and-sexual-abuse

See also http://www.huffingtonpost.com/nobuko-oyabu/

Chapter 26
Malarkey Time

Under the best of circumstances, there is no way to guarantee the outcome when a person goes forward to say or write what most people do not want to hear. There are always surprises in justice-seeking, whether in the courtroom or in a bishop's office. Things are usually more complicated than one would expect. Such is the nature of dissident writing.

As 2000 came to a close, I was putting the finishing touches on *The Truth about Malarkey*. This novelette, written by popular request from readers of previous work, had been fun to write. It was self-published through a popular new, environmentally-friendly means, called "print-on-demand." Someone said it was going to turn the publishing industry upside down, flooding markets with much-needed materials and stories for small audiences, which means anyone who doesn't have about 15,000 copies sold in a single year. Perfect for me, I figured.

By today's standards, it was still expensive--$1000, but that bought cover design and help with formatting, unlike Amazon's do-it-all-yourself-for-free option today, for multi-talented people with a ton of patience.

Every fictional character in the book was inspired by a survivor or advocate I'd met. It was a way to honor them all. Or dishonor, in the case of a few shady characters.

The story offered a bit of comic relief with a powerful, surprise ending, reviewers were soon saying. It was narrated by Grandma Cora, a great-grandma, sitting on her front porch, writing a very long letter to her seven-year-old great-grandson. As she began writing, she bemoaned the fact she had only seen him through photos. Yet still held out high hopes he might someday be interested in reading what she had to say in this otherwise only-for-grownups epistle.

The cover designer at Author House found the perfect picture for the cover. Two shiny white rockers sitting on the front porch of an old house, invited visitors to sit down and "listen a spell."

As soon as the book was released, with initial marketing in place, I made a trip up to Mankato, Minnesota. It was pay-back time—and I wanted to see the face of "Salty" Babcock as I handed her one of the first copies.

I had a selfish motive, too, wanting to first get a big bowl of homemade soup she always had waiting for any guest who might pop in. And, if she had it, I'd like some of her homemade berry cobbler before reading the story she had inspired, for Salty was the real Grandma Cora in my life, my spiritual grandmother, that is.

So, I did just that, sitting in the same rocker I'd sat in four years earlier when Ron and I had been her guests over the very stressful weekend in between Mayo appointments. Now, our hearts were merged into one.

And once again, forty-eight hours ago, when her most recent picture happened to arrive to grace our own kitchen table, front and center, as I put the finishing touches on this chapter in 2017. Next to my own mother and about the same age, she shines as the epitome of resilience.

A Positive Sign of the Times

In the process of getting that little story written, I was flooded with questions from survivors wanting to write their own true stories. Many had. Now, they only needed someone with expertise in the field and writing experience who would spend a few minutes looking over their "nearly-finished" story, as quite a few wrote to ask. Could I help? I was deeply humbled by these requests.

It was a nice problem for the survivor movement to have, but quite a dilemma for me. I could see an emerging issue none of them could have foreseen—one that I certainly could not have imagined ten years earlier.

Sadly, most of the stories sounded like duplicates, though every story had unique aspects, as they always do. In therapy, finding the uniqueness in a client or the story being lived is the key to overcoming for many, provided a therapist knows how to help in this process of self-discovery. In this case, while all of the writers seemed quite confident they'd have a corner on the emerging market, selling thousands of books, I knew this was all fantasy. There simply weren't that many corners to be had—at least, not that I knew of. Certainly, I didn't have one, as they seemed to assume.

It was actually a good sign. Unlike a decade earlier, with thousands of survivors now speaking out, and even collections of stories on the market already, the movement was getting where it needed to be—in the public arena. Survivors were starting to discover a wealth of information, thanks to the gradual media exposure. Markets were being flooded with all the new avenues for publishing, and that was the problem for would-be writers. Yet what a blessing for those of us who find reading to be our best source of information!

Few outside the movement were interested in reading what any of us had to say about abusive clergy, however, though we longed for things to be different. Most didn't want to know what "the lepers" knew, and it was likely to remain so for many years to come. Many survivors also shied away from others' stories because the triggers were too much.

This is the nature of any serpent. Five minutes on TV was enough time for anyone's sad story about anything, the way most people saw things, while the media kept producing plenty of evidence that the supply of stories was greater than the demand for learning.

Since most survivors had been isolating themselves rather than getting outside their shells for years, the chances of them getting back even a tenth of their investment was slim, thereby setting up some of the most fragile for a mighty fall in the end, I feared. So what would you advise?

Not wanting to discourage any who had found the energy to get this far, I also didn't want to lead them down a primrose path. Doing so would be akin to telling them what some clerics were saying—usually men with big hearts, attempting to be helpful by assuring survivors they could "expect to be heard" if they went to their local denominational official with a report. The reality was this usually served as a set-up, even when innocent and unintended to be so, and I often got the results in my inbox.

I decided to be upfront. They should certainly pursue their dreams, yet I wasn't in a position to help much, I explained time and again, until I finally put a page for these inquiries on my FAQ page.[1] It served two purposes: The fact the question was even there told searchers they were not in a unique situation, and it kept me from having to spend time letting each one down easy with what they might need to hear, but weren't ready to absorb. Once they considered the investment in personal resources to accomplish their goals, they could decide if it was worth all the effort. After all, that's what every survivor needs to know before coming to conclusions about any of the complicated issues in survivorship.

For some publishing was worth all the time and investment, even if they sold ten copies to close friends and select family members. For others, simply writing the story so it was out in front of them, for their personal use alone, was therapeutic.

Broken Trust

It's impossible for me to know how popular a booklet bearing the title "Broken Trust" ever became to its primary audience, Texas Baptists. I haven't heard from a single soul who ever read it. I find this surprising, considering that my work and website are sprinkled liberally throughout the document, which should have raised at least a few questions, if not a few eyebrows. It's still circulating on the shelves of Baptist institutions of higher learning in several states, according to interlibrary loan services, and in many ways it's a sterling accomplishment of Dr. Joe Trull, far exceeding anything Southern Baptists have yet produced, to my knowledge.

He refers to the problem of clergy sexual abuse as "clergy sexual misconduct," as Fortune commonly did almost exclusively in the 1980's and 90's. Unlike Fortune, he totally left out the possibility of minors being a part of a groundswell of concern as I predicted would soon be clearly revealed.

While some in the late 20th century, like Trull, were still declaring these sexual misconduct problems "not yet of epidemic proportions," Trull casts doubt on this by saying "not yet of *horrific* proportions."

The serious problem of "clergy sexual misconduct" of adults was well explained with no blame put on victims. He was especially wise to point out that ramifications for an entire congregation are vast and long-lasting, same as for survivors.

The wisest, most far-reaching recommendation he offers is his well thought-out "Covenant of Clergy Sexual Ethics." The form containing the covenant is printed in the book for churches or individual pastors to consider. Any denomination could and should require something of this nature, in my opinion, though true to Baptist polity, the SBC is as likely to disband as it is to do so. For the Convention's structure is not set up to nationally impose anything on individual congregations or church leaders. And even if an attempt was made to do so, independent-minded congregations could choose to simply withdraw from the Convention, as some do every year.

Furthermore, SBC congregations, like some mainline groups, are free to hire anyone they choose to, whether affiliated with the SBC or not—a problem few outsiders can understand, including many lawyers, until they are in the middle of all the frustration.

However, a code of ethics is needed for all professionals, not only members of church staffs with consideration also given to requiring every prospective Sunday School teacher to sign, if not to have a background check—something very few mainline congregations even do except for day care workers.

With adults, sometimes the senior pastor is understood to have far more power than the rest of the staff members and volunteers. To a minor, this is rarely the case. So, the damage done when a child is abused by a Sunday School teacher is high on the trauma scale for kids, especially for kids who don't have other reliable role models available.

This covenant goes beyond any state law, to include issues Baptists and many other Christians consider immoral, lumping it all together with the sexual abuse of individuals of any age, which is always a moral issue. No arguments there. In the document, there is plenty of room for adaptation, even for other denominations where congregations are more likely to be "open and affirming" toward LGBT clergy.

Perhaps there have been a lot of improvements made in Texas since "Broken Trust" was published. I really can't say. From 2000 on, I rarely heard from the BGCT about anything going on there, except through survivors who tested the system and came away very distraught.

However, since "Broken Trust" does still sit on the shelves of many institutions of higher learning, I feel it's important to offer some suggestions to address concerns and omissions. I'll start with the latter.

There's nothing to say that offenders usually have seriously messed up numerous times in some way, often including crossing sexual boundaries. Nothing suggests this fellow might never have been a good candidate for ministry in the first place, due to the very serious deficits in the screening processes in every denomination. Yet with Baptists, there's an even greater flaw—without even basic requirements in education and without professionals well trained to help in the determination beyond a statement of belief and no *known* record of a criminal record, it's very easy for a charismatic guy, good at charming a crowd, to be quickly ordained by his local congregation. That's right. The local congregation, often before a ministerial student even begins seminary, may be ordained. It happens all the time.

Most serious is the failure to point out that teenagers were some of the most likely victims. I'd done so in conversations with this ethics professor and writer on numerous occasions, each time coming away with the impression he considered cases involving teenagers to be flukes. Yet at least half the reports I was getting involving Baptist cases were from adults abused as kids by a member of the clergy, few of them by their own fathers. Perhaps this was because our story included adolescents, I often thought. Later, there would be an avalanche of cases coming to the attention of Christa Brown at stopbaptistpredators.org, soon after the Boston *Spotlight* story occurred in 2002, and some were more willing to talk to the press than the initial contacts I'd received via snail mail.

My greatest personal disappointment in "Broken Trust" was that his brief summary of my story skipped from the relatively "minor problem" of my sexual assault by a colleague, to the far bigger problem, the collusion, again leaving out entirely the adolescent victims. In so doing, he assisted the Board in minimizing, once again, denying that teenagers were even in the mix. Yet, it was the adolescents who should have been front and center, that got wiped out again as they have been by virtually every writer who has attempted to re-write *How Little We Knew* in summary form.

By failing to even mention the abuse of minors in this document, except in the covenant, keeping the focus only on adults recently abused who choose to report, minors are totally wiped off the slate. They do not exist in this story! While there should be no "partial blame" continuum, based on age, there is an increased vulnerability scale to help us be aware of the entire spectrum.

Keeping the focus entirely on adult victims, there is not even a mention of how some pastors begin grooming their young victims well before they reach the age of consent, then blatantly cross sexual boundaries as soon as these teenagers no longer fall under the jurisdiction of DHS or CPS in their respective states.

This common omission is worth mentioning again, especially as it pertains to the largest and fastest-growing group of churches—the conservative, evangelical—for reasons already given in Chapter 3.[2] What few recognize is that most of these girls are robbed of the opportunity to develop a normal interest in dating during this important stage of their development as their abusers lead them to believe they this relationship they are having with a minister or youth worker is extra special, even one to be treated as sacred.

The abuse of adult women by clerics is certainly an immense problem in the pastoral relationship. There's no denying this. However, failing to acknowledge the fact that sexual abuse of teens is also a widespread problem, in order to focus primarily on abuse of adults, is a huge mistake. It's like comparing the size of a massive tornado to a hurricane. We need to watch out for both and to be prepared for the potential for immense destruction that's inevitable in each, never minimizing the immense suffering of the victims in either.

Abuse of any minor, of course, should be reported to authorities. Even laity, though not mandatory reporters are *ethically* bound to report. Somebody needs to spell this out, as well.

Neither is there any coverage of the problem that causes the greatest degree of DIM thinking, often even far more than with women deemed to have recently had "a consensual relationship." This omission is the fact most minors do not report for many years, same as the Catholic victims coming forward now. Yet these late whistle-blowers should be taken just as seriously with accountability imposed after an investigation and reports made to law enforcement. Including this would also be a good educational piece, showing that the author is trauma-informed, understands why the delay occurs, and wants to be sure others do.

Another missing link: the fact that few adult victims ever report unless someone else discovers the problem and "squeals." And when someone does, be it a gossip or a truly concerned advocate or courageous survivor, if the case is either ignored or not well-investigated by an *outside* source, it will almost always be considered "false" or "unfounded."

In fact, there is no emphasis on the need to hire an outside consultant to assist in any investigation, like someone qualified in conflict resolution and sexual abuse to help the congregation process its feelings, teach them the very common dynamics of congregations, and work toward healing, regardless of the determination of the case.

Neither is there anything to say that Texas law already mandated churches to pass along information or to ask about any allegations in the process of hiring a new minister. Of course, Trull didn't describe other problems as I had when we'd last talked. He could have quoted me if he'd asked, though including my remarks wouldn't have done much for his own reputation and could have even created some serious financial woes for the BGCT. What I'd said was "the good ol' boy system works well in the Baptist system, helping clergymen to pass along recommendations to 'new places of service,' using well-developed grape-vines." I'd learned all about how this worked as a child, sometimes during anxious moments, listening from around a corner to Dad as he told Mom not to worry. After a few phone calls to men in his vast network, he himself, for whatever reason, was sure he could locate a less stressful group of congregants until he moved on to discover what Mom had been trying to tell him for years—they were basically all a lot alike. Unhealthy troublemakers, stuck in ruts, abounded right alongside the healthy and more progressive—the "wheat and tares" intermingled and often ensnarled together.

In the SBC, one recommendation is all it takes to get the ball rolling toward hiring a new pastor. And unlike with Methodists or even with the very conservative Missouri Synod Lutherans, there's no central person or clearinghouse with real clout at all. Plus, this Baptist system works 365 days of the year, for hiring and firing often without giving a cause for firing. This lack of checks and balances creates a whole layer of added anxiety for sexual offenders, as well as ethical pastors who may be simply trying to do their work with the utmost diligence. The sudden economic losses can be literally overnight, depending on the congregation's policies (or lack of them).

Economic loss of an alleged offender may be well covered by malpractice insurance along with powerful lawyers to come to the perpetrator's defense, as well as the insurance of the congregation for its own defense in case an adult victim finds economic means or a pro bono lawyer and the emotional energy to pursue a civil case if she even chooses to do so.

"Malpractice" is seldom a word used in documents like this, as opposed to those describing the behavior of medical doctors or counselors. However, it certainly should be there, same as the long-term economic impact and frequent disability or job loss sustained by victims, often for the rest of their lives and often exacerbated by church lawyers.

While there are clear recommendations that background checks be done when hiring a new pastor, not one word suggests any sort of informed consent being provided for members or potential new members when a "rehabilitated" offender is placed back into a pulpit after what's deemed by designated pastoral counselors to be an appropriate rehabilitation period either. Since Baptists often tend to think of women as property of their husbands, and since women may be minimally involved in the initial hiring or firing process of a pastor in most churches, I thought it would be good for the men of the prospective church to all be asked to consider: "Would I trust this guy to be in a room alone with my wife?" Of course, that would have been perceived as mere sarcasm, raising too many eyebrows, but I still believe it remains an appropriate question.

Also missing, a recommendation that the pastor *always* be required to step down and go on paid leave of absence during an investigation, though Trull does say that this is something to be considered by an individual congregation. Not nearly tough enough, according to other professions like police and school teachers. Just ask any journalist to explain the ethics in regard to public figures on this.

Neither is there a call for the congregation to be informed of the specific type of allegations if a pastor chooses to resign in order to avoid an investigation, which is very common. Nor a call for the nature of founded allegations to be made public once the investigation is complete, as occurs with any other public servant. No, that wouldn't be "Christian," folks say, as if secrecy that puts others at risk is? The only clear recommendation is that this should be done only if an alleged offender is found innocent. I certainly hope people understand the difference between "innocent" and having a case "unfounded." [3] (See Chapter 38 for more information.)

Also missing is the frequent issue of problem of blaming the wife and allowing an offender to do so, thereby putting her into a victim roll, as well.

One statement (on p. 19) is clearly an oxymoron, though I believe the wording is a mistake rather than intentional: ".... consensual sex is always an abusive act..." Instead it should read "no sexual action toward a parishioner or counselee should be spoken of as 'an affair' or 'consensual.'"

An important distinction should be made between "sexual immorality" and "abuse." Not all matters considered "sexually immoral" in faith groups are abuse, though all abuse or "misconduct" is immoral and never, when it involves a pastor, should it be considered a victimless act, whether it's covered by law or not.

A variety of violations of adult victims were given, including an entire page on sexual harassment.

With the omissions covered, there are not many corrections I'd suggest. Except for a very big one which I'd attempted to make clear to the ethicist to no avail, as noted in this text once previously in Chapter 16.

He seems to love the word "wanderer," as opposed to "predator." And like many more conservative ministers have, he has found individuals minimally-trained for this work, despite their academic credentials, who support his overly-optimistic view of potential rehabilitation. Not that I'm against rehab. As a nurse, that's high on my priority list for every person. I'm just not convinced that most offenders, even without minors among their victims, can be considered good candidates for returning even to supervised ministry for a very long while. And when they are, their return must be treated in the same way a new congregation decides to handle a new pastor who has embezzled thousands of dollars in funds from a previous congregation. How many are going to be willing to hire a guy like that, to have him stand as a "forgiven" role model for their children?

Unfair! Is that what you believe? Perhaps revisiting a set of values that puts the souls of vulnerable women as a lower priority than a few thousand dollars needs to be considered here.

Reading on, we soon discover a new terminology, the "lover," used to describe women not in counseling at the time of the "misconduct," but still the victims of sexual harassment—perhaps in the church kitchen or elsewhere than the pastor's study. Strangely, he considered them victims, so where he got this ridiculously confusing term I still do not know. It appears to be his own creation, and he refused to back down from my repeated suggestions he correct the error in his 2004 update of Ministerial Ethics.

If this had been one of the theses I was occasionally asked by a doctoral student to critique before printing, about the after-effects of abuse in individuals or churches, I would have praised much of the content he'd included and offered a few suggestions on matters I felt essential to change. He'd not given me that opportunity. Neither did the volunteer coordinator whom I'd met in Little Rock, a lady who showed interest in my work while admitting her experience with abuse issues was limited to the knowledge of a few cases. No doubt she had little power to override anyone else, but it would have been nice if she'd exercised her power, as women often forget they hold, and simply asked for my input as coordinator of this project. If so, I might have suggested that some of the space devoted to the needs of victims, which often vary greatly from one to the other. I would have cut to the chase with only three short sentences:

> Victims of trauma are likely to ask far less of you
> than you might expect. Make no assumptions.
> Simply ask.

I would ask he put a link to an article I'd given him, published on line by the time of Broken Trust's release. The title he appropriately listed as "unpublished" is "How could she?" In the article, I'd turned the question around to shine the light on members of the BGCT all the way down to every congregant, in the end posing a question so often asked by survivors: "How could *they*?"

Joe Trull left the door ajar for future research when he lifted what he saw as most important in the article: "Even less is available on what makes an individual in the institutional church vulnerable to colluding." Unfortunately, there was nothing to point readers to revelations of one of my most interesting respondents prior to the publication of Broken Trust:

> After finding my website, a lady named Dottie came under strong conviction that she should fully acknowledge to a survivor her behaviors of betrayal and express remorse. We corresponded for some time. I commended her for her rare courage and honesty.
>
> Eventually, it became evident that Dottie's motives were not entirely pure. She asked me to look over a letter she was hoping to send to the survivor. I did. To me, it seemed that she was most concerned with her own losses. There was no evidence, however, that the survivor was ready or ever would be ready to restore the relationship. My suggestion was that she remove the sentence expressing hope that the survivor would forgive her and once again be her friend. She needed to do that, I felt, because it was putting an undue burden on the survivor, who

might feel it as impossible and unhealthy for her to have the relationship restored as it would have been to restore fellowship with someone who had murdered her mother.

I told Dottie that it was appropriate that she admit what she had done. After that, there was only one thing remaining. She must grieve the loss of the relationship, relinquishing the luxury of putting the ball in the court of the survivor. Then, she must be willing to wait. Only if the survivor initiated a hope for restoration, could she pursue it. This was hard for Dottie, but she agreed that she could understand this. The story is still in the process of unfolding.

Meanwhile Dottie is working to bring good out of evil. Not only did she apologize. She is taking steps toward becoming an advocate within her denomination. She is determined that she will not collude again. And I believe there is a good chance that she won't. It has been an extremely painful education.

I leave you with Dottie's story, hoping that you will understand your vulnerability to both being victimized and to being blind-sided in the important work you are doing. In so doing, perhaps survivors who come your way will not be asking themselves "How could *they* .... ?"[4]

It was the betrayal of women like Dottie that had me most perplexed, even more than their male counterparts who also failed miserably in the empathy department.

Hope does spring eternal, as Kevin Gourley so frequently pointed out on the original advocateweb.org. So until a much younger Baptist drops into my life to update Joe Trull's historical first attempt, I hope these recommendations will be useful.

*****

[1] http://www.takecourage.org/articles/FAQ/FAQ6.htm

[2] The tendency in theologically conservative groups is to think of the "age of consent" as much lower than even the law indicates. Male privilege promotes a culture that expects girls traditionally to grow up and be responsible adults around the onset of puberty, whereas "boys will be boys" operates much longer—actually for life in the minds of so many.

[3] "Unfounded" does not mean those cases are false. It may mean no documentation was kept, perhaps purposely, and there's nobody willing to corroborate what the survivor is reporting.

[4] http://www.takecourage.org/howcouldshe.htm

Chapter 27
Pivotal Moments

There's nothing simple about advocacy. As any aspiring advocate will soon learn, having a network of individuals with advanced degrees in a variety of fields isn't just a luxury. It's an absolute necessity.

Robert Fulghum's wonderful, little classic, *All I Really Need to Know I Learned in Kindergarten: Uncommon Thoughts on Common Things*, is filled with gems that apply to the most ordinary, as the title clearly states. Everything he says also applies to the rather uncommon work of advocacy work. Yet there's so much more we really need to know before we take on this daunting work.

Like many kids born before 1950, I *never* went to kindergarten except for a few days—and Mom considered that "just for fun." It wasn't fun for me. It was absolute torture.

I wanted to be back with my mama, where things were comfortable, where I really fit in much too well—though neither my teacher or my prim and proper mother see this as a problem. In fact, this was also where my mama wanted me to be, I later figured out.

However, this put me at a real disadvantage when I got to first grade, around kids who had far surpassed me socially. Though not nearly as much intellectually, my parents, grandparents, and doting aunts all liked to proclaim, as if the one child in their lives was the smartest they'd ever seen and that was all that mattered.

Truth is, I was about the only child they'd seen in a long time, seven years the senior of the next child to come on either side of our extended family. Looking back, I suspect I was "spoiled rotten." Perhaps more so because of my role in my mother's side of the family. From what I now believe, having worked extensively with families who have lost a child to SIDS (Sudden Infant Death Syndrome), I served two generations—both my mother's and her parents', as "the replacement child" for Mom's older sister, lost only twelve years before my birth. That's not long at all for a grief so deep. In essence, I was spoiled rotten.

It was my mother who had the intellectual part well covered, long before today's concept of home schooling was in vogue. Her intent was not to protect me or to keep me from knowing the truth, I now understand, as much as it was for us to continue enjoying each other's company far more than was normal for most mothers and daughters. Mom needed me for good reason, as much as I needed her.

"I raised you as you finished raising me," she told me only weeks ago, as we took a ride down memory lane to the land her sharecropping father secured in her teenage years.

"Why haven't you shown me this place that you've spoken of so often?" I asked, as we pulled into the gravel parking lot of the old, historic, now deserted grocery store, standing as a relic.

"I thought you'd been here," she shrugged.

"If so, I was too young to remember," I say, as she retraces her lonely steps of eons past to a school bus that she tells me took her "far from home early each morning" at age fifteen. It didn't take long to establish that it wasn't really far at all—probably only twenty minutes if they'd gone straight into town at the speeds of the 1930's. Funny how perspectives change.

Mom's need to have her raising completed in adulthood is common for traumatized children who get stuck emotionally wherever the trauma occurs. So, she spent most of the next eight decades going back to the sounds and sights of horror she experienced in the same room where her sister died at age nine of diphtheria on a cold winter night, when Mom was only a year younger. She goes back there often still when she faces great adversity that causes her to regress much further than her linear years easily show on the calendar. Or in her dreams from PTSD that occasionally plague her, and last did in 2016, about the time of her sister's death.

Sadly, she understands the connections, and so do I, having often visited that trauma with her as a secondary victim, for as long as I can remember her telling the story. It followed me even in the deepest depressions for my mother, for which she received little treatment in my high school years, when I was forced to grow up fast to care for my two much younger siblings and mama, too, with my father's help, when she was too overwhelmed to handle the stresses their care required.

In much the same way as many families have spoken to me of experiencing "something like a death" when there is long-term sexual abuse of either an adult or child by priests, rabbis, or ministers, every life in my mother's family was deeply scarred from that day in 1934 forward, some more than others. Each twisted into a pretzel from which they seem never to have fully recovered, from the parents down and even to the baby sister, who was loved and coddled all the more by my mother as she tried to make up for her parents' inability to emotionally respond at times to the surviving children as each navigated along an uncharted course. Much of what happened at the time of the older sister's death was too painful for the family to talk about, so they acted out or suppressed their immense sorrow without the benefit of anything like the sophisticated therapy that more fortunate families of today are able to sometimes find.

Mom was left on her own to make decisions she'd always depended on her "twin" to make. They *were like twins*, in Mom's eyes and everyone else's, too. Only sixteen months apart, they even dressed alike and were considered so close in capability that Mom was promoted to sit beside her sister in the same class of their one-room schoolhouse by second grade.

How frequently I've been drawn back into those scenes so vividly described by my mother in the midst of The Great Depression! Yet, it wasn't until midlife, as I was recovering from my second bout with cancer that I was able to fully internalize the words of First Lady Eleanor Roosevelt, who epitomized enormous strength and character in an era when grief stretched from one shore to the other and around the world.

Soon I framed her words in a beautiful little plaque my daughter gave me, shortly after I'd clipped them. To me, they serve as a reminder of the resilience of the human spirit in people who have managed to more than survive despite the enormous sorrow I've witnessed in both sides of my family, in families coping with immense starvation in Africa, and those with some of the deepest wounds to the human spirit imaginable, due to betrayal and unspeakable abuses, all of which I've been privileged to know.

"I gain strength, courage, and confidence by every experience in which I must learn to look fear in the face," Mrs. Roosevelt declared. "I say to myself 'I've lived through this, and I must take the next thing that comes along.' We must do the things we think we cannot do."

More Uncharted Territory

Five years later, in 2001, we were on another uncharted journey, with much more to learn, as we once again faced the unknown together. Yet this time, more than ever before, we each appeared to some outsiders, as well as some close family members, to be deviating far off course going on two separate paths and even in opposite directions from where we'd been.

We really weren't. This, we knew without question. In spite of much shared grief, we were working hard to keep our channels of communication open and give each other the space to sprout new wings in advocacy far beyond anything we'd taken on yet, though our thoughts during the difficult days of 2001 were seldom centered on advocacy at all.

Ron needed to go on permanent disability. This meant that old house we'd bought for a getaway would soon be our primary residence. Yet how was I going to help make a living out there, we asked ourselves?

I wasn't, I soon declared. This situation was going to require some creativity, but I'd never needed to stay put in the city where we'd lived for so long more than now. Meanwhile, Ron needed the countryside equally as much. We would just maintain two residences and move back and forth between the two in a much simpler "long-distance marriage than some of our professional friends were doing. After all, forty-five minutes of separation four days each week could be good for us both, we mutually agreed.

A lovely apartment being erected near a secluded wooded area only blocks from where the parsonage stood allowed us to have the benefits in both the city with some elements of the countryside nearby. Without me nearby every day, Ron was free to make his own choices, based on his own energy level, venturing outside the confines of institutional church life, through volunteer work entirely of his own choosing in two distinct communities where we intermingled as we put down roots in our second home as our energy allowed.

This would include fulfilling a lifelong dream of even being a part-time DJ on a local radio station, becoming a city councilman once he'd become a little more stable physically, an advocate for change in mental health services and for children through a tutoring program and CASA (Court-Appointed Special Advocates), and even the presidency of Rotary International in nearby Atlantic, IA for a few years—all things he'd never had time to do with the daily grinds of the pastorate. Yet none of this he could have imagined those first few weeks after being forced to "retire."

The Day the World Stopped Turning

Of course, we were both as unprepared as anyone to cope on September 11, 2001, when tragedy struck our world once again. For Ron, it hooked his current, immensely personal grief. For he'd just preached his last sermon as a pastor and was out at the cottage, getting settled, supervising workers who were helping us turn it from a weekend getaway into a more comfortable, primary residence.

Emotionally, he was in the doldrums already that morning before he saw the first plane hit the World Trade Center. His body, rather than a powerful, corrupt system, had forced him to leave a career this time. Yet he was feeling close parallels with the prior career loss, he later explained. Thus, his current grief was hooking the trauma of thirteen years earlier, trauma that still remained at times as fresh as if it only happened yesterday.

In some ways, he was thrilled to be shedding the burdens of the pastorate that had become twice as heavy in recent years as he'd struggled to keep going with a body that was failing him miserably. We'd been blessed to discover the ABC had a better disability package than we ever imagined. Still, making ends meet wasn't going to be easy either.

It was only a process to get through, I told him. I knew the resilient guy I'd married was going to be fine, though I fully understood he was going to be struggling for a while as he searched for adequate support and a team of professionals to see him through all aspects. It was good we had some space and time to be alone, since he thrives on solitude and nature.

My attitude was somewhat like Kevin Gourley's about the time he found the CET article. He knew he could only support his wife through her struggles as he wrestled with his own. It was the words of Winston Churchill that got him through, he now tells me. "If you are going through hell, keep going."

Unlike Ron, I woke up on September 11 still in the parsonage, with a busy day of packing and teaching ahead, at a far different place emotionally than my husband. My day was all planned, and I could hardly wait to get started.

With the anticipation of a six-year-old, watching the clock for the first guests to arrive for her birthday party, I jumped out of bed, grabbed a cup of coffee and went straight to the computer, as I did most every morning. Eagerly, I prepared for one of my frequent chats with my friend, Olga, now living in England, though native Dutch. We'd become very close since meeting on Advocate Web's list-serve, and were hoping to vacation together soon in Florida, where she and her family would be visiting their daughter.

After my chat with Olga, I'd be going over to the new apartment to see what progress had been made as we anticipated moving what remained in the parsonage into that new place within six weeks. Coming back, I'd catch up with email from readers, put the finishing touches on a new article I was writing, and head out to my first student of the day. By nine o'clock that evening, I'd come home, catch up on the phone with Ron to see how his day had gone before settling in for a good night's sleep.

I glanced out the picture window, taking in the vibrant coral hues of the red oaks I'd soon be missing in the park across the street. I was enjoying the peaceful hour, much quieter than usual since I'd not even turned on the TV—something Ron usually did each morning to catch CNN. All the while, I took time to reminisce, reflecting on the roller coaster life we'd lived since coming to this place in 1990.

While I doubt anyone could fully understand what a tightrope we'd walked, taking a very controversial, often unpopular, stand, some of our congregants were still very supportive and had even asked for reports of my advocacy work from time to time. How grateful I was for these years that had sustained us!

Of course, September 11 didn't go according to plan for anyone. Yet I'm still trying to figure out, fifteen years later, why it never hit me until I called Ron that night. That's when he told me how he'd seen everything I'd missed, from the moment the first plane struck the Twin Towers, as he stayed glued to the television. As I look back, it's easy to understand how my denial and avoidance, not wanting anything else to mess up my complicated life, provided me with an alternative approach that I very much needed at that time in my life.

It wasn't just me. Strangely, not one person I met opened a conversation about the horrific events of that morning either. Above all, parents didn't, wisely not wanting to upset the children.

If it hadn't been for Olga, off in England that morning, I might not have even known of the tragedy. She was the first to speak of the story right after we greeted one another in a private chat room, the only internet means readily available for one-on-one conversation in those pre-Skype days.

"It's awful what's going on in your country this morning! Maybe this isn't a good time for you to chat," Olga began.

I had no idea what she was talking about, but as soon as she said it was in New York and might be terrorism, I remember literally shrugging. No problem, I told her, discounting her gracious concerns, in the message my flying fingers sent back in return.

"This isn't the first time, and it's no big concern for me. After all, New York's a long way from here. Haven't even turned on the TV this morning and probably won't, too much to do. Let's talk."

And just like that we shifted to family matters and the current events in our two little worlds, basking in the comfort of these precious chats, which had become for both of us as therapeutic an exercise as any two friends could ever hope for.

For the rest of the day, without ever turning on the television or radio, I moved across the city from one family of students to another until I finally got around to talking to Ron that evening.

Like millions of Americans who watched the entire tragedy unfold, it would be forever burned in his memory, he was certain. For me, just listening, was horrifying enough. He described it all, moment by moment, in great detail, even how he'd rushed outside to call the workmen in to share the pain and sorrow.

What about Cheryl and Greg, we wondered? We knew they lived in Manhattan, yet didn't figure there was much chance either of them had been near the scene of devastation. Totally wrong, I realized in an email exchange with Cheryl only days later.

She *was* in the WTC that morning, sitting at her desk when the first plane hit, leaving her physically unharmed but with a ton of emotional rubble to sort through. Still shaken, she felt grateful to have escaped. Added to the personal grief sustained from losses in her faith community, she now must also mourn the loss of friends who didn't survive the terrorist attack.

Olga and Cheryl, like Tom Economus and many other good friends, are Baby Boomers, same as me. Yet being born in 1946, I've often served like a "big sister" to other Boomers, a role to which I fall easily into being the much older sister in a family of five. It was no secret that we Boomers were changing approaches to many things, and talking about what others would prefer to forget was an overriding theme for most all of them. Yet, here I was at a time of immensely personal stress, choosing to skip the first-hand view of this most cataclysmic event that had captured the attention of the entire world that day. Somehow, I'm still not sorry I did.

Stepping outside my usual way of operating that one day helped me to comprehend the intense needs so many overloaded souls have for most of their lives, not even daring to look at issues in the middle of their own plate. And I've often wondered if our church pews are lined with more than the population's share of people like this, people who may be far more likely to cling to their faith because of the immense need for solace that's even above average? I've never seen studies on this. It's only a hunch; but if I'm right, would this explain why denial runs immensely deep in the faith community whenever leaders betray souls who are already desperate to survive? And why those deeply wounded by abuse and complicity in the church also grieve so deeply for this place of solace?

Might it take something as cataclysmic in to the "faith" community as the tragedy in New York City on September 11 before people in the pews began waking up to the massive abuse that still had not be exposed on the scale that those of us in the survivor movement knew from reports was going on around the world? If so, what would it be? I wondered. Where would it occur? That's what we activists were asking one another in private conversations that week, totally unaware that a rolling cauldron had been sitting on the front burner of the Boston Globe, about to boil over. Things had reached an iron-hot temperature for the Spotlight team. Yet September 11, as the movie clearly shows, forced this and everything else to the back burner for a little while. Neither journalists or viewers could handle anything more while we all braced ourselves for whatever was ahead.

Chapter 28
Openings and Closures

As the life of Tom Economus ebbed away in Chicago during the approaching Christmas season, Boston's Spotlight team was back at it, working on the biggest going-away present Tom could ever hope for. Multiple news articles about the abusive priests in the area began rolling out in January, as the final scenes of the Spotlight movie dramatically show. They continued until Tom's death the last Saturday in March of 2002, then just kept rolling as scandals continued to surface until the end of the year.

Attorney Roderick MacLeish, Jr. told Globe journalists Sacha Pfeiffer and Stephen Kurkjian for a January 28, 2002 article: "The focus of the archdiocese is solely on protecting members of the clergy, with absolutely no regard for those whose lives have been so profoundly and tragically altered as a result of this kind of abuse." [1]

"Everything we've been saying for years is finally getting into print," Gary Hayes told Bruce Egerton of the Dallas Morning News as he stepped into the leadership role of Linkup immediately following Tom's death.

The problem wasn't just Boston's. Nor was it limited to Catholics, Egerton knew all too well, living in Baptist territory. However, finding hard evidence of systemic patterns is difficult in a denomination so loosely structured as the Southern Baptist Convention, where there is no central authority to hold ordained ministers accountable for anything. This is the advantage the Convention continues to hold, which serves only as a grave disadvantage for survivors wishing to hold anyone accountable. The sense of hopelessness was profound and remains so to this day.

In May, I came in from a hard day to find a surprise on my answering machine from our son James. Haley, our first granddaughter, had just arrived and was waiting for us in Kansas City.

Four weeks later, I came home on my birthday to find another surprise call from Missouri, this time from St. Louis. It was Richard Ostling, a religion editor with Associated Press, wanting to get my opinion about some resolution just passed by the Southern Baptist Convention. I scratched my head and laughed out loud.

I'd not kept up on much the Convention had done for seven years nor where it was holding the enormous national meetings that always fell close to my birthday. As a kid, if our family had enjoyed a better-than-usual year financially, my father did his best to reward the family with an exciting little vacation, following days of us all sitting through long, boring assemblies in the civic auditorium of whatever city the SBC's biggest event of the year happened to be meeting.

What on earth was Ostling talking about? A quick internet search provided no clues. That seemed odd until I returned the call, eager to satisfy my curiosity, and soon realized the decision was so fresh it was yet to be written up.

"You're the first person I called for an opinion from the floor of the Convention," the editor explained before I confessed my total ignorance. I was both honored and amused. He could have chosen any number of people in power.

After I offered a humble apology for my total ignorance, he kindly read every word of the lengthy resolution to me.

It was because of Boston, of course. This was obvious from the very first sentence, which told how Catholics were "seeking to address the scandal of sexual abuse by members of their clergy." Next, "we acknowledge our own fallen-ness." It was nice of them to join the human race. Not much of a confession, though, since it did not state the problem of abuse perpetrated by Baptist ministers as a widespread problem.

Halfway through, the resolution called for "Southern Baptists to practice integrity and fidelity to God; urged accountability among spiritual leaders to the highest standards of Christian moral practice; urged seminaries and related educational institutions to emphasize ministerial integrity; encouraged religious bodies to rid their ranks of predatory ministers; called on civil authorities to punish to the fullest extent of the law sexual abuse among clergy and counselors; called on our churches to discipline those guilty of any sexual abuse as well as to cooperate with civil authorities in the prosecution of those cases; and urged our churches to offer support, compassion, and biblical counseling to victims and their families."

"It sounds fine on paper," I told him first thing. Later, what he put out on the wire that was picked up from the San Francisco Chronicle to the

New York Times, declared me to be "skeptical." It was quite an understatement!

My final remark to Ostling, if he chose to put it out, didn't get picked up at all, much to my disappointment: "I'd say this year's Convention is being held in the perfect location. Since Missouri's known as the show-me state, guess we'll have to wait for the SBC to show us what they really intend to do."

It was really the "biblical counseling" called for, as a necessary response to any case that I worried most about, I told this reporter and others that followed in several more interviews. I'd had plenty of so-called biblical counseling, same as other women, in the form of chastisement, mine coming from powerful characters at the Foreign Mission Board, who were upset to find an un-submissive woman on their hands, unwilling to cower to their expectations any more than I was to those of my violent colleague two years earlier.

The journalists who followed tended to ask some of the same ill-informed questions many of us had gotten for years. They were seeking answers nobody could give. Assuming that when I said "abused as minors," I was talking about pre-pubescent kids like the ones making news with Catholics, those were the cases they wanted me to find for them. Instead 98% of my contacts were fifteen or older at the time of their abuse. While hundreds of Baptist survivors had come my way briefly since 1993, few before the days of the internet had bothered to stay in touch. Even though the internet was now the most popular tool, allowing a degree of anonymity while seeking information, most survivors didn't want to be found. For self-protection, they often changed email addresses too, same as phone numbers, fearful of those they feared were out to get them. As for keeping up with most, I'd given up trying.

Oddly, most journalists wanted fresh cases as if there were parents whose kid had just come in to report last week's abuse. Bizarre to think how many failed to understand that most child abuse reports involving clergy aren't likely to be fresh cases. In fact, by the time the "kids" get around to revealing their ancient secrets, their parents may very well be dead and gone.

Yes, I understand these journalists need "real news." By their definition, I didn't really have much. Sorry. Did this prove that the abuse had all gone away now so the problem was fixed? Absolutely not! This was what folks wanted to believe, though. Half the journalists went away frustrated; the other half likely thought I was the biggest crackpot they ever met. I could understand that, too.

One day, when I was feeling a little more hopeful, I got a call from some AP journalist asking to talk to any Baptist survivor and offering to do so off the record, as long as their story was of child abuse—not teen abuse. Of course, most cases didn't fit that bill, anyway. Still, I agreed to see what I could do.

One survivor I located was skeptical. What good would it do her, she wanted to know? Well past the statute of limitations, there was no way the state could do anything. Baptists didn't care, she'd already discovered, and had no system to hold their pastors accountable if they did.

With another, I was sorry I'd called, for I'd obviously stirred up painful emotions.

Finally, a call came from someone asking for names of people who could verify my personal story. Wanting to better establish my credibility, he was disappointed and shocked when I told him I didn't know a single colleague I could count on to do this, even off the record.

I even doubted he'd find any written documentation at the mission board, even if he got a subpoena. For one of our colleagues, who'd talked on the sly to officials at the Richmond-based offices in 1987, informed me they weren't putting anything in writing and neither should I!

Most important, I explained, in case he wanted to pursue more, the Board and my former colleagues would all know me as "Delinda Ann Miller." Not that I'd purposely used a pen name. I'd been going by "Dee" since 1988 when some of my youngest patients, where staff all went by first names, had been calling me that, and it stuck.

Encouraged by the Spotlight story, I was hopeful he would take on an investigation, anyway. After providing him all the details I could, he declined my offer to fax him copies of my one-way paper trail from Africa.

He apparently had neither interest nor time or budget for such a goose chase, and I didn't blame him.

Whether it was confusion over the name, my inability to provide witnesses willing to talk on short notice, or the journalists' lack of interest in taking on a complicated piece of investigative journalism, AP's interest in my work ceased—at least for the moment. Those who had done their best to silence me fifteen years earlier had managed once again to evade public exposure, and I was stripped of the credibility needed to provide me with the platform for further advocacy in the wider arena that I longed to do while the greatest bulk of Baptist survivors were left without justice. Suddenly I was bluer than I'd been in years.

"Journalists never stay around long, and crop up when you least expect them," I could hear Jeanne Miller telling me again. "You never know what they're going to want. Problem is finding the right people to talk at the right time when you really need to be heard. Without a court case or some big news item, reporters quickly move on. Due to the confidences that must be kept, you'll always know much more than you can prove to the world."

I was deeply grateful to have my Catholic forerunners. Yet being the first and foremost survivor activist in the Southern Baptist Convention to speak for the children, as well as adults, was a very lonely position to fill.

Everything is about timing—in publishing and journalism same as it is with therapy. When the "stars align," things happen. The real secret is in the willingness to wait things out. Sometimes for generations if need be. So, I swiftly shifted back from high gear to second, and kept trucking.

Today I have witnesses from the 1980's who refer to me as "Aunt Dee." I'm certain some of them would talk off the record to any member of the press. The story took on much broader dimensions over time as younger members of our old "mission family" have sought me out. And who's to say what their children may decide to do with what they've been told.

Only during the course of writing this book did it dawn on me, while flipping through old scrapbooks, there was a person who would have vouched for me off the record in 2002. I had no doubt. If only I'd thought to provide the name of the psychotherapist in Richmond who was getting ready to retire five years earlier and "might not even be a Baptist anymore" if she'd followed through on those earlier feelings. She was the *only* true voice of advocacy I'd found yet among those still associated with Southern Baptists in this lonely work. Yet when AP asked for witnesses, I'd totally forgotten her telling me to let her know if she could ever be of help.

I figured chances were slim that she would even still be alive. Yet she was. Unfortunately, her age and memory issues seem to have prevented her from even remembering me when I finally tracked her down. In fact, she was confused, thinking I was one of her patients from years earlier when I emailed and later called. After several attempts to refresh her memory, she insists that I must be confused. "That kind of confrontation is out of character for me," she insists in a letter that adamantly denies any recollection of my 1997 phone call.

Yet in earlier conversation, she readily verified that the lady whose name I recalled as having sent me straight to her that night in 1997 was indeed her "best friend and adopted sister," as well as a former colleague. The two of them had worked together in the same Mission of the Foreign Mission Board, in fact. Her friend is now deceased. Now, the lady who helped preserve my sanity went further than saying she has no recollection of my call or of writing me a letter. She insists that she knew this old friend and colleague so well that she is absolutely certain the woman would never have believed that a small child could be held responsible for her own abuse if she crawled into a man's lap.

Despite the great disappointment, all of this denial and forgetfulness made sense to me. I know I did not dream up the remarkable conversation or the letter that I kept for many years and now deeply regret tossing along with many others I did not have room to save. Ron readily recalls all of this from twenty years ago, as well.

I also was shocked to experience a similar reaction only a few years ago. It was with a former male missionary colleague who was the most helpful in providing a sense of reality for us among any of our colleagues, though he never really stood *with* us because, as he told us, "I have to live with these people after you are gone!" It was a shock to hear him say this, for it was the first time either of us had ever stopped to consider we would be forced to leave our careers in order to keep our integrity.

This man, whom I call "David" in *How Little We Knew* denies he was even in Africa in late 1986 and early 1987. He insists he never knew anything about this case! Yet, I'm certain his children all know he was. To give him the benefit of the doubt, I choose to believe he has blocked the entire story out for self-protection, same as the psychotherapist who is certain she did not ever have a conversation with me about sexual abuse and foreign missions. This same woman says she only had "a few cases" of sexual abuse in her thirty-year practice as a psychotherapist. Reality is she only had a few that she *knew* involved sexual abuse. If she had been trained to do the sort of assessments that explore this possibility without even probing deeply, she would likely have discovered she had actually treated far more people suffering from these problems than she was ever aware. Yet avoiding such a line of direct questioning is not uncommon for someone trained in the 1980's, as she was.

Such denial, though not uncommon for a person traumatized by a personal experience they cannot accept, seems exceptionally odd to me in both of the above cases. It's not odd with mothers whose daughters insist they were clearly told the truth about a child's abuse case, however.

I think back to my psychiatrist-friend in Malawi and a question she asked about the perpetrator's wife in our story: "If she faced the truth, what would this require her to do?" In this case, I believe it would require these individuals to face their own roles in not coming forward to say publicly what they knew for so long.

Sadly, I cannot honor this lady by name in this text, as I had so hoped to do when I was thinking perhaps she would now be thrilled to be named as a heroine, same as David might have been after all these years, prompted after his wife had been in close contact with me for several weeks a few years ago. Horrified by the story her son had urged her to read for years, she'd finally gotten to it and now wanted to know who all these characters were—the ones with pseudonyms in *How Little We Knew*. Strangely, she didn't recognize herself until I pointed out an identifying detail I'd kept in the true story, one that could only be hers. I find it sad that neither she nor David were able to recall the contribution they each made to our lives, even by providing their minimal support or to believe they had been the exceptions, as the most supportive couple in our Mission. One would expect people on the wrong side of an issue historically to deny their involvement, but surely people would remember their very important participation on the right side of history that clearly shows a degree of character. Wouldn't they? Not necessarily, according to one expert I turned to for an explanation. [2]

I even have an email showing how this dear psychotherapist was indeed horrified again when I was able to provide substantial evidence of other things only she would have known, which she told me of in that phone call of 1997. And how she wavered back and forth about whether she should go back to her old colleague to discuss matters that now troubled her. Apparently, she changed her mind in the end, insisting I had the wrong person.

It's very possible for a person to do something heroic that is out of character. In fact, her choosing to do so in 1997, clearly illustrates this. It's a sign of character strength to step out of "character" for the greater good, an act of courage. By contrast, not choosing to do an act of justice when you've been presented with the facts is a character flaw so commonly demonstrated by colluding colleagues of professional offenders.

Ron Miller, normally a quiet, reserved diplomat by nature, also clearly demonstrated his ability to step out of his usual mild-mannered personality to act in character when he stood up to the family consultant and refused to back down.

To go one step further, if anyone had asked me to single out any person among our colleagues in 1984 (the year of my sexual assault) who I believed would even hesitate to insist that a sexual predator in our group be immediately terminated, I would have not been able to imagine—especially if the man had assaulted or molested teenage girls. Yet I'd never talked to any of our colleagues about this topic. Why would we talk about something we could not imagine at all? Therein is The Problem in a nutshell.

Likewise, the psychotherapist in the midst of her shock of that conversation in 1997, told me that she'd never discussed sexual abuse with her colleague who sent me her way. So, I can understand her believing she knew this woman to whom she was close. The truth is she did not know her as well as she thought. Otherwise, she would never have gotten a call and blessed my life so immensely.

In fact, none of us know how another may feel about something this serious unless we discuss our feelings freely and openly. What those of us who are seasoned advocates know: we should always prepare to be surprised at others' reactions.

How grateful I am now that I did not send Associated Press to this lady to verify what she knew in 2002! My hunch is that what I'd told her five years earlier and what she'd done out of character was too crazy-making for her to remember, even five years after that dramatic conversation we had on the phone.

Finding an Advocate

I always caution survivors: "Whatever you do, whenever you talk to someone within an institution, no matter how much you believe you can trust the person, be sure to take a witness with you, preferably one from outside the system." This buffer reduces the likelihood of secondary abuse, creating a more even playing field. It decreases the intimidation factor for survivors and diplomatically serves to put those with innate power on notice: secrecy is no longer acceptable.

Because power can be so easily obfuscated by those in charge, it's essential every victim chooses someone confident to serve as a witness to any proceedings. He or she will offer an extra set of ears and eyes.

Spouses should not bear this burden alone, though their presence may be extremely helpful. Nor will they be deemed credible by a system that's looking for excuses already to discount everyone they can. The option of having a dedicated advocate wasn't a luxury available to me in 1986. There was simply nobody I knew who truly "got it," at least not a soul the closed system would allow in. Certainly not the psychiatrist we knew, who kindly agreed to see Ron and me for free, then declared us to be sane and only in need of an apology we should not expect from the sick system. She was already on the system's black list when we turned to her.

Sometimes there's nobody today. Yet, thanks to increasing public awareness and sensitivity, it's more likely there will be.

Ideally an advocate should be assertive, a good note taker, and one with a calm presence. Taking another known survivor, no matter how much experience (s)he has may be counter-productive. Powerful systems with tendencies toward paranoia will likely view such an individual as a threat, no matter how much diplomacy is shown. In addition, triggers easily set off varying degrees of PTSD, severely impairing the most passionate survivor. Other survivors can still play a very significant role, helping to locate advocates without the emotional baggage and being available to debrief later.

Selecting a good advocate is tricky and one that will work in one situation may not be good in another. For instance, the more informed or educated an advocate is, the more likely an extremely insecure system will consider that person a threat, whereas a more balanced system is likely to respect credentials.

I encourage survivors to also work toward assembling an outside support system, made up of several people who may never cross paths with the institution, but can be readily available. Ideally, the combination will include one or two well-informed professionals in addition to good friends or family members. Of course, if there are on-going legal proceedings, an attorney will need to advise a client on how to best do this and who should be a part of this small circle.

While not often available, a strong, supportive man, other than a spouse, can provide a pillar of strength. Without the concern of gender bias, which is often disguised yet ever-present implicitly, such an individual who is willing to stand in the gap in a male-dominated system can make a huge difference. There is a big need for male advocates, yet a scarcity of men willing to take this role—a matter I'll have more to say about in the final chapter.

*****

[1] https://www.bostonglobe.com/news/special-reports/2002/01/28/church-settled-suits-priest/3bwisacFl7FB4x1dJ8SSzJ/story.html

[2] It's entirely possible that aging has something to do with these nearly unbelievable memory lapses. Outside of that, adding to our understanding of how memory works and why people are prone to forget significant things of the past, Gary Schoener provides much insight. It's all very complex, he says. Presented with a new topic outside of the past realm of possibilities or too difficult to comprehend, we may not even "have a place to file" the information. There may be nowhere in our personal memory bank where it can fit. It's very possible that previous trauma or a lack of past experience keeps the new input from registering. Sometimes the question in "filing" has to do with what file "folder" to even use. Creating a new file folder may be something we don't want to do at that moment, for whatever reason. Perhaps our "hard drive" is too full. Sorting things out requires us to stick with an unacceptable topic long enough to process or absorb what has just been said. Our individual capacity for doing this varies greatly.

"Arise, for this matter is
your responsibility.
We also are with you.
Be of good courage
And do it."
Ezra 10:4*

* an interfaith, international message for all generations,
and the cry of photo-journalist
Nobuko Oyabu
(See nobukoonline.com)

Chapter 29
Validating Voices

Persistently, patiently, we must cultivate relationships with other activists and members of the press, welcoming, nurturing, and empowering new voices in every endeavor in which we hope to make change in our world. While all of this takes lots of time and effort, over time, it eventually pays off.

Boston put the survivor movement on its feet in 1993. The tide wasn't in, but enough stories were washing ashore to get the attention of quite a few journalists, especially with an increasing number of lawsuits.

Nothing close to the impact of 2002, however. Boston's devastating news created by the persistent efforts of Phil Saviano and the staff at the Globe had a three-fold effect:

> 1) The *survivor movement* wasn't just toddling along anymore. The tide was obvious.

> 2) The increasing discourse on the street was noticeable, though church folks were the ones most likely to shy away from this most unwelcome topic. Both inside and out, *people were taking sides,* quite a few Catholics really angry at the promotion of incompetency when Cardinal Law was given a place of sanctuary to take on new responsibilities at the Vatican. I found it interesting, and still do, that many people saw 2002 as the cataclysmic year when "all of this started," rather than in 1985 when the Louisiana case should have shook all of Christendom.

> The news of all that Doyle and his friends had tried to do to awaken the bishops even reached us in Mombasa, Kenya, getting our attention in the middle of a much-needed vacation.

> Then, again, I suppose it's a bit like my experience with 9-11, when it didn't all hit me until I learned one of my friends was in the middle of the mess.
>
> 3) While many clergy members remained hostile, some were changing. There was more of a generalized anxiety now in 2002, mixed with shame rather than outright denial. This was unsettling. It was awkward, and *increasingly difficult for the profession to ignore.*

At times, I found it hard not to be amused at how some tried to deflect the "crisis," framing it as another "sign of the times," rather than a sign the profession's dirty laundry could no longer be easily white-washed. The blame for the "mostly Catholic problem" was laid at the feet of lawyers and trouble-making survivors "in this licentious day," a phrase Joe Trull used when warning churches to be cautious of these CSA problems.

"Survivors are just doing this for the money," other skeptics said. Or: "those liberal journalists only want to bring the church down." To others, their colleagues having "fallen into sin" only reflected the way "the world" was going. The solution was simply to protect institutions and pray this all through.

Our own case was "just a fluke" many denominational leaders besides Baptists, implied, as if there were no parallels in the pattern of collusion in other cases. These things don't happen in "the civilized world." I'd heard from the most naïve, some who assumed this had to be an African predator. It was impossible to convince most how commonly these same dynamics operated in virtually every institution, including most extended families, when facing incest, domestic abuse, or addictions.

It all offered many teaching moments, if only the "students" were willing learners.

With great denominational efforts from advocacy groups like COSROW and the Catholic organization, The Voice of the Faithful, resources and support were being spread around to meet the needs of the ever-increasing backlog of survivors pouring out from every corner of the world, faith-based or otherwise.

The needs for each survivor were different. Some sought only Biblical answers or "good Christian counseling." Others wanted none of this and ran from any semblance of it. I could offer some of both, yet my primary focus continued to be providing insights into collusion, the spiritual implications of such corruption for all concerned, and providing resources to assist every reader who came my way in their search for answers. This included anyone who might be seeking ways for institutional leaders to cope. Yet few of those seemed to be seeking help from anyone except lawyers. There was a strong trend in denominations across the board in the 1980's to have priorities align more with business models than the faith-based entities they had projected them to be previously. The worst thing an institution could imagine was financial devastation. Integrity seemed to be secondary and the well-being of the organization trumped individual concerns. Thereby, the personal devastation of individuals harmed by malpractice took a back seat in the "search of excellence."[1]

Meanwhile our own goals were committed to individuals who had been harmed by such a philosophy—like Cheryl and Greg who came to visit us all the way from NYC in the fall of 2002. During the visit we listened to Cheryl's chilling recall of the trauma still fresh for her from the World Trade Center. Yet we were amazed at how she was managing to integrate this with her past. Most telling were the connections she made to her survival in the faith journey. For that day in September, her very life depended on her ability to trust her gut, even going against instructions from officials that turned out to cost others their lives. Once again, Ron and I had switched roles, blessed to be students of someone with personal expertise in survival we could never have experienced otherwise.

Break Time

"There will be no cloning in our family," I was telling everyone when our last two grandchildren were born less than a year apart. Our daughter Renita gave birth to a third boy in 2003, and Kellyn joined her sister Haley ten months later, giving us a total of five, with Micah, the oldest, only eight. I was ready for things to slow down in advocacy. It was time to bask in the joys of grandparenting.

With survivors increasingly finding assistance with quality therapeutic service now and quite a few reporting far more empathetic responses, usually coming from females in leadership in mainline circles, I was ready to celebrate what had been accomplished.

Methodist, Lutheran, and other mainline survivors had no idea how far the movement had come in little more than ten years—actually in less than five, considering our shared sentiments at Boston College in 1998. Neither did they have any idea how much further behind those in conservative, evangelical circles were, with seemingly little hope of ever catching up.

When I attempted to comfort survivors, pointing out any exceptional response that had come their way, some escalated, focusing only on their disappointments. I couldn't fault them. They had a right to expect more, yet it simply wasn't realistic at this point. An increasing number were getting settlements outside of court, thanks to committees functioning far more ethically than anyone fifteen years earlier.

A most striking example of a positive outcome came from a young college student in the Pacific Northwest:

> *District Superintendent Tom Eberly saw that I got financial assistance for a retreat and therapy through the "Healing Care Fund." Meanwhile they called in Stephanie Hixon from COSROW, who acted as an advocate through the process. A consultant from Seattle helped the church leaders draft a letter, which clearly stated the nature of the violations and why the offending youth pastor was suspended, sending it to every member of the congregation!*

Going South

Increased interest came my way from a few women's studies departments. In 2003, with a growing eagerness to find out what sort of reception I might get in the Deep South, I made a trip to the Carolinas, visiting my good friend Sarah Rieth in the process.

With plans to speak at Meredith College and the University of South Carolina at Spartan, I thought it would be good to also have a book signing in Charleston and Savannah. Oh, what a fiasco it turned out to be, just finding places in Charleston! Even the board of the public library decided I was too hot a potato to handle! A survivor who had been practically barred from an Episcopalian church there also tried to find a place and failed.

In Savannah, though I easily found a reception at Barnes and Noble for a busy evening when the book store was full, only one person came near me even though the kind staff announced my presence repeatedly over their speaker system. Each time the announcement was made, over a two-hour period, I tried unsuccessfully to make eye contact with individuals as they looked skeptically in my direction. It was as if some scary creature from Mars had just dropped in to visit!

Finally, the middle-aged woman slowly crept from behind the shelf to my right. I smiled encouragingly, as she crouched before speaking just above a whisper: "I'm not here to buy your book. I only want to say 'thank you' for coming. You have no idea what it means to me."

"Thank you," I said, offering only a sincere smile and subtle nod as she turned and retraced her steps behind the shelf to a corner of the store.

It was a poignant reminder of how threatened entire geographical areas saturated with SBC congregations were culturally on these issues. I returned to Iowa with a heavy heart, though grateful for the warm, yet small, reception I'd discovered in the academic settings.

Another Test Case

It is not at all uncommon for a church, having discovered a perpetrator in their pulpit, to dismiss that person and later to hire another. The dynamics contributing to such problems are not easily cleared up in large institutions any more than in families.

So it didn't particularly surprise me when Christa Brown eventually discovered First Baptist Church of Farmers Branch, Texas, had hired another perpetrator after she had reported to a staff member her abuse as a teenager by the church's youth pastor, who was dismissed and went on to other "fields of service." The second known offender was the one who abused Deborah Dail.

Since Dail and Brown are attorneys, they were far more knowledgeable and prepared than the average victim. They knew what they should be able to expect when filing a report with the church.

In 2004, five years after Dail's report, Christa went back to Farmers Branch, the congregation of her youth, hoping to be heard. As in most local churches receiving a report, especially many years after the abuse occurred, they were not receptive.

There she found her hopes dashed over and over by "helpless" individuals in the usual closed-system dynamics, then, experienced further shock by what representatives of the BGCT and the Southern Baptist Convention had to tell her.2 The slow-paced responses, interspersed with statements that look good on paper yet are slow to translate into reality, are totally unacceptable, yet predictable. The rigidity plus the history of bigotry and misogyny always sugar-coated with Scripture and the heavy-handed tactics of the largest Protestant denomination in the world leaves little room for justice.

Wonderful Validation

Audra and Joe Trull pulled together a compilation of writers, with each of them also doing a chapter of their own, showing their strong stand in solidarity with Baptist women. It was published in 2003 and entitled "Putting Women in Their Place."[3]

I was especially delighted to find a chapter by ordained Baptist woman, Julie Pennington-Russell. While I'd not met her personally, I certainly knew of her. In fact, when I went to the national gathering of Baptist Women in Ministry in 1995, attendees were saying how it would be nice if more could have the success of this woman. Now, since 1998, she'd made history in Texas to become the first female pastor of a Baptist congregation in the state.

Several statements of hers in the book made me feel like I'd just stepped into a crystal-clear, mountain stream on a hot summer day. "When doors are slammed in your face, when your gifts are repeatedly discounted and dismissed....the effect can be devastating. .....Sometimes anger is the most appropriate response to injustice and the best motivating tool for action.....So much of what people have said and done is too ludicrous not to laugh!......I try to seek out and surround myself with people who keep my emotional balloon up in the air.[4]

Some of those words sounded almost identical to statements I'd made in the past. What a sense of kindred-ness is mine with this younger woman I've yet to meet!

Structural Issues

In many ways, the Southern Baptist structure works well for congregations. They can get many things done efficiently without getting bogged down in the bureaucratic quagmire found in denominations with multiple layers of hierarchy. The denomination is unsurpassed in its ability to mobilize people for outreach and to provide state-of-the-art literature to disseminate its doctrines and the teaching it promotes. It has big pockets in agencies, pockets well-protected so far from big lawsuits because of a structure that passes the buck and the burden easily to those with very small pockets, leaving very little help available in cases of devastating abuse. It all works well for the system, of course—which is the primary reason these cases haven't gotten a lot of attention, considering how journalists have needed "news" of law suits to warrant writing about the abuse problems.

Ironically, this polity generally works well to the advantage of liberals, provided churches don't care much about the approval of other Baptist churches, as well. "Liberal" and "liberated" do come from the same steam as "liberty."

However, there are two major problems—each feeding into the other and both appearing very strange to outsiders.

There is actually little security for ministers in the SBC. Nor for their families, as I explained earlier preachers' kids (PK's)—those with great fathers and those with not-so-great ones, all grow up at the mercy of any neurotic church member who can and do often hold more power over the congregation than the minister himself. This is totally the opposite of United Methodist pastors, who still have to be concerned about pleasing such folks. Yet the bishop adds an enormous layer of protection and also the power to sanction. They do well as long as the bishop isn't some neurotic—then things get to be a very different story. Most United Methodist pastors feel the system works quite well. They don't get shipped off somewhere in the middle of the year unless the bishop determines they have majorly messed up. "Shipments" of families occur in early summer, so few PK's ever experience what Baptist PK's can—becoming homeless, yes literally, in the middle of a school year. We were never homeless, but sure came close a couple of times.

The trick for pastors is to keep a viable network, for there's always a lot of politics involved with scores of pastors sometimes vying for the same position, while trying to keep any search for "greener pastures" a secret from their own parishioners for fear a means for improvement may not materialize. So much depends on being in good standing with peers, previously described in Chapter 24.

Those who strictly support such polity provide arguments closely paralleling those of states' rights proponents. Yet states' rights have not worked well on issues of civil rights. That's why we have national laws, which bigots detest.

In America, legislation to provide for safety from assault or sexual abuse is not entirely a local community issue, though enforcement of those laws is. Being safe from such matters is a civil right, no matter where it occurs, whether private or public. Enforcement and record keeping are another matter, but journalists often defy popular sentiments and wisely distribute information, especially on public figures. Ethical journalists and lawyers, the two biggest enemies of institutions, often serve as important instruments of justice and safety.

With the SBC, however, there are no "national laws." And churches tend to operate more like big dysfunctional families than one of the fifty states. There are some associations (similar to districts or areas in mainline denominations) where churches refusing to abide by an *un*written code of ethics are kicked out of the association. This doesn't mean they lose their property or building, though. Neither does it mean they can no longer govern themselves. That's what "local church autonomy" means—total independence, technically. Written codes have historically been frowned. In a sense, every congregation is a collective libertarian force to the degree nobody can force a congregation to stop calling itself "Southern Baptist." However.

Let a church ordain a woman or even ordain them as deacons and the association will likely "withdraw fellowship." Same goes for churches who welcome members of the LGBT community. "Withdrawing fellowship," however, is nothing more than publicly shunning a congregation. So a congregation that chooses to rebel may consider it a source of pride to be singled out like this.

The really big problem, the one I've spent a quarter of a century trying to expose, Southern Baptist congregations are one of the safest places for sexual offenders to hide. The thinking, especially in small, rural congregations is "We all know each other, so these things don't happen here."

Nowhere, nationally, by state, or association is a congregation required by denominational officials to share information about allegations of sexual misconduct or mismanagement of funds or any other crime with people in state or national offices, even when there is strong encouragement to do so. This is the way things operate in such a "libertarian" system. Neither are there sanctions or a withdrawal of fellowship from churches if they fail to report crimes like child abuse to law enforcement agencies. Situational ethics is in full swing with these matters, and the swing of the pendulum is very wide. Even participating in tracking the number and cost of CSA, as Catholics are requiring bishops to do annually since 2004, would be totally voluntary in this denomination of nearly sixteen million, making up half of all Baptist congregations total in the United States.

For instance, the majority of SBC pastors believe it is acceptable to return a pastor who has "had an affair" to the pulpit, according to a 2016 survey by Lifeway Research.[4] The very wording of the instrument and its interpretation shows ignorance, however. Notice I put "had an affair" in quotes. You don't have a victim with an affair. Affairs are consensual. Yet Baptists are still totally confused on this while Presbyterians leaders got their vocabulary up to political correctness, at least, twenty year ago. That's the first step to getting people to understand "sexual misconduct" should never be considered the equivalent of "adultery" and "an affair." To put it in simpler language, not everything immoral is abuse. Yet all abuse is definitely immoral and is considered a crime, even without a single minor as a victim, in a growing number of states—thirteen at present, to be exact.

Nothing is more naïve than believing local church leaders can be counted on to make public founded allegations of abuse any more than most families talk openly about incest among their own family members. That's the Baptist way, though, except for American Baptist Churches (ABC), comprising about two million members. It's also the way of most evangelical churches, those who have "Family Church" or "Community" or "Non-Denominational" as a part of their name. These autonomous congregations are, generally, the safest religious institutions of any for perpetrators because of loose or non-existent policies and failures in enforcement, as well as the greater propensity of abuse in theologically conservative groups, in general.[5]

It is not only evil to abuse a child. It is a crime. Shouldn't harboring criminals or those suspected of a crime, allowing them to continue in ministry without reporting them to authorities, be ample cause for formal sanctions far more than accepting a member of the LGBT or ordaining a woman? Likewise, shouldn't the same be the consequences for congregations that allow alleged sexual offenders to continue standing in the pulpit, regardless of the age of their victims, until they are cleared beyond the shadow of a doubt? I think so; I'm quite "unreasonable" compared to a lot of folks as you may have already concluded, however.

What about those who refuse to pass along the information to others—a matter Texas and several other states have clarified with legislation? These questions are not going away and cannot be defended by clinging to the old "letter" of the denominational system's laws.

By 2009, Christa Brown, in collaboration with SNAP had organized small marches outside annual meetings of the Southern Baptist Convention, appeared on 20/20, spoken to the Executive Committee of the SBC, and been declared the "public face" of victims of Baptist clergy sexual abuse wanting to force the Convention to acknowledge allegations and take concrete actions.[6] Yet forcing Baptists to do anything, she was soon to discover, is far more complicated even than forcing Catholics to reform their ways, thanks in part to church polity, but even more so because the propensity of this denomination's members to value independence far more than most denominations.

That year, in my review for her book, This Little Light, I tucked in a little prophecy, based on my own experience: "This is a book that Baptist leaders should not ignore. Still I predict they will."

The sacrifices Christa made cannot be measured. Her voice will go down in history as a public testimony. In 2008, she got the attention of Time Magazine after an Oklahoma Baptist pastor, Wade Burleson, officially proposed the Convention maintain a national data base for sexual offenders in ministry, which was first suggested by Christa. The *rejection* of this proposal made Time's list of the top ten under-reported stories that year.

This came only six years after I was silenced after giving my all trying to be heard. It was after women like Debbie Vasquez began speaking out to tell how she was persuaded to go before her church to apologize for being pregnant without telling the church their pastor was the father. Vasquez, same as many others, has now discovered the hands of the BGCT remain conveniently tied, unable to truly protect anyone from the pastor who ended up back in Texas, near Joe Trull's new place of residence in Denton, Texas. Ironically, it's the same city in this small world where Deborah Dail, who has since changed her name, resides and practices law and the same city where Trull's own church had a seriously mishandled case that was brushed off lightly.[8]

So far, the BGCT has managed to operate without incurring legal consequences, thanks to the lack of a clear line of responsibility beyond the local congregation. They have likely prevented many churches from getting into serious hot water. Hard to say how long this may continue with advice given by lawyers who may choose to "help" congregations and the BGCT simultaneously, which might appear to be a conflict of interest to most ethical attorneys. In all of this, women like Christa Brown get trampled in the process of preserving the status quo.

In her blog http://stopbaptistpredators.blogspot.com/ on March 3, 2016, Christa integrated the latest Academy-Award-winning movie with news about Ted Cruz' asking for support from Paige Patterson, a former classmate of my husband Ron, and now President of Southern Baptists' largest seminary, Southwestern in Ft. Worth, Texas. As you'll notice, Brown brilliantly ties all of this back again to 2008 when Patterson gave the biggest insult I've ever heard about childhood survivors of abuse by clergy. He called them "as reprehensible as sex criminals."

In so doing, he unknowingly gave activists a wonderful gift. By speaking *his* truth, he opened the door to expand the conversation, not just about child abuse, but about the bigotry that seems to know no bounds in the denomination of my heritage. Even as my heart bleeds for the destruction brought by such as this, how much more evidence do people need to either wake up and either run for the hills or join forces with those who believe there is still hope for change?

Today, though she continues to make her voice known, Christa has accepted her own limitations. Like me, she's a two-time breast cancer survivor. She's resolved herself to the fact the denomination of her heritage is not ready, and may never be ready, to take the steps that would put tighter security and keep records on founded cases alone. Yet she's still available, same as I am, from her website, with each of us ready to offer solace and help to individuals or congregations in need of information.

Who's to say what the next generation of men and women will decide?

*****

[1] In 1982, the Foreign Mission Board of the Southern Baptist Convention began to frequently refer to a new, popular book by Peters and Waterman, In Search of Excellence: Lesson's from America's Best-Run Companies (republished in 2006 by HarperBusiness). This book greatly shaped philosophies of management and increased the heavy-handed, more micro-management style that turned this largest evangelical mission board into what leaders of the FMB compared to a military organization as they turned increasingly to authoritarianism.

[2] Brown, Christa, This Little Light: Beyond a Baptist Preacher Predator and His Gang, (Foremost Press, 2009)

[3] Trull, Joe and Audra, Putting Women in Their Place: Moving Beyond Gender Stereotypes in Church and Home (Smyth & Helwys, 2003)

[4] See http://religionnews.com/2016/05/10/can-pastors-make-a-comeback-after-scandal-one-baptist-pastor-tries/

[5] See Chapter 3 of this text or Heggen, Carolyn, 2006, Sexual Abuse in Christian Homes and Churches, Wipf & Stock Pub; Reprint edition, p. 73.

[6] Austin American-Statesman, "Austin Lawyer Pushes Baptist Churches to Confront Sexual Abuse," by Eileen E. Flynn, July 9, 2008.

Chapter 30
Keeping Hope Alive

Fortunately, my own upbringing did not lead me to think about gender issues like Paige Patterson, who suggests that female submission be thought of as the equivalent of having an encounter with a police officer.

My father had his own issues leftover from his family of origin, and his education in a Southern Baptist college and seminary certainly didn't promote anything close to gender equity. He often failed to respect my mother's opinions and was often insensitive to her needs. Yet he had no idea what a seed he was planting the day he stormed into our living room one summer day, running right past me into the kitchen to find my mother.

"How on earth could that man have thrown away his calling like that?" he exclaimed.

This sounded plenty interesting to me. At sixteen, I was eager to find out what was going on as I approached the table where my father was now sitting. Whatever had happened, this obviously wasn't something he cared to keep at his office. The way he came in, like he was in the middle of a conversation with my mother, I gathered she knew as well as he.

"Who?" I asked. "And what's this about?"

"None of your business," Dad curtly replied. "You don't even know the man!"

Fair enough. It really wasn't any of my business, I said to myself. Whatever his colleague had done, though, it was obviously so reprehensible Dad considered it to be career suicide.

Actually, I *was* old enough to know, and this truth must have hit him almost as soon as he'd finished speaking.

"I might as well tell you," Dad said. "A pastor in our area ran off with the church secretary."

That was the best way anybody knew to frame the problem of clergy sexual misconduct in the early 1960's. What was missing from that description is as important as what my father did say. Most Baptist pastors in that day would have blamed the woman for leading the pastor astray, and quite a few would have set to work immediately to see how they could help the old boy with "geographical therapy" or "a new place of service."

Not once did he suggest the employee was to blame, not even in the tone he used to provide more information about his colleagues misbehavior in the ensuing conversation.

Equally significant, two years later in my freshman year of college, my parents were required to quickly vacate that same parsonage after my father refused to back down when two Sunday School teachers in the church were having an open affair. Totally inappropriate for them to continue in these roles, my father thought. Yet he stood alone. To most in the congregation, this was still "a personal matter," and my father should have looked the other way.

Never again did he pastor a church running over 300 in Sunday School. Yet the church also suffered. It went down to a very small fraction of membership in a few years' time.

A chilling coincidence: Dad was exactly the same age as Ron when we were forced from our own careers for a similar reason.

It was what happened in between those two incidents that was most educational and extremely disconcerting since my parents' decisions on how to handle this situation were entirely different than one might expect, considering what occurred in the other two.

In the same kitchen where I got my first introduction to sexual boundary violations and ethics a year earlier, I happened to be working only a few feet away from the phone when my mother picked it up and was soon gasping at what she was being told, obviously by a caller other than my father.

Once again, I received honest answers about what I'd overheard without even trying to eavesdrop. Yes, I'd figured correctly. This time the offender was the father of four, and I considered his entire family to be closer to our family than most of our blood relatives. What's more, he'd served as my father's role model for years.

The distraught lady on the other end of the line was a member of another local church, where the evangelist had been preaching a week's revival, with services morning and evening all week long, as was common in that day. Revivals were held at least twice a year in most every Baptist congregation, and good evangelists were well sought after.

The caller was also the next-door neighbor of a single woman who had let the evangelist in her back door two nights in succession during the revival, then letting him out the same entrance the next morning. There appeared to be only one explanation, my mother acknowledged, sad but certain there was no reason for her to doubt what she'd heard.

For years, I never knew what Dad did about the report. Nor did I ask. The matter was never brought up again in my presence; but I was quite certain from the undertones in our household that day, his reaction was the same as my mother's.

"It about killed him," she said several years after Dad's death, when I asked. "He didn't know what to do. He certainly never recommended him to anyone else, though." Since Southern Baptist pastors and evangelists (unlike missionaries) are basically "freelancers," there really was nobody to officially report to.

"Since he couldn't prove anything," Mom continued, he hated to admit to his colleague in town what he'd been told—chances are the woman who called told the pastor, too, Dad conveniently concluded. If so, however, the other pastor never spoke to your father about it."

Oh, the power of "the secret!"

It's doubtful the "hostess" of my father's friend saw herself as a victim. Though, in a very real sense, the caller who'd mustered the courage to talk to my mother certainly was. No matter how the incident was interpreted by the caller, she could never forget what she witnessed nor could she ever again hold this evangelist in the high esteem others had held him. And it must have impacted her ability to trust any others in this profession, still high on the credibility list in the 1960's.

Mom certainly couldn't bear to say anything to the evangelist's dear wife either. Never did. And to this day, I do not know if any of his children realized that their father's character might ever be in serious question.

I'm not sure what my parents could have done further in this dilemma, though I do believe my father should have at least talked with his local colleague and followed up with the caller. Perhaps the two pastors should have confronted the perpetrator together rather than my father simply distancing himself from this person he had admired for so long.

Even today, there is no protocol for handling men who still depend on word-of-mouth recommendations and may operate more like traveling salesmen. With a charisma like tele-evangelist Jim Baker that so many have greatly admired. For such men, there is absolutely no structural accountability—even far less than there is for pastors, where the gatekeepers are simply local leaders, stationed in every little church in every little hollow, who may also be counting the freewill offerings on which the visitor is depending for his livelihood.

The Problem with Unbridled Power

Running freely through the clerical culture, we find clear evidence of a conflict with an important set of principles Jesus taught about the greatness in the Kingdom of God.[1]

If one genuinely desires to right the wrongs in this world (or to "be great in God's kingdom,"), *power must submit* to the oppressed in true servant-hood, becoming "the servant of all." That's something very difficult for people who depend on personal power to operate. Submission isn't even in the repertoire of possibilities for most powerful men.

Therefore, without a strong victim's advocate with exceptional boundaries, and one still *inside* the system, there is little hope for justice inside the system, as any wise judge in a court of law can attest. Since justice is seldom served in organizations allowed to police themselves, lawsuits get filed. For even if someone inside the system tries to stand in the gap for the benefit of the victim, that person will soon encounter such opposition that it becomes nearly impossible to prevail.

Yet there are exceptions, though I've rarely encountered them in all the cases I've dealt with. There are certainly plenty of individuals in every society who make good choices because they have moral fiber. Get a bunch with power together, however, and things tend to go the opposite direction.

Systems in Christian churches have difficulty holding boundaries—period, for there seems to be something contagious about boundary violations of all kinds. There's also a resistance to keeping the hard-fast rules that professional ethics requires in these matters.

Abusers are the opposite of servants. They have a sense of entitlement that's not easily cured, even when sexuality isn't a part of the mix. So do those with a tendency to collude.

Once it begins, collusion spreads like a virus. One congregation decides in the course of things that all will be well if people are encouraged to just "not gossip." Since talking openly is discouraged, it soon appears that all is indeed well while everything festers. Meanwhile, a neighboring congregation, perhaps with another denomination, or maybe in another part of the state in the same denomination, sees how well things seem to be going and decides to follow this "fine example." Soon the virus has grown into a cancer that chokes out the good as anger and frustration come out sideways while "the secret" remains well hidden.

In a nearby state, colleagues protect an alleged offender and soon conclude that this guy is innocent despite a preponderance of evidence to the contrary. This all proves what these men have long suspected about other allegations. Just another example that women can't be trusted. Nor kids—now or later as adults—when they find the courage to speak.

So, when all else fails, exhausted survivors go to the courts. Yet court systems don't always right wrongs either. Without very tough hides, survivors can come away from the courtroom more devastated than when they begin. That's something Roger A. Canaff, an attorney who's devoted his life to the eradication of violence against women and children, tells clients who want to believe in "a just world theory."[2]

Canaff and Christa Brown, both abuse survivors themselves, have learned that justice comes in surprising ways. It can come in terms of a host of newfound, rich relationships that are forged in the course of advocacy. Or, it may arrive vicariously when a courageous survivor is able to achieve an outcome in the courtroom that others are unable to experience due to statutes of limitation or other barriers.

Totally Stuck

Christa Brown in collaboration with SNAP has organized small marches outside annual meetings of the Southern Baptist Convention. She and I have been on list-serves filled with Baptist preachers with disrespectful vile, bigotry, and DIM thinking like I've never seen. Often there is one man out of a half dozen attempting to be a voice of intellect and reasoning. Oddly, not one other woman except the two of us was ever present. Does this simply reflect what is going on in congregations across the Convention? I have no reason to believe otherwise until I hear from survivors who report having been well-received.

The sacrifices Christa made have been immense. The contribution she's made to the lives of thousands cannot be measured. Her voice has not been ignored, and it will go down in history as a public testimony.

Fast forward and you'll find she's still going with her blog.

At http://stopbaptistpredators.blogspot.com/ on March 3, 2016, she integrated the latest Academy-Award-winning movie with news about Ted Cruz' asking for support from Paige Patterson, a former classmate of my husband Ron, and now President of Southern Baptists' largest seminary, Southwestern in Ft. Worth, Texas. As you'll notice, Brown brilliantly ties all of this back again to 2008 when Patterson gave the biggest insult I've ever heard anyone make about childhood survivors of abuse by clergy, now standing in solidarity in SNAP. He called them "as reprehensible as sex criminals."

In so doing, he unknowingly gave activists a wonderful gift. By speaking *his* truth, he opened the door to expand the conversation, not just about child abuse, but about the oft-unspoken bigotry that seems to know no bounds.

So, what will it take before people of "faith" in our "civilized" world began to stand in solidarity against violence toward women and children? It seems that conservative evangelicals need much more than evidence before we begin imposing zero tolerance on our leaders, considering this group has been given more of the credit than any other for putting in the Oval Office a known sexual offender, even caught on tape bragging about his "achievements" with women he's blatantly harassed.

*****

[1] Mark 10:42-45 has even been turned into a popular song, "Servant of All" by Michael Ryan and produced by Maranatha Music in 1984. It's often used in Sunday Schools today. It begins: "If you want to be great in God's Kingdom, learn to be the servant of all."

[2] See http://rogercanaff.com/site/ for much, much more.

Chapter 31
Time to Sing and Celebrate

By early 2005, Ron and I had a lot to celebrate. We'd learned to find immense joys in our ministries, sometimes working inside the church, but mostly outside of it without particularly needing the blessings of those inside. Or anyone else, for that matter. Our freedom to carve out our own spaces with unique roles in each of the local communities where we resided—sometimes as individuals and sometimes as a couple—left us both smiling in spite of the challenges of working around Ron's increasingly challenging health issues.

In some ways, because of this newfound freedom, our life was the closest we'd ever had to "normal" by American standards. It was thrilling to see the huge difference in Ron's overall well-being now that he was out of the pressures of the pastorate.

Much to our amusement, his speaking voice, as strong as it had ever been, was increasingly recognized at businesses in the area by strangers who were shocked that the DJ they sometimes heard introducing the latest Bon Jovi hit or giving the local weather on the radio was well past middle age and noticeably "disabled." What few of those listeners knew was how this new identity fulfilled one of his childhood dreams—after he abandoned the idea of being a fireman, that is.

Music, in many forms, became the focus of our lives and outreach and showed up frequently in my blog entries. Thanks to contributions made to Advocate Web, I was able to do voice recordings of some of the more popular articles I'd written for that site. One was on about the therapeutic value of music I'd been privileged to witness on evenings when I'd provided live piano music years earlier to seriously-ill patients on a psychiatric unit.[1]

Ron splurged on a state-of-the-art Roland, primarily for himself, he quipped the day I arrived to find him sitting with a pre-recorded disc playing the digital "piano" at full volume, with the door wide open, so it could have easily entertained the entire neighborhood. Even though he'd never learned to play any instrument, he planned to learn all he could now. So, I added him to the roster of students I'd begun building in the neighborhood near the lake, as we filled our hearts with more frequent song including an occasional duet we mastered together.

How I loved the challenge of working with all ages, some with very special needs, including an autistic child who never spoke a word to me in five years, but learned the basics of making music!

For some, I became like an extended family member who dropped in weekly for a short visit, as well as a lesson, occasionally throwing in a word of advice to a parent who'd bent my ear. While some parents seemed to care little or were too overwhelmed to set limits, I had quite a few I felt cared too much. To these, I'd sometimes smile and shrug, after a kid had run out the door to kick a football. "You know," I'd say, "Put it into perspective. This isn't a matter of life and death. It's only music. It's gonna get better." In those families, it usually did.

What a contrast to survivor work, where the stakes sometimes seemed so high in terms of human lives. Decisions for some of my readers were grueling. Yet the work was highly profitable for me, except in a business sense.

How Little We Knew had reached the "wash" stage by IRS standards, having finally paid for itself and the occasional sales were supplying the small cost of my website. The real "pay" came from hearing that a single copy of a book had been passed around to scores in a support group until it was now needing to be replaced or when a doctoral student asked if I had time to read her thesis on spiritual issues of survivors of abusive clergy, inspired by *The Truth about Malarkey*, which she'd discovered on the shelf of her seminary library.

Thereby, my passion for teaching supplied one set of needs while the passion for advocacy work supplied the other. In that regard, I was one of the richest women in the world!

We also basked in the simple joys of grand-parenting as we recovered from the last wonderful time of frolic and made plans for the next with one or more of our five grandchildren. The tire swing outside our picture window served as a reminder of past memories and days to come. We made frequent trips to the picturesque lake and park where we often toted sand buckets along with fishing equipment and fresh-baked cookies, storing up memories. In summer, the boys sometimes pitched a tent out on our half acre, caught fireflies, and enjoyed the ring-side seats to one of Iowa's finest fireworks displays, easily viewed from our back yard. The girls adored the upstairs playroom. In the winter, if too cold to get out and make a snowman, we pulled out paints and encouraged any of the five to add to the continuous mural that ran around all four walls and across the ceiling of the kids' little upstairs loft room. What more could you want?

Between our country home and city apartment, we moved freely back and forth, enjoying the best of both worlds. Seldom did grandparenting conflict with teaching. By planning ahead, I often bartered a free piano lesson for baby-sitting. Or supplied a play date for one child who was glad to have company while I worked with a sibling to correct the musical discords everyone in the household had been enduring since last lesson.

Along with the music, I liked throwing in a little philosophy. My favorite was about how purposeful discords and the unexpected discords that come into our lives must be managed well. Classical musicians, same as modern rock stars, know the value of working discords into music for the surprise element. Yet few listeners can tolerate constant discord. We need to have purposeful discords resolved, and that's what good music writers do with their music. They bring us back to the center of things at some point, so we can enjoy cords or familiar patterns that are pleasing to our ears.

Though I never said so, what flowed in my teaching about discords in music came straight out of what I'd learned in the world of survivorship. I figured it just might someday be useful in the lives of my young students and definitely so in the present for any parents who might be listening over my shoulder, so I made a point of connecting the dots between the musical and the philosophical applications at every opportunity.

"In piano music, as in life," I explained, "we determine how to handle the discords we discover by giving each discord just the right amount of attention. It's the way we choose to touch the keys—our unique approach, that is—which determines whether the discord will be useful in the finished product. If we want others to pay attention to that discord, we apply a very strident touch. On the other hand, perhaps depending on our mood for the day, we may wish to use a slightly softer touch, to reduce the shock or the angst it would otherwise cause, thereby turning the music into something far more soothing. As budding artists who are always working to improve our skills at "playing" music or of navigating life, provided we are practicing both purposefully and persistently, we'll improve over time. Though never will we reach perfection. Nobody ever does.

For the greatest myth in piano is the same one held by idealists in life.

Practice does <u>not</u> guarantee perfection. It only makes improvement.

More Retreats

The fascinating thing about the Web is how it works when we're not. It's like having a virtual advocate and teacher all rolled into one every moment of every day.

"I can't explain it," one woman wrote. "I think I have half you've written on collusion memorized from off your website. I just need to go back and read it over and over, sometimes in the wee hours of the morning when I can't sleep, to get rid of the crazy voices people have put in my head."

Others, emailing for the first time, spoke of how hard it was to click "send." They'd received so much rejection that it was frightening to risk reaching out, even in cyberspace. One woman's message sat on her computer days before she found the courage to write to someone she'd never met. For many, I was the first person to whom they reached out with their story.

Some wanted resources. Others wanted to find other survivors. Many just wanted one person to validate their pain. That was the easy part, yet it was the part some who'd told their stories many times for years had never experienced. Not one soul I've heard from yet has heard anyone say: "We blew it." Which was what the psychiatrist-friend in Malawi had declared the two of us most needed to hear, but should not expect. I'd passed this along to many for validation.

Baptist survivors who often arrived at the site after putting "baptist" into a search might ask if they should go to a national office or only to their state offices to make a report. Who should they contact, they'd ask? Or who's in charge? That's when things got really difficult. I had to be honest, for I don't believe in keeping secrets. I didn't know of one single, safe place to turn. Neither did I know anybody truly in charge. They were all at the mercy of their local, incestuous congregation—for that's, unfortunately, what every one of their churches had become by the time they reached out to me.

Like any good mental health nurse, I could tell them the dynamics of incest and help them sort out options—the risks of not reporting, as well as doing so. Plus, the need to consider seeking legal counsel and locating a reliable therapist, if they didn't already have one, prior to doing anything else. Then, if they chose to report, they knew right where to find me when they returned.

Alternative Approaches

Even with accountability systems in place, not all survivors choose to make a formal report. As an advocate, I support this choice and do not consider it unethical, as some survivors do. It is not a requirement that a survivor bear the brunt of reporting, especially if she or he believes no good will come out of doing so. If an offender re-offends, it is not the fault of the survivor any more than the original abuse was. These choices do not come easy. Many struggle with the decision for years. They weigh what they hear from others, asking whether it's worth the effort, or if they would do better to put their energies elsewhere.

Renae Cobb was a Baptist who had lived with self-imposed shame for many years. With her limited understanding, she'd erroneously thought the same as the vast majority of people, assuming she had simply "had an affair" with the pastor of her church, starting in high school. The reality was, she'd been sexually abused from the beginning and had continued being into young adulthood. In 2007, she told her story for the first time to a popular spiritual retreat leader and writer, who helped her begin to see things differently.

Back home, this young mother of two, went straight to the internet, and soon found my website. Over the next several months, as we communicated back and forth, sometimes several times in a day, she began to question her old reality less and less while facing her deep wounded-ness more. Like Amy, those old emails remain on her computer, serving as a reminder of how far she's come.

Retreat Time

For some time, I'd had requests from readers around the country, with a heavy concentration from the South, asking when I might be coming to their area, perhaps for a survivor retreat. It wasn't that any of them knew others in their area who might be interested. In fact, most had never met another survivor of abusive clergy, though quite a few had joined incest survivor groups, yet realized they needed something more.

They were happy to consider coming to Iowa, yet almost all were really strapped financially, several having put every spare penny of personal funds into years of therapy without their counselors ever calling their experience "abuse." Those who had made a report to a church official had either been turned away in shame or gotten little or nothing to help with therapy. Since these were primarily cases where the abuse happened years earlier, same as Renae's, many had chosen not to report; some didn't even know where the offender now was. These were deeply wounded women who deserved to have help, same as the survivors from mainline denominations, who had often received scholarship money and even all travel expenses paid for a retreat.

Near our cottage was a large nicely-furnished farmhouse, available for special events or large family gatherings, with room enough for ten overnight guests if we squeezed in a cot or two. I reserved it, sent out invitations, and began making plans. Renae was the first to sign up.

Janet Clark, another writer and a Catholic survivor, was coming, too. She had recently joined SNAP and had published "Blind Faith"[2] a well-articulated novel about a Catholic case of priest abuse and the subsequent collusion from community and church officials, similar to the actual 1985 Gauthe case in Lafayette, Louisiana.

With all the interest my announcement initially generated, I was sure we'd have a houseful. Much to my disappointment, despite their eagerness, even with me donating my time, none of the others could scrape up airfare plus the modest charge to cover their room and board. While Methodists had provided hospitality and often helped other Methodists with air fare, none of these women had this kind of help available, even though some had asked. It was heart-wrenching.

One woman had the money, yet was very upset when she discovered on the simple application that I was not asking for sexual orientation. She refused to come, saying she couldn't handle it if she discovered she was sharing sleeping quarters with a lesbian. I wondered if she might feel the same way about the Jewish lady who came to one of the Methodist retreats.

With only the two of them coming, I expected Renae and Janet to back out. Neither was about to. This gave new meaning to "where two or three are gathered together." Despite the disappointment for the others, that weekend was one of the most memorable I've ever spent.

Through it, Renae came to some important decisions. She recognized the need for more intense work in therapy. She also felt she needed to begin working toward a career change from computer science. She'd been thinking of going back to school for some time. Now she could see it all happening and was certain of her future career plans. She wanted to empower others, struggling in isolation with issues of deep personal pain.

I'd never seen anyone so certain about anything. School had always come easy for her. She knew she could juggle it along with paying attention to her own needs of herself and her family, once she had begun to mend her own heart. Very well, I thought. These were fine aspirations, and maybe they'd work out in the end. Who was I to judge?

Without saying so outright, I did suggest that it might be too soon to be making any drastic decisions until she'd dug deeper to heal what I sensed she was somehow hiding from herself. There were many things she could choose from, and I'd be eager to hear more as things developed, I assured her.

She emailed me from the airport, thanking me for everything, including my very strong recommendation that she seek out a good therapist with a working knowledge of systems, as well as Carl Jung's theories, to work on any unfinished business she might have.

Within weeks, she'd located an outstanding counselor and was in process of enrolling at Southern Methodist University. In less than a year, she and her husband David decided to finance a second plane ticket from Dallas to Iowa so Renae could use her professional skills in web design to help restructure my site.

The results were lovely. Between the long list of frequently asked questions cutting down on the number of emails plus her standing by to help with technical support, keeping up soon became a lot less labor intensive, allowing me to make better use of the few hours I could eek out of my schedule each week to handle the most urgent concerns.

I started a blog,[3] taking on topics related to sexual and domestic abuse by clergy—things like power, shame, accountability, justice, advocacy, and many other neglected topics in the faith community that visitors can still access by category today.

Such collaborative efforts all through the movement were paying off—each of us empowering others in unique ways when we got together, then, connecting through technology in the interim. This new piece of "science fiction" the lady at the 1996 conference insisted I look into had become quite a connector!

I thought back to some of Economus' words during that same event—words that would have sounded like heresy to the Christian "purist."

"This is the church, what you see here at Linkup," he told us. "This is what it's supposed to be."

How exciting it was to be a part of this new frontier, expanding my own horizons, as we reached out to do what no church seemed able or willing to do because it was simply all too frightening. Yet Tom was right, as I see it.

This, too, is the work of the church. Or it could be. A difficult work, and a missed opportunity that the institution has often fled.

✶✶✶✶✶

[1] See http://www.takecourage.org/music.htm

[2] Janet Clark, Blind Faith (1st World Publishing, 2006)

[3] www.takecourage.org/blog offers hundreds of entries pertaining to advocacy and the intersection of spirituality, faith and power

Chapter 32
Faulty Assumptions

"The most common way people give up power is by thinking they don't have any."
Alice Walker

Like everyone, I grew up in an odd family.

Most kids begin figuring this out by their thirteenth birthday. About the time their parents decide the kids' grandparents were lots smarter than they ever assumed. It's those *kids* who are nuts, of course, the parents say.

Odd isn't necessarily bad. Some things are wonderfully odd. I had a mixture of both the not-so-good and the wonderful in my family—also in me. Maybe the same goes for you.

One thing rather odd was the spacing between me, as the only biological child, and my two siblings, both a half generation younger. I hated being an only child, but that was my lot for more than a decade.

It would be so much fun to have a bunch of siblings, I kept thinking. Like my cousins. There were six of them. Strangely, I later learned, at least a couple of them were envious of me for opposite reasons. I understand that now.

In 1955, a week before Christmas, our family had a dream come true. My darling little sister finally arrived on a snowy night at the airport after nearly twenty-four hours in flight, all the way from Korea. Sadly, her father, an American soldier, had abandoned her mother at the end of the war. In turn, her mother was forced to relinquish her due to the extreme stigma faced by single moms in Korea, making survival of the waif next to impossible.

To this day, Lydia yearns to find her biological mother just to let her know she survived. She even managed to visit the orphanage that housed her for seven months, but discovered no records were kept in those days. Like many childhood traumas, hers is impossible to fully resolve.

In 1960, my father came dashing into the house one day, all excited about another baby. This one, an American newborn, due in six months, when Dad's dream of finally having a son was fulfilled.

Tim presented a different set of challenges than my hyperactive sister, who was getting around like a live wire, making up for lost time. The two kids could balance a scale by his first birthday. Weighing thirty pounds before he could even walk, it was difficult for our ninety-pound mother to cope.

She soon developed a variety of health issues, with much of it related to a serious depression, I now believe to have been caused in part to the burdens of being a pastor's wife and mother. She spent much of my sophomore year in high school flat of her back. No problem, I assured her. I loved being a big sister, and found that stepping into a mothering role, though taxing, was also fun.

During those years, I felt closer to my father than at any time in my life as we worked together often in the kitchen. He thrived under pressure. My parents located excellent day care for the hours I was in school.

People in the church pitched in some to help, as well, serving as role models, nurturing me and my siblings, as well as my mother, allowing me time and space to also thrive as a church pianist during those years, playing for two choirs at our mid-size congregation.

Whenever I had a chance to get away from this routine, I'd either take in a ball game or pile into the tight quarters of my best friend, the oldest kid in her family of nine. Linda's baby brother Tommy, born the same day as my little brother Tim, often snoozed next to us as we girls all chattered away at the big "slumber party." The next morning I'd go home to our much more spacious house feeling like the luckiest big sister in the world!

This was only for a season, my wise teachers were careful to point out to me. Taking care of my family could not become my career, and I needed to find ways to cut the ties of concern after graduation and move on. Fortunately, that's how it turned out. As I made it clear to my parents that I was not abandoning or delaying plans for college, my mother began to rally.

Perhaps advocacy became an extension of my personality somehow due to these unique circumstances of my youth.

In some ways, I do believe I was better prepared to later take on responsibilities with more confidence because of the challenges of my high school years, having learned I could take charge when needed.

While this was not the normal, typical course of the average teenager in the early 1960's. And while my young siblings no doubt missed out by not having a more experienced caregiver in their lives, we all survived.

My own children would reach adolescence before it dawned on me how I'd sort of traded mine in. Yet, with my supportive parents, I never felt exploited. There simply wasn't much time in my teens to be a kid. And to this day, I have little patience for many American youth who seem to have everything handed to them except for the expectations that they live up to their potential.

Survival Skills

Adults who experienced multiple adverse experiences at a very young age, especially severe neglect, often say: "I don't know how *any* of us survived." By age nine, I was asking myself how on earth *my mother* had survived all the tragedies of *her* childhood.

How had she been able to cope with the sudden, traumatic death of her slightly older sister from diphtheria at age nine while my mother, only sixteen months younger, lay sleeping in the same room? I still can't imagine. The two girls had been raised like twins. It was "by the grace of God," my mother would be quick to tell you today, at 91. As the surviving "twin," her entire life has been impacted by this tragedy.

Suffering even yet from periodic episodes of PTSD, however, she still comes out occasionally with new bits of the sad story—the sounds, sights, and even recently the awful odor of creosote she'll forever associate with coming home from the cemetery on the dark, cold, January day to find freshly "disinfected" walls, blackened by government officials who also put a quarantine sign on their door, assuring no neighbors could come to console them. Twenty years ago, nearly a half century after her sister died and only days after the death of their father, she and a younger sister discovered all her deceased sister's clothing locked away in a trunk her parents had moved with the rest of their household possessions several times. In their unresolved grief, I was never allowed to even touch or ask about this mysterious object. For that matter, my own mother didn't ask either, though I suspect she knew on some level what was inside.

Somehow, she stood up to her overbearing father at seventeen when he demanded she come back home to the cotton-patch after financial hardship forced her to drop out of business college. "No way!" she told him as she went job hunting.

Yet out of all this, she manages to find happy memories. Those of her loving sister serve as consolation still. Like many children who grew up in one of the areas worst hit by the Great Depression, Mom expected little out of life. Her vivid memories of times she felt immensely loved are interspersed with "discipline" that would have most surely been considered criminal child abuse in my childhood.

No doubt, her personality was shaped both by love and trauma. Her resiliency is astounding. She remains a fun-loving keg of dynamite much of the time, a strong-willed lady for over nine decades, despite bouts of depression. Though seldom tipping the scale past 100, she's learned how to stand her ground, prides herself in functioning as independently as possible, even now with serious dementia, leaving others shaking their heads in disbelief.

As I reflect on her difficult life, the famous quote of Eleanor Roosevelt, sitting in a prominent place in my office, comes to mind once again:

"We must do the things we think we cannot do."

Navigating Toward Adulthood

I fully understand why some children learn to dissociate to cope with sexual abuse. Fortunately, this wasn't how my most creative skills developed. You see, I get bored easily, especially at church—always have. In the first place, I'm not a lover of ritual or routine. Yet I was forced to spend more time sitting still on a church bench than I ever had to kick a ball around. As a result, I've always lacked coordination.

A few other things, apparently commonly expected for kids to pick up at church, I somehow missed. Or maybe they just didn't sink in due to my selective listening combined with my acquired skill of faking attentiveness for self-preservation, which may have turned out to be an advantage in some ways.

Half-truths, or "secular scriptures"*, condemn anger, sadness, and "speaking ill of others" are some of the most common obstacles any whistle-blower must overcome in the faith community. "Nice folks" who are "faithful" just don't do those things, certainly not "nice ladies!" Since 95% of women who are now grandmothers have been carefully taught such, it's a wonder any woman in the church finds the courage to break these silly rules at all.

Unlike on Sunday mornings, I did listen to most everything I heard in a weekday gathering for early elementary kids, called Sunbeams, and later in Girls' Auxiliary. Until I was in third grade, my favorite church song was "Jesus Wants Me for a Sunbeam." That picture made perfect sense to me. GA's was a bit like Baptist Girl Scouts with no uniforms. Yet it was much more. With various divisions extending all the way through high school, we GA's studied how to "do missions." We had fun, too—as silly as any kids can be at the same time we were learning.

My leaders were strong on justice issues. It was about listening to exciting real-life stories, often about women who seemed to feel empowered—at least this is how I perceived the lessons. Nothing about gender equity particularly, except it really was. While nobody talked about gender equity in the 1950's, I couldn't help noticing how Baptist missionaries, whether single or married, appeared to hold the same status as men.

Unlike with Sunday School classes and church, there was nothing dry about GA's. This was down-to-earth practical Christianity, in fact, not a bunch of busy work or silly crafts. It was about doing something for others or learning about people who did. It was the highlight of my week.

Never in my life have I heard my mother say a single curse word. Yet I've seen her plenty angry for good reason, and when she's angry enough she uses a word that is totally unacceptable for nice ladies to say. "How stupid!" she exclaims, same as I do myself out of the same long-time habit I caught from her, dating back to my preschool years. In Texas culture, women are expected to be "nice." In professional circles the "stupid" word is offensive. Neither my mother nor I intend it to be so. Today, the "S" word is more likely to be spoken than ever in Mom's world of dementia. Yet never does she say a person is stupid—that's not her intention at all. It's the *thinking* that sometimes is. How we think is a choice, as Mom sees it. Yet we can separate ourselves from our thoughts and choose to be upset or not.

Following Jesus meant *getting upset* at certain injustices, locally and around the world, according to my GA leaders, as well as Mom. It's okay to call injustice "stupid." While nobody in GA's used the word "anger," our female role models showed a fair amount of outrage as they spoke of the unfairness due to abusive governments where freedom was scarce.

"Missions" was a good word—always. Nobody suggested that missions might ever support the sin of oppression, especially in the pre-revolutionary days of African nations, when colonialism reigned supreme. This history wasn't taught any more than true Southern Baptist history that had supported slavery, the KKK, and Jim Crow. Those secrets were kept so very well, I doubt most of my GA leaders even knew these things themselves. Yet, to their credit, neither do I recall any of them making racial comments or talking badly about other cultures. If they believed American culture was the answer to all the world's woes, these commonly-held ideas weren't transmitted to me either—not by leaders or by literature. So, concepts of racial justice weren't a part of our conversations. And that was stupid, to borrow my mother's language. Or "Stupid, stinkin' thinkin'," my friends in Alcoholics Anonymous might say in reference to such avoidances.

The highest calling a woman could have, according to Southern Baptists, was to become a foreign missionary. Even before my little sister came to us from Korea through the joint efforts of the Holt agency and SBC missionaries, I was hooked. All I talked about being for many years was a missionary-nurse.

Doing justice wasn't a topic I ever heard anyone take on in the pulpit. Apparently fighting injustice was more of a girl thing with Baptists, though I never considered this until I was forty. All those years, I thought it was a Jesus thing. I still do.

Once, when we were on a road trip with me in the back seat, my mother had to remind Dad to watch his driving when he turned all the way around and looked me directly in the eye. "You know, it's too bad you were born a girl," he declared. "Otherwise, you could have made a mighty fine lawyer." Apparently, he didn't know there'd been women practicing law in the United States for almost 100 years, and neither did I. Yet I've never had a desire to pursue a career in law in spite of my great admiration for those who do.

In a day when few women stood up to male oppression, my mother did, often several times per week whenever my father showed a sense of entitlement or became emotionally abusive to her or any of us kids. It was mostly my mother who bore the brunt, though. And from an early age, I knew she needed an advocate, for I could easily see how this subtle form of domestic abuse was very injurious to her. I couldn't stand it, so I'd call his hand and somehow get by with it. Oddly—something I never could understand, growing up—Dad would usually soon back down when I spoke up to let him know I didn't like the way he was treating my mother. Yet he seldom did so until I stepped in to stand in solidarity with her, ironically borrowing from my father's own sense of determination for a totally different purpose. It was a strange "dance" we did. Like all kids, I didn't stop to think this set of dynamics was particularly odd, though I had nothing to compare it to, of course.

Often, he'd be stunned as the impact of what he was doing must have somehow dawned on him for a little while. Then, he'd soon mellow, sometimes for weeks—this I understand now as the cycle of abuse, though it played out rather atypically and, fortunately, not with physical violence.

After the first Iowa survivors' retreat I attended, I called my mother. "You did me a real favor," I told her. "I only realized this yesterday in listening to some others. Thanks for never telling me it's wrong to get angry."

"Why would I?" she asked. "That's not what the Bible says. It talks about being slow to anger or being angry, but not sinning because of it."

Mom has never been nearly as good at self-advocacy as she is in advocating for others who've take advantage of her —no doubt because of the violence she experienced in her own childhood. As a kid, I would try to coach her, thinking that's all she needed.

I doubt she ever heard the word "advocacy" until I started using it long after Ron and I were doing it in the civil rights movement. And the first time she heard me talking about it, she noted it was something she'd found hard to do all her life and felt guilty when she did. Yet she often did it, anyway, demonstrating a fortitude that was greater than many women her age, I now understand.

While both my parents often failed to channel their anger appropriately when they lashed out, I never saw them strike one another. If so, I would certainly have gotten a much different message than I did. I cannot imagine growing up with the daily threat of physical violence any more than waking to find your sister dead in the next bed.

On our better days, as I grew older, Dad and I sometimes made a game of debates, similar to how he and his siblings did in those moments when their angst with one another was at a minimal level. In fact, though he'd appear to be totally exasperated with me at times, I had a sneaking suspicion he secretly enjoyed the challenge as much as I reveled in annoying him, same as most teenagers.

Miscalculating

Through all of this, I was set up to believe many myths about myself and my world, at least one or two created entirely on my own:

1. Though I never heard the term "advocacy" or "injustice" applied to church work, I erroneously understood it as something built into the female DNA, simply because of the role models I had. My mom and the GA leaders all would have stood up for anyone, especially any other woman, I assumed. Neither could I have imagined for one moment my grandmother or aunts would fail to stand up for me either. That's what women did in my world, though none used the word "solidarity," this word I understood well the first time I heard it used. Later all of this got easily re-enforced by Ms. Wiebe, the clinical director of student nursing, at the school I attended. There I also drew the faulty conclusion that all nurses being trained in the 1960's would also stand together against health inequities and abuse in the workforce.

2. In my idealism, I took a bounding leap to another erroneous deduction, believing any educated person would automatically aspire to be the wisest, most competent and ethical person possible—especially people with deep religious conviction.

To be otherwise less than this would be to show ignorance, as I naively saw things. Educated people do not have to be taught to be ethical, especially Christians. This is an assumption shared by virtually every Christian I've ever met; and in the evangelical world, missionaries, already considered to be altruistic, competent and trustworthy, as well as educated would certainly have no problem sorting out what was wise, I reasoned.

"Naivety to the hilt," you say. You're right. I was, and I find it difficult to know just when I began to change. I only know I had a lot to learn and still do.

If there was anything treasured by the vast majority of Baptist men I met in my first forty years, it was naïve women. It was quite convenient, actually, as long as everyone stayed in their respective places by gender and lived by the rules.

Intellectually, I understand it's extremely dangerous for women in leadership roles or professional ministry to stick their necks out and speak boldly about the vulnerability of females in many conservative theological circles. Yet I do believe things are changing.

So I'm still looking around, in hopes of finding the exceptionally brave, ready to step up to the plate like so many Catholic women now have.

*****

* "Secular scriptures" was a concept introduced in 1986 by Jordan in "Taking on the Gods" (Abingdon Press). He's referring to destructive lies or distortions of the truths we need to confront in order to maintain an emotionally, spiritually healthy, safe world. For example, one of the most common in the evangelical world is: "All problems are spiritual and can be solved without seeking help from the 'secular' world."

Chapter 33
The Ultimate Betrayal

The recent Women's March on Washington shows that American women *can* stand in solidarity with women all over the world. The sad thing is that far too often we have wasted many opportunities to do so.

More than fifty years after the founding of the National Organization for Women, we are still struggling to hold on to what we have achieved along with the precious little amount of power that has been bestowed on us by male-dominated systems that want to go back to "the way our Founding Fathers set things up." As power increases, true courage often decreases in both genders, while the opposite would seem to be true.

Like many men, women of moderate power believe there is only so much power to go around. Sharing power is a threat to someone at the top of a pyramid, large or small. Sadly, the people who are in positions to address violence and gender oppression the most show themselves to be powerless to stand with other powerful women among their own peers. Shackled with time-consuming and often mundane details of life, there is little energy or time left for us to take charge of our own lives, let alone to improve our lot in life.

We women know what it's like when we stand to support one another as an alternative to male competitiveness. Yet, it's much safer to stand with oppressed women far away and most dangerous to stand with the women we rub elbows with every day. Then, when our role models let us down, it feels like the ultimate of all betrayals.

The most painful, personal example of this took place in 2007. It was even more painful than the betrayal of my female colleagues, too intimidated twenty years earlier to stand up to incompetent, insecure men who were more interested in protecting male privilege than protecting vulnerable females. Surely much more powerful leaders would have learned to do much more by now, I told myself.

Two years earlier, when I received a call from Dr. Diana Garland, the founder and dean of social work at Baylor, I was embarrassed to have to ask her to tell me who she was.

While I knew the SBC's long-standing Carver School of Social Work had been forced to close due to conflicts between the standard expectations in the practice of social work with Southern Baptist beliefs on matters such as homosexuality, I had no idea Carver School had essentially relocated in Waco under a new name due to Garland's leadership. Nor had I kept up with the various personnel in most SBC agencies since leaving for Africa nearly forty years earlier. I'd even stopped reading "Baptist Today" by 1997, finding it too painful to learn of the heads that were still rolling due to the "conservative resurgence."

During the same months that I was writing for "Baptists Today," Diana explained how she and her husband David had been trying to decide what to do with the rest of their lives. As the Carver School closed, forcing Diana out of her career there, her husband David experienced a similar fate as many others at the nearby Southern Seminary that year, also too progressive to fit into the strictly conservative agenda being imposed there. So, David joined the staff of the newly founded George W. Truett Theological Seminary at Baylor about the same time Diana was re-establishing her own career.

I was fully taken back when she explained that she'd known of my work all along. In fact, *How Little We Knew* was one of the first books she ever picked up having anything to do with sexually abusive clergy. Plus, for years she'd been on the board of Marie Fortune's Center for the Prevention of Sexual and Domestic Violence (now Faith Trust Institute). While I'd known none of this, I was certainly happy to now. For the first time in over a decade of doing this work, I had a female reaching out to me who had also suffered the loss of a well-established career in the SBC. What's more, she now wanted to step into a more public role as an advocate among Baptists. I finally had company!

She was in the initial phases of planning for an extensive survey, which would be funded by the Ford Foundation with approximately 5% being funded by the BGCT. Unlike most surveys in the past that had only polled clergymen, asking for them to "tell on themselves" for either abusing or for their association with an offender colleague, this one would interview women, most specifically to show what percentage of survivors of abusive clergy a pastor might have in his or her congregation. She believed it might be far more than most pastors assumed. She also hoped to find out how common the problem was in African-American congregations.

Why not poll women in the general population and keep the questioning centered there to determine what nobody yet had, I asked. Wouldn't it be more useful to learn the overall percentage of women who have been sexually abused by clerics, not just the percentage of victims among all who attended church at least once monthly? After all, that would be only a small percentage of total victims.

I also wanted her to show a breakdown of families who had experienced the abuse of a minor by a clergy person vs. the abuse of an adult. And to go further and substantiate those in more conservative denominations vs. mainline, something to further back up what Carolyn Heggen, Marie Fortune and several other scholars had verified as common understanding among clinicians about the greater likelihood of abuse in theologically conservative families. I wanted Diana to apply this to clerics specifically.

In time, she would do more surveys, acknowledging that this was only a start.

From that first phone call until late summer of 2015, when I heard from her for the final time, giving me the devastating news that she could no longer do anything except get through the process of dying of pancreatic cancer, Diana was available almost instantly anytime I need her. Oh, how I miss her! And how I wish she could now be by the side of her husband David as he stands at the helm of Baylor, facing the challenges of the university's "sex scandals."

While I can only imagine what Diana must have known, I'm certain she most certainly tried to push for reform at every opportunity at the university, same as every other area where her professional life has been impacted by issues of violence against women.

Perhaps some of her students are already picking up where she left off. If not, somebody somewhere needs to. I hope to see much more follow-up questionnaires in the next few years, perhaps breaking down survivors abused as adults from those abused as children—something sociologist Anson Shupe also did not do when he established 4.6% he polled during door-to-door surveys in 1996 right in the heart of SBC territory, in Dallas and Ft. Worth, knew of a family member or friend abused by clergy. [1]

The weekend retreat with Renae and Janet left me more passionate than ever about this work. There were hundreds of women needing this opportunity, I was certain. Still, need did not constitute availability of resources. Most survivors could not afford to come halfway across the continent and pay retreat expenses, as well. If Methodists could do this, and do it even on an ecumenical basis, what about Baptists?

I called Diana and told her about the Iowa retreat ministry. I was thinking—dreaming, to be exact—about how Baptist women had the resources to do this on a limited basis.

While there was a nothing like COSROW (United Methodists' Commission on the Status and Role of Women), the closest thing to an empowerment group in the largest of Protestant denominations was Woman's Missionary Union. One of their most impressive projects currently was an extensive ministry to victims of human trafficking overseas. That's exactly what I was dealing with—human trafficking in the SBC.

"Not that I expect them to agree," I told Diana. "I would just love to hear what they'd tell me if I asked for help with my ministry. Just an experiment. Got any ideas?"

"I think they might surprise you," she said. "Let's set up a conference call, invite the leadership of the WMU to join the two of us on this."

I laughed. Was she serious? She was indeed. At a recent nationwide meeting, she'd led a small break-out session on CSA. Not many attended, but it was a good start. Since a former graduate student of hers had recently joined the staff, she would first contact the young social worker to tell her of this great idea. That led to several of the top leaders at the WMU wanting to join in after seeing my proposal.

"We're holding the ropes for you," the WMU liked to tell missionaries. I reminded them of this now. "Twenty years ago my ropes were cut," I said. "Now, I'm asking you to throw me another for women likely to even be your own membership."

They listened to me talking, initially very enthusiastically, so happy I was offering the retreats. They agreed that a hot line was needed. In fact, those on the line all could think of some CSA survivor they'd personally known. The moment of truth was at hand.

$2000 for scholarships this year would go a long way, I told them. In addition, a hot line was needed. I wasn't asking them to take any action, only to provide survivors with a listening ear and healing resources. I wanted the hotline publicized, as well as my retreats.

It suddenly got very quiet before one of them explained the problem.

"We walk a tightrope these days," she said.

This I knew, I assured them. My sister-in-law, still very active in the WMU, kept me informed. This women's auxiliary, organized independently and led out in more justice ministries than The Brotherhood, the SBC men's auxiliary, had even come close to doing. They'd never asked for a red cent from the SBC, though since the "conservative resurgence" began, the male leadership of the Convention was now trying to take over the organization as the women fought to keep from being emotionally and structurally gang raped.

Between these mighty forces and the fact many in WMU leadership were also married to Baptist clergymen, anything they chose to do as a positive response to my request would be perceived as an act of war. Nobody said this. Nobody had to.

It was the moment of truth. Calm as a cucumber, I had nothing more to say. Neither did Diana. All I wanted was an honest answer. So I waited for these gracious women who had already told me how much they appreciated what I was doing and knew the need.

After several awkward moments, a brilliant idea was thrown out, a way for them to help raise awareness and present the need without the WMU committing itself directly with funds. I could work with one of their editors to write an article about my ministry, including the retreats. This would be great publicity, raise awareness, and might even indirectly result in some funding from an external source. Agreement was immediately echoed. This would be no problem at all.

An editor would be contacting me soon, someone promised.

I was prepared for a "no" to my proposal. I wasn't expecting to be set up and then dropped on cement, however. That's what it felt like a month later when I finally accepted the fact that what had been so enthusiastically promised wasn't going to happen.

I'd never had abandonment issues before—betrayal issues, yes—but this felt more like abandonment. Nurtured by the WMU since Sunbeams and GA's, both organizations totally under their auspices, this auxiliary served as my collective mother. Yet they were nothing like the mother woman who raised me.

This collective "mother" had suddenly gotten rid of me, thrown me under the bus, and left me feeling totally "cut-off." There was no misunderstanding here. The message was crystal clear. I was not a perpetrator. Neither was I acting as a victim.

These women, steeped in a culture intended to leave us all with a sense of learned helplessness, were the real victims, and I was free. I only got caught in the middle of their latest assault that had left them with their hands tied behind their backs unable to remove the duct tape across the mouth of each one.

All Diana could provide was a genuine "I'm sorry." She was deeply disappointed.

I was also, for a season; but relief for my personal misery was on the way.

*****

[1] Anson D. Shupe, Jr., William A. Stacey, and Susan E. Darnell (eds.) Bad Pastors. Clergy Misconduct in Modern America. New York: New York University Press, pp. 187-213

Chapter 34
Soul Restorations

In spite of all we do or say, changing systems with deeply ingrained histories may not be possible—at least in a single lifetime. Personal, internal change always is. Sometimes it comes slowly, sometimes it comes like a keg of dynamite, blasting away what we've been needing to have removed in our thinking for a long time and clarifying what's been hidden beneath our full comprehension.

Advocates sometimes have the opportunity to serve as a keg of dynamite, as well. I believe that's what Susan Shaw did for me nine years ago:

My complimentary copy of Dr. Susan Shaw's book arrived unexpectedly one bright, spring day 2008, a few weeks prior to my sixty-second birthday. What a present!

I'd totally forgotten it was coming, even totally forgotten about my interview with the professor. She'd explained how she first found me and decided I should be on her list of 150 women to interview, women who'd found ways to cope and thrive in spite of the shared experience of growing up in the Southern Baptist Convention. What I didn't tell her and haven't until this day, the woman who recommended she include me in the 150 women to interview was the very same lady who'd told me in a round-about way, back in 1997, that she believed I was partially responsible for my own sexual assault by a missionary colleague, same as every little child ever sexually abused. God does work in mysterious ways.

The title of the book had me captivated. It was perfect. So was the timing after my experience with the WMU. What fun it would be to show this book to the three women coming to my next retreat.

I could just envision the laughs, especially from Phyllis, the latest SBC survivor to pop into my inbox, who was flying up from Tennessee. "God Speaks to Us, Too"—those five small, simple words packed a powerful message while the subtitle told exactly who was bringing the message of the day. This was a book filled with the voices of "Southern Baptist Women on Church, Home & Society," the subtitle revealed.

Why hadn't I thought to say "God speaks to me, too, Davis Saunders" when I sat across a table in Kenya with one of the top executives of the Foreign Mission Board, telling me he was struggling to decide if the assaults and abuse of teenage girls he was claiming he knew little about were moral problems, though he acknowledged he was certain homosexuality was? Of course, I would certainly have been written up for insubordination because if I'd gotten that far, I would have gone on to add "so you better listen," right after suggesting he was telling a bald-faced lie about not knowing any of the facts in this case.

I wanted to take the day off, just to read this new book to see what every one of my "sisters" had said. This would be like getting caught up, or learning things I never knew, about a whole bunch of relatives in faraway places. Like a letter from home, I suspected—though I was quite sure, knowing what I did about Susan, this letter would not be nearly as disturbing as one I'd gotten from a distant relative "back home" more than a decade earlier. That epistle chastised me. After all, I "should know that we Southern Baptists don't believe in sexual misconduct."

I don't recall answering. If so, I'm sure my answer was short, same as what I said to Ron with a chuckle the day I received it: "Exacto! Southern Baptists *don't* "believe" in sexual misconduct. This is why I wrote the book."

Before I got too excited, though, I better see what this professor of women's studies at Oregon State University, with a PhD from Southern Baptist Theological Seminary in Louisville, might have decided to say. What could I possibly have said, if anything, that was worth including? After all, this scholar had likely been forced to delete 99% of what 150 outraged women said to get it into less than 300 pages. Listening to so many of us, at various stages of awakening, telling how we'd all struggled to cope with the illusions of our heritage must have made her ears burn.

The fact she'd even taken time to really listen to me longer than any one woman of her caliber ever had was a great gift in itself, no matter what I failed to remember of that long-ago conversation. Seeking a clue, I went first to the index. There I found four pages listed next to my name.

The most important of all had much to do with my current ministry. If a vote were taken, I was quite sure almost every single woman in this book would agree with me on that. While 95% of men in the Convention

would not. It also specifically had to do with the recent political climate of
the SBC, which only complicated what I'd tried to do:

> *Dee Miller, a former Southern Baptist missionary*
> *to Africa, realized early on that women would be*
> *a central issue in the Controversy. "Back in*
> *1982,"she explained, "when we were on*
> *furlough, the pastors often would confide in me*
> *their concerns. I heard rumblings from some of*
> *them about how the 'women's issue' was going to*
> *be the downfall of the SBC. I began thinking,*
> *back then, that the inerrancy issues really had*
> *nothing to do with inerrancy. They were only*
> *raised because of the 'women's issue.' We were*
> *being perceived as such an awful threat to the*
> *establishment, of course."* [1]

By nightfall, I was shaking my head in awe at how Shaw had
empowered each of her contributors to speak. Our voices, mostly of
dissension, would be considered suspect, arrogant, or downright rude by
the male establishment we had been forced to cower to in a culture most of
these women found impossible to think of leaving. It was a culture we'd
often been discouraged to question out loud because of our "original sin"
of being born female. Yet the men and even the boys had a right to do so.
And they definitely could more easily get by with disparaging words and a
whole lot of true vices—if only they dared.

I was so proud of Christa Brown! She harmonized perfectly with my
own voice, as Shaw showed clearly. While I'd been the first to open the
public discourse about clergy sexual abuse in the denomination, Brown had
come along nine years later as I'd reached the point of near-exhaustion and
pushed through the resistant crowds, speaking to a press now more
sensitized and far less resistant than the one I'd encountered at the end of
the last century.

In truth, God speaking to every individual, down to the smallest
child, is a precious tenet taught by all congregations who give more than
lip service to "the priesthood of the believers." Historically this tenet has
been considered sacred to Baptists as the Declaration of Independence

saying "all men are created equal." Therein was the problem—no "priestess-hood" existed, one of many characteristics making Southern Baptists close cousins with Roman Catholics these days, more than either wanted to admit.

Nobody would have thought of having me preach about the topic of my current volunteer ministry in 2008. That was a sharp contrast to 1988 when, before our resignation, I was being honored with that privilege granted to females *only* if we were missionaries. To ask me to do that now, giving my current testimony, would be at least as upsetting to most congregations than having a lesbian fill the pulpit.

I was happy to see how Shaw framed the issues of the lesbian participants in this masterpiece of hers, concentrating on April Parker, an ordained minister and co-pastor serving with heterosexual Amy Mears of Nashville's Glendale Baptist Church, now affiliated with American Baptists and The Alliance of Baptists. Glendale was one of several open and affirming, formerly Southern Baptist, congregations Shaw pointed out. She went further to honor The Alliance's 2004 renewal of its pledge to "create places of refuge and renewal for those who are ignored by the church" by taking a stand in support of "our sisters and brothers" for same-sex marriage.

The Alliance had also welcomed my work informally in 1994, when I called Stan Hastey to tell him about a proposal from Linkup, which Ron and I soon decided we could not actually commit to. It was for the two of us to move to Kentucky to help establish and personally staff a retreat center for survivors. Stan Hastey, The Alliance's longtime leader, promised he'd try to locate "seed money" for this project so fully in keeping with the organization's mission.

In 2015, someone else closely related to Shaw's project would re-enter my life as an author. J. T. Collins, an MK now in her fifties, whose mother was my closest friend at the time of our rude awakening, was just beginning her own ministry as an activist and one of the lesbian members of Glendale. She and her partner Kim would visit us, doing a little marketing on the side for her new book "Face in the Mirror." It's a slightly fictionalized description of her journey from "a childhood as a missionary-kid in the African bush into the American jungle of life as a lesbian," including how she managed to achieve acceptance in every important arena of her world.

"The Universe at work!" I could hear Fran Park saying all the way from Connecticut. She's also the one who a concept I've come to treasure, the idea that our lives can become a prayer when we put feet to them. If so, this reconnection with Janet felt like mine had been answered.

By the time Janet and I got connected again, Ron had taken on the cause locally of advocating for LGBTQ individuals in our metro area and was getting some clout on Facebook for what he was posting on their behalf there. This was merely an extension of where we had been for many years, going back to his Iowa pastorate, where he'd first had the joy of working alongside a lesbian musician on our staff and had later supported a young man and his family who struggled in the shadows with some of the members of our church who quietly voiced their own bigotry in a congregation still conflicted over the issues, same as many remain today.

A Final Word for the SBC

I couldn't help wondering how many of those 150 women perhaps might be silent victims of collusion with abuse in the faith community, might have been validated, just knowing of my ministry. I suspected dozens.

With the affirmation of "God Speaks to Us, Too," my soul was fully restored even if the majority of the women in this text might hesitate to stand beside Christa Brown now, as she worked so hard to raise awareness in a far more public role than I was currently able to do.

My long, hard journey with the SBC was over at age sixty-two. The final knell in the coffin, marking a twenty-year, painful death process, came at a time that would seem to some a moment of victory. My relationship with this denomination had been on life-support since 1988. I'd hung on for a good cause. I had "fought a good fight" with this inheritance of mine

I could move forward and now on to bigger and better things. First, I wanted to write a book review for Shaw's masterpiece and send it to Joe Trull, now the editor of Christian Ethics Today since 2000, the same year he'd left the seminary and officially joined with the BGCT to address clergy sexual abuse.

With that accepted and published, I had one more article I wanted to write that summer as I reflected on the past twenty years. Not that I expected to make any new connections from it—unless another Kevin Gourley happened to be out there.

I wanted one last word—actually I wanted several thousand last words, I told myself, when I approached Trull about another article for Christian Ethics Today. For I had plenty to say about the statement that came from Morris Chapman, President of the SBC Executive Committee, as he addressed the need for churches to cooperate fully with civil authorities in reporting child abuse and to remove child predators from ministry. His message was intended as a portion of the response of a committee charged with the task of studying whether it would be wise for them to keep a data base on ministers who had committed sexual abuse against minors, a proposal made by Pastor Wade Burleson. I could write several more books on the whole topic of this powerful denomination's failure to come up with feasible, realistic plans for keeping abusers out of the pulpit, not to speak of protecting vulnerable adult women from abuse by their pastors.

That was the problem: I really had so much to say I couldn't readily collect all my thoughts, though I tried for weeks before finally sending what I explained was still a rough draft.

It didn't make a bit of sense to him, he told me. What on earth was I trying to say? I was hoping he would *help* me make sense of it, I told him.

In all fairness, this latest set of frustrations wasn't all about him. I was still extremely traumatized from the WMU betrayal that particular afternoon when I sat in a windy park on a cell phone, yelling partly out of frustration with myself at this man who I perceived to have the capacity to understand the intersection of ethics and professional power beyond most of his colleagues.

He suggested I call him back when we had a better connection. I decided it wouldn't make any difference. We'd really "lost our connection" years ago for all practical purposes.

What had the retired professor most puzzled in that article was what I thought was the most profound. It was by my an excerpt from a children's book, telling the familiar story of The Lion King:

> "Simba," asked Pumbaa, "do you like being the
> Lion King? I mean, isn't it an awful lot of
> responsibility?"
>
> "Well, sure," answered his friend. "But I like
> having everyone depend on me to keep them
> safe. It makes me feel as if I'm doing something
> that matters." [2]

He couldn't understand why this was even applicable to the article.

I was using the illustration in a section of the article that indirectly addressed the data base issue while referring back to an article in CET from a year earlier that I found deeply troubling. Yet it was one that nobody else had bothered to do so.

Charles McGathy, a military chaplain, still held that revelations to clerics about all abuse should be "privileged," same as Catholic priests had tried to claim years earlier! That combined with Chapman's declarations and the decision on the data base, all tied together, raised a myriad of issues about secret-keeping to deflect responsible actions at the expense of vulnerable children. This, in a big nutshell, was the premise of the article.

I knew that Joe didn't agree with what McCarthy wrote. He told me so, though in the spirit of CET, he'd printed it as an opinion. It was the fact that not one reader had bothered to challenge it which bothered me most.

With men like McGathy around, still espousing such dark-ages ethics like many others in the SBC, it didn't matter what anybody did with the structure. There would always be somebody in this conservative denomination, same as with Catholics, trying to protect secrecy at the expense of children.

In spite of the condescension shown toward me and some of the people for whom I've advocated, Joe Trull really did believe, same as I had years earlier, that the Convention might be able to address its problems with widespread abuse without structural change and without outsiders being brought in to help find the blind spots of those inside the system.

From what I was seeing in other systems, I wasn't convinced that any particular structure could adequately do the job—not to police itself. Structures were only as good as the people who were a part of it. It was still going to require major changes in attitudes. The arrogant attitudes of denominational leaders, who often projected those attitudes onto powerless survivors, would need to be addressed.

Men trying to "fix things" had to quit thinking like abusers or like abusers wanted them to think. They had to stop patronizing women, too.

I never got back. In time, I did some revision and posted the results on line.[3] I wanted this article easily found for decades to come rather than tucked inside a hard copy of a journal likely soon to be tossed aside.

Would other survivors step forward to build on what Christa Brown and I had done? Or survivors like Deborah Dail? Or Debbie Vasquez? If they read our web sites now, I'm quite sure few will. Instead they're likely to run to creative lawyers like Ron Weil and Adam Horowitz of Florida, Neal Smith and Tahira Khan of Texas, and others in the upcoming generation. What other choices are left?

Follow-Up on Renae

Renae followed through with every one of her original career goals plus more. The mending from long-term abuse turned out to be a lot more work than she anticipated. It always is. Yet she never wavered, refusing to skip any steps.

She drove many miles over the years to work with a top-notch analyst, got through school with flying colors, became fully licensed, and eventually got into private practice. Somewhere in the middle of that process, she began to struggle with counseling other abuse victims and urgently worked to get past that.

While the perpetrator was no longer in ministry of any kind, having been forced to leave the pastorate after abusing an adult congregant several years after her own abuse, she still needed closure.

"I decided I needed to see if I could stage a conversation to confront what happened to me," she tells me now. "I had mutual friends with one of the offender's daughters on social media, so I messaged her to say I was looking for people who had influenced my life. She contacted him for permission and sent me his phone number.

"I left a message for him, and he called me back, agreeing to my request to attend a session with me and my analyst. Unbeknownst to him, I invited a friend to sit in that session as a silent witness. I was sort of surprised when he showed up. I said what I needed to say; he made halfhearted, lame excuses, offered an apology and paid for the session at my request."

That encounter fully empowered the budding psychotherapist, putting her on a firm foundation, able to move forward in confidence.

Despite a full practice, she's now making frequent trips to Switzerland, working toward becoming an official Jungian Analyst—all with the encouragement and shared financial support of her husband David, who is a very active partner, integrating all they've learned together as they relate to their two very active teenage daughters. This has all been on their own without assistance from either the denomination of her heritage or the perpetrator who brought so much devastation to her soul.

Just as most women in Susan Shaw's book, Renae has managed to remain a Baptist. Yet she struggles with that decision constantly and re-evaluates it frequently, weighing into it what's best for her family now and what she will be able to live with in the future.

Her decision raises the dilemma of many women—not just Baptists, but many mainline Christians, and Catholics, as well as those of other faiths. Some questions for those who wake up in mid-life with a family already entrenched in an extremely misogynous religious system are: Can I and my family survive better by staying or by leaving? If I stay, how do I cope? Most of all, how do I manage to keep myself and my children safe, especially if there are no strong policies and procedures for handling reports of abuse? By leaving, will I make a greater impact on the system? If not, is there hope of doing so by staying? Am I content to live with the frequent silencing of women I have so frequently experienced in the past? Who is going to listen to my prophetic voice or be willing to hear my witness if I stay? How can I best nurture my own soul in this environment? If nobody does, how long will I put up with that?

By staying in the system, mothers like Renae, with daughters to raise, may make their very best contribution as role models, boldly speaking out and teaching their daughters to do the same. In the end, whether those daughters decide to stay or leave, they are likely to become the salt of the earth as they join other "squeaky wheels," such women in autonomous congregations hold some of the greatest potential in this world for turning patriarchy totally upside down.

A Shining Example

One of my closest friends in the survivor movement is an amazing musician and school teacher, also a poet in England. She reminds me a lot of Bette Rod because of her passion to watch out for the little ones, which has been sharpened even more in very healthy ways, after years of hard work to confront her own childhood trauma.

Nobody in her family wanted to hear her speak of the trauma from criminal neglect or of how she had managed to overcome it, however both were very important to her. This was her life after all, the serious neglect and the victory over it.

She has a photo for proof of the neglect, and many photos now showing evidence with her genuine smile of her recovery. The one from her childhood shows her trying to occupy her three-year-old mind with a bicycle parked within reach of where she was chained to a water-pipe for confinement. This is how her mother coped with her own serious mental health issues for which the child was not responsible, of course.

Things seldom go as expected in cases like this. Usually there's only greater disappointment. Often a total cut-off comes closer to achieving peace of mind. For a time, it seemed the best to hope for. After struggling for years to hang on to what fragments remained of her relationship with her family, that's exactly what happened during her daughters' teenage years.

Yet that's not where this story ends. That's what makes it the exception.

In 2009, a relative involved in Olga's mother's care reached out to my friend in a loving manner. She'd noticed a mellowing in the old woman and wondered if there might now be some resolution at long last.

So the middle-aged daughter went, not with high hopes, but she knew she could now handle whatever her mother and the rest of the family might dish out. Wholeheartedly, without failing in any way to own any part of her daughter's grievances, this mother took full ownership for her role in the child's neglect, which also extended to several older relatives who did not own their part. In fact, they were distraught that their mother had reversed her attitude toward her abused child.

When she died less than a year later, she did so in peace. At the same time, her daughter felt her life had come full circle. She was now whole. In that whole process, inter-generational healing took place. For during the time my friend struggled most intensely, she had sustained deep psychological damage from a nun, posing as a counselor. This had put the woman, already with a high ACE score, in such a regressed state she was unable to care adequately for her own children.

The ending isn't picture-perfect because most of her surviving family members have remained complicit with her abuse and neglect as a child. Yet the power is in the court of this vibrant woman who reflects it, empowering me and so many others now.

I have seen this only one other time—when the cut-off imposed by his teenage daughter, until she was well into adulthood, persuaded an abusive father, after many years, to stop drinking in order to meet this young woman's long-established boundary for restoring their relationship. In that case, it was the arrival of a new grandson that persuaded the old man to realize just how much he had to live for and how much he'd be losing unless he did an about-face. Once he proved his sobriety over time to his daughter, he not only saw the boy, but has maintained a strong relationship with both the grandson and the child's mother for over a decade now.

Both of these stories show that change is possible when tough love is extended over a period of years. Yet the sorrow, appropriate consequences imposed, and the great losses experienced by the offender can never be totally erased from memory. This is what accountability is all about, and it has nothing to do with forgiveness.

Icing the Cake

Also in 2009, I eagerly accepted Renae's invitation to join her at a workshop in Houston with another Texan with the last name "Brown" and a first name that rhymed with "Renae."

Brene Brown, already a world-renowned speaker and writer, specializing on issues of shame. So there I sat after following my young friend to the front row of a room with about seventy-five other participants.

To her left, was the first retreat leader she'd turned to in the retreat that led her on an internet search that brought her like a breath of fresh air into mine. I'd met the older woman only a half hour before Brown stepped to the front of the room and announced we were going to begin by having each person stand for a brief   introduction. That could take half the morning, I was thinking, as I looked at the crowd of around seventy-five before she finished her instructions.

"Not just your name, though," she explained. "Tell us something about yourselves—what you do, why you're here. Let's start right here."

With that, she pointed toward the left side of the room to the front row where I was sitting. I was now in a panic, despite having made many extemporaneous speeches, even filling the pulpit with only five minutes' notice one recent Sunday morning when Ron's sub didn't show up. I'd come to sit back and learn, not to be "on stage." What "something" should I choose that would be acceptable at this conference about shame?

My panic only increased after the first two stood, as the renowned leader introduced Renae's other friend as an author, wife and daughter of Baptist ministers, and a popular retreat leader with whom Brown had herself been privileged to work recently.

After Renae did a fine job describing her situation as a current student who had taken an interest in Brown's work, my moment of truth arrived.

"I am also a writer and a native Texan, married to a Baptist minister," I blurted out. "We now live in Iowa as American Baptists. My specialty in writing is collusion with clergy sexual abuse, and my greatest moments of shame come when I am forced to admit I was ever associated with Southern Baptists."

A nervous laugh rippled across the crowd as Brown, an Episcopalian, worked to contain herself before turning to the first woman in the second row, much to my relief. The awkward moment I'd managed to create wasn't only *unforgettable* for me. It turned out to be one of the most defining of my life.

Reactions to my self-revelation of shame came forth uninvited over the next hour. Several stood to weigh in proudly as Southern Baptists while just as many chose to identify with my sentiments. Some sought me out at break time, eager to share more. With ample lead time, I'm certain I would have been much more diplomatic. Yet diplomacy wasn't my top priority that day. Neither was my intent to shame others. Authenticity, on the other hand, was.

It served as a reminder. In spite of awkward moments, we all have choices. Speaking out as individuals isn't easy. We can stand together in solidarity. We can insist on change. We can pull forward or pull out. Or we can stay, quietly hoping someone else will step up to the plate, depending upon the situation. Once we speak to a crowd, who's to say what the outcome may be.

*****

[1] Susan Shaw, God Speaks to Us, Too: Southern Baptist Women on Church, Home & Society (The University Press of Kentucky, 2008), p. 156.

[2] From the children's book by Lisa Ann Marsoli, The Lion King: the Pal Patrol (Advance Publishers, 1998)

[3] Wishful Thinking: Southern Baptists 2008 Plan to Eliminate Child Abuse by Clergy (plan for adult victims still "pending") http://www.takecourage.org/WishfulThinking.htm

Chapter 35
Challenges Beyond Belief

Advocacy is not bound to a single cause. Nor does it require we move at full speed constantly. Even when we are forced to shift to a holding pattern or join others in worthy causes, the seeds of past efforts continue to sprout.

If we intend to move from the role of bystander to one of advocacy for any cause, it's essential to consider the perception of the disenfranchised. Seeing ourselves as "the other" who is privileged, we learn to help the world adjust to this new reality we would not have otherwise seen.

By late 2009, Ron's dependence on high doses of narcotics to cope with severe pain had me increasingly worried about leaving him at the cottage alone. This place that had been such a source of joy was fast losing its charm. Life was a burden for both of us.

Then, when his mother died suddenly in the summer of that year, we managed the difficult trip for the funeral and returned to Iowa, where we began packing to vacate two residences at once—the lovely apartment and the cottage where we'd invested so many happy hours, as we prepared for a move into a rent house, closer to specialists in the city. I braced myself. Whatever the struggles ahead, I needed to keep up my full-time teaching schedule for another year, take care of the two of us, and continue to maintain two residences—the one we occupied and the one we desperately needed to sell.

Nobody was more surprised than our real estate agent when a single mother with a special-needs child declared our place was exactly what she'd been looking for. Mother and child arrived, ready to move in the same day movers took the last of our things away.

While we were still in the midst of this immense personal whirlwind, our daughter had her own acute crisis. Grieving over a lost marriage, she faced the stresses of being a single mother to our three grandsons. As a family, we pulled together even over the long distances as Ron and I prepared for my semi-retirement and another move to the city where we now live—Lawrence, Kansas, near the campus of the University of Kansas.

Meanwhile, back in Iowa, we set to work, making medical appointments and taking trips to hospitals in between students. Except for answering an occasional email, advocacy work had fortunately dropped to a trickle. Christa Brown had picked up much of the slack along with hundreds of others who had joined the survivor movement, now more easily finding voice after years of "advocacy training" we'd done with journalists.

By Christmas, after three hospitalizations, Ron was finally feeling better than he had in years. Thanks to his surgically-implanted pain pump, he was fully alive now. Our spirits soared as we looked forward to establishing a new life closer to our children and grandchildren.

Our joys were short-lived. Four months after the pain pump was implanted, his legs gave out one day with me watching, too far away to do anything before he was flat of his back in a parking lot. Doctors were as puzzled as we were, though they determined that whatever the problem, it was neurological.

Totally out of the loop, not even staying in touch with Christa anymore, I never knew until recently about the huge breakthrough that occurred while we were struggling with our personal confusion. Oh, how I could have used some good news back then!

Christa's blog captured her feelings of elation. Three Baptist journalists in the past week had written op-ed columns "decrying the problem of clergy child molestation and cover-ups in Baptist churches!"[1] To Christa, and the growing number of visitors to her website, www.stopbaptistpredators.org, it looked like a real breakthrough. Surely all the work that she had done, on the heels of my own attempts, was going to finally produce action beyond a conversation—at least, one would think so.

A New Home

By August of 2011, as Ron began sinking further into life as a paraplegic, we moved into our newfound home in Lawrence, with a lot of help from our son James. Meanwhile, we were hopeful a new set of doctors in the Kansas City area would be able to build on the exploration Omaha doctors had begun.

The little culprit causing big problems at least had a name, we discovered, though its exact location remained a mystery. It was a rare condition, technically a spinal arterial-venous fistula or "AVF," only vaguely familiar to most doctors, most having only encountered a case via a textbook. What could be done about it remained to be seen. The only comfort was it would not be fatal. At least not for *him,* I told myself. With a little luck, maybe I'd survive, as well.

I no longer needed to get to the gym or walking track. The activities of daily living were plenty to keep me in reasonable shape physically. My emotional state was another matter. So was Ron's. This serpent was a monster.

Still without solid answers after consulting with a top specialist at the University of Kansas, we left boxes sitting and turned again to Mayo, as worried as we'd been fifteen years earlier when facing my cancer recurrence.

Our son James, who drove up to join us, was by our side to offer another set of ears on Monday morning when we saw the surgeon, who totally smashed the optimism another Mayo physician held only days earlier. This was not a "simple" AVF, the surgeon explained. In fact, it was so rare he'd only seen one other like it.

Whatever we chose to do, there was little hope for improvement, even if the surgeon managed to stop the disease process with yet another risky surgery, once he found his way through the massive scar tissue from past operations.

Back home, after several days of weighing the limited options, Ron phoned Rochester to say we'd not be returning. While we chose to do nothing more surgically, this didn't mean we sat down to cry in our coffee mugs, for there wasn't *time* to do that either—not with the danger of a fall each time he tried to go across the living room, even with a walker. We had much to learn and expensive equipment to locate.

As I unpacked the last box, Ron hired several carpenters who soon installed an aluminum ramp to the front door, a stair lift inside, and a safer and more accessible bathroom on the main floor, giving him the full run of our new abode. Thanks to craigslist, we found two essentials: a power wheelchair to make do while we waited for a custom-built one; and a good, used van with a ramp system.

The new chair that would double as a driver's seat in the special van would not be arriving for months. So, we learned to allow extra time each time we left the house to get the make-shift chair safely secured to forego the likelihood of it becoming a flying missile in case of an accident.

Meanwhile, as the eye-opening Penn State case hit the news, Ron stayed glued to the television, keeping me informed of every horrific detail, calling me to come quickly when anything new was revealed. As a sports fan, he was especially distraught when famed coach Joe Paterno's role in the complicity broke. What a contrast the news coverage was now in 2011 from the reticence that abounded in past institutional scandals, from the days when Anita Hill was leading the way as an unintended spokesperson on the issues of sexual harassment. To when church or military officials had been permitted copious amounts of prime-time news coverage to freely tell the American public how everything was being "handled well" while collusion was being minimized in the press. No longer was it politically correct to do this. Nor was the well-informed press, well-versed in the dynamics compared to past decades, so easily manipulated. Neither was the public nearly so gullible, only saddened by such news.

The two of us shifted gears, back and forth, as we sought practical ways to deal with peripheral neuropathy and limited mobility with the help of newfound friends, all veterans at coping with severe disabilities, at a local advocacy group known as Independence, Inc. There, inspiring members range from professional caregivers functioning independently from wheelchairs to those with very limited educations, including some with intellectual disabilities who still manage to cope with amazing resiliency.

Advocacy took a whole new set of purposes now. Ron grieved, of course. So did I. For him, losses included having to abandon dreams, including his desire to establish ties again in his previous fulfilling work with CASA[2]. This advocacy group continually cries for volunteers for children, often in foster care and needing support while courts trying to sort out what's in their best interests through the justice system. His challenging mobility issues prevented him from even getting up the stairs to the CASA offices in Lawrence, let alone into the homes of the children.

Soon he traded in this passion, taking on a combination role of self-advocacy and advocating for others with special needs. The advantage was that we'd each had plenty of training and experience in overall advocacy to build on, starting back in New Orleans. Easing into these new ventures, Ron soon realized he'd had ten years of already living with disability, though still on his own two feet.

What we'd both learned about DIM thinking in professional circles also applied to the general population in regard to ADA issues. People who have never "crossed over" tend to assume that everything is already fixed for these "troublesome" folks who keep voicing complaints about disability, not stopping to think through barriers now very visible to us— not only the physical barriers, but the intense problems people with multiple debilitating illnesses and limitations may have that we'd looked right past previously ourselves. Ron had seen this also when advocating for the chronically mentally ill, as a person with disability himself, while living in Iowa.

In fact, it took me getting into the Ron's power wheelchair and trying some things myself before I began comprehending some of the dilemmas.

Not all of DIM thinking is due to apathy, I soon concluded. Much is from the fear of identifying. "How would I cope in this situation if it were me?" When it comes to a serious disability, nobody wants to think of this for long anymore than to think of being a victim of a violent crime.

Yet, true advocates do not turn away, but simply develop a new set of eyes. People do not understand how perceptions naturally change when one feels on display or has to ask for help, for instance. Simply having to constantly ask for help, when much of the asking could be easily remedied with better accessibility, discourages many from even leaving their homes, thereby adding to the invisibility of this growing population. Few recognize the discrimination felt due to barriers that forbid autonomy and free access. To the "disabled," there might as well be a sign at the doors of many structures, saying: "Do not enter." When it comes to disabilities, it takes a lot more energy for a person with a disability to be heard than it does for those without visible disabilities.

In a church setting, it's much easier for Ron than for the majority, however. He knows how to make his voice known there and often does. His experience combined with special knowledge of church systems, in fact, makes him a natural as long as he's wheeling up and down the halls of a friendly congregation. Sometimes he finds it downright entertaining.

Like recently, when he came speeding toward me with joystick in hand to report a conversation five minutes earlier with a friendly lady down the hall. He was there on an advocacy mission, he explained, to help the congregation with any accessibility issues he might observe. He didn't say he'd been there on the same mission earlier. Nor did he voice a complaint that he still couldn't get into a single restroom in the church.

Instead he focused on another concern: The double glass doors into the sanctuary were a barrier for wheel chair users. "Though I'm sure the Board will do the right thing when I tell them," he said.

"No they won't," the kind lady replied with deadpan confidence as she walked away.

Doing the right thing for disenfranchised folks does require a re-arrangement of priorities. It can be quite inconvenient and sometimes expensive, even when it's as simple as replacing double doors with a single. It's much easier to do things right in the beginning, of course; but resistance to making amends is not always high on the agenda of church systems or any other institution.

Most participants in his water therapy class were women older than he is, so it was thrilling when another man about his age joined a few weeks after he did on a morning when Ron was in unusually high spirits.

"There was this guy in the locker room today," He shakes his head, laughing as soon as he sees me. "That guy says, 'If I was in your shoes, I'd just find a gun and shoot myself!' Can you believe that?"

My sense of humor didn't match Ron's that particular day.

"People like that need to grow up. I've told some so," said Dot Nary, who's both a professor and professional advocate, having lived and coped with spina bifida all her life.

I've thought a lot about Dot's remark, how it can apply to any of us with a variety of matters and settings. It explains much of the problem with collusion, in fact.

Everyone needs to grow up. Some are forced to very fast.

The Challenge of Mind-Changing

Growing up is a lifelong process, a universal need for each of us. Changing minds is an inter-generational process totally related to the individual.

Raising awareness is difficult, raising concerns and changing attitudes, much harder. This especially applies to churches, who are often limited in creativity as well as a willingness to prioritize for the many people who stay isolated in their homes, no longer even attempting to go to houses of worship where apathy and ignorance still abound more than a quarter of a century since ADA became law.

Of course, attitudes can't be legislated. People aren't arrested for crude remarks made to victims of any life-altering circumstance.

Churches are sometimes exempted for good reason from following the laws about building requirements. Older buildings on the historic registry are a prime example. Other churches simply prefer to disregard what they obviously can address.

Just as Baylor University chose to do with Title IX from the beginning, disregarding requirements intended to protect students, educating them, and holding offenders accountable in a fair, but swift process, accessibility issues on campuses, city streets, and even new public buildings are frequently overlooked.

Strangely, inspectors fail themselves, even with brand new structures and newly-laid parking lots. Which is why when Ron says: "Let's go check that new place out," he'll be referring to parking, timing on automatic front doors, or—one of the biggest annoyances of all—the much-too-heavy rest room doors or inaccessible areas of the rest room that the "expert" architect and builder overlooked before the inspector came along.

Self-advocacy, for accessibility, is essential for Ron. I can get by fine without it—if I leave him at home, that is. Sometimes, too tired to fight discrimination along with the constant physical discomfort and personal challenges that plague him, he chooses to stay home as many do far more often than not, resorting to lives of near-total isolation. If I were in his shoes—or in his seat—I might hibernate completely.

Since he doesn't suffer from PTSD like many of the previously-abused women and men who no longer go to church like Salty, and since one of his greatest remaining strengths is a strong set of healthy vocal cords, he's quite visible and vocal, too. Since he's got a healthy self-esteem hewn from years of experience living *without* a severe disability, he makes an added effort to speak his own needs as an act of advocacy for those who cannot speak, as much as for himself. Yet it's still very tiresome. And can be deeply personal.

His greatest focus has been organizing the Faith Accessibility Task Force for the entire city of Lawrence. Its purpose is to educate clergy and other church leaders to not only make their buildings full accessible wherever possible, but also to break down the barriers keeping people with special needs in social isolation because they don't feel totally welcome in any church.

Because of this task force, advocates without severe disabilities have joined in to organize a day-long workshop for the past two years at the United Methodist church.

It's difficult to see how Ron's advocacy work and mine are so closely related. His is much more visible. He can't be entirely ignored or silenced anymore in this new community. It's much harder to see the silent sufferers, such as children who have either experienced or witnessed sexual and domestic abuse. Since these survivors aren't in wheel chairs, they are truly invisible, and often in emotional isolation because faith groups "manage" these "special needs," too fearful to bring them into the daily discourse of the congregation.

The Beauty of Shared Visions

Much of our encouragement during those early days of adjustment came from long-time friends in other states, especially people with whom we had strong ties through the survivor movement.

When Amy Kasmar came down from Chicago only months after Ron got his new wheels, the little plaque she brought as a housewarming gift said it all:

> Life isn't about waiting for the storm to pass.
> It's about learning to dance in the rain.

It was just what I needed five years later, when I awoke the morning after this last Presidential election, as well. I referred to it as I took readers back to the days of the Moral Majority in a guest blog I wrote for Marie Fortune.[3] The blog reflected on the personal challenges of our family during another very volatile era, when the theological leanings in our nation had suddenly hijacked what many of us understood to be both moral and just, thereby impeding progress in areas of human rights that some of us had taken for granted.

Just Following Orders

Having no plans for future writing, I began teaching again, making plans to only take on a few students. Meanwhile we settled down to take in everything we could in this grand, historic, university city of Lawrence.

One afternoon I meandered into the local library, picking up a book nearly half the size of an old unabridged dictionary about the most infamous fellow who ever entered the city limits here. He was William Quantrill, a confederate guerrilla who led four hundred men on a raid of Lawrence in 1863. This guy is known today even to most kindergarteners in our city. Older kids, same as any adults paying attention, can soon learn the gruesome details of how those men left 250 children fatherless in one morning. They may also know the sanctuary of the Methodist church was quickly converted to a temporary morgue.

Yet the part I'd missed, now suddenly on the page before me, had me totally dumbfounded. I knew nothing about the 20,000 others, living in three counties less than an hour's drive from where I was sitting, who had been forced into homelessness by an executive order, issued only four days after the raid in Lawrence. Most shocking, the majority of those out on hot dusty roads, dealing with horrific drought and hunger, were thirsty children.

And it was the children I had to write about, crossing genres for the children of today, many coping with bullying, homelessness, and an array of injustices. This wasn't something to sit around thinking about. I was totally smitten. And much more so when I discovered I'd missed nothing in the museum on previous visits there.

Yet, come August, Order No. 11, as the massive eviction notice was called, would be among the topics of new displays, I was assured, just in time for the 150th anniversary of the disasters that played havoc on both sides of the border. This way, the children would be provided new understanding of war, identifying with children of the past, essential to facing the truth early on.

Only weeks into my research, I'd identified a wise, peace-loving minister in Missouri, known by few people today. He'd had relatives in Lawrence who'd been fortunate to escape a close call in the struggle of that awful morning. Just like that, I was off and running, writing full-time again for the first time in over fifteen years. "Just Following Orders," as I named it, was soon enlarging conversations among middle schoolers and their teachers, at festivals, historical societies, and even in churches.[4]

Anyone looking closely—really closely—and reading detail in the museums of eastern Kansas will soon recognize the ironies of history here, especially when it comes to racial injustice. Around 1850, outsiders from back east wanted to stamp out slavery before it ever got a stronghold in this new territory, the story goes. Yet, looking very closely at the reasons for this desire and for what subsequently happened once the Civil War was fought, the area "secured for freedom," then going on to see how racial oppression soon became the established way of thinking—all of this intrigued me. Especially interesting were things played out in the civil rights movement, with the clearest evidence being the landmark case about school integration. Brown vs. Board of Education took place one-half hour's drive from Lawrence, a city that had made such great sacrifices to fight for abolition a century before.

Someday, I'd do a sequel to this book, I told myself—another story about justice, carrying strong elements of DIM thinking easily borrowed from the survivor movement. This would certainly broaden my own horizons. As my first busy summer of marketing came to an end, I prepared to spend most of the following winter with research and plot development.

That was the plan, anyway .....

*****

[1] http://www.ethicsdaily.com/catholics-and-baptists-have-different-sacraments-but-similar-child-abuse-scandals-cms-15868

[2] http://www.casaforchildren.org/site/c.mtJSJ7MPIsE/b.5301295/k.BE9A/Home.htm

[3] See http://www.faithtrustinstitute.org/blog/252

[4] http://justfollowingorders.takecourage.org

Chapter 36
Blessed Distractions

Totally out of the blue, I was drawn anew into the fray of advocacy work in a whole new way. Though this new thing initially seemed to have little connection to my writing—nothing to do with either history or with issues of abuse in the faith community. It came from a faith-based organization, one 100% devoted to bringing people together, regardless of theological differences, to take bold steps to seek present-day justice on a local level, spreading it like a healthy virus into the entire community over time.

DART, as it's called, stands for Direct Action and Research Training.[1] It's really advocacy with a capital A. The principles, drawing from spiritual, sociological, and political insights, are solid as a rock. And it's all about empowering people of faith to work for positive change outside the walls of the church.

While houses of worship are often heavily involved with mercy ministries, few ever focus on the underlying causes of violence, poverty, hunger, and a multitude of other injustices causing misery for people both inside and out of church, and even more so for those too disenfranchised from society to even enter a church building or ask for help from any agency.

Mercy ministries feed the hungry, for instance, taking care of the symptom needing immediate attention. By contrast, justice ministries look for the reasons people may not have enough food. The focus is on a diverse set of solutions, best discovered by thinking very systemically. This requires research.

Solutions for hunger could involve setting aside land for community gardens, advocating for higher wages, or finding ways to cut through the barriers that keep many, many Americans from getting food stamps despite their eligibility—things like a general unawareness of qualifications or difficulty in filling out applications due to poor literacy skills.

Yet these solutions, though they may spread from one community to another are reached and implemented only at a local level. While DART is a national program that holds great potential for becoming widely international, its success is totally dependent on what people at the grass roots decide to do, and succeed at doing, at the local level. This puts it closely in line with the international Hesperian Foundation[2], whose materials I devoured and witnessed working in Africa through numerous small, grassroots projects.

Despite DART seemingly being tangential to my writing ministry, I had a hunch my time investment was going to somehow flow back into print through the work of my own fingers. Yet, whether it did or not, what was about to begin in Lawrence was right up my alley. Ron's too. It incorporated much of our personal philosophies, whether in nursing, mental health, pastoral ministry, or writing. That philosophy had worked for us on two continents since civil rights days in New Orleans, where we tried to do "the impossible" —which, if our efforts had been successful, would have led to the integration of one of the first Southern Baptist churches in the South.

With Ron's six wheels and my two feet, we jumped right in. Since child abuse of all sorts is a huge piece of many puzzles in every community, I figured maybe on down the line .... say in five years .... abuse could also be a part of this program.

Instead it quickly became front and center. And within months, it dawned on me what we were discovering through this "DART work" was going to ultimately be a gift to me and many of my colleagues in advocacy work in two specific arenas: applications for prevention of sexual abuse by professional ministers *and* helping explain to outsiders the depth of trauma experienced by individuals who were ever sexually abused by clergy in childhood or youth.

Justice Matters

DART asks every faith group represented to hold small group meetings each year in a process that gives each participant voice in identifying persistent, community problems reflecting injustices too large for any one individual, church or agency to fully tackle independently. Multiple areas of concern are listed and voted on. Here in Lawrence, three emerged in the first year: mental health, affordable housing and children's issues.

DART also asks every participating community to choose a unique name before individuals begin forming research teams to help determine potential solutions. Here in Lawrence, we voted to call ourselves "Justice Matters." Depending on voice inflection, these two words can either be a declarative sentence or give a simple description of what we do. We use it both ways: *Justice matters* to each of us as we work on the *justice matters* we have chosen to address. Simply having people representing thousands, from faiths as divergent as Catholic to Muslim to conservative evangelical to Quaker, was itself an amazing feat.

I immediately chose to put my energies with children's issues, hoping somehow children's mental health might get a *little* attention and assuming the group designated for mental health would be focusing primarily on adults. As it turned out, childhood trauma, which naturally correlates closely with the mental health of all ages, encompassed *everything* we decided to address.

ACES

"You have two rivers flowing here, and they both need attention," Becky Williams tells young seminarians. "There's the personal and the interpersonal in your congregation. It would be much better if you pay close attention to the personal in the beginning rather than wait years to discover the need."

Williams isn't a seminary professor. After thirty years in private practice as a psychotherapist, she's now Director for Sexual Ethics and Advocacy with United Methodists' General Commission on the Status and Role of Women (COSROW). Passionate about preparing faith leaders to reach their highest potential to incorporate personal integrity and ethics, she's convinced focusing on the impact of early trauma will go a long way toward this task.

Ideally, this work will provide a great advantage—not just in prevention of professional boundary violations, but allowing professionals to turn their own traumas into a tool for personal empowerment, first of themselves and their families. Then, ultimately of those they serve.

In the process, even the ones fortunate enough to have escaped serious trauma in childhood may learn to better draw on their strengths, same as those who have learned to integrate unfortunate experiences, discovering unique survivor skills in that process. This end result may potentially lead to modern-day miracles through the phenomenon of "shared wisdom," which Pamela Cooper-White has written much about in a book by that title.[3]

This is all related to the very study one hundred professionals here in Lawrence are going to be trained to incorporate into their practices with children who have also experienced trauma. It was one of our solutions reached after many hours of collaboration with scores of experts far and wide. And it was announced and accepted at an assembly less than a year after the ecumenical group organized, where over 1700 people gathered in our city's largest auditorium, located on the campus of The University of Kansas.

So how did we come to that conclusion? Let me explain by telling you about this study we discovered.

Back in the fall of 2014, even those of us who had somehow invested years in prevention and early intervention with issues of abuse and neglect found ourselves suddenly intrigued by a very scientific set of findings professionals in a variety of disciplines need to know about, though far too few do. Yet the knowledge is spreading like another good virus at this point—not only here in Lawrence, but around the world.

Understanding ACEs offers doctors, mental health providers, teachers and community leaders a chance to change how they operate. In 2016, it's now reached Capitol Hill, where legislators are being urged to give it consideration in public policy.[4]

Since I'm always thinking of how often justice gets neglected *within* churches, as well as out in the community, I'm now bringing it to the discussion of clergy health and abuse, hoping it will be used to promote *internal* justice.

In fact, I'm absolutely certain this can make a huge difference in both the personal lives and outreach of professional ministers, young and old, inevitably trickling down to most congregants through Sunday morning sermons that are as practical to the lives of those sitting in the pews as anything one can imagine. Yet without it, commonly-held myths which church attenders cling to in regard to violence and abuse being "out there somewhere" are likely to leave regular church attendees more vulnerable to family violence than those who never darken the doors of the church.

Here's the caveat professional ministers are likely to appreciate more than everything else: For those congregations who dare open these discussions, finding ways to bear one another's biggest burdens that have long remained hidden, the entire infrastructure of any group—church or otherwise, cannot help but become healthier in the end.

Our adverse childhood experiences very definitely make a difference in the health and well-being of us as adults for the rest of our lives, especially if we remain ignorant of the impact of these experiences on our current lives. Prolonged, intense childhood trauma can actually change brain development, according to the Centers for Disease Control and Prevention .[4] This was the determination established through a two-year study undertaken by the CDC through Kaiser Permanente in 1995. The organic impact actually shows up through technology as images of the brains of victims of childhood abuse are compared to others.

To help establish all of this, an extensive questionnaire was distributed to more than 17,000 adults. It covered several broad categories of common ACES (adverse childhood experiences) — psychological, physical, or sexual abuse; violence against a child's mother; or sharing a household with an individual suffering from mental illness, substance abuse, suicidal attempts or imprisonment.   Individual results were calculated along with another set of factors commonly experienced in adulthood, such as poor work or academic performance, chronic physical illness, substance abuse, financial distress, domestic abuse, etc.

The results were shocking. The greater the ACE score, the greater the chance of negative outcomes, including premature death. The tabulated conclusions may surprise you.   Roughly two out of three respondents identified at least one ACE. More than one in four females reported *three or more* while less than one in four males reported this number. Of course, three or more can spell several disasters later in life for either gender.

Not surprisingly, females have a significantly higher incidence of sexual abuse on ACE scores. Physical violence was only factor higher in males than females. Emotional abuse for females came in at 13%, almost twice that reported by males. Make no mistake about it: the impact of misogyny begins very early.[5]

In neither the extensive questionnaires, available through the above link, or in the simpler screening instrument,[6] was it impossible to include every potential trauma. Therefore, ACE scores would be even higher for some of us than what the instrument shows. For example, nowhere does it ask how often a child had to pick up and move to a new community, as most preachers' kids do multiple times before leaving for college. Nor does it ask if a child was ever in a car accident with serious injury. Yet I was, and it happened in the process of a major move. So I personally count multiple moves as one ACE and the car accident that put me on crutches as I entered a new school in the middle of seventh grade as another. That's two in addition to two more common ones from my own childhood.

While my children were never in a car accident growing up, they both are TCK's (Third Culture Kids), which means they've struggled trying to fit into the culture they were born into, just as they sometimes did in their adopted culture, while now feeling most at home with other TCK's who all share a common language not spoken in any one country. Try adding up those ACE's when "changing cultures" isn't even mentioned in the questionnaire. Neither is being a child in a mixed race family, though the stigma society imposes on these children is often experienced as trauma.

Now, let's go one step further, applying this to victims of childhood sexual abuse by clergy. How would you score that one? While you're answering this question, I'll ask another. Know what pieces are missing from the ACE instrument that I believe are common in faith communities in general?

OK. Time's up! The answer to the second question is "spiritual abuse and spiritual neglect." Both of those must always be added to sexual abuse by clergy, giving a total of three, even if the victims didn't have a single ACE before the abuse, which is seldom the case. For, as anyone who saw the movie Spotlight knows, perpetrators seek out the very kids who *do* have multiple ACE's.

Spiritual abuse, a common problem even for adults, is the topic of several writers.[7] This type of abuse, often dished out along with other forms of child abuse, even lacing it into religious education at time, serves as a double whammy. Those who have grown up with shame of this nature need to look at how often we've passed this on, without thinking, to the next generation in order to stop the cycle. There's nothing spiritual about spiritual abuse at all.

Since being able to isolate victims is especially important to child predators, children in boarding schools of any kind may be more vulnerable than those in traditional educational settings. Allow me to focus momentarily on MK's (missionaries' children) who often already feel deeply abandoned or emotionally neglected by being sent far away from home, especially at an early age. Imagine how their very survival every hour of every day entails being away from the watch-care of their parents, where severe corporal punishment has been used for the slightest misbehavior, in a remote area outside their own culture. Want to try quantifying the ACE score for a child abused in this group?

OK—ready to go one step further? Or do you need a break? Take one if you need it, but don't you dare stay away from this for long.

Let's look at the average adult victim of professional sexual misconduct who has gone to a minister for counseling. Because help is so often sought following trauma, even if the trauma is recent, there's a strong likelihood a person struggling to cope with life may have a high ACE score in the first place. In other words, unresolved or partially-addressed childhood trauma greatly impacts the ability of many people to cope with subsequent traumas. High ACE scores make many adult counselees particularly vulnerable to sexual abuse; and the abuse can occur even if the help comes informally, in the process of another church activity, from a pastor who claims he was not "doing counseling."

Add to this the propensity for a clergy member with unresolved childhood trauma to cross sexual boundaries and you have the "perfect storm." Yet having a high ACE score does not provide an excuse to abuse. It only invites to us to look at what Becky Williams describes as a "personal river" to be attended to *before even taking on the enormous responsibility that professional ministry inevitably entails.*

For the professional is always the one to be held accountable, not the client. It is essential that bystanders understand this, as much as the professionals. The message is very clear: professionals, whether nurses, clergy, lawyers, teachers, police officers, counselors, or any other public servant better be prepared before taking on these roles. In other words, these responsibilities are not for kids. Nor are they for anyone who has not grown up.

Not All ACEs Are Created Equal

Here's the most positive news about this whole study: children who have many positive experiences, even if they encounter great adversity, can develop resilience. Also, adults at any stage can work toward reversing the impact of past traumas—to some degree simply by connecting the dots, experts say.

When the reality of the science dawns, when we recognize the unhealthy patterns rendered by our own ACEs, we can begin to change habits, seek professional help, talk to spouses, friends, and our offspring, incorporating our understanding into formal and informal speech and sermons, teaching and encouraging others to join the dialogue. There's the good virus spreading, once again. In so doing, we can develop much more a sense of personal, internal control, regardless of the faith we espouse.

Having positive experiences or empathetic responses to childhood trauma constitutes only one of many variables as we attempt to quantify individual impacts. By genetic makeup, some kids manage to have more trauma resiliency than others in the first place. Certain personalities combined with the effect of positive role models may allow another to seemingly sail through untouched. Yet these are the exceptions. The fact these exist should not be used as a reason to blame those whose lives remain in shambles, even with decades of intense state-of-the-art therapy.

In the future, we need to look more closely at the adults who have ended up with fewer negative outcomes than their ACE score might predict, as well as those who continue to suffer, same as we study causes of cancer—not to blame those who haven't survived, but to find out the reasons why some of us have. Wouldn't this be a great study for an ambitious student to undertake?

While I Was Sleeping

In September of 215, a year into Justice Matters, I had an experience reminiscent of 2008, when Susan Shaw's book dropped into my life long after she interviewed me at length. I suddenly realized I'd somehow been published by the World Council of Churches in a collection of writings in a book entitled When Pastors Prey: Overcoming Clergy Sexual Abuse of Women. How did this happen? I wondered.

Most uncanny—the book had been released in April of 2013, the very month I was so smitten by the story of the people ordered into homelessness that I began turning into *Just Following Orders.*

Assuming something I'd written long ago had been re-published, I ordered the book to see, and soon discovered I was in fine company with several good friends—Marie Fortune, Gary Schoener, and Margaret Kennedy being among them. To top it all off former President Jimmy Carter, a man from my own theological roots, was the foreward writer! I could hardly contain myself, though I still couldn't imagine how this all happened.

Seeing Diana Garland's research[9] on the extent of clergy sexual misconduct of adult women in the third chapter summoned tears to my eyes even as it sent new sparks of inspiration through my soul. How I longed to help move her work forward after her recent, untimely death!

When I finally reached, Valli Boobal Batchelor, the editor of *When Pastors Prey*, I found her traveling in a remote area of the globe, where she'd been for some time without access to internet service. I could certainly relate to that.

As I suspected, she'd first reached out to me about the time of all the chaos with Ron's latest major health crisis, asking my permission to re-print some of the work on my website. I'd quickly agreed, of course. Now, despite my memory lapse, I was thrilled to learn of the recent release.

My personal contribution to the collection, Chapter 5, is simply entitled "Systemic Collusion." In it, I've compared collusion to anemia in Africa. While both are common, neither should be accepted as normal. What do low hemoglobin levels and the failure to protect the vulnerable have in common? They are both signs of serious sickness. In the case of anemia, there's physical illness in an individual. In the case of collusion with sexual or domestic abuse, we have a spiritually sick system suffering from a thinking disorder (DIM thinking).[10]

In early, 2016, a few weeks after I saw the Boston story on the big screen, I phoned Richard Sipe to tell him how I loved SPOTLIGHT and also what Batchelor had chosen to publish from his writings. His reaction was identical to mine earlier:

"What!" he exclaimed, laughing out loud. "I have no idea what you're talking about! What on earth did I say, Dee?" So I snatched the book from my desk and read to him words I'd underlined from the seventh chapter, entitled "Speaking Truth to Power." In it, he spoke of how we gain power by turning to the "higher power of truth;" and how the Gospel provides guidance.....The "battle is not easy. There is always a price to pay." He went on to talk about Jesus, how He experienced powerlessness, yet "instructed his disciples in a lesson they would have to know well—not to fear the powerful people; to trust the power of truth, even harsh, demoralizing truth spoken by the powerless."

Sipe went on to chide church authorities, saying they "still have not heard victims. They have learned to 'deal' with complaints. They have increased their public relation efforts and skills." Next, he takes on the "bishops' lawyers, who insult, accuse, discredit, and demean victims, re-abusing them through the process. In all my years, I have never met a more compromised group...."[11]

In the end, he summarized my own sentiments from the last thirty years, which I suspect he'd already come to understand before Ron and I ever took off for Africa in 1978. These could just as easily apply to the thousands of men and women who hold positions of considerable power in Southern Baptist institutions, same as Catholics. Yet other denominations, even those who have worked extremely hard and greatly improved their responses, also need to be reminded of his prophetic message:

> *"Reform will come not from power, but from truth.*
> That is the power of Christian powerlessness."[12]

That message applies to each of us, as individuals who make up systems that have the potential for serving us all well, as they are intended to do. Systems, especially family systems, hold the power to greatly empower. They also hold the power to dis-empower.

*****

[1] http://thedartcenter.org/

2 http://hesperian.org a health education resource, producing a wide variety of practical, easy-to-comprehend, and amazingly thorough, well-researched information, especially useful in areas around the globe where doctors may not be readily available. These resources can be life-saving in emergencies. They are intended to empower people with limited or even no training to take charge and work together for change in a variety of community health issues.

3 Pamela Cooper-White, Shared Wisdom (Augsburg, 2004)

4 www.preventchildabuse.org/images/docs/2016FPPA.pdf

5 Information on the history, details of interpretation and the original, extensive questionnaire is recommended for professionals. http://www.cdc.gov/violenceprevention/acestudy/

6 A bare-bones ACE instrument for a fast screening can be found at https://acestoohigh.com/got-your-ace-score/

7 Stephen Arterburn and Jack Felton, Toxic Faith (Shaw Books, 2001), David Johnson and Jeff VanVonderen, The Subtle Power of Spiritual Abuse (Bethany House Publishers, 2005). Both have extensive bibliographies to assist in further study.

8 Dee Ann Miller, Just Following Orders: Escape from Guerilla Warfare in 1863, (CreateSpace, 2013) is for middle school students with the same story, simplified and under a different title, Mighty TALL Orders, is for upper elementary. See http://justfollowingorders.takecourage.org for enhancing activities and supplementary info on cultural issues of the AmericanCivil War.

9 https://www.baylor.edu/social_work/news.php?action=story&story=60932

10 For a more complete description of DIM Thinking, including symptoms, interventions and parallels between familial/systemic issues with substance abuse addictions, see www.takecourage.org/CollusionMain.htm

11 Valli Boobal Batchelor, editor of When Pastors Prey: Overcoming Clergy Sexual Abuse of Women (WCC Publications, 2013), p. 55

12 Ibid, p. 5

Chapter 37
Come Now, Let Us Reason Together

So here we are. Almost at the end. Hopefully, pointed in the right direction. We have many miles still to go, however. Nobody's arrived. In spite of all the work, the changes and implementation of policies, the press coverage and big lawsuits, everybody's still got a lot to learn in every faith group. All of us.

For example, after years of ongoing, mandated training in boundary violations, United Methodists still paid $100 million to settle lawsuits due to collusion with clergy sexual misconduct for the first ten years of the 21st century[1]—and that's not counting anything handed over to victims to help compensate for losses, rendering law suits unnecessary. We know this thanks to the active watch-care of COSROW, a strong denominational entity with a powerful voice that's been working toward changes in the status and role of women in the second largest Protestant denomination. These women and men who refuse to keep secrets aren't going away. Oh, that we had a group like this in every denomination!

Of course, that's a drop in the bucket to what Catholics paid. From 2004 to 2010 *alone,* these "organized" crimes and coverups, which have amount to nothing more than human trafficking cost them nearly $2 *billion.*[2]

The big secret—something that would make a great research project—is how many hard-earned dollars went to settle cases in some 50,000 Southern Baptist Convention and Cooperative Baptist Fellowship congregations (made up of folks like those at the BGCT who chose to withdraw from the SBC, yet with polity that leaves local congregations most vulnerable to being sued). Yet for this project, the research could be very tricky since most of these agreements are made in secret, same as the Catholics were able to do for so long.

When you mix CSA issues with a structure that often puts people with very little training in positions of decision-making in a chaotic system without built-in accountability, it's easy to understand why true experts in the social sciences throw up their hands and run for the hills. This, of course, is exactly what promotes the status quo with most communities where sexual and domestic violence thrives—people running.

We must learn new habits, practice new skills, and stop taking the same old avenues for "resolving problems" like this. Indeed, the Church—and this applies to those committed to keeping traditions, in general, "thinks in centuries." That's why it took so long for the SBC to face its own history at long last. That is, to admit this denomination of my heritage, an American-born denomination, was conceived in ante-bellum days, not because of missions, but because it wished to preserve the century-old practice of slavery. Elitism without merit must be surgically removed through such confession before it can gain what it has never truly possessed—authenticity.

Perhaps our greatest failure so far, as a society, as well as in each of us, as individuals, has been in thinking too small. Is it possible to go into our own pasts to find a new vision for the future? What if we decided to even call in outsiders to help?

First the Questions Close to Home

"It is easy to be brave a thousand miles away. But now I must face the question at short range," wrote Rev. Richard Cordley[3], a Congregational minister here in Lawrence. The year was 1859. The problem was at his doorstep, and it begged an immediate answer. Her name was Lizzie, a runaway slave, needed a place to hide. Chances are good she'd heard the Cordleys were friends to runaway slaves. They'd helped others.

Richard was newly-ordained and newly-married. Yet he'd committed himself to justice—to stand against slavery and support women's suffrage—banding with three other seminarians before graduating from Andover.

The Cordleys had a choice. They could play it safe like many of their neighbors were doing. It went against natural instinct to do otherwise. It was life-threatening to them, same as it was to Lizzie. Besides that, they were breaking the law if they chose to intervene.

This was political, but far more. As the pastor saw it, he had a responsibility to be a role model, which meant taking sides, lining up with what he believed about slavery. All indications are his wife Mary agreed.

So they protected Lizzie through the anxious night, helping her get away before the U. S. Marshall arrived to arrest her.

Throughout history, clerics have had a problem at their doorstep that is life-threatening, but not to them personally. It's not against the law to address the problem from the pulpit, as it was in 1859 with slavery.

The daily problems of sexual and domestic violence, which will be down the street or on the nearest college campus if not at the door of the parsonage, require an immediate answer. They're more than political. "In the context of violence against women, religious teachings and communities will play a role; they will never be neutral," says UCC Rev. Dr. Marie Fortune and Rabbi Cindy Enger in an online article entitled "Violence against Women and the Role of Religion," which also offers numerous sermon ideas on the topic. [4]

These are issues of violence and often death. That's why pastors have an obligation to stand publicly on the side of the powerless on this, even if it means somebody will get upset. Even if it means men who are assailants will leave the church, which does make taking a stand quite scary, same as standing up to their abusive colleagues, holding them accountable, imposing very stiff consequences, can be.

As one victim of domestic abuse, very faithfully involved in her congregation says: "I wish I could say I was one of those people who would like to go forward, to open up the eyes of the people in my church, but I'm wearing a disguise so I wouldn't be recognized and I haven't told you the name of my church because I'm so afraid of the repercussions for me and my children." [5]

Yet 42% of US Protestant pastors "rarely" or "never" address domestic violence in their churches, according to a 2014 LifeWay Research study. Another 22% speak to the issue only about once per year. Among pastors who address domestic violence, 75% believe it's not a problem in their churches. [6]

Considering the Gallup poll findings from the past few years' credibility of professional ministers,[7] it might be a good thing to think of reversing this trend, given that one in three women sitting in the pews will become victims of domestic abuse sometime in their lifetime. And a good possibility that little boys sitting beside them will grow up to be abusers if they witness such abuse.

However, even for men who have suffered serious trauma, either personally or as a witness in their childhood home, this situation is particularly scary, even if they are *not* abusers themselves. Meanwhile, churches and schools alike would do well to remember that children's safe options for speaking out about violence at home are often more limited even than adults; yet these institutions should be safe havens for reporting, and far more likely to be if the problems are talked about openly, even in the pulpit.

While grown men were often victims of child abuse, most often perpetrated by their fathers, they are even more likely to carry deep scars from seeing their mothers beaten and being unable to physically intervene. Intense fear often trumps anger in these little boys. As they get older, the anger that's built up for years comes out sideways with aggression. If it gets turned inward and there is no opportunity to process it, a deep sense of helplessness may be the result.

There's also the shame factor. Shame is a universal experience, Brene Brown [8] tells us. Through her scholarly work on shame resiliency, she has successfully empowered many of us to find new ways of framing old garbage, recycling it into a life of authenticity to discover a host of applications.

Men's shame is hooked by trauma. Whether it's imposed internally or by others, the shame is connected to a perception of weakness, increasing the difficulty men have in speaking of their shame. With women, it's likely to present itself around body image and competing or conflicting expectations.[9]

The shame element, as I see it, is closely related to why it's so difficult for many men to develop empathy with victims, a fact that Pamela Cooper-White writes about in much more depth in *The Voice of Tamar*.

It would be most helpful if somebody could study this problem as it exhibits itself in male clergy. While more research is needed to substantiate this, I suspect the ACES scores as they relate to child abuse and witnessing domestic abuse are as high, if not higher, for clergy and those in other helping professions than even in the general population. If so, this may explain why the men of this profession, which has a golden opportunity to make a difference on issues of violence against women and children, neither takes a stand in the pulpit nor tends to take a stand against their own abusive buddies.

While it's certainly not against the law to confront past serpents, doing so can feel even more formidable than the dangers Cordley's faced with Lizzie. Yet, having walked beside many men who've decided to do so, I've witnessed the enormous spiritual growth and courage that can come when one decides to do so—not only for oneself, but for many others.

Miracles at Walla Walla

If you were a citizen of Walla Walla, Washington, chances are good you'd know your ACE score. You and your neighbors would have ACES as a part of your vocabulary, possibly even discussing it across the back fence. You might very well discuss it with your doctor, too, and talk about your own resiliency concerns and how that relates to your present health.

Your children's teachers might even ask how ACES has impacted your family and your parenting. Maybe you would see the intergenerational patterns and be able to intervene in different ways when your offspring are upset.

I wish I'd known a lot more about ACES fifty years ago. Like abuse issues, ACES is important for community discussion, as well as for personal exploration.

"Resilience trumps ACES!" That's the cry of Walla Walla. Years ago, they stopped asking, "What's wrong with this person?" and began asking, "What has this person gone through?"

It makes all the difference when we are trauma-informed, we know how to provide empathetic responses and interventions and where in our community these can be found. We extend our love. We put limits on behaviors that come from trauma—yes. We also teach alternatives. We teach resiliency. We have an explosion of education.

Walla Walla sets an example—not just for a city, but for communities of faith--above all for leaders. It suggests we find the courage to speak what we have experienced, the courage to listen, and courage to confront. In the process, we overcome our DIM thinking. For we stop denying and minimizing trauma as we cease to be ignorant.

For professional ministers seeking best practices, this means finding the courage to educate others by speaking intelligently about issues of sexual and domestic abuse from the pulpit. It invites each person to consider sharing, as personal testimony, past personal traumas and experiences of transformation whenever possible and appropriate to do so. In that process, we empower others to speak their own truths.

Walla Walla is not a small town. Its population is over 30,000. Together by encouraging ACES education to permeate the conversations in every institution all over town, they've reduced domestic abuse by 33% with teen suicides and high school dropout rates being reduced at almost twice that rate.[10]

When high school students are "in the red," says Jim Sporleder, high school principle, there's no way they can deal with their problems. They must wait until they cool off before they can start to address the problems at hand.

If this is true with high school students, it's also true with clergy members and other professionals who are not prepared to hear of the trauma an abuse victim has gone through. They will half hear and begin to super-impose their own past experiences onto the current narration, rushing to judgment, without having a background to even process the story. They act out of fear because they are filled with DIM thinking: Denial that says this could not possibly have happened. Ignorance that says, "If it did, this person would have done something different than she did. Besides, even if what I'm hearing is true, it can easily be addressed if we can only get her quieted down."

Imagine the alternative. Can you envision how concepts of ACES and resiliency might be applied if professionals faced their own personal issues, then incorporated all of this into the workplace or speaking platform, from school to the counselor's office and even into the pulpit?

Finding the Courage to Listen

Not only is it possible for us to hear and understand difficult stories, it's essential. Yet, unless we begin listening with fresh ears, we will have missed the whole point of Spotlight.

Sometimes it takes even *more* courage to listen to stories of trauma than to speak of our own. This is another way we collude, projecting onto others what we have not resolved in ourselves. That's why these problems require us all.

If it takes a village to raise a child, it takes a village to abuse one.

When we do listen, we may find the world shifting, as Peter Grant learned in 2008 before he began working with Restored[11]. He went to Mexico City for the World AIDS conference that year, not realizing that the entire focus of his work with AIDS was about to change dramatically.

It happened when Herlyn Uiras, a 24-year-old Namibian woman suffering from the deadly disease, stood to explain how so much of her life had been destroyed by three different men from two different cultures through rape. Peter listened as she poured her heart out for a full hour, then, quickly concluded this story had to be about men. For him it came as a dramatic calling.

"Never have I felt the presence of God so much!" he exclaims. "I had two questions. Where is the Church in this? And where are all the men? Suddenly it became about me. I had to do something."

That's why he partnered in 2010 with Mandy Marshall, a woman who was passionate about working for change through Christian churches to respond effectively to the world-wide problem of gender-based violence from domestic abuse to GFM, genital female mutilation. They do it by partnering with many other organizations, providing resource material, inspiration, and consultation through www.restoredrelationships.org Above all the organizations I've mentioned in this book, I invite you to look at the program "First Man Standing," on Restored and how it invites men to take against gender-based violence in their faith communities.

Both the Walla Walla program and Restored offer us alternatives to silence and collusion. They give us tremendous hope. Change is possible.

*****

[1] Facts revealed in a 2010 address by Garlinda Burton, top executive of the National Commission on the Status and Role of Women for United Methodists. For more info, contact journalist David Briggs newsdesk@umcom.org or see http://archives.gcah.org/xmlui/bitstream/handle/10516/1244/8437677.htm?sequence=1

[2] http://www.bishop-accountability.org/reports/2004_02_27_JohnJay/index.html

[3] Four years after providing Lizzie refuge, 250 children of the city of Lawrence were left fatherless in one morning when 400 drunken, gun-slinging,

crazed Confederate guerrillas tore through the city on horseback. With an out-pouring of donations, mostly from afar, the historic building of the Plymouth Congregational Church was soon erected. It remains a beautiful sanctuary, preserved for an active, socially-progressive, justice-seeking congregation, attempting daily to face the questions at close range or far away.

[4] This article and a multitude of resources can be found on the National Online Resource Center on Violence Against Women (Vawnet.org)
http://www.vawnet.org/applied-research-papers/print-document.php?doc_id=411

[5] From the discussion guide and documentary, produced by United Methodists, "I Believe You: Faith's Response to Intimate Partner Violence."

[6] http://blog.lifeway.com/newsroom/2017/02/20/good-intentions-lack-of-plans-mark-church-response-to-domestic-violence/

[7] http://www.gallup.com/poll/1654/honesty-ethics-professions.aspx and "Honesty and Ethics Rating of Clergy Slides to New Low" by Art Swift at http://www.gallup.com/poll/166298/honesty-ethics-rating-clergy-slides-new-low.aspx

[8] Brown is a popular author, and public speaker, currently a research professor at the University of Houston Graduate College of Social Work.

[9] See https://heartworks.training/review-of-i-thought-it-was-just-me-but-it-isnt-by-brene-brown-ph-d-lmsw/

See also https://onbeing.org/programs/brene-brown-the-courage-to-be-vulnerable/

[10] See https://www.facebook.com/ResilienceTrumpsAces/videos/vb.194804447282921/894994250597267/?type=2&theater

[11] See http://www.restoredrelationships.org/

Chapter 38
Remaining Matters

One of the major reasons it takes trauma-informed lawyers, psychotherapists, and courageous investigative journalists to teach folks what they should know in the first place is that men in power, unless they *are* trauma-informed, tend to define the problems quite differently from most females. Women may also fail to understand if they've somehow managed to avoid the first-hand experience of feeling traumatized or vulnerable.

"We can handle this," male-dominated systems have insisted for years. Oh, how they work to convince us! It would seem they could, since most of the actors in these stories are male. Therein is the problem—the primary actors with professional sexual abuse *are* male. They are men with big problems and long track records, usually well disguised. Refusing to be educated beyond academic degrees, these folks create even bigger problems for people they're hired to serve, people who have often been taught since the cradle to trust without question, who buy into the same myths that keep the oppressed in place, subservient to the men or women in charge.

These are the "good patients" in hospitals, the quiet, "well-behaved" students who would never dare question authority, even if the authority was obviously in the wrong.

Dr. Venida Chenault, President of Haskell University here in Lawrence, Kansas, knows all too well when it comes to Native American issues. There is a constant tug of war between those who may never have experienced any form of oppression and those still suffering from generations of living beneath the rubble.

Even when change is made, there is still the problem of assimilation due to a failure to resolve the past. "The question is 'When do we agree to sit down and live at peace in harmony on an equal playing field?'" says Chenault as we discuss the on-going issues with which we must all wrestle—issues of inter-generational suffering due to collective hate crimes of the past. Matters which many would prefer to ignore with "let bygones be bygones."

Yet, even in communities where racial oppression abounds, issues of sexual violence get complicated. It's very easy to blur the lines because of the double-bind of oppressed people caught in systems where more than one oppression exists. This happens with the abuse of African-American women, for instance, in an African-American male-dominated subculture. How can you possibly betray one's support group by calling out a member of it as a perpetrator! And if the person in power to whom one turns is a female drawing power from a male-dominated system herself, it gets even more complicated.

Where we draw the line with each issue of abuse and oppression depends on the willingness of all of the privileged to acknowledge, disown patterns of the past, and find ways to reach out as recipients still benefiting from history gone awry.

I'd venture to say it can only end when those who have suffered injustice in both genders can be *forgiven for repeatedly speaking* what the more privileged among us do not want to hear while those still suffering from inter-generational suffering can clearly enunciate to those of us belonging to privileged in-groups what justice might look like if it is ever achieved. Otherwise, we're all caught in impossible games of projection and mind-reading.

Yet how many times does SNAP or MK's living in recovery have to tell people what they do not want to hear? How long will it take for the Church to forgive survivors for holding them responsible for the past with matters that aren't close to being corrected despite all the posturing? All because these matters make "others" very confused and uncomfortable.

Issues for Professional Ethics

It still baffles me: if Ms. Wiebe was smart enough to build boundaries and ethics into nursing education fifty years ago in nursing school, how come it's taken so long for male-dominated professions to get these basics? So lately I've been thinking maybe we should get elementary kids to go to universities, law schools, medical schools and seminaries to teach adults what is now considered basics in our public school anti-bullying programs. Teaching adults not to bully shouldn't be any harder than teaching kids.

The biggest problem in this whole pile of manure is that the majority of men still see these crimes as "children's issues" or "women's issues." This puts the children and the women as the primary actors rather than the most likely offenders. Sexual violence is primarily a "men's issue," or a problem for males to own up to rather than deflect and hide behind female advocates like me. How many times have I heard a man tell me: "Keep up the good work!" Why is this considered "women's work," may I ask?

If "gender is the last frontier," as Susan Shaw[1] declares, then we better not take our eyes off the horizon. We cannot turn away from the obvious fact that gender works against female victims of sexual abuse, especially in the church.

"Let's just focus on the problem of power," some say. "With so many women stepping into positions of power these days, women need to stop using the gender card in regard to sexual violence."

Patrick Wall has a lot to say about such comments. He wants the world to know that the vast majority of victims in the Catholic Church are female, and they face enormous barriers to justice compared to all the male victims he's seen.

Wall is a canon law expert who left the priesthood as repulsed as Tom Economus after a few short years, tired of being sent from one parish to another to pick up the pieces left by another perpetrator wherever he was assigned. Today, with attorney Jeff Anderson[2], he spends his time listening, comforting, and hoping to educate wherever possible.

Women have very good reasons for their reluctance to bring a case forward, he says, even though they may be less reluctant than male victims to reveal their abuse to close friends.

Much of the problem females have can be laid at the feet of defense lawyers, "quick to paint the survivor not as a child but as a whore," he explains. "This makes the female survivor out to look promiscuous or a woman who entrapped some poor guy, just naïve about the ways of the world.

"Added to this burden, female victims' past sexual experiences are often used against them. They may be in a good relationship now, yet have good reason to "fear being painted as damaged goods and wonder if their partner will treat them differently in the future because of the public exposure," he explains.

To top this off, "The Church even "allows girls as young as 14 to be married with permission of the parents. The real root of this practice is the Mary Magdalene complex many clerics have towards women. When Bishop Norman McFarland of Orange, California was asked why he put a priest back in ministry who preyed upon minor girls, he stated that many adolescents are fully developed and precocious."

Wall tries to be optimistic: "The idealist in me says these (practices) can stop with this generation. The pragmatist says that unless and until several Roman Catholic Cardinals, Bishops, Provincials and Abbots go to jail for failing to report childhood sexual abuse, the cycle of violence against our children, especially girls, will continue."

Christa Brown learned how this works with Baptists, too. A journalist told her she was being painted as a whore, same as Monica Lewinsky was.

Men who are accustomed to being in charge must accept the role of a student—yes, a role of much lesser power, without assuming a lifetime of experience counts as "good experience," as Foy Valentine initially did.

Becoming a true expert doesn't come necessarily come with academic degrees, though academic training can certainly enhance expertise. http://nomas.org/history/ is a prime example of what happens when men, through education, become concerned about gender-based issues. Nomas got its start when a group of young men merely decided to take a women's studies course. Imagine that!

Does this mean they cease to care about issues of oppression that impact men—of course, it doesn't. It simply means that they recognize how much gender inequality impacts all of society.

Pamela Cooper-White, author of *The Cry of Tamar: violence against women and the church's response*, tells of a male pastor she knew who was brought up not to ever be afraid because fear was considered unmanly. Therefore, it's been hard for him to stay with someone in fear without trying to soothe or fix the fear. She stresses the importance of drawing on our past experiences, bringing them into conversations when appropriate, for the good of an individual currently in pain.[3]

By networking, we are able to gain confidence in our ability to take on any issue that perpetuates the inter-generational cycle of abuse, including male aggression and gender oppression. As we become advocates rather than helpless bystanders, we encourage survivors to speak publicly. Pro-active churches do not shy away from these topics and welcome their ministers taking them on with sensitivity from the pulpits on Sunday morning, in everyday conversations, and in small groups.

It's not a matter of "dealing" with victims or pacifying them, and certainly not a matter of convincing them that things are sure to get better if they stay or return to the abusive situation. That's insanity, not faith.

This does not mean we cease to acknowledge the existence of male victims and female perpetrators. It does mean that we should remember that even with male victims, the majority are assaulted by other males. If we focus on the gender of the perpetrator rather than that of the victim, we have the same perpetrator issues.

It *is* about power, and the day may come when it will no longer be about gender. When that day comes, when females are equally in charge and the problem of male aggression can somehow get removed from the whole spectrum of the conversation, we can cease to focus on gender.

Focusing on the least likely scenarios isn't going to help us find solutions to gender inequities that make blaming virtually inevitable worldwide. On the other hand, male victims need to work on their own support networks, even as they also try to join cross-gender groups like SNAP, where these issues are often more freely discussed.

The Problem of False Accusations

False accusations *are* a big problem, same as lack of forgiveness— primarily because that's where most prefer to stay focused. It's easier for the Church to do so than go further into discussions. So, victims are the ones most often falsely accused. Of lying and/or seducing the perpetrator, that is, then seen as spiritually rebellious because they won't "forgive." Ironically, the latter is mere projection on the part of self-righteous critics who are more prone to shy away from survivor testimonies as incomplete that do not incorporate the same definition of "forgiveness" as others into everyday speech.

We *do* need to be concerned about falsely accusations whenever we're dealing with judicial matters in any form. Members of minority groups, already powerless to defend themselves due to our prejudicial court systems, are frequently falsely accused due to racial profiling.

When it comes to allegations against a person held in a position of high esteem and power, "If the glove doesn't fit, you must acquit" is the default position rather than the preponderance of evidence. Thus, when our daughter and her husband started trying to talk to Baptist preachers in Oklahoma in the mid-90's about issues of abuse, they ran into nothing but DIM thinking. The guys knew plenty of CSA stories. "All turned out to be false accusations." That urban myth remains strong, and they continue collecting "evidence" of this in chat rooms I've visited. Without a solid system to hold men accountable, I fear the lack of evidence to the contrary will continue to mount and go unchecked, especially with the examples of politicians leading the band wagon with such thinking.

Not easy, however, for the U. S. Conference of Catholic Bishops to claim now after they commissioned a study that didn't come out the way many had hoped. Only 1.5% of allegations against priests were found to be false according to a survey completed by the U. S. diocese themselves.[4]

While 18% of cases were deemed unfounded due to lack of sufficient evidence, same as far too many child abuse allegations are determined to be with an investigation, this does not mean those cases are false. It may mean, there was purposely no documentation kept and nobody willing to collaborate.

Since there is no standard procedure and no central office for record-keeping, there's no way to track predators in the SBC. Nor a way to do an annual audit, as Catholics have been doing since Spotlight got worldwide attention.[5]

In some cases, as with O. J. Simpson, where journalists do long-term follow-up, "justice" comes later.

Bringing the Conversation into Our Living Rooms

So what's keeping us from having these discussions at home? If we can do that, might we learn to welcome stories of trauma into our churches, even into our pulpits?

Maybe we could even squeeze it in between all our discussions about sports scores and the weather we can't control. If we all did this for at least a half hour per week, do you suppose we could start a non-violent revolution? How would this impact the next generation of men, who might pick up a small portion of what they hear us saying as they get caught up on the latest action game on line.

Little boys, expected since toddlers to brush it all off, are experts at deflecting vulnerability. As they grow into big boys, those who get hurt on the football field are our heroes. They just get up and shake it off, right? We really like to see that—mothers as much as fathers.

Of course, the trauma of being hurt on the football field, unless it is a very serious injury, is just considered "a part of the game" .....unless it's intentionally inflicted.

Since we don't allow boys to lick their wounds for long, too often they work their issues out with bullying. All too quickly, they grow into men who soon "forget" what it feels like to be a victim. Far too many make a bounding leap into adult bullying, which is what "an abuser" is, regardless of the violation. Standing by, protecting and institutions at the expense of the vulnerable is another form of bullying.

Confusing Fantasy with Reality

The fear of being found out is petrifying. The fear of "stepping over the line in a moment of weakness" is an often unspoken issue because of the tendency to confuse normal sexual fantasies with acting on them.

Having fantasies and committing violence, however, unless pornography gets pulled into the mix.

Male-perpetrated violence is curtailed when men talk about all these issues among themselves, teach one another about them in daily conversation, dare to even talk more openly about their own experiences of victimization to one another, and stand in solidarity with women. While the discussions of victims may begin behind closed doors with a therapist, where everything remains "a secret," we can encourage those who want to bring the discussion into the light of day and even welcome them doing so.

Getting Tough

Since 2009, The National Organization for Women has officially called to criminalize sexual exploitation by clergy, holding them accountable the same as all physicians and licensed counselors. [6]

Defense that clings to the old "letter" of the denominational system's laws of "church autonomy" would be rendered irrelevant if this should pass. Perpetrators could be taken straight to the courtroom by criminal prosecutors. With church systems no longer able to own the secrets, the dynamics of a huge incestuous "family" would offer little protection. Justice would fall under the jurisdiction of outsiders. Though churches could still decide to hire criminals, even after conviction, this would mean abusers, regardless of the age of their victims, would be more like likely to be hiring someone on sex offender registries, provided local public prosecutors were doing their jobs.

Male on Adult Male Abuse

While most of this book has been centered on violations against minors or adult females, I was recently reminded of how complicated a case can become when it fits outside the usual mold of clergy sexual abuse. It happened only days before this book was set to go to press.

Suddenly I was scrambling to find resources for a congregation with multiple adult male victims of a trusted bishop. Each one of these young men were assured that they were among God's chosen to help lead and would need to be mentored by the older cleric who provided them with "opportunity" for retreats and one-on-one consultation that groomed them and led them on to where he wanted to go with each of them.

Where this case will end, it's hard to know. Of one thing, I'm certain. I will learn much if these dear souls stay in touch, as I hope they will.

The perception in this quite conservative community, most likely filled with homophobic members, is likely to be skewed toward blaming these young men and even ostracizing them due to what will, no doubt, be considered their choice to engage in homosexual behavior.

Exaggerating the Meaning of Accountability

"You can't take my right to earn a living!" a repeat offender, now a chaplain told an adjudicatory committee a few years ago.

This is a commonly used tactic for someone facing the possibility of defrocking, a consequence sometimes used in mainline denominations to remove the credentials of a clergy person. The equivalent for some denominations, including Southern Baptists, is "lifting of ordination," though this is very, very rarely done in the SBC (I'm not aware of a single case). Once a person is believed to be "called" and the congregation agrees, it's permanent. After all, it would be strange to think God might "un-call" a person, especially if the man grew up in the congregation of his ordination, as Ron and many others have.

Of course, lifting credentials can't prevent anyone from earning a living, only from earning a living as an ordained minister. Yet the chaplain in this story was successful in playing on the emotional vulnerabilities of his colleagues, who made an ill-informed decision to place him where he could be "more easily monitored." For all I know, he may still be there. If so, I hope all the vulnerable people have managed to stay safe in the nursing and rehab center where he worked.

The Problem of Child Safety in Churches Extends Beyond Clergy

In the course of finalizing this book, I was called by SNAP to join a press conference at Westside Family Church, one of a the largest megachurches in the Southern Baptist Convention, a church that has grown by 20% in the past three years. A lawsuit had just been filed by the parents of two young girls, claiming the church should have done more to keep their daughters safe from a convicted sex offender in his late teens. If they'd known he was working in Vacation Bible School, they could have easily kept their daughters home.

Since they didn't and church officials "didn't feel comfortable" asking too many questions to follow up on rumors they admit they heard, the offender is back behind bars, now convicted and serving a seventeen-year sentence. The girls are "in for life," with attempts being made to blame the victims and punish the family for speaking out publicly, calling for them to identify their daughters by name rather than the usual "Doe" that survivors of sexual violence are usually allowed to use. This is a case that bears watching closely, a study in collusion, specifically as it plays out in the SBC.

I can hear Tom Economus speaking to Westside's attorney, same as he did when a lawyer for the Church scorned those justifying a plaintiff's lawsuit twenty-five years ago.

"This is ridiculous!" he exclaimed to Tom. "You can't put a price tag on a person's life!"

"No," agreed Tom. "But we could certainly *try*."

Physical disability is visible. Emotional and spiritual wounds, equally disabling, are likely to be just as permanent as physical, however. That's what churches and their lawyers fail to acknowledge in their own DIM thinking. Law suits are designed to level that playing field—or at least try, as Tom would be quick to remind us.

The Westside story reminds us that pastors aren't the only ones who can cause grave damage to the souls of victims through their blatantly abusive acts. In spite of the great positive impact they have on our children, volunteer youth leaders and Sunday School teachers are often the problem, both those who fail to protect children from abusers and the primary culprits, who may even be older teenage boys in some churches. They can also be mothers, as much as fathers, with no record at all.

Linda Crockett knows this all too well. She clearly demonstrates, however, that it's not what you've been through but what you do after trauma that really matters.

Crockett, who has chronicled her own discovery as a childhood survivor of maternal sexual abuse[7], is now a leader in an interfaith movement through a program out of Samaritan Counseling Center in Lancaster, PA. "It's gone from local to regional to a national training platform so fast my head spins sometimes!" she says.

"For the past 5 years I have been working with about twenty organizations across the country which were initially organized and funded by the Ms. Foundation for Women in their groundbreaking strategic initiative to end child sexual abuse," she writes. "Samaritan SafeChurch is stepping up to protect children from sexual harm by shifting culture in their congregations so that all adults become educated about child sexual abuse and how to prevent it - not only in churches but in the community." She does it by travelling across the country to provide a 3 day Safe Church facilitator training.

Added Confusion with Issues of Sexual Orientation

Over time, conversations we could never have had thirty years ago are more likely to be in our comfort zones. Thanks to vast strikes in neuroscience over the past decade, we can now see the biological effects of childhood maltreatment through structural neuroimaging studies.[9]

This, along with the ACES study, has done much to raise awareness.

In the past decade, it's also become impossible for scientists to deny that sexual orientation is a biologically fixed trait. OK, you say, what's that got to do with a discussion on abuse? More than you might think, actually.

Regardless of how you feel about the LGBT population, we need to look at four areas often overlooked, where the vast majority of us may agree. Even if you don't agree with it all, I hope you'll be open to looking anew at each area of conflict:

1. Homosexual activity between two consenting adults, though still considered an immoral, sexual perversion by many, is *never* abuse.

2. Sexual activity between a professional and a client of any age is *never* consensual. Though the ramifications for the offender and his or her spouse will also play out as an affair, it's always abuse, always malpractice, and often a criminal offense.

3. Individuals in the LGBTQ often have issues related to victims of sexual abuse: internalized homophobia, emotional and spiritual abuse due to gender orientation, shunning. The greatest discrimination often comes from family. Heterosexual minors who stand with them as advocates often endure similar abuses. So while we're on that topic, let's get this very confusing matter cleared up. No matter which side you stand on, whether you declare homosexuality "immoral" or not, can we not agree that mutually

consensual acts of homosexuality do not fall under the category of "abuse?" Only by untying that thread, can we have a rational conversation about sexual abuse.

4. Equating or confusing homosexuality and sexual abuse adds greatly to the confusion that exists in some faith groups. For ultra-conservatives, homosexuals post a danger to children because of their perceived tendency to prey on others. For the liberal, there's also confusion. Having a "let's not judge" or "anything goes" view of issues surrounding sexuality can lead to a greater tendency to overlook sexual misconduct/abuse, considering it to still be "a private matter" same as homosexuality or a true affair.

The Fallacy in 21st Century Stats

It would be nice if any faith group could lay claim to eradicating abuse in all its forms. Some idealists believe we've come close. Some think we even have evidence to show we're close. I'm not one of them.

Though I would like to hope it is true, thanks to all the education, prevention and early intervention, we're still in no position to let our guard down. We're all guessing and often making guesses on faulty assumptions, despite the studies. Here's why:

Kids are still extremely vulnerable to sexual abuse, especially needy kids. In spite of all the efforts we've made to alert them to dangers, encouraging them to tell if anything weird happens, finding the courage to tell is still hard. Kids wait for years, even decades—anyone working this field in any capacity knows that. Some journalists and a lot of other professionals, especially overly-optimistic clergy, don't seem to have gotten that message. Nor do they understand that if a kid (or adult victim) chooses to tell someone who does not have the courage to hear, it may be decades before they talk again, if ever.

Patrick Wall is convinced there has been a drastic decrease in the number of youth abused by priests since the massive clean-up that began being undertaken several decades ago. He has plenty of data to study now and can track it by dates when the abuse was said to have happened, thanks to mandatory reporting that's strictly enforced on the bishops—that, and the fact fewer middle-aged people today, coming to the age when awareness and sufficient strength can be mustered to make a report, are doing so.

So, who is tracking abuse of minors in Baptist circles? Without a mandatory reporting system and nobody in charge, it seems we can only rely on cases brought to the courts. And that's certainly not a reliable predictor if what Wall says is true about gender bias and the fear of reporting. Even if there should be a reliable tracking system that could be enforced, this denomination is still decades from being able to compile the data.

Finding the Courage to Change

I'm an optimist. If I'd not been, I would never have invested the last thirty years of my life in this oft-discouraging work. Nor would I have ever been found venturing onto Boston's drive-time radio during the Christmas season of 1993.

What we can change, one person at a time, are the attitudes in every faith group if we are willing to enlarge our conversations.

How grateful I am that women like Christa Brown, much younger than I, have found the energy to pick up, going when I could no longer go at full speed. During those years, when mainstream journalists were finally off and running to catch up, I could only pray in wordless groans.

Now it's time for others—men and women alike.

This all brings to mind the analogy of the retreat leader, Elizabeth Stellas, who explained to me the flight formations of geese—how one leads the way for a while, then drops back as exhaustion takes over, though still in the flock. The geese take turns because none can sustain the force of the heavy winds without pulling back at times.

Now, as the younger generation comes in to blaze new trails, facing their greatest fears, daring to feel vulnerable, may they find the courage to also speak, the courage to listen, and the courage to change.

Over-turning DIM thinking in all its forms in every institution in every community on our planet most definitely requires us all.

*****

[1] Shaw, a prolific author and professor at Oregon State University for twenty years, is a scholar in several fields. With a PhD in Theology from SBC's Southern Seminary, she remains an ordained Baptist minister, but now makes her congregational home with United Church of Christ. She also holds an MAIS (Master of Arts in Interdisciplinary Studies) from Oregon State. Much of her focus has been on women's struggles as they intersect with spirituality and patriarchal systems. She is Director of the School of Language, Culture, and Society. In addition to God Speaks to Us, Too, referred to extensively in Chapter 33 of this text, her writings include Reflective Faith: A Theological Toolbox for Women (Smyth & Helwys, 2014) with an companion workbook, available for purchase separately.

[2] Jefferson Anderson & Associates, based in St. Paul, Minnesota, has taken a leading role in litigation for victims of clergy sexual abuse, empowering victims, thereby effectively bringing interventions that have led to institutional justice over time.

[3] See suggested reading list at back of this book for information on Cooper-White's Share Wisdom, as well as The Cry of Tamar, previously mentioned in this text.

[4] http://www.bishop-accountability.org/AtAGlance/data.htm#falseallegations

[5] For more info on locating these reports, contact United States Conference of Catholic Bishops or http://www.usccb.org/

[6] http://now.org/about/conference-resolutions/2009-national-now-conference-resolutions/#call

[7] Linda Crockett, The Deepest Wound: How a Journey to El Salvador Led to Healing from Mother-Daughter Incest (iUniverse, 2001)

[8] http://scclanc.org/safechurch/

[9] Of all the resources in this book, one stands above all as a must-read, for it is related to the broad scope of abuse and how it impacts adult functioning, as evidenced in neuroscience. "Neuroimaging of Child Abuse: a critical review" by Heledd Hart and Katya Rubia in Fundamentals in Human Neuroscience, March 19, 2012, and available online at
http://www.ncbi.nlm.nih.gov/pmc/articles/PMC3307045/

Next.....

Old advocacy writers, like old soldiers, never really die. Perhaps we do just fade away. That's what I'm counting on, at least.

"It all stopped me dead in my tracks." That's how I started a guest blog I found gut-wrenching to even write. It was for Marie Fortune at Faith Trust Institute[1] last November, but related to what had transpired to keep me from finishing the book you've just read.

"NO!" I kept screaming in early June to everyone around—then all summer long, until two weeks ago, when I finally came up for air.

"For crying out loud! Not NOW!" I yelled, as if there's ever a good time for a case of abuse, made more baffling when both victim and perpetrator keep saying: "Don't worry. We've got everything here *well covered.*"

Did they ever! That was what had me worrying night and day.

I knew full well what I was "seeing" from hundreds of miles away. It didn't matter what authorities said after spending only a few minutes on the front porch of my ninety-year-old mother in Texas, where she believes the sun still rises and sets (and is determined to stay).

How this gracious woman managed long ago to get the art of pretending down to a science, I can explain easily. It's an "occupational hazard" for any woman married to a minister for forty years. Now, with Dad long gone, my little brother, at fifty-five, with his own forty-year history of drug addiction, sleeps half the day, screams when he's awakened, then gets up to be sure Mom still understand he's *still taking care of* her, tells her he's again not hungry enough for the supper she's lovingly prepared. Then, guzzling a half gallon of milk and an energy drink (two favorite drug-enhancers of many addicts) before he goes out to find his next fix.

It doesn't really matter what I know. I'm just my mother's daughter. No need to say how much of my life, through nursing and writing, I've spent working on interventions in hopes of stopping the widespread collusion with abuse that's so common with all professionals whose duty it is to protect the vulnerable. As for elder abuse, I could write a book on this topic.

Which would be somewhat of a joke to anyone who knows me well, considering why I was screaming in early June, as entire life was being hijacked. It happened just as I was putting finishing touches on a book I believe to be one of the most important projects of my life....."

This blog went on to explain that Mom was in a far better situation, under the watch-care of a faithful advocate in an institution where she was safe. At that point in November, I assumed what I'd been through was about to come to an end.

Instead, my mother's whole world fell apart soon after the blog was published. And when an elderly mother's life falls apart, for the child who has always been by her side emotionally, ready to pick up the pieces again and again if need be, that's what I found myself doing....again....and again....and again.

In each time of crisis since November, I've been forced to re-examine priorities. Each time looking at my mother's sense of values and my own, discovering that there is now very little difference in the two, despite the vast differences in our theological beliefs.

Safety is now Number One for my mother, as reflected in the precious note she sent a few weeks back. "It's so nice to be where I'm safe, well fed, and have friends." Keeping her safe and cared for is paramount. Guarding her mental health is equally important. And having her in a place where we have funding to cover all of this—that is the biggest challenge of all. Funding, related to the universal health care coverage that should be available to every American is one of the biggest barriers in keeping our seniors safe and as healthy as possible.

Yes, someday, if I live long enough to complete a sequel to this book, it will be on elder care—applying the very principles I've sprinkled freely throughout Enlarging Boston's SPOTLIGHT to the growing crisis that families across America are facing.

In the meantime, I hope to be speaking on these issues of advocacy in an institution near you.

Stand by .....

Dee Ann Miller
www.takecourage.org
1946writerdee@gmail.com

*****

[1] faithtrustinstitute.org/blog/248

A Short Book List

James S. Evinger's extensive bibliography on clergy sexual abuse provides an in-depth look at all that's been written over the past thirty years, specific to this topic. He has worked tirelessly to keep this important list up to date. You will find this, along with many other resources provided by Faith Trust Institute.

See   http://www.faithtrustinstitute.org/resources/bibliographies/ clergy-sexual-abuse

Throughout the text of Enlarging Boston's SPOTLIGHT, there are references to many authors whose book titles are listed below for your convenience:

- Arterburn, Stephen and Felton, Jack, 2001, *Toxic Faith*, Shaw Books.

- Bates, William, 2014, *The Cemetery of My Mind, Create Space*.

- Batchelor, Valli Boobal, editor, 2013, *When Pastors Prey: Overcoming Clergy Sexual Abuse of Women*, WCC Publications.

- Brown, Brene, 2008, *I THOUGHT IT WAS JUST ME (BUT IT ISN'T): Telling the Truth About Perfectionism, Inadequacy and Power*, J.P. Tarcher, Penguin & Putnam

- Brown, Christa, 2009, *This Little Light: Beyond a Baptist Preacher Predator and His Gang*, Foremost Press.

- Clark, Janet, 2006, *Blind Faith*, 1st World Publishing.

- Cooper-White, Pamela, 2012, *The Cry of Tamar: Violence Against Women and the Church's Response*, 2nd edition, Fortress Press.

- Crockett, Linda, 2001, *The Deepest Wound: How a Journey to El Salvador Led to Healing from Mother-Daughter Incest*, iUniverse.

- Fortune, Marie, 1989, *Is Nothing Sacred? When Sex Invades the Pastoral Relationship*, 1st edition, Harper & Row.

- Fortune, Marie, 2005, *Sexual Violence: the sin revisited*, The Pilgrim Press.

- Hawthorne, Nathaniel, 1850, *The Scarlett Letter*, Ticknor and Fields.

- Hefley, James, C. 1991, *The Conservative Resurgence in the Southern Baptist Convention*, Hannibal Books.

- Heggen, Carolyn, 2006, *Sexual Abuse in Christian Homes and Churches*, Wipf & Stock Pub, (Reprint of previous edition 1993).

- Johnson, David and VanVonderen, Jeff, 2005, *The Subtle Power of Spiritual Abuse* Bethany House Publishers.

- Jones, Serene, 2009, *Trauma + Grace*, Westminster John Knox Press

- Kaiser, Robert Blair, 2015, *Whistle: Fr. Tom Doyle's Steadfast Witness For Victims Of Clerical Sexual Abuse*, CreateSpace Independent Publishing Platform.

- Maes, Yvonne, 1991, *The Cannibal's Wife*, Herodius.

- Oates, Wayne E., 1987, *Behind the Masks: Personality Disorders in Religious Behavior*.

- Rutter, Peter, 1989, *Sex in the Forbidden Zone*, Ballentine Books.

- Schoener, Gary, 1989, *"Psychotherapists Sexual Involvement with Clients"*

- Shaw, Susan, 2008, *God Speaks to Us, Too: Southern Baptist Women on Church, Home & Society,* The University Press of Kentucky.

- Sipe, Richard, 1990, *A Secret World: Sexuality and the Search for Celibacy,* Routledge.

- Trull, Joe "Broken Trust" http://www.worldcat.org/title/broken-trust-confronting-clergy-sexual-misconduct/oclc/52525668

- Trull, Joe and Carter, James E., "Ministerial Ethics," Broadman and Holman, 1993

- Trull, Joe and Audra, 2003, *Putting Women in Their Place: Moving Beyond Gender Stereotypes in Church and Home,* Smyth & Helwys.

- Young, William Paul., 2007, *The Shack: Where Tragedy Confronts Eternity,* Windblown Media.

Finally, the author's previous books related to SPOTLIGHT are listed for your convenience:

Miller, Dee Ann, 1993, *How Little We Knew: Collusion and Confusion with Sexual Misconduct,* Prescott Press.

Miller, Dee Ann, 2000, *The Truth about Malarkey,* Author House.

www.ingramcontent.com/pod-product-compliance
Lightning Source LLC
Chambersburg PA
CBHW050433290526
45786CB00006B/2021